Cambridge studies in mediev

THE POLITICAL THOUGHT OF
BALDUS DE UBALDIS

Cambridge studies in medieval life and thought
Fourth series

General Editor:
J. C. HOLT
Professor of Medieval History and
Master of Fitzwilliam College, University of Cambridge

Advisory Editors:
C. N. L. BROOKE
Dixie Professor of Ecclesiastical History and
Fellow of Gonville and Caius College,
University of Cambridge

D. E. LUSCOMBE
Professor of Medieval History, University of Sheffield

The series Cambridge Studies in Medieval Life and Thought was inaugurated by G. G. Coulton in 1920. Professor J. C. Holt now acts as General Editor of a Fourth Series, with Professor C. N. L. Brooke and Professor D. E. Luscombe as Advisory Editors. The series aims to bring together outstanding work by medieval scholars over a wide range of human endeavour extending from political economy to the history of ideas.

Titles in the series

THE POLITICAL THOUGHT OF BALDUS DE UBALDIS

JOSEPH CANNING

*Lecturer in Medieval History,
University College of North Wales, Bangor*

The right of the
University of Cambridge
to print and sell
all manner of books
was granted by
Henry VIII in 1534.
The University has printed
and published continuously
since 1584.

CAMBRIDGE UNIVERSITY PRESS

CAMBRIDGE

LONDON   NEW YORK   PORT CHESTER
MELBOURNE   SYDNEY

PUBLISHED BY THE PRESS SYNDICATE OF THE UNIVERSITY OF CAMBRIDGE
The Pitt Building, Trumpington Street, Cambridge, United Kingdom

CAMBRIDGE UNIVERSITY PRESS
The Edinburgh Building, Cambridge CB2 2RU, UK
40 West 20th Street, New York NY 10011–4211, USA
477 Williamstown Road, Port Melbourne, VIC 3207, Australia
Ruiz de Alarcón 13, 28014 Madrid, Spain
Dock House, The Waterfront, Cape Town 8001, South Africa

http://www.cambridge.org

© Cambridge University Press 1987

First published 1987
Reprinted 1989
First paperback edition 2003

A catalogue record for this book is available from the British Library

Library of Congress Cataloguing in Publication data
Canning, Joseph.
The political thought of Baldus de Ubaldis.
– (Cambridge studies in medieval life and thought;
4th ser. v. 6)
Bibliography.
Includes index.
1. Ubaldi, Baldo degli, 1327? – 1400 – Contributions
in political science. I. Title. II. Series.
JC101.U23C363   1987   320.1   86-9608

ISBN 0 521 32521 8 hardback
ISBN 0 521 89407 7 paperback

For my parents

CONTENTS

Contents

PREFACE

The first study which I produced of Baldus' political thought was my Ph.D. dissertation. After a lapse of some years I returned to the subject in order to publish a full-scale treatment. This book represents my recent thought about Baldus' political ideas and entirely supersedes my dissertation. I found that my own ideas about Baldus and indeed my understanding of medieval political thought had radically changed in the interim with the result that this book is very much a new venture: I have entirely rewritten and rethought my interpretation of Baldus. Not only that, I have also included much more information from the primary sources, both from Baldus himself and from other jurists.

In order to reach a wider audience I have in the text translated into English all the quotations from primary sources. The original Latin versions will be found in the Appendix. In order to save space I have made shortened references to books and articles in the footnotes: full details will be found in the bibliography. In referring to the *Corpus Iuris Civilis* I have followed the edition of T. Mommsen, P. Krueger, R. Schoell and W. Kroll as regards the numbering of books, titles, laws and *novellae*. In quoting, however, from the *Corpus Iuris Civilis* I have used the text of the Venice, 1497–8, edition because this is derived from the medieval Vulgate version (*littera Bononiensis*).

I owe a great debt of gratitude to my research supervisor, Walter Ullmann, who first suggested this subject to me, asked me to write this book, but sadly did not live to see it published. Over many years I have experienced David Luscombe's kindness and have derived much benefit from his editorial comments for the final draft. I should further like to thank Nicolai Rubinstein, Michael Wilks, Peter Stein, Jimmy Burns and Anthony Black for their generous advice; successive librarians of Queens' College, Cambridge, Mr A. C. Spearing, Dr J. Diggle, Professor J. Riley-Smith and Mr I. Wright who have been most helpful in providing me with access to the Old Library; the librarians of the Wren Library, Trinity College, and of Gonville and Caius College for their permission to consult early printed books; and the following libraries for microfilms of manuscripts – the Biblioteca Feliniana Capitolare at Lucca, the Joseph Regenstein Library, University of Chicago, the Biblioteca Apostolica Vaticana, the Preußische Staatsbibliothek at Berlin and the Bodleian Library, Oxford. Cambridge University Library through its unfailing efficiency and helpfulness has greatly facilitated this work. I also wish to express my gratitude for the research grants given to me by the University College of North Wales at Bangor, and the British Academy.

Lastly, I must record my many debts to my parents, and to Roberta, my wife, for their constant support and encouragement and to my children, Lucy, Martin, Peter and Polly for their patience.

Bangor, J. P. C.
All Souls Day, 1985

x

ABBREVIATIONS

Add.	*Additio*
Auth.	*Authentica ad Codicem*
C.	*Codex Iustinianus*
Clem.	*Clementinae Constitutiones*
Coll.	*Collationes Authentici*
Cons.	*Consilium*
D.	*Digesta Iustiniani*
D.V.	*Digestum vetus*
Decr. Grat.	*Decretum Gratiani*
Def. pac.	Marsilius of Padua, *Defensor pacis*
Eth. Nic.	Aristotle, *Ethica Nicomachea*
Feud.	*Libri feudorum*
gl.	*glossa*
Inst.	*Institutiones Iustiniani*
M.G.H.	*Monumenta Germaniae Historica*
Nov.	*Novellae Iustiniani*
Pol.	Aristotle, *Politica*
Rep.	*Repetitio*
Sext.	*Liber Sextus Decretalium Bonifacii P. VIII.*
Specul.	Guilielmus Durantis, *Speculum iudiciale*
S.T.	Thomas Aquinas, *Summa theologiae*
X.	*Decretales Gregorii P. IX. seu Liber Extra*

INTRODUCTION

In a subject as well established as the juristic contribution to medieval political thought the relative neglect of one of its major exponents, Baldus de Ubaldis, may cause surprise. The political thought of his teacher and colleague, Bartolus of Sassoferrato, is so well known that in the pantheon of late medieval political thinkers he ranks with Aquinas and Marsilius of Padua; and indeed no treatment of medieval political thought is complete without a consideration of his ideas.[1] Yet Baldus who was certainly the juristic peer of Bartolus has received a scattered and piecemeal study of his political ideas rather than any systematic treatment aiming at completeness. Indeed Baldus' contribution as a whole to legal history lacks its historian.[2] This is so despite the fact that Baldus shared with Bartolus the greatest fame and influence amongst the Commentators, the school of jurists which originating in the late thirteenth century dominated Roman law studies in the late Middle Ages, and indeed as the *mos italicus* (Italian manner) remained highly influential throughout the sixteenth century and beyond.[3]

[1] For Bartolus' political theory see especially Woolf, *Bartolus*, and Ullmann, 'De Bartoli sententia', and also Baskiewicz, 'Quelques remarques', and David, 'Le contenu de l'hégémonie'. For Bartolus' place in general histories of political thought see, for example, Ullmann, *History of Political Thought*, pp. 214–19, and Skinner, *Foundations*, I, 9–12, and 59–65.

[2] There exists only one published monograph on an aspect of Baldus' ideas, Horn, *Aequitas*, although *L'opera di Baldo* provides a useful collection of essays to mark the five-hundredth anniversary of Baldus' death. As regards Baldus' political ideas Wahl gives some treatment of his theory of monarchy: 'Baldus' concept of state'; 'Immortality and inalienability'; and 'Baldus and foundations'. See also Curcio, 'La politica di Baldo'. Baldus' theory of citizenship has also attracted some attention: see Rummer, 'A fourteenth-century legal opinion' (this concerns an autograph *consilium* of Baldus); Kirshner, 'Ars imitatur naturam'; id., 'Between nature and culture'; and Canning, 'A fourteenth-century contribution'. For Baldus' theory of tyranny see now Quaglioni, 'Un "Tractatus de tyranno"'. Bonolis, *Questioni* provides useful material for Baldus' political thought. For a piecemeal treatment of Baldus' political ideas see Gierke, *Genossenschaftsrecht*, III, passim; and R. W. and A. J. Carlyle, *Medieval Political Theory*, VI, 19–22, and 85–7. For aspects of Baldus' political ideas, notably on kingship, see Riesenberg, *Inalienability*, and E. H. Kantorowicz, *King's Two Bodies*. For a list of some further articles devoted to Baldus see Horn, 'Legistische Literatur', p. 273.

[3] For the importance of the *mos italicus* see Holthofer, 'Die Literatur', pp. 107–14.

Furthermore Baldus (unlike Bartolus) was also a canonist of renown. This inadequate modern treatment of Baldus' ideas means that it has so far proved impossible accurately to assess Baldus' general stature as a jurist.[4] Since Baldus in his legal commentaries ranged over the whole gamut of those aspects of contemporary society relevant to juristic treatment, the total picture of his contribution to jurisprudence will surely emerge through specialised studies of specific aspects of his thought; and it is within this larger context that this book, being a study of his political thought in particular, should be located.

For an historical understanding of political ideas knowledge of the historical context in which they were produced is crucial. This is very much an historian's point, and one which provides a key-note for this study;[5] those solely interested in assessing the philosophical status of a past writer's political theory, or indeed the internal logic of his ideas are free to adopt a different stand-point.[6] Baldus' political conceptions only surrender their historical meaning if the reader bears in mind the particular institutions, entities and relationships with which the jurist was actually concerned. In this respect Baldus is typical of all medieval jurists: their political ideas are of such a nature that their interpreter, unless he keeps contemporary medieval reality firmly before his eyes, can be led into constructing flights of fancy far removed from a jurist's original meaning.

The political and legal world that Baldus experienced was that of mid and late fourteenth-century Italy. He was born in Perugia, the son of a medical doctor, Franciscus Benvenuti, and a member of the established Perugian family, the degli Ubaldi or Baldeschi. It has become traditional to refer to him as Baldus de Ubaldis; but in his juristic writing he always referred to himself as 'Baldus de Perusio', a practice which it might be better for modern writers to follow. As with so many

---

[4] For differing modern assessments of Baldus' work see Calasso, *Medio evo del diritto*, p. 578, where he compares Baldus with Bartolus, 'Rivaleggiò col maestro, e, certo, lo superò per alcuni aspetti. Per esempio, per la versatilità dell' ingegno e l'ampiezza d'orizzonte...È sopra tutto meraviglioso per la intensità del pensiero, che porta constantemente i segni di un travaglio interno non comune... Tuttavia, fu meno profondo di Bartolo'; and W. Ullmann in his review of Horn, *Aequitas*, in *Tijdschrift voor Rechtsgeschiedenis*, xxxvii (1969), 281, 'By any standards, Baldus was a jurist and writer of brilliance, ability, depth and width, and had a mastery of the purely juristic material which made him rank far above his teachers, including Bartolus, and his contemporaries.'

[5] For a recent exposition of the methodological significance of this contextual approach see Skinner, *Foundations*, I, x–xiv.

[6] See A. J. Black's review of Skinner, *Foundations*, in *Political Studies*, xxviii, 3 (1980), 453–4.

figures of the Middle Ages we do not know when he was born. The date of 1327 is quite possible. It is, however, certain that he died at Pavia on 28 April 1400.[7] He studied at Perugia and, possibly, Pisa. Johannes Pagliarensis, Franciscus de Tigrinis of Pisa and Bartolus taught him Roman law;[8] Federicus Petruccius was his master in canon law.[9] Baldus was, therefore, the recipient of a form of 'apostolic' succession in legal training by the best juristic authorities: Dynus and Franciscus Accursius taught Cynus; Cynus taught Bartolus; and Bartolus taught Baldus. Domenico Maffei has shown recently that less is now known about Baldus' early career than was previously believed.[10] It had been accepted that Baldus received his doctorate *in utroque iure* (in both laws) in 1344, and that he thereupon took up his first chair at Bologna. This interpretation was based upon a passage in the *Practica iudiciaria* attributed to Baldus.[11] Solmi, following up doubts expressed in the sixteenth century, accepted that the work was in fact by Tancredi da Corneto, but maintained that the biographical information had been inserted by Baldus himself.[12] Maffei has now shown that Baldus had no hand at all in the *Practica*, and that the biographical material is a complete forgery which was added by Celse-Hughes Descousu to make it appear that the *Practica* was by Baldus, a clear example of the practice common amongst early modern printers whereby a juristic work was attributed to a famous writer in order to secure more sales.[13] There is therefore now no evidence that Baldus received his doctorate in 1344, nor that he ever lectured at Bologna at this time.[14] The only secure date is 1351 when he was certainly lecturing in law at Perugia and was made one of the *Savi dello Studio* together with his younger brother, Angelus, who was then given a chair at the same university, the start also of a famous juristic career.[15] The previous acceptance of the date,

---

[7] For the reconstruction of Baldus' life see notably Scalvanti, 'Notizie e documenti', and also Cuturi, 'Baldo degli Ubaldi in Firenze', and Savigny, *Geschichte*, VI, 208–48.

[8] See Baldus ad *Feud.*, 2.26, fol. 52r (ed. Pavia, 1495).

[9] See Baldus ad C.1.3.48, fol. 40v (ed. [Lyon, 1498]).

[10] 'Giuristi medievali e falsificazioni editoriali', pp. 26–33, and 71–4 (Appendice IV: 'Su alcuni nodi della biografia di Baldo degli Ubaldi').

[11] Rubr. 'De questionibus circa appellationem', qu. 1.

[12] Solmi, 'Di un'opera attribuita a Baldo', p. 434.

[13] 'Giuristi medievali e falsificazioni editoriali', p. 33.

[14] Some writers had always expressed caution about the Bologna professorship. Diplovataccius in his life of Baldus made no mention of the passage in the *Practica iudiciaria*, nor of any professorship at Bologna (see his *De claris iuris consultis*, ed. Schulz, Kantorowicz and Robotti, in which Baldus is treated). Tiraboschi, *Storia della letteratura italiana*, v, ii, 486, doubted the Bologna chair because of lack of evidence at Bologna and was followed by Vermiglioli, *Biografia degli scrittori perugini*, I, 116–18.

[15] See Scalvanti, 'Notizie e documenti', pp. 191 and 280. For Baldus' and Angelus' lecturing careers at Perugia see also Ermini, *Storia*, pp. 122–31.

1344, for Baldus' doctorate had caused serious problems of biography. For if the date, 1327, were accepted as that of his birth then he was, really, far too young to receive his doctorate in 1344. This led to the postulation of some date before 1327 as the date of his birth.[16] With the demolition of the 1344 date it is now quite possible that Francesco Baldeschi's date for Baldus' birth (1327) could be correct.[17] Baldus, therefore, as far as we know, began his lecturing career at Perugia in or before 1351. Indeed both Baldus and Angelus may well have commenced in that year because it marked the revocation of the Perugian statute prohibiting the commune from paying salaries to Perugian citizens who taught Roman or canon law.[18] Maffei's discovery illustrates that there is a great deal of biographical research still to be done on medieval jurists. This is a very broad and involved subject, and only those aspects of Baldus' career which are relevant to the study of his political ideas will be mentioned here.

Baldus was a professional teacher of law for the rest of his life. It was a profession which encouraged mobility as cities and *signori*, emperors and popes competed to attract the services of the best jurists; in this respect Baldus' career proved no exception. He remained at Perugia probably until 1357, and then taught at Pisa, probably from 1357 to 1358. On 25 June 1358, the Signoria invited him to a chair at Florence; his appointment was confirmed in 1359 and he taught there until 1364.[19] He then returned to Perugia and lectured there from 1365 until 1376. From 1376 to 1379 he was professor at Padua, whence he again returned to lecture at Perugia. In 1390 he took up the invitation of Giangaleazzo Visconti to lecture at Pavia where (apart from a stay in Piacenza for a few months in 1399) he worked until he died. Thus from the point of view of gaining practical experience of different political systems Baldus through his peregrinations around Italy lived under several forms of city-republic, and at Pavia had first-hand acquaintance with the *signoria* of Giangaleazzo Visconti.[20] Furthermore his lecture-room must have acted to some extent as a clearing-house for information about a wide range of political systems, because after the death of Bartolus in 1357 the way was left clear for Baldus to develop

16 See, for instance, Scalvanti, 'Notizie e documenti', pp. 188–92.
17 Francesco Baldeschi, writing in the second half of the sixteenth century, mentioned in his *Ricordi* these words which, he claimed, had been extracted from a volume of Baldus' *consilia* transcribed by Zanobius, Baldus' son, 'Oritur Baldus an. dom. 1327, die secunda mensis Octobris' (see Scalvanti, 'Notizie e documenti', p. 188, n. 4).
18 See Scalvanti, 'Notizie e documenti', p. 280.
19 For details see Cuturi, 'Baldo degli Ubaldi in Firenze'.
20 See Bueno de Mesquita, *Giangaleazzo Visconti*, p. 183.

his reputation as the most famous jurist in Europe, a reputation which attracted pupils from the rest of Europe as well as Italy. Indeed, some of his students achieved eminence in their own right: they included Pierre Roger de Beaufort (who later became pope Gregory XI), and the jurists, Petrus de Ancharano and Paulus de Castro.

Baldus was not, however, just an academic teacher of law. His opinion was sought on a wide variety of legal cases; and there have survived about two and a half thousand of his legal opinions (*consilia*) – the largest number of any medieval jurist. These *consilia* provide an immensely rich and valuable body of sources for Baldus' application of legal theory to the political conditions in which he lived, as is true for his thought on any subject.[21] The question arises whether the *consilia* are less speculative than his commentaries and more tied down to existing legal tradition because they are designed for the practical purpose of winning legal cases. No such general trend is discernible in Baldus' *consilia* in so far as his political ideas are concerned; but certainly the *consilia* do contain fuller treatment of some aspects of his political theory than do his commentaries, notably of the topics of kingship and the rule of *signori*. Certainly Baldus' *consilia* on political matters reveal that he was involved in delivering his professional opinion on current questions of government, politics and public law. In the twenty-eight years or more of his public life spent at Perugia Baldus was also involved in the practical affairs of his city in other ways. Perugia was essentially a guild-republic,[22] and Baldus was deeply involved in this aspect of the city's life as the retained advocate of the merchant guild.[23] From time to time he held public offices; and most important the city (following the practice common in Italy) used its most famous jurist on crucial diplomatic missions. For instance, in 1370 at the crisis of its war with pope Urban V, Perugia, having in March elected Baldus as one of the *Tre della guerra*, chose him on 3 September as a member of an abortive embassy to Urban at Corneto, and again in November sent him on a successful embassy to Bologna to sue for peace with the pope's brother, Cardinal Albano.[24] Likewise from 1379 to

---

[21] For the medieval juristic *consilia* see in particular Engelmann, *Wiedergeburt der Rechtskultur*, pp. 243–330; Riesenberg, 'The consilia literature'; Kisch, *Consilia*; and Coing, *Handbuch*, I, 249–50, 336–41, 359–60, 379 and 382. On Baldus see Lange, 'Consilien des Baldus'.

[22] See especially Blanshei, *Perugia*.

[23] Baldus, *Cons.*, 3.435, fol. 124r (ed. Venice, 1575). See also Scalvanti, 'Notizie e documenti', p. 243.

[24] Peace was concluded on 23 November and on 4 December at the cardinal's request Baldus gave before the university of Bologna a *repetitio* ad C.2.3.27 which is dated (for full details see Maffei, 'Giuristi medievali e falsificazioni editoriali', pp. 71–2).

1381 Baldus served on occasions as the city's ambassador to Charles III of Durazzo. Baldus may therefore be seen as both jurist and man of affairs with a considerable practical knowledge of politics.[25]

That Baldus' political ideas can only be fully understood by seeing their relationship to the political world which he knew of either directly or indirectly, is further indicated by a fundamental characteristic of his works. Baldus' main intention in writing, an intention he shared with the whole school of the Commentators as well as canonists, was the accommodation of legal science to contemporary reality. Baldus saw jurisprudence as being concerned with the works of man:

> Every art takes nature for its material...but the jurist takes the works of man for his material...Again, he interprets them; and thus our law is founded upon accidentals, that is on cases which emerge...for laws are born of facts...But the common material [of legal science] is not concerned with the works of nature but of man.[26]

This was an essentially this-worldly orientation and was an aspect of the form of humanism which can be detected as a characteristic of legal science from the time of Irnerius onwards.[27] Baldus considered that in human affairs nothing was immutable, and that the natural world suffered change through time.[28] Thus he was acutely well aware that human laws and the conditions which brought them forth also changed with time. He was concerned with studying law and human society as they were in his own day. He had therefore a clear sense of the historical gulf between the ancient world and his own period. But he used this understanding not as an inspiration for trying to examine Roman law of the republican or classical periods in its historical context, but as a reason for turning his back on the past and concentrating on the present.[29] Thus his historical sense led him to precisely the opposite

---

[25] For Baldus' public offices and above all his diplomatic activity see Scalvanti, 'Notizie e documenti', especially pp. 197–220, and Ermini, *Storia*, pp. 126–8. For Perugia's relationships with the papacy and other Italian powers in Baldus' life-time see Heywood, *History of Perugia*, pp. 182–283; Fop, 'Il comune di Perugia' (for Baldus' service on embassies to the papacy see pp. 71 and 91); and Partner, *Lands of St Peter.*

[26] Ad D.1.1.Rubr., fol. 4r (ed. [Lyon], 1498).

[27] See Ullmann, *Medieval Foundations*, pp. 50–2. Cp. Cynus ad *D.V.*, Proem, n.8, fol. 2v (ed. Frankfurt, 1578) on legal science: 'Disponens subiectum sive materia nihil aliud est quam actus hominum...quia et dispositum nihil aliud est quam actus hominum.'

[28] Baldus, *Cons.*, 3.278, fol. 86r, ed. Brescia, 1491 (= *Cons.*, 1.328, ed. Venice, 1575).

[29] Ad D.1.3.32, fol. 18r (ed. [Lyon], 1498): 'Dico ergo quod iura nostra considerant tempus, et in tempore fundant leges suas. Tempus enim quod valde recessit a memoria hominum, perinde reputatur ac si non fuisset, quoniam deletum est, et diverso usu consumptum. Quid enim attinet nobis Cesar, an Pompeius iustius regnaverit? Certe nihil ad nos. Sub Cesare enim vixerunt maiores nostri; igitur et nos vivamus. Non

conclusion from that drawn by the sixteenth-century legal humanists who attempted to study Roman law in its historical context, and to some extent (but not universally) condemned the Commentators for their interpretation of the Roman law in terms of contemporary society.[30]

The nature of Baldus' writings furnishes a further clue for their interpretation. He did not set out to write political theory as such: his works are entirely juristic in nature. Unlike Bartolus he wrote no professedly political tracts.[31] Ideas and arguments which the modern interpreter may consider to come under the heading of political theory have to be sought out in Baldus' treatment of public law. Any resulting construction of Baldus' political thought is thus an interpretation of evidence extracted from discourse which is juristic in nature and purpose. Any such interpretation must give due weight to the specific universe of discourse within which Baldus' works are located. The significance and meaning of Baldus' ideas can only be understood in the context of that specific juristic language which was part of a tradition and was directed towards a particular juristic audience. For this reason his ideas have to be understood in the context of the writings of previous and contemporary jurists. Indeed his works form a kind of debate with jurists living and dead. Only if this is realised can any originality on Baldus' part be discerned, and the significance of any addition he might make to the stock of juristic ideas be assessed. A great attraction of studying the political thought of the late medieval civilians and canonists is that they provide a model case-study of a group of writers sharing a common language-structure, or universe of discourse. The political thought of these jurists provided a major and specific contribution to the traditional role which law played as a vehicle for the expression of medieval political ideas – a dominant one earlier in the Middle Ages but still highly important in the thirteenth and fourteenth centuries.

The sheer volume of Baldus' juristic writings is prodigious (somewhat

sunt radices perscrutande, quoniam omnium dei operum nullam potest homo invenire causam. Tempus quod dat sibi vitam, dat sibi legem. Tempus vero quod semper accedit ad nos, illud dat nobis mores, illud dat nobis legem, illo [illo *ed. Venice, 1616*; illa *ed.* [*Lyon*], *1498*] vivimus, nutrimur, et sumus, ut dicit Iulianus in hac lege.'

[30] See Maffei, *Gli inizi dell'umanesimo giuridico*, and Kelley, *Foundations of Modern Historical Scholarship*.

[31] Bartolus' political tracts are *De regimine civitatis*, *De tyranno* and *De Guelphis et Gebellinis*. Quaglioni provides the most recent discussion of the texts of these tracts: 'Per una edizione critica'; 'Il "Tractatus de tyrannia" di Bartolo'; 'Alcune osservazioni'; and *Politica e diritto* (critical edition of all three tracts, pp. 130–213). Bartolus' *Tractatus represaliarum* also contains much which is relevant to political thought.

in excess of seven million words), and may well constitute the largest output of any medieval jurist. As regards the quality of Baldus' work only Bartolus bears comparison with him. Certainly Baldus is unique among the medieval jurists as regards the scope of his works: he wrote commentaries on the Roman law, canon law, feudal law and the Peace of Constance, as well as producing his *consilia* and several tracts.[32] As regards Roman law Baldus wrote commentaries on the *Institutiones, Digestum vetus*,[33] *Infortiatum, Digestum novum*[34] and *Codex*, I–XI.[35] His commentary on the *Libri feudorum* became the *glossa ordinaria*. As regards the canon law Baldus' major work is his commentary on the *Decretales* of Gregory IX;[36] he also wrote a *Margarita* on Innocent IV's commentary on Gregory's *Decretales*,[37] and part of Baldus' commentary on the *Liber sextus* is known in manuscript.[38] Baldus also composed *additiones* to the *Speculum iudiciale* of Guilielmus Durantis. Our knowledge of when his various works were written remains very imperfect. His commentary on the *Libri feudorum* was, according to

[32] The tracts, *De pactis* (dated 1350) and *De constituto*, are bound with Baldus' commentaries on the *Corpus Iuris Civilis* in the Lyon, 1585, and the Venice, 1615–16, editions. For Baldus' famous and extremely lengthy *Repetitio* ad C.1.1.1, which amounts to a tract on the question of statute-law, see the modern edition with an introduction in Meijers, *Tractatus duo*. For the other tracts (*De syndicatu officialium, De iure protomiseos, De substitutionibus et earum apparatu, De additione cum inventario, De carceribus, De tabellione* and *De questionibus et tormentis*) see *Tractatus universi iuris* (Lyon, 1549) or *Tractatus illustrium iurisconsultorum* (Venice, 1584), collections which also include *De pactis* and *De constituto*. There is some overlap between Baldus' commentaries and his tracts. *De syndicatu officialium* = D.1.16.4 with some verbal differences. The same applies to *De constituto* (= C.4.18.Rubr.), although in the version of *De constituto* inserted in the commentaries material on *statuta mercatorum* is added which is lacking in C.4.18.Rubr. This overlap is not uncommon among the Commentators: Horn, 'Legistische Literatur', pp. 346–7.

[33] We possess both a final version of his commentary on the *Digestum vetus* and also a *lectura antiqua*.

[34] His commentary on the *Digestum vetus* is his fullest: that on the *Infortiatum* ends at D.1.35.1, and the relatively thin one on the *Digestum novum* at D.46.8.

[35] The commentary on I–IX is very full; that on the *Tres libri* (i.e. *Codex*, X–XII) is more scanty, and ends at C.11.5.6. The Commentators commonly neglected the *Tres libri* in similar fashion, the great exception being the Neapolitan jurist Lucas de Penna's lengthy and vastly learned *Commentaria in tres posteriores libros Codicis* (see Ullmann, *Medieval Idea of Law*, and id., *Law and Politics*, pp. 113–14). Bartolus' commentary on the *Tres libri* is much fuller than that of Baldus.

[36] This gives a very deep and extensive treatment but ends at X.3.2.8.

[37] In the printed editions the *Margarita* is arranged by alphabetical entries. Baldus' *additiones* to Innocent's commentary on the *Decretales* contained in MS. Cod. 187, Biblioteca Feliniana Capitolare, Lucca, are also found in the *Margarita*, but are arranged according to the order of titles of the *Decretales*: it seems most likely that this is the earlier ordering and that the *Margarita* is derived from it.

[38] In the Vatican Library (Codex Vat. Lat. 5925, fols. 1r–23v): see Izbicki, 'Notes on late medieval jurists'. It should be noted however that on the fly-leaf of this manuscript a denial of the authenticity of the ascription to Baldus is inserted in another hand.

the Pavia, 1495 edition, produced while he taught at Pavia. The commentary on the Peace of Constance was also produced at Pavia as in it Baldus refers to his commentary on the feudal law as having been already completed. The commentary on the *Decretales* was definitely written in the later 1390s.[39] A number of *consilia* can be dated: many clearly date from Baldus' time at Pavia and refer to Giangaleazzo Visconti as lord. Individual *additiones* and *repetitiones* are sometimes dated.[40] There are clues to dating elsewhere in Baldus' commentaries, the most notable being found in his commentary on C.6.40.3 at the end of which he refers to leaving Padua on 3 November 1379. The problem is, however, that the appearance of a date or a datable event in a commentary does not necessarily prove conclusively that the dating of the whole commentary can be inferred therefrom,[41] a *caveat* which

---

[39] Baldus ad X.1.3.25, n. 13, fol. 53v (ed. Lyon, 1551) commences an *additio* concerned with the Great Schism thus: 'Et novissime MCCCXCVII. Rex Francie subtraxit obedientiam domino Benedicto' (this subtraction was in fact finally decreed on 28 July, 1398: Swanson, *Universities, Academics*, p. 134); ad X.2.24.1, n.15, fol. 298r (ed. cit.) Baldus says, 'Cum legebam Florentie iam sunt fere anni quadraginta'; ad X.2.24.5, n.1, fol. 299v (ed. cit.) Baldus refers to his commentary on the Peace of Constance; and ad X.3.1.11, n.5, fol. 378v (ed. cit.) Baldus clearly mentions the Bianchi movement of 1399. He also mentions his surprise that he is almost at death's door with the Great Schism unresolved (ad X.1.6.42, n. 23, fol. 97r, ed. cit.). The impression given is that he composed this commentary in the few years before his death, and that death interrupted him in the middle of it.

[40] Apart from his *repetitio* ad C.2.3.27 (above, n. 24) see for example Baldus ad D.2.15.11 (additio), fol. 141v: 'Istam legem sic ordinavit dominus Baldus de Perusio cuidam scholari suo qui eam habuit in punctis in regio studio Padue, in Mccclxxviii. [Mccclxxviii *ed. Venice, 1616*; Mccclxviii *ed. [Lyon], 1498*] indictione prima. Amen'; id. ad D.1.14.3 (additio), fol. 48r, dated 1366; and his *repetitio* ad C.2.1.3 given at Padua in 1378.

[41] It would clearly be unwarranted to assume that Baldus composed his commentary on C.1.1.1–C.6.40.3 at Padua, and the remainder of his commentary on the Code on his return to Perugia thereafter: ad C.4.19.23 he says, 'in ista scilicet civitate Perusii', and ad Auth., 'Habita' (ad C.4.13.5) mentions 'hoc territorium perusinum'; furthermore his commentary on C.9.2.7 appears to have been written in Florence – 'Dux Athenarum fuit hic tyrannus'; 'ista civitas ivit in exercitum contra Lucam'; 'dum Pandulphus fuit hic generalis capitaneus guerre' – and that on C.8.1.3 is dated 1365 and could thus have been delivered at Florence. Baldus' commentary ad C.7.39.7 is, however, clearly written between 1378 and 1389 since he refers to the 'schisma quod est inter Vrbanum sextum et Clementem septimum'. Tamassia, 'Baldo studiato nelle sue opere', pp. 4–5, accepts Savigny's opinion that the commentary on the first part of the *Digestum vetus* was the course which Baldus taught at Perugia after his return from Padua (see *Geschichte*, VI, 222–3). There is however no strong evidence to suggest such a precise dating. Vague indications exist: for instance ad D.1.3.3 Baldus remarks, 'si papa Vrbanus hodie resurgeret non recuperaret papatum' (he could be referring to Urban V or Urban VI); and ad D.1.7.15 he mentions 'illi duces infidelium qui iure belli submiserunt se hoc anno regi Vngarie' (all that can be said is that this most likely refers to a campaign of Lewis I [d. 1382]). We do in fact know that there existed several versions of Baldus' commentary on the *Digestum vetus*: apart from his main commentary

clearly does not apply to his commentary on the *Decretales*. Given the great length of Baldus' academic career, the certainty that there were several versions of the commentary on the *Digestum vetus* and the probability of the same as regards that on the *Codex*, an obvious problem of interpretation arises: to what extent did he change and develop his ideas on political matters? In general our scanty knowledge about the dates of composition of the various parts of his works does not permit acceptable answers to this question. Those few occasions, however, on which the view expressed in a known late work clearly differs from what appears to be an earlier opinion, will be noted. Otherwise the *corpus* of Baldus' writings has to be accepted as something given without considerations of the dating of the various parts.

Baldus' works present a vast textual problem. There exist no modern critical editions of his writings, the only exceptions being those of a few individual *consilia* and his commentary on C.1.2.16.[42] In this respect Baldus shares the fate of all the Commentators: with tiny exceptions[43] their works lack critical editions. As a result modern research on Baldus and other Commentators has been based on early modern printed editions with some small reference to manuscripts. A few autograph *consilia* by Baldus survive;[44] but there appear to exist no holographs of Baldus' commentaries.[45] The sheer size of the

the editions contain excerpts from a *lectura antiqua*, a *lectura secunda* and *additiones* (which could have been composed before or after the main commentary and could in part be fragments from other *lecturae*). This illustrates that Baldus produced different versions at various stages of his career. Indeed the main commentary on the *Digestum vetus* may well have been a final one which he produced towards the end of his life – see his concluding remarks in *Cons.*, 1.84, fol. 33r, ed. Brescia, 1490 (= *Cons.*, 2.217, ed. Venice, 1575) which from internal evidence was written after 1388: 'Vltimo rogo vos quod alia vice mittatis mihi tot chartas, quia non occupat me tantum lectura maioris libri digesti veteris quantum scriptura vestrarum chartarum.' We do not however know for certain the dates of composition of the various versions of this commentary. Likewise one possible solution of the internal dating problems of his commentary on the Code would be to suggest that it may be a later composite of parts of different lectures given at a variety of times and places.

42 See the works of Rummer, Kirshner, Quaglioni and Bonolis cited above, p. 1, n. 2, and Kirshner and Pluss, 'Two fourteenth-century opinions on dowries'.

43 Notably Quaglioni's work on the text of Bartolus' political tracts (see above, p. 7, n. 31).

44 For example that transcribed by Rummer (see above, p. 1, n. 2). See also H. Kant-orowicz, 'Introduzione: la vita di Tommaso Diplovataccio', pp. 43*–44*, and 80*.

45 This is only to be expected since it is the case with the other Commentators. For the complicated problem of the extent to which the commentaries of Italian jurists were the *reportationes* of lectures given (most commonly sketched out in advance in writing by the jurist and subsequently worked up by him) or were composed in full by the jurist himself see Horn, 'Legistische Literatur', p. 321. Certainly in the editions of

problem of establishing a critical text of Baldus' works is indicated by the large number of printed editions in existence ranging from very early ones, such as the Venice, 1474, edition of his commentary on *Codex*, I–III (held by Cambridge University Library) and the Naples, 1476, first edition of his commentary on the *Digestum vetus*, to the Venice printing of all his Roman law commentaries in 1615–16,[46] and also by the vast bulk of manuscripts of Baldus' works known to be scattered across Europe and America.[47] The enormous task of establishing a critical text could only be accomplished by a team of scholars. This textual study urgently requires to be done because of the textual discrepancies among the editions[48] and the manuscripts. The establishment of a critical text of Baldus' works has not been the purpose of this study which is based on fifteenth-, sixteenth- and early seventeenth-century printed editions of the works of Baldus and other jurists, although some reference has been made to manuscripts where printed editions are lacking.[49] A few textual emendations are here suggested where textual corruption has clearly resulted in nonsense or grammatical error; all such emendations together with the original reading are noted and are introduced as sparingly as possible. C. N. S. Woolf when confronting the same problem in the works of Bartolus considered the variations between editions to be merely verbal and therefore of little account.[50] Such an attitude must be received with some reservation: a critical text remains highly desirable. Yet there is currently no prospect that such a project is going to be started let alone finished within a foreseeable period. In any case even if a critical text were produced the possibility that there might be some element of *reportatio* in Baldus' Roman law commentaries means that we could not even then be totally sure that his original words had been established. It seems necessary, therefore, to proceed with the major task of examining Baldus' ideas on important topics so long as it is realised that the state of the text

Baldus' commentaries the terms *commentaria* and *lectura* are interchangeable and do not indicate the presence or absence of *reportatores* (I agree with Horn, ibid., p. 321, n. 9). Whatever the possible role of *reportatores* in the transmission of his other commentaries, that of the *Decretales* gives the very clear impression of having been composed by the jurist himself. Baldus' *additio* ad D.2.15.11 (above, p. 9, n. 40) appears to be a *reportatio*.

[46] For some details see Horn, 'Legistische Literatur', p. 327.

[47] For MSS of Baldus' works other than his commentaries on the canon law see Dolezalek, *Verzeichnis der Handschriften*, III. No such wide-ranging list of MSS of his canon law works as yet exists; but for some details see Fiumi, 'Alcune ricerche sui manoscritti'.

[48] This becomes rapidly obvious to any student of Baldus' works: see, for example, the remarks of Maffei, 'Giuristi medievali e falsificazioni editoriali', pp. 72–3.

[49] Apart from the MS of the commentary on the Sext already mentioned some *consilia* exist only in MS (see below, p. 14).   [50] *Bartolus*, p. xiii, n.1.

puts some distance between us and Baldus. Norbert Horn maintains that the modern scholar, because of the textual problems, studies not the original jurist directly, but the jurist of historical tradition, that is the canon of his works as accepted in early modern editions:[51] this is really a way of presenting the problem stated. The question remains of whether all the works attributed to Baldus are indeed by him. Research at present suggests that only the *Practica iudiciaria* and some *consilia* are by other hands. In this respect Baldus appears to have escaped far more lightly than Bartolus whose name was often ascribed to juristic works in the late Middle Ages to provide them with a more distinguished paternity.[52]

Unless otherwise stated I have used the [Lyon], 1498, edition of Baldus' commentaries on the *Digesta* and *Codex*, I–IX (held in the Old Library of Queens' College, Cambridge); the Venice, 1615, edition of his commentary on the *Institutiones*; the Pavia, 1490, edition of his commentary on *Codex*, X; the Pavia, 1495, edition of his commentary on the feudal law and the Peace of Constance; the Lyon, 1551, edition of his commentary on the *Decretales*; the Lyon, 1525, edition of his *Margarita* on Innocent IV's commentary on the *Decretales*; and the Frankfurt, 1592, edition of his *additiones* to the *Speculum iudiciale* of Guilielmus Durantis. I have used throughout the Brescia, 1490–1, edition of Baldus' *consilia* (held in the Library of Gonville and Caius College, Cambridge). This edition is in five books: 1, 2 and 4 were published in 1490, and 3 and 5 in 1491. Between 1486 and 1653 there were produced numerous printed editions of his *consilia*. In comparing editions I have noticed considerable variation in the ordering of *consilia* within the overall structure of five books: the same *consilium* can, for example, appear in a different book in different editions. Much confusion exists: *consilia* are, for instance, combined together or separated in a different manner in different editions. To be able to say with accuracy that one edition of the *consilia* corresponds completely with another it would be necessary to compare every word. From 1516 the editions of Baldus' *consilia* were enlarged by the addition of the

---

51 'Legistische Literatur', pp. 318–19.
52 For the complex problem of false attributions to Bartolus see Calasso, 'Bartolo da Sassoferrato', p. 645; Paradisi, 'Le glosse di Bartolo da Sassoferrato'; Ascheri, *Saggi*, pp. 28–73; and Horn, 'Legistische Literatur', p. 317. It is particularly relevant to Bartolus' treatment of public law (and hence his political thought) that modern scholars accept that much of the commentary on Book I of the *Digest* attributed to Bartolus in the printed editions is not in fact by him but is put together from the works of several jurists (the commentaries on D.1.1.9 and D.1.3.32 form however crucial exceptions: they are by Bartolus), and that the commentary on the *Institutes* also attributed to Bartolus is in fact by Jacobus de Ravannis.

previously unedited *consilia* which Cardinal Savelli claimed to have obtained from Baldus' great-grandsons: whereas the Brescia, 1490–1, edition purports to contain 2040 *consilia*, the [Lyon], 1543, edition (held in the Wren Library, Trinity College, Cambridge) and the Venice, 1575, edition purport to contain 2518 *consilia*.[53] The references which I have seen to Baldus' *consilia* in modern secondary works appear to correspond with the ordering of the [Lyon], 1543, and the Venice, 1575, editions. I have, however, used the Brescia, 1490–1, edition as my basic one because the state of the text is very good (better, for instance, than that of the other editions mentioned), and because it is the one used by Diplovataccius in his life of Baldus.[54] Modern legal historians attach great weight to the judgment of Diplovataccius. It may be significant that Diplovataccius, whose *De claris iuris consultis* was put into final form after the appearance of editions including Savelli's additions, nevertheless persisted with the Brescia edition.[55] Diplovataccius maintained that Baldus himself originally divided his *consilia* into five books.[56] The editors of the Brescia edition claim to have reproduced the *consilia* from Baldus' original manuscript.[57] The internal ordering

[53] For a discussion of Savelli's role see Bonolis, *Questioni*, pp. 4–5: the [Lyon], 1543, edition (but not the Venice, 1575) notes at the beginning of Book 1 of the *Consilia*, 'Inter alias curas Baldi quoque eterne memorie iurisconsulti libros si quod ille occultius scripsisset a Petro Juliotto atque Antonio pronepotibus eius et per lineam heredibus conquisivit [i.e. Joannes Baptista Sabellus]. Neque magis letari unquam visus est quam cum illius viri consilia in triginta sex amanuenses (ut ita dixerim) libros congesta consequutus est que statim in quatuor volumina exscribi curavit denique inter delicias habuit.' I have also used the Lyon, 1559, edition: whereas this in the main corresponds with the [Lyon], 1543, and the Venice, 1575, editions, it also differs in some respects from these in internal ordering. Lange in 'Consilien des Baldus', p. 18 also notes these variations in the editions of Baldus' *consilia*, although he does less than justice to the Brescia edition: 'Einige Ausgaben enthalten sehr viel weniger *Consilien*. Z.B. bringt die Ausgabe Brixiae nur 926 Gutachten' (n. 76) – Lange may well only have had access here to Books 1 and 2, which purport to contain 927 *consilia* (the British Library, for instance, possesses a volume consisting solely of Books 1 and 2). Baldus' two *consilia* on the Great Schism are not contained in the editions of his *consilia*, but are printed elsewhere (see below, p. 22, n. 18).

[54] This is made clear in Diplovataccius, *De claris iuris consultis* (ed. cit.).

[55] For the dating of this work by Diplovataccius see the full discussion in Ascheri, *Saggi*, pp. 100–9. Another possibility (in the light of Ascheri, p. 103) is that the *vita Baldi* was completed before 1516 and not revised.

[56] 'Item volumina quinque consiliorum composuit' (ed. cit.), p. 298.

[57] Books 1 and 3 claim to be 'ex proprio originali suo exemplata', and Book 5 begins, 'Excellentissimi Iuris Cesarei pontificisque interpretis domini Baldi perusini Consiliorum quinta pars: hac prima impressione ab elegantissimo originali suo in lucem edita', and ends, 'Excellentissimi Monarche domini Baldi Perusini iuris Cesarei pontificisque Interpretis: Consiliorum quinta pars nuperime elucubrata ac diligenti castigatione emendata cum ipso originali collatione habita.' It is not however known whether Diplovataccius' statement that Baldus composed five books is derived from the Brescia edition or sources unavailable to us.

of the *consilia* in the Brescia edition on the one hand, and that in the [Lyon] and Venice editions on the other are very different; yet all these editions claim to be drawn from such an original manuscript. The Brescia edition may well follow Baldus' original order; what is certain is that the later editions incorporating Savelli's additions do not, but insert the new material into a changed ordering of the *consilia* found in the Brescia edition. So as not to confuse readers, and to facilitate the following up of my references, I have wherever possible indicated cross-references between the Brescia, 1490–1, and the Venice, 1575, editions, because the latter is readily available in a modern reprint.[58] I have made it clear when I refer to a *consilium* contained in this Venice edition but not the Brescia one. I have also used a manuscript of purportedly 443 of Baldus' *consilia* held in the Biblioteca Feliniana Capitolare at Lucca (Cod. 351), and containing many *consilia* which are not found in printed editions, and also another manuscript including 160 *consilia* ascribed to him (MS 6, Joseph Regenstein Library, University of Chicago).[59] It is not possible to know exactly how many of Baldus' *consilia* survive, a problem which is complicated by doubts about the authenticity of some *consilia* attributed to Baldus in the editions,[60] and the overt inclusion of some *consilia* by other jurists.[61] Certainly about 2500 *consilia* survive, and it may be as many as about 2800.[62]

In the Latin quotations from Baldus' and other jurists' works in this study I have consistently used 'e' for 'ae' since this was the spelling they used. Further I have often had to rationalise punctuation because of its erratic state in the editions and manuscripts.

[58] Anastatic reproduction, Turin, 1970.

[59] Bonolis, *Questioni*, provides details of this Lucca MS, and transcribes the following *consilia*: nos. 95, 112, 150, 204, 249, 262, 342, 358 and 442. For information on MS 6 see Kirshner, 'Messer Francesco di Bici degli Albergotti d'Arezzo', pp. 87–8, and id., 'Between nature and culture', pp. 179 and 204.

[60] Whether *consilia* purport to be signed or unsigned in the editions provides no clue: the editors could have inserted the signatures.

[61] For instance, in the [Lyon], 1543, and Venice, 1575, editions *Cons.*, 2.476 is by Franciscus de Spoleto; *Cons.*, 4.400 consists of two *consilia* by Bartolus and Cynus on the same subject; and *Cons.*, 5.64 is two *consilia* by Rogerius de Perusio and Franciscus (de Spoleto?). Furthermore material not from *consilia* is inserted: for example, in the above editions *Cons.*, 3.371 is an acknowledged quotation from Cynus ad C.1.14.4. Also a few *consilia* are repeated by the editors (e.g. *Cons.*, 1.456 = *Cons.*, 3.277, ed. Brescia, 1490–1), and some are unnumbered (e.g. that commencing 'In puncto iuris communis dicte allegationes' being the second of two *consilia* between *Cons.*, 4.251 and 4.253, fol. 64r, ed. Brescia, 1491).

[62] Bonolis, in the light of the Luccan MS cited, estimated that there were about 300 *consilia* by Baldus in this MS unpublished in Italian sixteenth-century editions of the *consilia* (*Questioni*, p. 5). See also Campitelli and Liotta, 'Notizie del Ms. Vat. Lat. 8069', for four unpublished *consilia*; and Rummer's transcription of an autograph *consilium* (above, p. 1, n. 2).

The format of Baldus' commentaries poses a major methodological problem for the reconstruction of his political ideas (and, indeed, his views on all subjects). His commentaries follow the order dictated by that of texts of the Roman law, *Decretales*, *Libri Feudorum* and the Peace of Constance. This means that there is no extended and systematic development of political argument in these commentaries. Likewise material for establishing Baldus' political ideas is scattered throughout his *consilia*. His political theory has thus to be pieced together from all parts of his works. It has been necessary to read every word he wrote because material relevant to his political thought can be found almost anywhere in his works. This characteristic of Baldus' commentaries is, of course, shared by those of the whole school of the Commentators; in contrast the treatment of Roman law according to subject-matter was to be a distinguishing mark of the commentaries of the sixteenth-century legal humanists,[63] although the Commentators in their tracts were able to develop extensively argued discussions of specific questions.[64]

Baldus' works are scholastic in form as are those of all the Commentators and canonists, in the sense that they applied to books of authority methods of systematic treatment derived ultimately from Aristotelian logic.[65] Indeed, it was in jurisprudence that fourteenth-century Italy made its major contribution to scholasticism. Baldus was above all the master of this craft being able to manipulate a massive array of legal authorities without being dominated by the wealth of his material: his immense knowledge and expertise endowed him with a supreme self-confidence which permitted him both to explore the most speculative aspects of jurisprudence, and to examine exhaustively the *minutiae* of specific legal problems.

Because Baldus was concerned with political and legal reality he was not an apologist for any one form of government, but rather sought to provide juristically acceptable explanations of the forms of government, jurisdiction and political organisation which existed in his own day. This book in its structure has set out to reflect Baldus' own preoccupations. Quite apart from their intrinsic interest, Baldus' political ideas merit a full-scale study because they provide an excellent

---

[63] See Holthofer, 'Literatur', pp. 114–31.

[64] Discussions of legal points divorced from the texts are also to be found in the Commentators' *Quaestiones*.

[65] For medieval civilian jurisprudence as a form of scholasticism see Weimar, 'Legistische Literatur', pp. 129–32; and Horn, 'Legistische Literatur', pp. 262–4. The Glossators can certainly be described as scholastics; but the Commentators applied a more developed understanding of Aristotelian method.

locus for considering the major political questions exercising the minds of fourteenth-century jurists, and thus further illuminate the crucial contribution which late medieval civilians and canonists made to the development of political thought, a contribution which retained influence into the seventeenth century.

Chapter I

UNIVERSAL AND TERRITORIAL POWERS: THE FUNDAMENTAL STRUCTURE OF BALDUS' POLITICAL THOUGHT

Baldus' political thought possesses a fundamental structure which underlies and informs his whole treatment of public law: the acceptance that universally sovereign authorities, in the form of the emperor and the pope, coexist with territorially sovereign entities, that is independent city-republics and kingdoms. The explanation and elaboration of the origin, nature, operation and interrelation of these two forms of sovereignty form the core of his political ideas. It could be objected that adherence to the notion of universal sovereignty precludes the recognition of a genuinely territorial kind, on the grounds that the so-called territorially sovereign power would thus have a superior which would be a contradiction in terms: that the two ideas are in short mutually exclusive. This, however, would be to apply a modern view of sovereignty. When seen from an historical perspective sovereignty is a term whose meaning has changed through time: Bodin, for instance, considered that no jurist or political philosopher writing previously had been able to define the concept (and thus really understand it);[1] yet Bodin's own interpretation would not have passed muster in, for example, Austin's eyes;[2] and Austin's own definition is no longer adequate for expressing the intricacies of state-sovereignty in the interdependent world of the late twentieth century. The detailed examination of Baldus' theory will reveal that he was operating with a specifically late medieval concept of sovereignty which permitted the simultaneous acceptance of both universal and territorial forms, and that this concept can justifiably be termed one of sovereignty so long as the precise meaning attached to it is understood. Furthermore his theory of sovereignty also enabled him, as we shall see, to solve the other

[1] *Les six livres de la république*, ch. 8, p. 85.
[2] According to J. Austin's concept of sovereignty as a supreme coercive power without effective limitations (see his *Lectures on Jurisprudence*, I, esp. p. 263) Bodin's idea of sovereignty, with its recognition that *la police*, *la religion* and *la justice* constitute some form of restraint on that power, would appear limited and therefore a contradiction in terms. For this aspect of Bodin's thought see Skinner, *Foundations*, II, 293–7.

17

apparent conundrum of ascribing universal sovereignty to both emperor and pope.

Overall Baldus' conception of sovereignty resulted from his reflections on *trecento* political reality in the light of the juristic traditions he inherited. In his active life-time the actual power of the emperor fell far short of the claims to universal authority which the Roman law made for him; yet in north and parts of central Italy there was still a role for the emperor to play as the superior of territorial states. For to the north of the papal patrimony the emperor possessed a real jurisdictional authority, but admittedly in a very specific sense. The days of imperial attempts to exercise effective governmental and political power in Italy were over: in reality the empire never recovered after the death of Frederick II in 1250. Henry VII in 1312 and 1313, and Lewis IV between 1327 and 1330 had attempted to reestablish imperial power in the whole peninsula yet with no lasting effect, while Charles IV on his brief visit to obtain the imperial crown in 1355 had in agreement with the papacy never intended to resurrect the ancient imperial claims to rulership in Italy.[3] Real political power north of the papal patrimony lay with the independent city-states and *signori*. Nevertheless, although the emperor was in truth nothing more than the ruler of part of Germany and but a pale shadow of the Hohenstaufen in their prime, in that part of Italy his ultimate powers of jurisdiction were accepted, in the sense that he remained the ultimate source of legal legitimacy but did not possess the capability to be an active political power: he was the ultimate sovereign in a theoretical rather than a practical sense. This position of the emperor is shown by the way in which cities sought confirmation of their liberties from him, and indeed also procured imperial vicariates, as did *signori* (in their case either to legitimise their regimes or to break the constitutional link with the commune).[4] Thus when Charles IV came down to Italy in 1355, the response of the city-republics showed that his authority was real because they flocked to purchase from him privileges confirming their liberties and constitutions: Florence, for instance, paid 100,000 florins for this purpose and the revocation of Henry VII's ban,[5] and Perugia through an embassy led by Bartolus himself bought specific liberties from the emperor.[6] The rash of signorial requests for vicariates ensured the

---

[3] See, for instance, Barraclough, *Origins of Modern Germany*, p. 315.

[4] For extensive details on both cities and *signori* see Ercole, *Dal comune*, especially pp. 273–328; and for *signori* in particular see Jones, 'Communes and despots'.

[5] See Ercole, ibid., p. 282, n. 1, and Seibt, *Karl IV*, p. 236.

[6] See Segoloni, 'Bartolo da Sassoferrato', pp. 654–5.

continuation of valid imperial jurisdiction in Italy, a process which culminated in Wenceslas' grant of an imperial dukedom to Giangaleazzo Visconti in 1395. This grant of jurisdiction was considered to be real both in Italy, where it raised the Visconti to a level of magnificence above other *signori* who were mere vicars, and in Germany, where it was considered by the Rhineland electors to constitute a genuine dilapidation of the empire and grounds for Wenceslas' deposition as king of the Romans in 1400.[7] For his part, Wenceslas certainly considered that he had real jurisdiction throughout Italy, because in his grant of an imperial vicariate to Sigismund in March, 1396, he included Apulia, Calabria and Sicily.[8] Furthermore the Italian feudal structure, so vitally important for the *signori*, and for the nobility and ambitious men in both signorial and republican regimes, depended for its effectiveness on the validity of both imperial and papal jurisdictions, because the emperor and the pope underpinned feudal titles.[9] Not only that, the continuing existence of the emperor's jurisdiction was seen as being intimately connected with Roman law's status at that time as Italy's common law (*ius commune*): the contemporary Roman emperor was considered to be the direct successor of Augustus or Justinian, and thus the *princeps* of the Roman law which was a living law, and by no means a dead relic from antiquity. It is true both that the Roman law, because it was accepted as valid, facilitated the recognition of an actual emperor, and that the emperor, because he existed, breathed extra life into the law, a process which had earlier been aided by Frederick I's application of the revived study of Roman law to bolster his imperial claims, and the continuation of this policy by Henry VI and Frederick II.

What is important for establishing the context of Baldus' political ideas is not the German monarch's view of his role in Italy, however minimal in practice from his point of view, but how regimes in Italy north of the papal patrimony understood the emperor's function and the use they made of him. For them the emperor's ultimate sovereignty was of this legitimising rather than a ruling kind. The crucial political fact was the almost unbroken absence of the emperor from Italy: Charles IV, for instance, made only one brief return (1368–9). This habitual absence ensured that the emperor had no real power in Italy, a situation in which Charles was only too happy to acquiesce, having fixed his attention above all on the consolidation of his rule in Bohemia.

[7] See Buisson, *Potestas und Caritas*, pp. 320–2; and Offler, 'Aspects of government', p. 219.

[8] Offler, ibid.   [9] See Ercole, *Dal comune*, pp. 313–14.

The reality of power in Italy north of the papal patrimony was that theoretically subject cities and *signori*, where they enjoyed practical independence, attained effective sovereignty. The emperor was in reality used by the cities and *signori*. An imperial grant of jurisdiction served merely to increase the authority of its recipient without giving the emperor any real influence: he could not determine how that power was used, nor limit its possessor in the exercise of it. Yet the emperor was willing to participate in this sale of titles for the revenue it raised. In reality therefore this part of Italy presented a scene of competing independent territorial powers. *Signorie* had been supplanting communal forms of government from the mid-thirteenth century; and a decreasing number of republics survived in Baldus' time, notably Florence, Venice, Siena, Lucca and Perugia itself. Among city-republics Perugia claimed to be a unique case in that it protested its freedom both from the emperor and the pope,[10] although it lost its liberty to the papacy in 1370 through the treaty negotiated by the embassy on which Baldus served. Perugia then revolted in 1375, and in 1378 managed to obtain better terms from the pope.[11] Thus in Baldus' life-time, besides the surviving republics, the *signoria* was a long-established form of political authority, with the major example being the Visconti state under Bernabò and then Giangaleazzo beneath whose rule Baldus ended his days.

The other power with universalist claims was, of course, the papacy. The popes' possession of universal and supreme spiritual jurisdiction was still accepted in Latin Europe, whereas papal hierocratic pretensions to an ultimate sovereignty in the Christian community in matters both spiritual and temporal were singularly out-of-date in the fourteenth century and were generally rejected; but such hierocratic claims still existed in canon law, as is shown for instance in Boniface VIII's *Unam*

[10] See Bartolus ad C.11.31.3, n. 2 (fol. 35v) and ad C.10.32.61, n. 1 (fol. 18v): 'Facit hec lex quod civitas perusina non subsit ecclesie nec imperio...nam imperator donavit eam ecclesie...et ex privilegio ecclesia liberavit eam' (unless otherwise stated I have used the Turin, 1577, edition of Bartolus). For discussion of the vexed questions of the historical origins of this claim and its legal standing see Scalvanti, 'Un opinione del Bartolo'; Ercole, *Dal comune*, p. 332, n. 1; Baszkiewicz, 'Quelques remarques', pp. 16–17; David, 'Le contenu de l'hégémonie', p. 209; and especially Segoloni, 'Bartolo da Sassoferrato', pp. 567–671. Segoloni maintains (p. 655) that in 1355 Albornoz probably conceded to Charles IV the *ius administrationis* over Perugia, with the result that Perugia was (temporarily at least) no longer part of the lands of the church, a theory developed further by Fop, 'Il comune di Perugia', p. 48. Partner, *Lands of St Peter*, p. 342, n. 1, completely rejects this thesis for lack of evidence. For the position of Perugia in Baldus' treatment of popular sovereignty see below, pp. 123 and 126.

[11] See Scalvanti, 'Notizie e documenti', pp. 209–10 and Heywood, *History of Perugia*, pp. 264–8.

sanctam[12], and in the works of papal apologists such as Augustinus Triumphus.[13] Its universalist claims apart the papacy maintained its right to direct temporal government in the papal patrimony in central Italy, an ancient claim supported by the forged Donation of Constantine and made reality from Innocent III's policy of recuperations onwards.[14] In stressing their own temporal sovereignty in the patrimony the popes upheld the exclusion of the emperor from their lands, and thus imposed a territorial limitation on imperial jurisdiction, a view rejected by Lewis IV who claimed to rule in Rome itself,[15] but accepted by Henry VII[16] and Charles IV who in deference to papal desires on his coronation day fleetingly entered Rome after dawn and left it before night-fall thus demonstrating that he had no pretensions to real jurisdiction in the city, nor indeed in the papal lands as a whole. There was, however, often a major discrepancy between papal rights of jurisdiction in the patrimony and the realities of power there. The papal exile at Avignon during which Baldus was born was itself largely the result of the papacy's inability to establish and maintain effective control over its Italian lands, a predicament which far from being new was endemic; indeed, as is well known, the city of Rome itself posed the popes their worst problems, so much so that between 1100 and 1304 they spent one hundred and twenty-two years out of Rome and only eighty-two in residence.[17] In its absence at Avignon the papacy lost control further over the patrimony to the advantage both of cities like Perugia and of *signori*; and grants of papal vicariates like imperial ones in northern Italy and Tuscany benefited the recipient rather than the donor. John XXII spent most of his revenues on Italian wars to re-establish papal power there; but the spectacular recovery of papal authority in the patrimony was achieved later through the campaigns of Cardinal Albornoz, and his reorganisation of the government of these lands through the so-called Aegidian Constitutions. As a result Urban V's premature return to Italy was made possible to be followed by the final home-coming of the papacy in the person of Baldus' pupil, Gregory XI in 1377. The outbreak of the Great Schism in the next year made this triumph short-lived producing rival papal courts at Rome and Avignon and an accompanying loss in power and prestige for the papacy. Baldus supported the cause of Urban VI producing in 1378

---

12 See especially Ullmann, 'Boniface VIII'.
13 Wilks, *Problem of Sovereignty* contains an authoritative study of Augustinus Triumphus.
14 Out of a massive literature see especially Partner, *Lands of St Peter*.
15 See Wilks, *Problem of Sovereignty*, pp. 78–9.
16 See Davis, *Dante and the Idea of Rome*, pp. 191–2.
17 See Renouard, *Avignon Papacy*, p. 37.

and 1380 two of his most famous *consilia* in order to justify Urban's claims to be the valid pope, but did not live to see the schism resolved.[18] Nevertheless as far as the political complexion of Italy was concerned Baldus did see in his life-time the universal power of the papacy re-establish its territorial temporal monarchy in the centre of the peninsula.

The territorial limitation of imperial power, accepted in practice by Charles IV, recognised another political fact of the fourteenth century: the sovereignty of the secular monarchs of western Europe. In Italy the two kingdoms of Sicily furnished prime examples. The papacy certainly favoured the independence of the Neapolitan kingdom. Thus when Henry VII on the basis of his imperial claims to universal jurisdiction sought to treat King Robert of Naples as a rebel against the emperor and thus guilty of *laesa maiestas*, Clement V in the bull, *Pastoralis cura* (*Clem.*, 2.11.2), of 1313, maintained that the kingdom of Sicily was outside the territory of the empire. Robert like all kings of Sicily was, as the pope said, a papal feudal vassal, vicar and legate, and as such it might seem that he could not be considered to be a sovereign ruler. Yet for all practical purposes he was sovereign.[19] There is, as regards practical sovereignty, great similarity between the relationship between King Robert and his papal overlord, and that existing between an independent northern or Tuscan republic and the emperor. The two kings of Sicily enjoyed territorial sovereignty as did the great western monarchies beyond the Alps: France, England, the Spanish kingdoms and Scotland. Indeed, as we shall see, the theory of the territorial sovereignty of kings made rapid strides from the end of the twelfth and throughout the thirteenth centuries. The papacy, commencing with Innocent III's decretal, *Per venerabilem* (X.4.17.13), which accepted as a fact the temporal sovereignty of the French king in his kingdom, supported the claims of monarchs to territorial sovereignty at the expense of imperial claims to universal superiority. The French monarchy especially maintained its sovereign independence

---

[18] The 1378 *consilium* is printed after the rubric in Baldus' commentary on C.6.34; it is also contained in Raynaldus' ecclesiastical annals in Theiner (ed.), *Annales ecclesiastici*, XXVI, anno 1378, nos. 36–7 (pp. 304–9), as is the *consilium* of 1380 (pp. 581–99). A full discussion of both *consilia* is to be found in Ullmann, *Origins of the Great Schism*, pp. 143–60; see also Swanson, *Universities, Academics*, pp. 24–5. For the political aspects of Baldus' treatment of the Great Schism, that is his proposals for the involvement of lay-rulers in ending it, see below, pp. 41–3.

[19] For the juristic position of the king of Naples relative to the emperor and the pope, together with the significance of *Pastoralis cura* see Calasso, *I Glossatori*, and Ullmann, *History of Political Thought*, pp. 195–9.

from the emperor, a theme which was reiterated emphatically in the French pamphlet literature produced during the conflict between Philip IV and Boniface VIII,[20] and had indeed led the French to claim in the period after 1276 that the empire should be in the hands of a French monarch rather than the German, and in the period up to 1347 to interfere continually in elections of the king of the Romans by supporting French candidates. The general papal policy of championing the territorial sovereignty of monarchs marked a fundamental change of direction from its earlier support for the universal nature of imperial jurisdiction, a *volte-face* brought about largely by its disappointment in the attitude of successive members of the Hohenstaufen dynasty, the threat that Henry VII was perceived to have posed to papal independence despite an initial papal invitation into Italy, and the extended conflict with the excommunicated and execrated Lewis of Bavaria. Just as however its earlier support for the emperor rebounded to the papacy's disadvantage, so its favouring of the French monarchy did not prevent the emergence of conflicts culminating in Boniface's humiliation at the hands of Philip IV.[21] Nevertheless in the realm of theory the papacy considered that all monarchs were subject to an ultimate sovereignty which was not the emperor's but its own.[22]

THE UNIVERSAL SOVEREIGNTY OF THE EMPEROR

Two major forms of solution were proposed by civilian jurists to cope with the universalist jurisdictional claims of the emperor and the pope, and the territorial sovereignty of kings, cities and *signori*; solutions which were conditioned to a considerable extent by the forms of regime under which these jurists lived. The first retained the universal sovereignty of the emperor or pope in some sense, and accounted for the sovereignty of cities and kings within this context: it was the tradition within which Baldus wrote following the main outline laid down by Bartolus. It was produced in the city-state environment of north and central Italy. The emperor's claim to be universal sovereign, *dominus mundi*, was founded of course on the text of the *Corpus Iuris*

---

[20] For details see the fundamental studies of Scholz, *Die Publizistik*, and Rivière, *Le problème de l'église et de l'état*.

[21] Indeed, in the midst of his dispute with Philip, Boniface turned in reaction to the emperor-elect, Albert I, and expressed opinions favouring the universality of the empire (M.G.H., *Leges* IV, *Const.* IV, 1, pp. 139–40).

[22] For papal theory in the thirteenth and fourteenth centuries see especially Buisson, *Potestas und Caritas*, Ullmann, *Principles*, Wilks, *Problem of Sovereignty* and Watt, *Theory of the Papal Monarchy*.

Civilis itself and could not therefore be ignored by the civilians.[23] Clearly the mainstream of juristic interpretation was to accept this claim as something given, as is shown by the works of the Glossators[24] and the early French Commentators, Jacobus de Ravannis and Petrus de Bellapertica, and then their interpreter for Italy, Cynus de Pistoia, and following him Bartolus himself.[25] Baldus clearly shows himself to be an adherent of this tradition: 'It is very true that the emperor is lord of the world with respect to all kinds of jurisdiction and supreme power, as in [D.14.2.9; C.7.37.3; C.1.14.12; & X.1.33.6]'.[26] For these jurists the contemporary Roman emperor was the true successor of Augustus and Justinian, and the Roman law the valid law of his empire, with the result that the attributes of the *princeps* in the *Corpus Iuris Civilis* applied to the present-day emperor: in stressing the imperial jurisdictional rights the Italian jurists at any rate were reflecting a legal reality in Italy which the study of Roman law had historically helped to shape. The reader of Baldus' works gains the cumulative impression that imperial jurisdiction was for him a living and pervasive reality; any interpretation which neglects the fundamental role he attributed to the emperor's jurisdiction distorts his jurisprudence and his political thought in particular.

There existed, however, a deeper reason for affirming the universal sovereignty of the emperor or the pope: both were held by these jurists to have been divinely instituted. In the case of the pope this needs no further explanation; the case of the emperor is somewhat more

---

[23] D.14.2.9 (*l. Rhodia*). [24] See, for instance, Ullmann, *Law and Politics*, pp. 90–5.

[25] This is to mention just the major exponents of this tradition. A few examples must suffice: Jacobus de Ravannis ad C. Rubr. 'De emendatione Codicis Iustiniani', ad v. 'Augustus', fol. 1r; Petrus de Bellapertica ad C.1.1.1., n. 3, p. 8; and Cynus ad C.1.1.1., n. 2–3, fol. 1v. The reliance of Cynus on Petrus de Bellapertica has long been recognised: for a recent discussion see Gordon, 'Cinus and Pierre de Belleperche'. Maffei's discovery of the long-lost *Lectura super Digesto veteri* by Cynus reveals that in this work (as opposed to his commentary on the *Codex* and his other fragmentary lecture on the *Digestum vetus*, as printed for instance in the Frankfurt, 1578, edition), he shows far greater independence from Petrus: see Maffei, *La 'Lectura super Digesto veteri'*, p. 49, n. 137, where he dissents especially from Meijers' disparaging assessment of Cynus' dependence on Petrus (*Etudes*, III, 99, 102 and 120). A full-scale assessment of Cynus' work in the light of Maffei's discovery remains to be done: indeed, it appears that Cynus in the *Lectura super Digesto veteri* produces political theories highly divergent from those to be found in his commentaries on the *Codex* and the *Digestum vetus* in the Frankfurt, 1578, edition (Maffei, ibid., pp. 48–56).

[26] *Cons.*, 4.436, fol. 103r, ed. Brescia, 1490 (= *Cons.*, 5.300, ed. Venice, 1575). He also says of the emperor: 'Habet namque imperium in universa ditione, que ascendentem videt et descendentem solem, et que ex utroque latere est: id est meridie et septentrione, ut in auth. "Vt omnes obediant iudicibus" [Coll., 5.20, 1 = Nov., 69, 1]' (*Cons.*, 1.418, fol. 129v, ed. Brescia, 1490 (= *Cons.*, 3.218, ed. Venice, 1575)). See also id., *Cons.*, 3.283, ed. Brescia, 1491 (= *Cons.*, 1.333, ed. Venice, 1575).

complicated. The Roman law puts forward two sources of the emperor's authority. The legal construction known as the *lex regia* states that the Roman people was the original source of the emperor's jurisdiction;[27] yet the *Corpus Iuris Civilis* also stresses the divine source of imperial authority: the Code and the Novels are redolent with the language of Caesaropapism.[28] Baldus is typical of mainstream juristic interpretation in habitually attributing a thoroughly theocratic origin to the power of the emperor, who is God's vicar on earth: 'Note that we are all bound to the emperor because God, just as he is the emperor in heaven, has also set up the emperor on earth as his vicar and ruler in faith, truth and justice... Moreover sacred scripture says, "Let every soul be subject to the emperor".'[29] Indeed, the most extreme expressions of the theocratic nature of the emperor's power are to be found in Baldus' works, as, for instance: 'Note that everyone who takes an oath does not do so against the emperor, just as he does not against God. And thus an exception is made of the emperor in every oath of fealty, because he is the emperor of the world, and so to speak a corporeal God for the world.'[30] Identical and similar statements are legion in juristic discourse.[31]

[27] Inst., 1.2, 6; D. Const. 'Deo auctore'; D.1.4.1; D.1.9.1; and C.1.17.1, 1. The *lex regia* was an *ex post facto* juristic construction to explain the legal origins of the emperor's power and appeared to be the Roman people's original grant of its jurisdictional power whereby the empire was set up – it was this view which was known to medieval jurists. The *lex regia*, as it appears in the *Corpus Iuris Civilis*, never existed in reality and is distinct from any historical *lex de imperio* which granted specific powers to an individual emperor. See the recent discussion in Lucrezi, *Leges super principem*: he both considers that there was no *lex regia* at the time of Augustus, and denies the widespread view amongst modern scholars that there was a series of *leges de imperio*, and thus maintains that the *lex quae dicitur de imperio Vespasiani* was unique (text in Riccobono, ed., *Fontes iuris romani anteiustiniani*, 1, 154–6). See also Ullmann, *Medieval Foundations*, p. 138 for Cola di Rienzo's discovery of this text in 1347 and his belief that it was the *lex regia* of the *Corpus Iuris Civilis*; and for the importance of this distinction between the *lex regia* and any historical *lex de imperio*, in interpreting Accursius' treatment of the *lex regia*, see Tierney, 'The prince is not bound by the laws', pp. 389–90.

[28] See, for instance, C.1.17.1; C.1.17.2, 18; Nov., 6, Praef.; and Nov., 73, Praef., 1.

[29] *De Pace Constantie*, ad v. 'Imperialis clementie' (fol. 88r). See also id., *De Pace Constantie*, ad v. 'In nomine sancte et individue trinitatis' (fol. 88r); id. ad D.1.1. Rubr. (fol. 4r); and id. ad X. Proem, ad v. 'Rex pacificus', n. 11 (fol. 5r). The biblical text alluded to here is Romans, 13:1 ('Omnis anima potestatibus sublimioribus subdita sit'), one of the major sources for the theocratic theme: see Ullmann, 'The Bible and principles of medieval government', and id., *Individual and Society*, p. 10. Bartolus also similarly adapts this text by applying it to the *princeps* in particular (ad Auth., 'Sacramenta', n. 15, fol. 85v, ad C.2.28). [30] *Feud.*, 2.55 (fol. 86r).

[31] Out of a vast number of examples see, for instance, Cynus ad C.1.1.1, n. 3 (fol. 1v); id. ad C.1.14.4, n. 6 (fol. 26r); Bartolus, *De regimine civitatis*, p. 167 (ed. Quaglioni, *Politica e diritto*); and id., ad Const. 'Ad reprimendum', ad v. 'Totius orbis', fol. 1r (ed. Venice, 1497).

The *lex regia*, on the other hand, seems to propound a purely human source of the emperor's authority: it is in essence the peculiarly Roman example of the derivation of governmental authority from the *ius gentium* (the law of peoples) in that the Roman people ultimately draws its jurisdiction and its power to institute government from this source.[32] Two interrelated questions immediately arise: how did imperial authority initially derived from the people come to be considered theocratic in nature; and how can the popular and theocratic sources of that jurisdiction be reconciled? This constitutes a usual problem in juristic discussion, and Baldus makes a strong and clear contribution to a well-established line of argument. For his solution he draws on Roman law, canon law, and the New Testament. He sees no conflict between the popular and divine origins of imperial jurisdiction because the people passed the *lex regia* at God's behest: 'Note that the emperor's authority depends on the *lex regia* which was promulgated at divine command; and thus the empire is said to be immediately from God.'[33] The people, in short, acted as God's agent. This suggests an important point of interpretation for medieval theories of the origins of governmental authority. While the use of the dichotomy between the popular and the theocratic sources of authority is often useful as a model for interpretation, the people can also in some contexts be seen as deriving its authority from God and acting as the channel for the divine effusion of ruling powers to the monarch.[34] The relevance for the contemporary emperor is that, because the constitutional law from which his authority derives was enacted at divine command, God is established as the immediate source of his jurisdictional powers. Elsewhere, commenting on *l. Bene a Zenone* (C.7.37.3), Baldus gives further details of how, in the process of creating the empire, God involved himself in human

---

[32] Like any other people: 'Ex hoc iure gentium introducta bella, discrete gentes, regna condita, dominia distincta ...' (D.1.1.5).

[33] Ad C.1.14.4 (fol. 50v). Cp. Cynus ad D.1.4.3, n. 1, fol. 8r (ed. Frankfurt, 1578): 'Ab ipso deo [imperator] immediate processit, unde inter imperatorem et deum non est ponere medium...nec obstat quod dicitur supra [D.1.4.1], quod lege regia dicitur princeps creatus, quia hoc est permissione divina...nec est absurdum, quod sic a populo et a deo, tanquam ab agente universali...et solutio vel melius dico, quod imperator a populo est, sed imperium, cuius presidatu imperator dicitur divinus, a deo.' Cp. Accursius ad Nov., 73, Praef., 1, ad v. 'Quia igitur de celo' (fol. 60r), where he considers the apparent discrepancy between the divine and popular sources of imperial authority to be more apparent than real: 'Immo populus romanus de terra, ut [Inst., 1.2, 6] que est contra. Sed deus constituit permittendo, et populus dei dispositione.' This resolution of the problem was not confined to jurists: see John of Paris, *De potestate regia et papali*, c. 19, p. 173 (ed. Bleienstein).

[34] See the important discussion in Kantorowicz, *King's Two Bodies*, pp. 296–7.

affairs, and human beings acted out the divine plan. He explains what 'at divine command' means:

In the text there, 'at divine command',[35] note that the emperor like the pope is divinely constituted, and the empire proceeded from God. And thus the empire and the church fraternise, as in the beginning of the constitution 'Quomodo oporteat episcopos' [Coll.,1.6 = Nov.,6]. Innocent [IV] however said that he does not know whence the empire derived its origin. You can say that it had its beginning from the sword with divine permission, for he wished the whole world to be subjugated to the Roman people. Thereupon the Roman people set up the emperor and transferred all its power to him, and afterwards this was confirmed by the express word of God, when he said, 'Let the image of God be rendered unto God and the image of Caesar unto Caesar'. And this was also approved afterwards by the church.[36]

Here historical, theological and legal arguments are combined to reveal four stages in the process. Originally the rulership of the world was in the hands of the Roman people who possessed it by divine permission, and it was in this sense derived from God. Next the people, still with divine permission, transferred their power to the emperor. The confirmation by Christ then established the rule of the emperor as the will of God, while ecclesiastical approbation, as we shall see, came to be institutionalised in the papacy's role in the making of the emperor. Baldus elaborates the relationship between the original setting up of the empire and the source of the contemporary emperor's power: the developing character of its divine source is revealed, from permission, through direct confirmation to approbation by the Church, with the result that the contemporary emperor, like the pope, is understood to be divinely constituted. Although historically speaking the empire was not initially directly instituted by God, the culmination of its historical development is that in its contemporary form it is a divine institution which it is beyond the capacity of man to suppress: 'And again that supreme dignity was instituted by God, and cannot therefore be suppressed by man. This is the reason why the empire is sempiternal as in Auth. "Quomodo oporteat episcopos" [Coll.,1.6 = Nov.,6] at the end.'[37] It is because this divine origin guarantees the continuing existence of the emperorship, that Baldus has to accept the living validity of imperial jurisdiction as a basic assumption of his juris-

---

[35] 'Nutu divino imperiales suscepimus infulas.'
[36] Fol. 201v. The text of Angelus de Ubaldis, ibid., n. 1–2 (fol. 198r) is the same with only small verbal variations.
[37] Baldus ad D.V., Proem, ad v. 'Quoniam omnia' (fol. 1v). Cp. also id. ad *Specul.*, 2.2.7 (p. 376).

prudence, whatever set-backs the power of the *princeps* may suffer in
practice. Christ's confirmation is the crucial turning-point; and Bartolus
had maintained that anyone who denied this confirmation was a
heretic.[38] The argument featuring Christ's confirmation, in that it refers
to an historical event, reveals that for jurists such as Bartolus and Baldus
the divine origin of imperial authority became manifest through a direct
intervention by God into human affairs. The divine origin of the
emperor's sovereignty which had previously been discernible through
an ideological construction, that is the divine mission of the Roman
people, thus became an historical fact; and who were Baldus and
Bartolus to deny this? This view places theocratic emperorship on a
completely different plane from theocratic kingship, which was not
understood to have obtained its authority from direct confirmation by
Christ, but to derive from divinity through the mediation of the church
in the order of coronation, and on the warrant of certain Biblical
passages.[39] Every emperor, therefore, since Christ's confirmation of the
empire shared the distinction of direct divine approbation with the
other universal sovereign: the pope.

How extensive is this divinely sanctioned authority of the emperor?
For Baldus the emperor is lord of the world; but does this phrase mean
literally what it says, or has it for him a more restricted significance?
In his commentary on *l. Cunctos populos* (C.1.1.1), which for any jurist
is a *locus* of central importance for discussing the emperor's authority,
Baldus explains that the emperor is the *universalis dominus* in the sense
of being the universal lord of all Christians. His argument is similar
to that in his commentary on C.7.37.3, but is only in part historical,
and, using scholastic categories, analyses dialectically the senses in which
the contemporary empire derives from God.[40] The argument from

---

[38] Ad D.49.15.24, n. 7 (fol. 228r).

[39] Most notably 1 Cor. 15:10, 'Gratia autem Dei sum id quod sum'.

[40] Ad C.1.1.1 (fol. 3r), 'Nunc videamus an presuppositum sit verum quod imperator sit
universalis dominus...Ego addo et dico quod cesareum imperium est a deo, ut in
Auth. "De non alienandis aut permutandis ecclesiasticis rebus", § "sinimus" [Coll.,
2.1, 2, 1 = Nov., 7, 2, 1], et hoc tripliciter: primo permissive, secundo approbative,
tertio formaliter et effective. Dico primo quod permissive, nam hoc est permissum a
deo propter bonum universale, quia entia nolunt male disponi, nec bonum pluralitas
principatuum; unus ergo princeps ut ait Aristotiles. xii. Metaphisice, ad finem. Hoc
enim permissum est a deo sub ratione finis ut mundus optimis legibus regatur, nam
secundum phisicam regulam cuius finis bonus est ipsum quoque bonum est. Omnia
enim rectificat finis; iustum est enim a fine denominari omnia secundum Aristotilem.
Secundo dixi quod imperium est a deo approbative; Christus enim approbavit
imperium dum dixit, "imago Cesaris reddatur Cesari", ut habetur in evangelio, nisi
enim approbasset illa imago non esset Cesaris, nec deberet restitui iniusto et violento

permission reappears here as a means of retaining an ultimately divine source for justifications which essentially have nothing to do with religion. By introducing the idea of the *bonum universale* (universal good) Baldus is using the traditional medieval conception that government has a moral aim; this view could be expressed in religious or (as here) secular terms. It is no accident that he provides Aristotelian justifications for political arrangements meeting with divine approval: both Aristotle and Christian teaching shared the teleological view that government possessed a moral purpose. The contention that the common good requires the rule of one man was of course one of the classic medieval arguments in favour of monarchy. The way in which Baldus uses Aristotle shows how useful a treasure-house the philosopher's writings were for providing texts to support a variety of political views. Because Aristotle accepted as valid monarchical, mixed and popular forms of government, passages from his works could be used (as here) to advocate a monist view favouring monarchy, or, as we shall find in Baldus' treatment of city-republics, be incorporated in arguments elaborating the sovereignty of the people. The second and third arguments are specifically Christian; and it is the third which explains directly the emperor's lordship of all Christians ('the empire is formally and effectively from God'). This is an authentically theocratic argument in that it is the faith of the church which both accepts and reveals the divine source. Indeed the form which the empire takes is the church in the sense of all the faithful as a collectivity; and the belief of this body reflects its divine head's will to which his vicar, the pope, gives practical effect through his approbation of the emperor. This is a traditional explanation of the emperor's rule over Christians; but does he enjoy it over non-Christians as well? Partly in response to the expansion of the geographical vision of western Europe resulting from the Crusades and long-distance trade the Hohenstaufen emperors had laid claim to universal emperorship in the literal sense.[41] Is there any echo of this in Baldus' works? There are passages which state simply that the emperor is *dominus universalis*

creditori, quia violentus possessor non fuisset defensus a deo in impropria possessione. Tertio dico quod Romanum imperium est a deo formaliter et effective, nam cum tota collectio Christianorum hoc teneat, licet quedam regna non obediant, non est putandum aliud, nisi quod etiam ipse deus hoc disponat, qui est caput illius collectionis; et post deum est imperator apostolicus immediatus qui hoc approbat, ut [X.1.6.34]. Ex quibus apparet suppositum esse verum quod imperator Romanorum est dominus universalis Christianorum.' Baldus' argument met approval among canonists: see Panormitanus ad X.1.6.34, n. 18 (fol. 142r).

[41] See Wilks, *Problem of Sovereignty*, pp. 411–12. For Frederick I's conception of universal emperorship see *M.G.H., Const.*, I, n. 191, p. 271.

without further qualification;[42] but the problem is not solved because in *Cons.*, 1.418, ed. Brescia, 1490 (= *Cons.*, 3.218, ed. Venice, 1575) he is content to describe the jurisdiction of the emperor as being both apparently unrestricted in geographical extent, and as applying to territories where the Roman law and the Catholic Church are operative (it is not clear however whether the one proposition is included in the other or is antithetical to it).[43] The problem was an obvious one, and a subject of juristic concern notably to Bartolus who identified the emperor's area of jurisdiction with Catholic Christendom, and mentioned those *populi extranei* (peoples outside the empire), who do not recognise the emperor as *dominus mundi*, without reaching an argued conclusion as to their status as regards the emperor ('those outside are of small concern to us').[44] Baldus appears to have nothing of importance to add on this point: for all practical purposes he operates in his jurisprudence with the concept of the emperor as the universal lord of Catholic Christendom.

THE RELATIONSHIP BETWEEN THE EMPEROR AND THE POPE

The thesis of the universal sovereignty of the emperor is thus fundamental to Baldus' political thought, yet the divine origin of imperial authority raises the problem of the jurisdictional relationship between the emperor and the pope. It emerges that the powers of the two divinely instituted authorities, *princeps* and pope, form for Christendom the basic constitutional law within the context of which all discussion of governmental power and political relationships ultimately takes place. Baldus recognises papal jurisdictional claims but in such a way that imperial sovereignty is also maintained through a peculiarly medieval acceptance of a hierarchy of sovereignty existing between the two powers, and limitations on the sovereignty of both parties.

Baldus certainly adopts a pro-papal stance throughout his writings; but he is no apologist for any truly hierocratic interpretation of papal

---

[42] Ad C. Const., 'De novo Codice componendo', Rubr. (fol. 1r); ad X. Proem, ad v. 'Rex pacificus', n. 4 (fol. 5v); and *Lectura antiqua* ad D.14.2.9 (fol. 94v).

[43] The immediate continuation of the passage quoted above, p. 24, n. 26 is, 'et in omnibus insulis que ad oceani recessus extenduntur...et in omnem terram quam Romanorum continet lex et catholice ecclesie sanctio'. The same wording occurs in id. ad D.V. Proem, ad v. 'Quoniam omnia', fol. 1r (see below, p. 44, n. 87).

[44] Ad D.49.15.24, n. 6–8 (fol. 228r). See also Woolf, *Bartolus*, pp. 25–8, for Bartolus' discussion of these questions. The problem derives from a contradiction in the *Corpus Iuris Civilis* itself: the emperor is described as *dominus mundi* yet it is accepted that there exist *populi liberi* outside the empire, as in D.49.15.7.

jurisdictional authority such as that found for instance in the works of Augustinus Triumphus.[45] Whereas the treatments of papal claims by hierocratic publicists and canonists tended to be purely theoretical in nature, Baldus' discussions feature an interpretation of practice in the second half of the fourteenth century in the light of the relevant texts of both civil and canon law: there is an appearance of that note of realism which characterises all aspects of his political thought. His own inclination and his role as a canonist led him to accept the ancient papal claim to *plenitudo potestatis* (plenitude of power), that is sovereignty absolute in the sense of being freed from positive law, but limited by higher norms:

[The pope] is not only a bishop but the chief of bishops and of others whom the intellect can imagine. To him has been given the full power of the keys and that highest and unrestricted power which is called power freed from all constraints of canon law and from every limiting rule except the law of the gospels and the apostles.[46]

Divine and natural law limit the pope's freedom of action: 'For the statement that the pope can do all things should be understood to mean that he so acts using the key of discretion which does not deviate from the rules of the divine law and the precepts of the natural.'[47] The question remains whether the pope's sovereignty within this moral framework extends to things temporal as well as spiritual. Of papal spiritual sovereignty there can be no doubt;[48] and Baldus can use the pope's unique relationship with God to justify his complete superiority over all secular rulers without exception as he does in a discussion of the case of a king who is a minor:

Concerning a kingdom whose king is going to be a boy, the pope can declare both his own intention and that of his predecessors, since he is not like other earthly men, and I do not exclude the emperor. For the pope is the principal vicar of Jesus Christ and possesses power beyond human nature, power which proceeds from the mouth of the most high [Eccl:23], and therefore he is the prince of the kings of the earth [Apoc:1].[49]

---

[45] See especially Wilks, 'Idea of the church'. Baldus does, however, ad C.1.19.7 provide a jurist's litany of the powers of the pope.

[46] Ad X. Proem, ad v. 'Gregorius', n. 3 (fol. 3r). See also id., ibid., nn. 6 and 34; id. ad X.1.3.22, n. 12 (fol. 51r), 'Contra libertatem plenitudinis potestatis pape nihil statui potest. Papa denique non solum habet plenam potestatem ut tutor, sed summam sive supremam'; id. ad X.2.24.33, n. 4 (fol. 315r); and id. ad X.2.26.2, n. 1 (fol. 325v).

[47] Id. ad X.2.24.18, n. 5 (fol. 303r). Cf. id. ad X. Proem, ad v. 'Gregorius', n. 4 (fol. 3r).

[48] Baldus ad X. Proem, ad v. 'Gregorius', n. 1 (fol. 2v).

[49] Ad C.6.30.19 (fol. 85v). For the history of the title, *vicarius Christi*, see Maccarrone, *Vicarius Christi*. This formula, although used by the papacy from the time of Eugenius

The emperor's vicariate of God is clearly subordinate to the pope's vicariate of Christ because of the special nature of the Petrine commission which gives to the pope a power which is of a superior and different kind from that otherwise available to human rulers. Yet closer analysis of Baldus' arguments elsewhere reveals that his detailed treatment of the relationship between temporal and spiritual power is not so simple. He is almost exclusively concerned with those aspects of papal temporal jurisdiction which are at issue in Italy – the relationship with imperial jurisdiction and the status of direct papal temporal rulership in the peninsula; and his treatment takes full account of the situation confronting him.

In considering the relationship between papal and imperial jurisdiction he develops his own line of argument. The crucial question is whether the nature of the pope's role in the making of the contemporary emperor means that the pope mediates imperial power from God. From what we have seen so far the major trend of his arguments states that imperial power derives directly from God, while there is also mention of papal approbation which would indicate the possibility of a hierocratic mediatory function for the papacy. Baldus' solution accurately reflects the practice current in his life-time, and is incomprehensible without knowledge of it; and he weaves together those elements in juristic tradition which best explain it. Fundamental to his argument is the distinction between the position of the *Rex Romanorum* and that of the emperor. The Diet of Rhens and Lewis IV's decree, *Licet iuris*, followed by the Golden Bull in 1356, had confirmed in a permanent manner as part of the constitutional law of the empire that election by the electoral college of princes gave to the *Rex Romanorum* full powers of imperial jurisdiction. The existing papal claim to approve the choice of the electors, of which the major statement in canon law was Innocent III's decretal, *Venerabilem* (X.1.6.34), was simply ignored. The *Rex Romanorum* was thus constituted emperor in all but name by the sole will of the electors; and the papacy had in practical terms no choice but to acquiesce. It was however recognised by all concerned that for the *Rex Romanorum* to become Roman emperor as such it was necessary for him to be crowned and anointed by the pope or the

III, became an official title of the pope under Innocent III (see Ullmann, *Growth of Papal Government*, pp. 26; 342; 428, n. 4; and 443–6). In the modern dispute over the interpretation of Innocent's usage, Ullmann is the chief representative of the view that it formed part of a hierocratic claim to plenitude of power in both temporal and spiritual government (see for instance, *Principles*, p. 52), whereas Maccarrone and Kempf (*Papsttum und Kaisertum*, especially pp. 280–313) in particular deny that Innocent claimed thereby for the papacy any direct temporal power outside the papal patrimony.

papal representative. In imperial eyes this gave the king no more power but only the honorific title. Of the six kings of the Romans in the remainder of the Middle Ages, two went through this process to become emperor as Charles IV had done in 1355: Sigismund in 1433 and Frederick III in 1452; but in 1508 the pope allowed Maximilian I the imperial title without coronation. Thus the hierocratic papal claims to constitute the holder of imperial power and if necessary depose him remained in canon law, but were in practice a dead letter.

Among civilians and Decretalists different answers were produced to the question of the origin of the electors' power to choose the *Rex Romanorum*: the imperial view, as represented for instance by Cynus' commentaries on the *Codex* and the *Digestum vetus* (ed. Frankfurt, 1578), maintained that the electors acted in the place of the Roman people who had originally constituted the emperor, and that there was thus no question of papal mediation:[50] as Cynus so memorably put it, while the empire itself now derives immediately from God, the choice of emperor stems from the people (through the medium of the electors).[51] The Decretalists were divided between a hierocratic interpretation and a dualist one rejecting papal mediation of imperial power, although it appears that the main line of Decretalist argument was hierocratic holding that the pope by virtue of his divine vicariate had transferred the empire from the Greeks to the Germans in the person of Charlemagne in 800, and had given to the German electors the power to choose the emperor-to-be; but that their choice had to be approved by the papacy and involved no compulsion on the pope to make their candidate emperor: the pope retained a totally free hand in the making of his creature, the emperor. The majority of thirteenth-, fourteenth- and fifteenth-century canonists in short elaborated the position of Innocent III.[52] Baldus combines both views. At one point

---

[50] Ad C.7.37.3, n. 5 (fol. 446v). For the exclusion of any medium in the divine derivation of imperial power see id. ad D.1.4.3 (above, p. 26, n. 33), and ad D.1.1.5, n. 4, fol. 4v (ead. ed.), 'Imperium non est a papa sed pariter procedit una cum sacerdotio ab eo deo.'

[51] This is the meaning of 'imperator a populo est, sed imperium, cuius presidatu imperator dicitur divinus, a deo' (ad D.1.4.3). Cp. Albericus ad C.7.37.3, n. 19 (fol. 109r), where he denies that the empire depends on the papacy and maintains that the emperor derives his power directly from God, supporting his argument by referring to Dante's *Monarchia*, and John of Paris' view in *De regia potestate et papali* that there were kings before there were priests. Cp. with Bartolus' rejection of Dante's contention that the empire did not derive from the church (ad D.48.17.1, n. 3–4, fol. 189v), a passage ·:·hich become well-known: see, for instance, Panormitanus ad X.2.1.13, n. 13 (fol. 32v).

[52] For a recent survey of the relevant literature see Walther, *Imperiales Königtum*, pp. 65–8. For elaborations of Innocent III's position see Innocent IV ad X.1.6.34,

he certainly follows this canonist view: 'And setting all the obscurities of the law to one side, I think that the empire is conferred by election and not by succession [X.1.6.34; X.1.35.5]...But those who elect in this way have received the authority to elect from the apostolic see.'[53] Yet in his commentary on X.1.6.34 itself he says, '[Note] that phrase, "from the apostolic see": that is from the catholic church and the people together.'[54] While recognising the papal source of the electors' power he retains the popular origin of it. As we have already seen, Baldus accepted that the Roman people was historically the initial source of imperial authority; and there was no question in his mind that the church had in any sense supplanted the people as the first human source of that authority. The church for Baldus is the mother of the empire in the sense of its conservator or protector not its creator:

But is the church the mother of the empire? Say that it is...The church is therefore its mother in that it conserves it rather than generates it, for the empire proceeded immediately from the people, as in Auth. 'De instrumentorum cautela et fide' [Coll.,6.3 = Nov.,73], and at the beginning of Auth. 'Quomodo oporteat episcopos' [Coll.,1.6 = Nov.,6]. The church is therefore its mother through protecting and approving the imperial insignia or crown.[55]

It was in the role of conservator that the church translated the empire and in the process passed on to the electors the power to elect which had originally been possessed by the Roman people. As elsewhere Baldus strongly senses the continuity between the present Christian empire and the original pre-Christian one: his view is the reverse of any suggestion that the church through the *translatio imperii* created a new and different kind of empire derived from and subject to the church, an idea which the pro-imperial civilian, Albericus de Rosciate, had

n. 1 (fol. 65v), and Panormitanus, ibid., nn. 1 and 18 (fol. 141r–142r). For a classic exposition of the hierocratic interpretation of *vicarius Christi* see Innocent IV ad X.2.27.(27) (c. *Ad apostolice*), n. 6 (fol. 317r–317v), ad v. 'Privamus'. For a civilian exposition of the hierocratic view-point see Cynus, *Lectura ad D.V.*, ad D.1.3.9 (ed. Maffei, *La 'Lectura super Digesto veteri'*, p. 56).

53 *De pace Constantie*, ad v. 'Hoc quod nos' (fol. 90r).

54 n. 5 (fol. 78r). Cp. X.1.6.34 (ed. Friedberg, col. 80): 'Verum illis principibus ius et potestatem eligendi regem, in imperatorem postmodum promovendum, recognoscimus...praesertim, quum ad eos ius et potestas huiusmodi ab apostolica sede pervenerit.'

55 Ad C.1.1.1 (fol. 3r). For the church as *mater imperii* see Guilelmus de Cuneo ad D.V. Proem (ed. Brandi), p. 107, where he also describes the church as *soror imperii*, for whom the Donation of Constantine was a dowry from her brother. Baldus ad D.V. Proem, ad v. 'Quoniam' (fol. 2r) expressly rejects Guilelmus' view of the church as *soror imperii* and denies the common opinion that the Donation was a dowry. For Baldus' understanding of the Donation see below, pp. 47–55. Elsewhere however Baldus observes that the church and the empire '*fraternizant*' (above, p. 27).

rejected as an error of the papalists.[56] The papacy to Baldus' mind had been looking after the empire which had existed since the time of Augustus.

Baldus makes a fundamental distinction between the status of the *Rex Romanorum* and that of the emperor. It was in the fourteenth century the *communis opinio* of the civilians that the *Rex Romanorum* possessed full powers of imperial jurisdiction, and that papal coronation and unction only added the honour of the imperial title. Whereas, however, Jacobus de Arena and Cynus held that papal confirmation was not required for the king to have valid exercise of his power, Bartolus maintained that it was.[57] The law of the empire, certainly as set down in the Golden Bull, clearly accorded with the interpretations of Jacobus and Cynus; and it was these jurists, therefore, that Baldus chose to follow. Baldus' major statements come from the end of his life: in his commentary on the *Decretales* written more than forty years after the Golden Bull he states unambiguously, 'The king of the Romans as soon as he is elected also has fully formed imperial authority and power, although he awaits the crown.'[58] The electors, therefore, give imperial power: through their election the essence of emperorship is conferred, and the granting of the imperial title through papal coronation only increases the emperor's honour and glory – it adds nothing concrete to his powers of jurisdiction: 'In the case of the emperor coronation adds only glitter and increased honour. He derives the true essence however solely from a harmonious election...It follows from this that administration can precede the election as well as follow it.'[59] Other jurists in attempting to define the nature of the

---

[56] Ad C.7.37.3, n. 19 (fol. 109r).

[57] See Woolf's discussion: *Bartolus*, pp. 30–4. See Bartolus ad Const., *Ad reprimendum*, ad v. 'Reges' (fol. 1v) where he says of the imperial concessions given to Perugia by Charles IV while still *Rex Romanorum*, 'que littere sunt Perusii sub bulla aurea; et predicta vera postquam persona est electa in Romanorum regem, et per sedem apostolicam fuerit approbata'. Cp. Cynus ad C.7.37.3, n. 5 (fol. 446r–446v). At the end of this commentary Cynus claims to have inserted the *disputatio* of Jacobus de Arena which discusses whether the *Rex Romanorum* has imperial power; Jacobus' commentary on C.7.37.3 is missing from the Lyon, 1541, edition of his *Commentarii in Vniversum Ius Civile* available to me. See also Cynus, ibid., and Albericus de Rosciate, ibid., n. 12 (fol. 108r), for the argument that just as consent is the constitutive element in matrimony, the *Rex Romanorum* through accepting election gains full imperial rights.

[58] Ad X. Proem, ad v. 'Rex pacificus', n. 4 (fol. 5r).

[59] Baldus ad X.2.24.33, n. 6 (fol. 315r) – for this decretal see below, p. 48. Cf. id., *De pace Constantie*, ad v. 'Hoc quod nos' (fol. 89v). In, however, *Cons.*, 3.276, fol. 83r, ed. Brescia, 1491 (= *Cons.*, 1.326, ed. Venice, 1575), which because it discusses Giangaleazzo's dukedom was written in or after 1395 and was thus more or less contemporary with these passages from the commentary on the *Decretales*, Baldus

king's imperial jurisdiction described it in terms of the administration
of the empire, as Baldus does here, and also in his commentary on the
words, 'we crown', in X.1.6.34 itself, where he clarifies the effects of
election and coronation:

The emperor is crowned with three crowns. The gold crown however is not
necessary for conferring on him the power of administration which he
possesses as soon as he has been legitimately elected in harmony or by the
majority. What effect does the crown have? I reply that it is the final
confirmation... You are to say that the last crown of gold which is conferred
at Rome gives the ultimate perfection and is the chief of all crowns which
are beneath heaven.[60]

Administratio imperii is therefore a formula useful for describing the
king's possession of imperial jurisdiction without formally being the
emperor. Baldus is mostly careful to maintain this distinction between
the king and the emperor; but because they possess the same power
it is a difference which can become obscured. Indeed, in his discussion
already mentioned concerning the conserving function of the church,
in order to stress the imperial powers of the *Rex Romanorum*, he
identifies him with the emperor, a loose usage to make a specific point:
'But is the church the mother of the empire? You are to say that it
is, because the emperor should receive his imperial insignia from her,
although he is the emperor even before this.'[61] Strictly speaking, the
king through possessing 'imperium plene formatum' is emperor in all
but name:[62] to obtain the *forma* of emperor he requires papal coronation
and unction. The role of the pope does not however appear to be that

indeed accords imperial power to the *Rex Romanorum* but still associates confirmation
(presumably papal) with election in the process of creating imperial power: 'Corona
enim est signum cuiusdam demonstrationis et glorie, sed non est substantia essentie,
que in electione inicitur et in confirmatione substantiatur, licet in coronatione suscipiat
incrementum maiestatis et honoris.'

[60] n. 5–6 (fol. 93r). Cynus ad C.7.37.3, n. 5 (fol. 446v), maintained that papal consecration
gave only spiritual benefit not jurisdiction, and Albericus de Rosciate, ibid., n. 19 (fol.
109r), on the same basis denied that such consecration gave any jurisdiction or power
of administration. Under the influence of events canonists, applying the concept of
administratio, came increasingly to accept the *communis opinio* of the civilians: see, for
instance, Panormitanus ad X.1.6.34, n. 26 (fol. 142v). For the twelfth-century canonist
roots of this use of *administratio* see Kantorowicz, *King's Two Bodies*, p. 323, n. 27 for
Rufinus' distinction (ad *Decr. Grat.*, D.22, c.1, ad v. 'terreni simul') between
administratio (possessed by the emperor directly from God), and *auctoritas* (conferred
on him by the pope at the imperial consecration).

[61] C.1.1.1 (fol. 3r). Cp. Guilielmus Durantis, *Specul.*, 2.1.9: 'Imperator enim ex sola
principum electione etiam ante confirmationem aliquam verus est imperator et
consequitur ius administrandi' (quoted in Woolf, *Bartolus*, p. 34).

[62] '[Rex Romanorum] est imperator causatus, licet non sit formatus in nomine' (Baldus,
Cons., 3.277, fol. 84v, ed. Brescia, 1491 (= *Cons.*, 1.327, ed. Venice, 1575)).

of the mediator and source of imperial power: the *translatio imperii* is not seen by Baldus as having established for the papacy a title to mediate the *imperium* as such – the assumption lying behind his treatment of the *Rex Romanorum* is that the *translatio* was an historical act of conservation of the empire whereby the human participation in the empire's origin was preserved, a participation perpetuated in the role of the electors.

Baldus is not, however, completely consistent in his treatment of the powers of the *Rex Romanorum*. In his commentaries on C.7.37.3 itself he follows Jacobus de Arena in so far as he accepts the powers of general administration over the empire possessed by the *Rex Romanorum*, but he then denies to the king imperial *plenitudo potestatis* or *suprema potestas* (supreme power). Thus Baldus here denies to the *Rex Romanorum* certain powers which are possessed only by the emperor, notably that to transfer private property. Yet elsewhere Baldus is happy to accord imperial *suprema potentia* (supreme power) to the *Rex Romanorum*.[63]

It might well appear, however, that the difference between the king and the emperor was in practical terms meaningless by this time; that Baldus and other jurists were making a mountain out of a mole-hill; and that his loose usage in C.1.1.1 indicates that the distinction in his mind between the two was not as important as the use of the concept of *administratio* might elsewhere suggest. Such scepticism neglects, however, the role of the pope. In hierocratic theory papal deposition of secular rulers in general was justified ideologically by the Petrine commission and reinforced through the development of this doctrine by means of the elaboration of the significance of the vicariate of Christ. This argument, precisely because it was an ideological construction, had in the medieval context less force than the far more immediate reason

---

63 Three commentaries by Baldus on C.7.37.3 are printed: a long one (fols. 201r–201v, ed. [Lyon], 1498) followed eight folios later (in the [Lyon], 1498, Lyon, 1561, and Venice, 1615, editions) by a shorter one, and also an *additio* to the first commentary found in the 1561 and 1615 editions, but not in the 1498. See second commentary (fols. 209r–209v, ed. 1498): 'Simpliciter tenet [Jacobus de Arena] quod eoipso quod est electus imperator tenent eius privilegia. Sed ipse non distinguit inter supremam potestatem et generalem administratorem [administrationem *ed. Venice, 1615*] ut facio, quia hec lex innuit quod non possit dominia rerum auferre dominis, quia ista sunt de suprema potestate'; and *additio* (fol. 28v, ed. 1615), for the same argument. For the emperor's power to transfer private property see below, p. 81. In his *consilia*, however, dealing with Wenceslas' grant of the privilege of a dukedom to Giangaleazzo Visconti Baldus makes it crystal-clear that Wenceslas as *Rex Romanorum* granted a full imperial privilege: see *Cons.*, 3.276, fol. 83r, ed. Brescia, 1491 (= *Cons.*, 1.326, ed. Venice, 1575); *Cons.*, 3.277, fol. 84v, ed. Brescia, 1491 (= *Cons.*, 1.327, ed. Venice, 1575) where he attributes supreme power to the *Rex Romanorum*; and *Cons.*, 3.283, fol. 88r, ed. Brescia, 1491 (= *Cons.*, 1.333, ed. Venice, 1575) where Wenceslas in making the grant is identified with the emperor.

why the pope could claim to be able to depose the emperor: he crowned the emperor, whereas, except occasionally in the case of papal vassals, he did not crown kings.[64] As one would expect, both forms of argument are to be found in Baldus' works. It is true that on purely hierocratic grounds, using the well-tried sun–moon allegory, he justifies the papal power to depose the emperor, a sure sign of papal superiority:

[The Roman emperor] has no one above him except God from whom however he may expect punishment if he commits injustice. From time to time the pope has deposed him for enormities in his rulership, as in [*Sext.*, 2.14.2], because the pope is more the vicar of God than the emperor is, for the pope is equated with the sun which is greater than the moon in quantity, dignity, office and sublimity.[65]

The emperor's divine vicariate is trumped, as it were, by the pope's. In strict hierocratic theory, however, this passage is illogical in that the pope as the superior vicar would be above the emperor's head. Baldus is clearly envisaging an extremely rare form of papal action: *Sext.*, 2.14.2 refers to the deposition of Frederick II by Innocent IV in 1245 at the First Council of Lyon. Amongst civilians there was disagreement about the applicability of the sun–moon allegory to the relationship between the emperor and the pope. Guilelmus de Cuneo, for instance, whom Baldus much admired had given it prominence: 'There are two luminaries, a greater one, namely the church or the pope, and a lesser one, namely the emperor, as in Auth. "Quomodo oporteat episcopos", § "quia vero" [Coll., 1.6 = Nov.,6]';[66] whereas Albericus de Rosciate referring to Innocent III's famous decretal, *Solite*, unsurprisingly approves Dante's denial of the papal interpretation: 'Although what the chapter, *Solite* [X.1.33.6], has to say about the sun and the moon is commonly accepted, Dante himself however denies that it is true that the priesthood and empire are represented therein, and he proves this in the said *quaestio* with subtle and convincing reasoning.'[67] Elsewhere Baldus reinforces his argument by maintaining that the pope through his role of approving, anointing and crowning obtains the power to depose the emperor: 'Examination, however, promotion, unction,

---

[64] See Ullmann, *Short History of the Papacy*, p. 214 for that of Peter II of Aragon by Innocent III.

[65] *Cons.*, 3.283, fol. 88r, ed. Brescia, 1491 (= *Cons.*, 1.333, ed. Venice, 1575). Cp. this sun–moon allegory in Gregory VII, *Registrum*, 7.25, pp. 505–6 (ed. Caspar), and Innocent III's decretal, 'Solite': *Registrum*, 1.401, p. 600 (ed. Hageneder and Haidacher).

[66] Ad C.1.1.1 (fol. 2r).

[67] Ad C.7.37.3, n. 19 (fol. 109r). See Dante, *Monarchia*, c. 4, pp. 365–6.

consecration, coronation and the laying on of hands belong to the lord
pope, as in the said [X.1.6.34]...The lord pope will therefore with cause
be able to depose the emperor, as in [*Decr. Grat.*, C.15,q.6,c.3].'[68]
Through undergoing this process the *Rex Romanorum* places himself
directly in the power of the pope: there is a fundamental distinction
to be made between his position as king, which does not derive from
the pope, and his status as *imperator formatus*, which entirely depends
upon the will of the pope. Indeed, papal confirmation of the *Rex
Romanorum*, the first stage towards imperial coronation, signifies the
superioritas of the pope:

Note further...that nothing is greater and holier than the empire with the
understood exception of the apostolate of St Peter. For since the pope confirms
the emperor this is a clear sign of his superiority, as in Auth. 'De defensoribus
civitatum', § 'interim' [Coll.,3.2 = Nov.,15], and thus the emperor swears
fidelity to the lord pope [X.1.6.34; *Clem.*,2.9.1].[69]

Thus the *Rex Romanorum* becomes subject in a unique way to the pope
from the moment of papal confirmation; but his *imperium* obtained
through election does not have the pope as its origin. For this reason
it is the electors who can depose the king after his election, but only
the pope can do so after papal confirmation:

But I ask here whether the emperor could renounce the empire and place it
in the hands of the electors. And I say that he could not because they are not
his superiors...But after the emperor is confirmed and crowned or merely
confirmed the electors do not have the power to deprive him. It cannot
therefore be renounced and placed in their hands.[70]

What therefore emerges is that Baldus' view draws on a range of
juristic sources to elaborate an argument to accommodate the two
crucial facts, namely that, when he wrote, the *Rex Romanorum* through
his election alone gained full imperial jurisdiction, and that only the
pope could confer the imperial title. He does not follow Cynus[71] and
Albericus, for instance, in denying the pope's jurisdiction over the
emperor, nor does he approach the extremely hierocratic statements
to be found in Bartolus' commentary on *Ad reprimendum*, statements
of which the most ardent papal apologist would have been proud.[72]

---

[68] *De pace Constantie*, ad v. 'Hoc quod nos' (fol. 90r) – this is the immediate continuation
of the passage quoted above, p. 34.

[69] Baldus ad C.1.14.12 (fol. 55r). See also id., *Cons.*, 3.303, fol. 98v, ed. Brescia, 1491
(= *Cons.*, 1.353, ed. Venice, 1575).

[70] Baldus ad D.1.14.3 (fol. 47r).

[71] i.e. in his commentary on the *Codex* and the *Lectura ad Digestum vetus* (ed. Frankfurt,
1578).   [72] Ad v. 'Totius orbis' (fol. 1r).

39

While it is true that for Baldus the pope's power to depose the emperor, as derived from his confirming and crowning him, must ultimately depend on his vicariate of Christ, there is no deduction of any wide-scale temporal jurisdiction for the pope on the basis of this vicariate. The pope's universal temporal power, that is his sovereignty over the universal emperor, is clearly limited. It is not a claim to actual universal rule in any sense, but a right of confirmation, coronation and ultimately of deposition in extreme crisis. Furthermore, the pope's sovereignty is hedged around in two crucial respects. He does not have a completely free hand as regards deposition of the emperor: a deposition without just cause is invalid: 'The emperor can therefore be deposed...But if the pope deposes the emperor through deceit or personal ambition without a legitimate and grave cause, that deposition is null in law.'[73] It could be argued on hierocratic principles that the pope's power is not thereby diminished, because it is up to the pope to decide whether the cause is just, there being no institutional restraints to make moral limitations on the pope effective. Baldus is, however, suggesting that there is a norm of justice against which such papal actions can be judged, and if necessary found wanting; that papal jurisdiction like all true jurisdiction is a moral power. The practical questions would be, what precisely would constitute injustice on the pope's part, and who would decide whether he was acting unjustly? Baldus does, however, introduce a far more specific limitation on the pope's power over the emperor: because at the imperial coronation both parties had entered into a feudal relationship the pope is governed by feudal law in his dealings with his vassal, the emperor. Whereas the requirement of a *iusta causa* for a deposition places no practical restraint upon the pope, feudal law provides the emperor with the remedy of a right of armed resistance against the pope if the latter acts unjustly in feudal terms, as Baldus says in the continuation of this passage:

And there is another reason: the church has a reciprocal obligation to its vassal, and cannot harm him [i.e. the emperor] as regards his empire. Indeed the pope shows himself unsuited to his power if he does not render such justice to the emperor who swore fealty to him... And the emperor can defend himself with his army.

This right of resistance exists essentially because the feudal bond creates a reciprocal relationship of rights and duties. The employment of feudal concepts here can cause no surprise since in the thirteenth and

[73] Baldus, *De pace Constantie*, ad v. 'In nomine Christi membrum' (fol. 94v). Cf. id. ad C.1.14.12 (fol. 55v).

fourteenth centuries the idea had become increasingly widespread that the emperor's oath of *fidelitas* to the pope created a feudal bond between them.[74] Essentially and originally the relationship between the pope and the emperor had not been a feudal one from either the papal or imperial point of view: Frederick I for instance had at the incident at Besançon firmly repudiated any suggestion of feudal subjection to the pope, while in the high and late Middle Ages the papacy maintained that the emperor was its unique officer whose function was justified and was to be accepted on the grounds of *fides* in the sense of Christian not feudal faith. Indeed, the papacy took great care to differentiate between its feudal relationship with its vassal kings and that with the emperor.[75] The emerging prevalence of a feudal interpretation reveals how deeply embedded feudal conceptions were in the late Middle Ages, so much so that the relationship between a *superior* and an *inferior* tended to be seen in feudal terms, especially where any oath of fidelity existed between the two: the element of *fides* became feudalised. Indeed, thirteenth- and fourteenth-century Italy saw new life breathed into feudalism: the *signori* tended to be drawn from the feudal nobility, and the imperial and papal vicariates they sought were considered to be feudal in nature.[76] The vitality of feudal conceptions finds expression throughout Baldus' works. His statement of the emperor's feudal rights against the pope is very strong, if not extreme, and is a clear reflection of his respect for the rights of the emperor. He places a major limitation on the pope's freedom of action, because the vassal may decide whether the pope is acting unjustly or not and act accordingly: the papal power which limits that of the emperor has its own limitations.

Furthermore at the end of his life, and in desperation at the continuation of the Schism, Baldus in two passages (ad X.1.3.14 and X.1.3.25) expressed the view that the emperor and kings could force both popes to submit if they refused to end the Schism, whether through resignation, convening a council or accepting arbitration.[77] He makes it perfectly clear that this does not imply any superiority of the lay rulers over the church: they would act to help the church in an extreme and unique circumstance, that is to say they would be forcing the two popes as individuals for the good of the church as an institution. There is no suggestion that the lay rulers as such can end the Schism:

[74] See Wilks, *Problem of Sovereignty*, p. 321.
[75] See Ullmann, *Growth of Papal Government*, pp. 337–43. For the 'incident' see id., 'Cardinal Roland and Besançon'.
[76] See Dean, 'Lords vassals and clients'.
[77] Ad X.1.3.14, n. 7 (fol. 40v), and ad X.1.3.25, n. 18 (fol. 53v) – this forms part of what is strictly speaking an *additio* (see above, p. 9, n. 39).

he favours a general council.[78] The justifications he produces for this lay role are thin. In his commentary on X.1.3.14 he justifies the imperial action on the grounds that the empire is the *patronus* of the church because it gave it a dowry (the Donation of Constantine). Elsewhere Baldus had earlier rejected this dowry argument;[79] furthermore his whole treatment of the Donation does not accept the element of lay superiority implied by the term, *patronus*. Not only that, it is difficult to see how the Donation, the role of which for Baldus was to establish papal temporal jurisdiction in the patrimony, also justifies imperial interference in the exercise of the papal office over Christendom as a whole. In his commentary on X.1.3.25 Baldus justifies this imperial role on the grounds that the emperor is the 'friend, brother, patron and debtor' of the church. Here as in the commentary on X.1.3.14 the impression given is that Baldus is searching for whatever justifications may come to hand: although he did once refer to the empire and the church as 'fraternizing',[80] his major view is that the church is the mother of the empire, thus meaning that she is superior not equal to the empire, as a sibling relationship would imply.[81] The view that the emperor is 'friend' and 'debtor' does indeed reinforce the imperial role of aiding the church, but Baldus' consistent treatment of the role of the emperor shows that this should be exercised in subordination to the spiritual mission of the church. In his commentary on X.1.3.14 Baldus implies that kings should participate in compelling the recalcitrant popes. His justification is that a form of feudal bond overlays the relationship between the papacy and secular monarchs in general (quite apart from those which are papal vassals strictly speaking). Again, the theocratic origin of regal power formalised through ecclesiastical unction, which is essentially non-feudal, has become feudalised,[82] a further reflection of the contemporary extension of feudal conceptions. Baldus' general statement is in itself by no means unusual for his period: Aquinas, for instance, had expressed a similar opinion which was well-known.[83] Essentially this feudal relationship would subordinate kings to the papacy, and indeed Baldus' apparent identification of the

---

[78] This is the impression given by his lengthy discussion of the role of the cardinals in calling a council (ad X.1.3.25, n. 20, fol. 53v), on which passage see also Tierney, *Foundations*, pp. 216–17; Wahl, 'Reluctant conciliarism', pp. 27–9; and Swanson, *Universities, Academics*, p. 138.

[79] See above, p. 34, n. 55.

[80] See above, p. 27.   [81] See above, p. 34.

[82] The development of this view may have been facilitated by the terminological identity between the monarch's *fides* in the church and feudal *fides*.

[83] *Quaest. quodlib.*, 12, qu. 13, art. 19 ad 2, 'In isto tempore reges sunt vasalli ecclesie' (ed. Spiazzi, p. 232) – see the discussion in Calasso, *I Glossatori*, p. 135.

ecclesia with the pope suggests that he is adopting a hierocratic interpretation. The precise references to the *Liber Decretalium* are, however, strange in that they do not relate to his point, and the application to France would not in any case be acceptable to the French monarchy. The point however is that in the context of the passage as a whole Baldus is in these remarks seizing on an available argument, and, irrespective of the niceties of the feudal relationship between pope and kings, is using this feudal bond to justify the vassal's aid to the institution of the church as such without thereby implying any superiority on the vassal's part. Overall in these two passages Baldus does not infringe his general view of the supremacy of the pope in spiritual matters. As he says in his commentary on X.1.3.14, although there is this role for secular force, ultimately the popes cannot be coerced into giving up their rights. Yet in a third passage (his commentary on X.1.6.34) Baldus' patience seems exhausted and his words are blunter: 'Note that the office of the emperor is to defend the church, as here, and to exalt the pope...For this reason, lest the Catholic people come to ruin on account of the schism the emperor can so apply remedies from without (I do not say from within) that he may dispose of the papacy...Note that every persecutor of the Catholic church is to be exterminated, something which goes against the popes who are controlling the schism.'[84] Thus in this crisis Baldus says that the emperor can dispose of the papal office. What he means however is that it is the role of the emperor to enforce papal cooperation in the face of a general council called by the Roman cardinals, a council at which the emperor (or more correctly the *Rex Romanorum* in the case of Wenceslas), kings and princes would be present, and which would solve the Schism: 'A council is necessary in this case so that the Roman clergy, amongst whom all the world's true and indubitable cardinals are contained, would have to convene it and call the king of the Romans to it and all kings and princes whom it concerns.'[85] Baldus' remarks in his commentary on X.1.6.34 taken at their face value contravene everything he has said about the relationship between empire and papacy; but just as his arguments in his commentaries on X.1.3.14 and X.1.3.25 are unsatisfactory and the product of a despairing concern for the church, Baldus is at X.1.6.34 driven by hopelessness, and his solution to this crisis cannot be taken as undermining his general conception of the relationship between imperial and papal authority.

The overall view that emerges in Baldus' works is that, while the

---

[84] n. 10 (fol. 93r).   [85] Ad X.1.6.42, n. 16 (fol. 97v).

pope possesses an ultimate form of universal sovereignty which appears most dramatically in moments of extreme crisis, the emperor also enjoys a real universal sovereignty, which is the necessary basis of the fundamental constitutional law of Christendom, and which remains valid whatever the ultimate relationship of emperor and pope. This view is not a dualist one but rather a form of hierarchy of sovereignty, and as such unacceptable to imperial publicists such as Dante or Marsilius, or pro-imperial jurists like Albericus. It would also be unattractive to extreme hierocrats in the fourteenth century who would maintain that full sovereignty could lie only with the pope.[86] Baldus' conception of the precise and limited senses in which the pope is the emperor's superior has shown that he considers that the canonist view of papal supremacy has to be distinguished in the scholastic sense: indeed, he expressly tells us that the canonist view cannot be accepted *tout court* but has to be interpreted in such a way that the temporal sovereignty of the emperor is retained.[87] There is, however, a major statement by Baldus which if taken in isolation would appear to be dualist in nature:

But the emperor has a superior, namely the pope... A just pope is the supreme vicar of God. Anyone who says to the contrary is a liar. As regards the world the emperor is greater than the pope, and the pope, if he is just, is greater as regards God: he is not greater than the emperor in this world.[88]

The pope's ultimate superiority deriving from his divine vicariate is clearly spiritual in kind, whereas the emperor in the secular sphere is superior even to the pope. Indeed, the phraseology is strongly reminiscent of the Thomist *duplex ordo in rebus* (double order in things) and thus directly apposite for expressing the distinction between spiritual and temporal powers.[89] It is quite possible that this passage is evidence of inconsistency in Baldus' thought; but if it is taken in the context of his overall view it can be seen to stress that temporal sovereignty lies with the emperor whereas the pope's ultimate superiority has a spiritual base. Most interestingly the idea of the moral limitations on papal authority is taken a stage further: the pope only enjoys a spiritual superiority over the emperor if he is a *papa iustus*. Thus it is no longer a question of denying the validity of papal actions

---

[86] See Wilks, 'Idea of the church', pp. 40–9.

[87] Ad D.V. Proem, ad v. 'Quoniam omnia' (fol. 1r), 'Et non est negandum quod papa qui habet claves celi et mundi sibi traditas ad iusticiam est maior imperatore et nomine et re *secundum quid sed non simpliciter.* Imperat enim cesar de iure in universa ditione etc.' (See above, p. 24, n. 26, and p. 30, n. 43.)

[88] Ad D.1.14.3 (fol. 47r).   [89] See S.T., 1a, qu. 21, art. 1 ad 3.

on the grounds of injustice, but an attack on a crucial presupposition of the hierocratic theory: the distinction between the papal office and its human incumbent, whereby the moral unworthiness of the holder did not affect the validity of his jurisdictional acts as pope.[90] Baldus indicates that the question of whether a pope is just or not affects his powers of jurisdiction, the implication being that the pope may be judged as a man for his moral imperfections. The historical significance of this view is clear in the context of the controversies concerning the nature of the papal office from the thirteenth century onwards, when the papacy was increasingly attacked and judged at the weak point in its defences – the quality of the individual popes.[91]

THE TEMPORAL POWER OF THE POPE

Yet throughout Baldus' career the great and ever-present political reality which directly affected his life was papal temporal power in all its vicissitudes: its successes and its defeats, its recuperations under Albornoz and its problems during the Great Schism, its war with its natural ally, Florence, and its swallowing up of the liberty of Perugia. The question of the juristic relationship between the emperor and the pope in the second half of the *trecento* was strictly theoretical and of no practical importance whatsoever as regards Italy. After Lewis IV's incursion which brought the last papal–imperial dispute into the peninsula, and which, as Maffei speculates, may have encouraged Cynus to abandon a pro-imperial for a papalist stance, the greatest political issue of the high Middle Ages, the relationship between pope and emperor, in actual terms withered away as being irrelevant in a Europe in which territorial states were becoming more consolidated, and the empire itself tended to be seen even by its rulers as more German than universal. Thus the question of the pope's ultimate universal sovereignty was no longer of pressing practical importance for Italian jurists; nor indeed did they have to concern themselves with any direct exercise of real temporal power in Italy by the emperor. It was the pope's actual territorial power in the patrimony of St Peter which demanded and received Baldus' attention.[92]

---

90 On this crucial distinction see Ullmann, *Principles*, pp. 38, 50, 102–3 and 304.

91 See Ullmann, *Short History of the Papacy*, pp. 269–70, and 327. Judgment of the pope for his personal defects was proposed by Frederick II: see *M.G.H., Const.*, II, n. 215, p. 297.

92 See Ermini, 'Diritto Romano comune', p. 63, for the sharp contrast between the reality of ecclesiastical temporal power in Italy, and the theoretical nature of imperial power there, in the period after 1250.

The existence of this direct papal temporal jurisdiction confronted Baldus with two fundamental juristic problems: how could the basic proposition of the emperor's universal secular sovereignty be reconciled with the pope's rule in central Italy; and how in the light of his conception of the nature of the papacy's universal authority did the popes obtain a right to temporal power in this area? The answers to both questions are woven together in his discussions. Having accepted the first principle of the universal temporal authority of the emperor, the remainder of Baldus' political thought can be seen as a detailed modification of this proposition in order to retain it as true in a crucial and necessary sense while justifying and accepting the authority of the other bearers of political power in the fourteenth century, the papacy, kings, cities and *signori*: in Baldus' structure of the constitutional law of Christendom the universal sovereignty of the emperor remains logically necessary, yet has to be reconciled with the fact that the contemporary emperor's direct power is limited to certain territories in central Europe. The papacy's temporal jurisdiction attaches to imperial authority a limitation which deserves to be considered first because of its position at the heart of his political theory, and its unique justification which derives from the very foundation of Baldus' world-view.

As we have seen, viewed on the universal scale temporal jurisdiction as such is for Baldus an imperial rather than a papal possession, so much so that temporal authority remains imperial in a fundamental sense, whoever exercises it and by whatever justification: 'It is certain...that temporal jurisdiction is, as it were, rooted in the emperor.'[93] He maintains however that this *imperium* is not universally exercised by the emperor but is divided with the pope in such a way that each is sovereign within his own territory, whether it be the *terrae imperii* (lands of the empire) or the *terrae ecclesiae* (lands of the church):

The emperor possesses imperial majesty everywhere because majesty is not divided, as is neither character nor fame. But he does not have imperial administration everywhere, for he has an *imperium* divided with the pope in such a way that the lands of the Roman church are not subject to the emperor either directly or indirectly... Again, just as the pope does not legitimise in the lands of the empire, neither does the emperor in those of the pope, as in the said [X.4.17.13], for in the papal lands the emperor is reduced to a status like that of a private person, and if he has no jurisdiction he cannot therefore grant privileges.[94]

---

93 Ad *Specul.*, 2.2.7 (p. 376).
94 *Cons.*, 2.37, fol. 11v, ed. Brescia, 1490 (= *Cons.*, 4.40, ed. Venice, 1575). See also id. ad X.2.28.7, n. 2 (fol. 349r); id. ad C.6.42.14 (fol. 125r); and id. ad D.1.4.1 (fol. 21r).

Bartolus also, as is well known, had previously adopted precisely this territorial division of temporal jurisdiction in Christendom, a position which reflected the realities of power so far as papal jurisdiction was concerned, and accommodated the canon law contention maintained since *Pastoralis cura* that imperial jurisdiction in Italy was territorially confined.[95] What is perhaps not so obvious is that this division of jurisdiction means that a single form, and therefore kind of authority is being exercised by two different people: the emperor and the pope. This is clearly Baldus' meaning; but it is explained with greater lucidity by Bartolus who says of church jurisdiction in the papal patrimony: 'In those lands the Roman church exercises jurisdiction which belonged to the Roman empire, and it admits this. They do not therefore cease to be part of the Roman people; the administration of these provinces, however, is conceded to another.'[96] Imperial authority, however, remains universal despite this territorial limitation on the exercise of the emperor's jurisdiction; thus Baldus maintains that *laesa maiestas* can be committed against the emperor anywhere including the city of Rome,[97] and Bartolus holds that the emperor retains a regulatory function in the *terrae ecclesiae*, thus adhering to the original papal conception of the imperial role of protecting the church.[98]

Baldus did not derive the pope's temporal jurisdiction hierocratically from the latter's vicariate of Christ, which, as we have seen, possessed according to Baldus an essentially spiritual nature issuing in the pope's conserving role: the justification of the papal *imperium* was a human measure, the Donation of Constantine. This was logically necessary since for Baldus the title to that jurisdiction, which was derived from its first human source, the Roman people, lay validly with the emperor who in the person of Constantine had transferred it through the Donation to the pope. The Donation of Constantine was of course a *locus classicus* of medieval civilian and canonist jurisprudence, and all jurists discussed it.[99] Even given this welter of words about it Baldus' contribution to the discussion in the fourteenth century is of the first importance, and stands out clearly especially in comparison with those

---

[95] See Woolf, *Bartolus*, p. 99. Bartolus' hierocratic stand-point however in his commentary on *Ad reprimendum* led him even so to give the advantage to the pope who, he considered, could cite in the *terrae imperii*, whereas the emperor could not cite in the *terrae ecclesiae* (ad v. 'Per edictum', fol 5r).
[96] Ad D.49.15.24, n. 4 (fol. 228r).   [97] Ad C.1.3.32, and ad C.7.53.8.
[98] *Ad reprimendum*, ad v. 'Totius orbis' (fol 1r).
[99] The main modern study is Maffei, *La donazione*. Considerable reference to juristic discussion is also to be found in Laehr, *Die Konstantinische Schenkung bis zur Mitte des 14. Jahrhunderts*, and id., 'Die Konstantinische Schenkung in der abendländischen Literatur des ausgehenden Mittelalters'.

of Cynus and Bartolus. Cynus issued contrary opinions on its validity.[100] Bartolus' treatment is generally recognised as being one of the weaker parts of his political thought being vitiated by his *caveat* in two crucial passages that he wishes to please the church in whose territories he is speaking; as a result it is not possible for his interpreter to be completely certain of his true meaning, although the general impression given to his reader is that he did not consider it to be valid.[101]

The whole direction of Baldus' treatment is to justify the Donation's validity. This was necessary because the Donation appeared to contravene what the civilians agreed was a fundamental duty of the emperor, that he should not alienate part of the empire.[102] Baldus is scrupulously fair to those jurists who do not agree with him: in two prominent places in his commentaries, those on the Proem to the *Digestum vetus* and the rubric, 'De novo Codice componendo', initiating the *Codex*, he examines exhaustively the juristic arguments for and against the Donation's validity before reaching his own solution favourable to it.[103] Important discussions occur however throughout his works, and his position is encapsulated in his commentary on X.2.24.33, Honorius III's seminal decretal, *Intellecto*, which became the *locus classicus* for canonistic

---

[100] See Maffei, *La donazione*, pp. 136–45. See Cynus ad C.7.39.6, n. 1–2 (fol. 448r) where he denies that the Roman church could have prescribed the jurisdiction supposedly given by the Donation (for the question of such prescription by the church see below, p. 53). Of this passage Maffei says, (p. 139), 'L'accertamento della imprescrittibilità sembra coincidere implicitamente con quello dell'inalienabilità.' Whereas in his *Lectura super Digesto Veteri*, ad D.1.8.9, and ad Proem, Const. 'Omnem', he justifies the validity of the Donation (see Maffei, La '*Lectura super Digesto veteri*', p. 51). Jacobus Butrigarius also both affirmed and denied the validity of the Donation (Maffei, *La donazione*, pp. 163–9), as Baldus remarks (below, pp. 54–5).

[101] See Bartolus ad D.V., Proem, Const. 'Omnem', n. 14 (fol. 3v), and ad Auth., 1.6 (= Nov., 6), fol. 10v: Maffei (*La donazione*, pp. 185–90) maintains that it is impossible to make out his true opinion in these passages. Indications, however, that Bartolus might have accepted the validity of the Donation are provided by his division into *terrae imperii* and *terrae ecclesiae*, and his commentary ad D.49.15.24, n. 4 (fol. 228r), where he says of those peoples subject to the Roman church through the Donation, 'posito pro constanti quod donatio tenuerit, quodque revocari non possit, adhuc dico istos de populo Romano esse' (the passage quoted above, p. 47, is the immediate continuation of this). Baszkiewicz ('Quelques remarques', pp. 12–13) maintains, however, that Bartolus certainly defended the Donation partly because he considered the independence of Perugia to be founded on an imperial grant of the city to the church which in turn had given it its liberty (see above, p. 20, n. 10).

[102] See below, pp. 86–8.

[103] Maffei gives an extensive treatment to Baldus (*La donazione*, pp. 193–207). At p. 200, n. 19 he gives lengthy reasons for doubting whether Baldus wrote the final lines of the commentary on C. Rubr., 'De novo Codice componendo' (as contained in the editions) in which he suggests what he claims are two hitherto unheard-of arguments for his opponents. Laehr only paraphrases Baldus' commentary ad D.V. Proem (*Die Konstantinische Schenkung bis zur Mitte des 14. Jahrhunderts*, pp. 133–5).

discussion of the role of the coronation oath in the monarch's duty of non-alienation:

Note that a king's oath even while he is alive does not harm the rights of his kingdom. The Donation of Constantine goes against this. But in that case Constantine had not sworn not to alienate, and it was a miracle for the sake of the defence of the Catholic faith. Modern emperors however first confirm the donation with the pope's authority, and afterwards they give an oath, and saving this they then swear as is contained here. Others say that the church is in usurpation, but this opinion is not a good and Catholic one because the supreme authority of the pope and the Catholic church seems to be excepted from the operation of every law and constitution, and the pope is not understood to receive an oath against himself, as above [X.2.24.19;D.33.8.6,4]. This question has never been so resolved as to remove the doubts of those favouring the empire, because the empire cannot be diminished, for the whole of it could for the same reason be dissolved bit by bit. This line of reasoning is a very difficult one to disprove and Accursius bases his argument on it in his gloss on the beginning of Auth. 'Quomodo oporteat episcopos' [Coll.,1.6 = Nov.,6], and no one ever says that Accursius would have been a heretic on this account. We also see that these days the empire is much diminished; but whatever is said against the universal church's well-being, upon which the empire and the whole world depend, is nothing but dreams.[104]

This is a frank recognition that the alienation problem cannot totally convincingly be solved within terms of Roman law. One possible solution could be to distinguish between the grant of a substantial part of the empire (a *quota*), which would be by definition invalid, and the donation of individual possessions (*res particulares*), which could be valid. Here Baldus clearly considers that the granting of *res particulares* still counts as invalid alienation. Elsewhere his views on the usefulness of the distinction to show a way out of the problem are contradictory: while he can ridicule it,[105] he can also use it as an argument for the Donation's validity.[106] Such juristic niceties are not going to provide Baldus with his real solution. As this passage (X.2.24.33) shows so well,

---

[104] n. 4 (fol. 315r). X.2.24.33 both condemns royal alienations of a kingdom's rights and declares that any oath made by a king to support such alienations is invalid because it contravenes his coronation oath. For Baldus' treatment of X.2.24.33 in his discussion of kingship see below, p. 219. See Riesenberg, *Inalienability*, pp. 113–44, for the significance of *Intellecto* and the commentaries on it.

[105] Ad *Feud.*, Proem, ad v. 'Expedita' (fol. 2v).

[106] Ad *Specul.*, 2.2.7 (p. 376). In his commentary ad C. Const., 'De novo Codice componendo' (fol. 1r) he uses the distinction but comes to no clear conclusion and refers to Accursius' contrary glosses on the Donation's validity – ad D.1.12.1, ad v. 'cum urbem' (for), and ad Auth., 'Quomodo oporteat episcopos' (Coll., 1.6, praef. = Nov., 6, praef.) (against). See Maffei, *La donazione*, pp. 69–74, for the apparent contradiction in Accursius, which was also noted by Bartolus (ad D.1.12.1, n. 1).

the answer is provided by the attitude which pervades his political thought: the simultaneous acceptance of political facts and respect for the claims of the church. It is highly revealing that Accursius in the famous passage to which Baldus refers here, and which denies the validity of the Donation, expressly rejects a solution in accordance with the facts (a quintessentially Glossatorial attitude),[107] whereas Baldus as a Commentator *par excellence* considers that the fact of the empire's greatly diminished extent as a real political power at the end of the fourteenth century must be recognised as a basic consideration. That is to say, he makes a distinction here between the universal empire in a juristic sense, which remains constitutionally necessary in Christendom, and the actual power of the emperor. The letter of the Roman law cannot provide a solution: it has to be interpreted in the light of reality. Reality, however, for Baldus was not simply a this-worldly one; he accepted the religious claims of the Catholic Church as being divinely given truth and therefore real in a special sense, and that therefore any attack on the well-being of the church as an institution must be illusory because it was directed against the spiritual authority upon which the whole world-order, the empire included, depended by divine decree ('somnia sunt [etc]...').[108] Any denial of the validity of the Donation would clearly be such an attack. Since it was in this exalted position, the church, as he says, could not be bound by any restrictions in civil law, and extraordinary measures breaking through the normal constraints of Roman law were justified for the defence of the faith (the 'miracle' of the Donation). This was his mature view as is made clear by a passage in his commentary on the *Libri feudorum* written earlier in the 1390s where he maintains that the Donation, because it derived from the Catholic faith, possessed a validity which being an alienation of the empire it could not have had under Roman law alone:

---

[107] 'Sed licet solutio facti ad nos non pertineat, solvimus de iure quod non valuit talis collatio sive donatio' (quoted in Maffei, *La donazione*, p. 67). This was his main view. Cynus in his *Lectura super Digesto veteri* (Maffei, *La 'Lectura super Digesto veteri'*, p. 51) was happy to dismiss Accursius' objections to the Donation's validity.

[108] That Baldus intended this form of spiritual interpretation here rather than any direct claim by the papacy to universal temporal jurisdiction is shown by the inclusion of the phrase, 'universalis orbis', and is supported by id., *consilium* on the Great Schism (ad C.6.34), fol. 103r): 'Quomodo enim mundus sine capite spirituali stare potest a quo cuncta dependent? Si navicula Petri submergitur ubi erit animarum solamen? Apud quem erit administratio sacramentorum, imperatorum confirmatio et consecratio, regum inunctio, absolutio et remissio peccatorum?... Certe apud neminem esse potest nisi apud Petrum clavigerum Iesu Christi. Nunquid Odoacer conferet sacramenta? Absit [C.1.2.16].'

The writers of old resolved that question by touching on this one concerning the donation made to the church, and which owed more to divinity than to human nature. They said that as far as the expropriation of territory, dignity or jurisdiction was concerned it was neither valid nor possible; but that the advantages attached to these and the right to use them could be conceded, always saving recognition by the empire and good faith. For it would be a form of fatuity to maintain that the emperor should mutilate himself, that is amputate limbs of the empire from himself... And thus if the Donation of Constantine had not proceeded from the Catholic faith, as indeed it did proceed, but merely by right of the imperial office, the head of the empire, that is Rome, could not have been cut off from the other members, because decapitation involves the destruction not of a part but of the whole.[109]

This religious justification, however, applies only to the Donation, which was a unique case, and not to alienations by other monarchs who remain in this respect restricted by limitations in civil law.[110]

The monarch's duty of non-alienation was in the medieval period formalised by the coronation oath. Because the emperor swore a coronation oath, it might be thought that this placed on him the same duty of non-alienation that it imposed upon a king; and it is through the discussion of this point that Baldus in the passage quoted from his commentary approaches the Donation. After brushing the objection aside in the case of Constantine on the grounds that he had sworn no such oath, Baldus states that modern emperors confirm the Donation before they take their imperial oath, and that therefore the contents of the Donation are excluded from those things which they have sworn not to alienate ('hoc salvo iurant'). This contemporary observation has important implications. It reflects fourteenth-century practice: Henry VII's confirmation of all his predecessors' grants to the papacy including the Donation was included in the *Corpus Iuris Canonici* (*Clem.*, 2.9.1), and Charles IV in 1355 had repeated the confirmation. Thus juristically the papal claim to direct temporal jurisdiction in the patrimony rested not only on a supposed imperial constitution made in the distant past, but was reinforced by repeated and recent reenactments of it. Both in legal reality and Baldus' interpretation the papacy's claim was

---

[109] Ad Proem, ad v. 'Expedita' (fol. 2v). For the idea that Constantine could have conceded the use of the papal territories see Jacobus de Ravannis ad C. Rubr., 'De emendatione Iustiniani Codicis', ad v. 'Augustus' (fol. 1r).

[110] Baldus, *Cons.*, 1.359, fol. 109v, ed. Brescia, 1490 (= *Cons.*, 3.159, ed. Venice, 1575), 'Quicquid dicatur de donatione Constantini que fuit miraculosa, si similes donationes fierent a regibus non[non *ed.* 1575; ideo *ed.* 1490] ligarent successores quibus regni tutela non dilapidatio est commissa.' For Baldus' conception of the king's tutorial function see below, p. 219. *Sext.*, 1.6.17 is a probable source for the idea that the Donation was miraculous (Maffei, *La donazione*, p. 203, n. 21).

strengthened. Furthermore, it is another proof of the continuing real jurisdictional power of the emperor. It is not entirely clear, however, what Baldus means by maintaining that the confirmation takes place 'auctoritate pape': it most probably signifies that in this the emperor acts at the pope's behest, and under his supervision, thus fulfilling a required precondition for coronation. Certainly Baldus' view here is consistent with his overall theory of the imperial source of papal temporal jurisdiction, and the form in which the pope's superiority is shown at imperial coronations.

This argument from modern confirmation is obviously only effective if the fundamental arguments justifying imperial alienation to the papacy are accepted. Baldus suggests that the papacy sought a new donation from Charles IV because it had doubts about the original one:

Solution. Prescription by the church is not possible against the emperor who claims temporal jurisdiction by divine institution. The church certainly possesses tithes by divine institution, but temporal jurisdiction by human institution and foresight. But because the church has doubts about the old donation it has had the emperor Charles make it a new one, against which new donation prescription through time cannot be adduced, because it is a recent donation.[111]

What precisely Baldus considers these doubts to have been is not absolutely clear: it is more likely to be reservations about the genuineness of the Donation of Constantine as a historical fact, rather than doubts about its legal validity, because in terms of Roman law Charles IV would have no greater legal authority to donate the patrimony than Constantine had possessed. There may be here an approach towards the denial of the original Donation's genuineness by Nicholas of Cusa and Lorenzo Valla in the fifteenth century; but there is no evidence that Baldus knew of earlier disbelief such as that expressed by Otto III and in the early twelfth century by Gregory of Catina.[112] It is significant that Baldus locates this doubt in the mind of the church to explain why it sought this new donation; there is no suggestion in Baldus' works that he himself doubted either the

---

[111] Ad *Specul.*, 2.2.3 (p. 248). By referring to the donation as 'recens' Baldus makes it clear that he refers to Charles IV. This passage is not mentioned by Maffei in *La donazione*.

[112] See the famous diploma of Otto III (*M.G.H.*, Legum IV, Const. I, n. 26, p. 56). For Gregory of Catina see Laehr, *Die Konstantinische Schenkung bis zur Mitte des 14. Jahrhunderts*, pp. 41–4, and ibid., p. 67, for Wezel's letter to Frederick I expressing the denials of the Donation's validity current in Rome at the time of Arnold of Brescia. Cusa and Valla produced systematic proofs of the Donation's falsity as opposed to the isolated statements of disbelief punctuating the almost seven hundred years of belief in its validity.

genuineness or the validity of the original Donation.[113] The passage contains a very clear statement of Baldus' fundamental view that temporal jurisdiction is an imperial possession claimed from God; and that the papacy therefore derives its temporal jurisdiction from the emperor. It is perfectly logical for Baldus, given his acceptance of the reality of imperial jurisdiction, to derive papal temporal power in the patrimony from a donation from a contemporary emperor.

Because of the juristic difficulties associated with the validity of the Donation of Constantine, the question of whether the papacy had in any case prescribed its jurisdiction in the patrimony had become a common topic amongst jurists, who as always differed: Cynus, for instance, in one passage, as we have seen, was prepared to deny the validity of papal prescription, whereas Albericus both affirmed and denied it.[114] Baldus' denial in this passage is, for him, unusual: his normal and major opinion is to accept the validity of papal prescription. The fundamental objection that the emperor's jurisdiction as universal superior could not be prescribed was held by Baldus to be of no weight because the pope was in no way the inferior of the emperor:

Papal prescription weakens the right of the emperor forever... And although an inferior could not prescribe regalian rights against his superior, as in [C.7.39.6], the pope can however prescribe regalian rights against the emperor and his subjects because he is capable of bearing supreme power, just as one king can prescribe a king's regalian rights against another.[115]

This is a purely secular argument viewing the pope as a temporal sovereign monarch, and as such it illustrates that the prescription argument is of a different kind from the religious justification of the Donation. It is essentially of an auxiliary nature: even if the Donation had not been valid (which according to Baldus it was), the papacy would have legally prescribed temporal jurisdiction in the patrimony anyway; or alternatively prescription may be added to the Donation as a source of the papacy's jurisdiction. Papal temporal jurisdiction is justified not only by imperial grant but also by the choice of the pope's subjects:

[113] Ad D.V. Proem, ad v. 'Quoniam' (fol. 1v), 'Et licet imperatores innovent istam donationem hoc non fit ad diminuendum, sed ad approbandum eandem donationem.'

[114] Cynus ad C.7.39.6 (above, p. 48, n. 100). For Albericus see Maffei's discussion, *La donazione*, p. 178–85: ad D.V. Prima Const., Rubr., n. 8, fol 3v, Albericus supports papal prescription (bolstered by imperial acquiescence in and subsequent confirmation of the Donation which was originally invalid *de iure*), and ad C.7.37.3, n. 32–4 (fol. 110r) denies the possibility of such prescription.

[115] Ad D.V. Proem, ad v. 'Quoniam' (fol. 1v).

For it is agreed that provinces elect themselves a king according to natural reason and the law of peoples, as in [D.1.1.5]. And thus what has been approved from the beginning is judged to be according to the law of peoples. But that oath of fealty to the pope himself was always approved and given by the provinces and cities; therefore such provinces and cities are subject to the lord pope by the law of peoples according to natural reason. And I take this side and affirm it, because, if for argument's sake the Donation had not been valid, the church would have nevertheless prescribed [its jurisdiction] despite [C.4.21.20], because a subject is not prescribing as in that case, but the church is equal to the empire.[116]

Precisely because the pope's temporal jurisdiction is secular in character it is possible for Baldus to ascribe to it the same origins as those of any other secular rulership; and in turning here to natural reason and the *ius gentium* he is using his fundamental explanation for the emergence of government, a line of reasoning which, as we shall see, has immense implications in his political thought. The argument here mixes together two themes. The cities and provinces choose the pope as their ruler; but their continuing choice in itself is not said here to prescribe imperial jurisdiction. It is because they have chosen the pope who is at least the emperor's equal that this prescription is possible; and the pope enjoys this position not through the *ius gentium*, but as a result of his religious authority. It is, therefore, the pope who prescribes imperial jurisdiction; but he is in a position to be able to do this because he has been chosen as ruler by his subjects. The cities and provinces have changed their superior, not through the direct exercise of their own will, but through the authority of the monarch they have chosen. Thus in this prescription argument the secular and the spiritual aspects of papal authority meet: papal temporal jurisdiction can be prescribed because it is secular, but the effectiveness of that prescription depends ultimately on the pope's spiritual authority.

The pope's status relative to the emperor is crucial for the durability of the Donation. As we have seen, Baldus often represents the pope as being not just the emperor's equal, but in certain senses his superior; thus the emperor as the pope's inferior cannot revoke the Donation which has become his superior's right:

If the emperor should have the task of increasing [the empire] and does the opposite, he is then doing what he should not do, and thus he does not prejudice [the rights of] his successor, because in addition he is an officer and not the outright owner... And Jacobus Butrigarius in his lecture at this point held this opinion saying that the alienation is not binding either on the emperor

---

[116] Baldus ad C. Const., 'De novo Codice componendo' (fol. 1v).

himself or his successor, although according to him it is less doubtful in the case of the successor. Afterwards he rightly changed his opinion because, since the pope is the superior, the right has thus been acquired by a superior, and as a result the inferior cannot revoke it.[117]

Because the basic relationship between the emperor and the papacy remains the same, the contemporary *princeps* can make to the church further donations which would be irrevocable, while the church can if it wishes relinquish the Donation or be understood to have abandoned claim to part of it through desuetude, in which case the emperor can reassert his jurisdiction,[118] whereas papal enjoyment of the Donation is seen as confirming its validity.[119]

THE 'LEX REGIA'

Baldus' acceptance of the role of the Donation in irrevocably validating papal temporal jurisdiction in the patrimony assumes even greater importance in his political thought because it helps to explain certain crucial aspects of his theory of the *lex regia* itself, and thus relates to the fundamental constitutional law of Christendom. One of the major topics for debate amongst civilians in the thirteenth and fourteenth centuries was whether the *lex regia* had been a revocable grant, and whether in consequence the Roman people retained the sovereign capacity to make laws generally valid throughout the empire;[120] the implications however of the jurists' divergent views on this question are far from obvious. Amongst Baldus' predecessors there was a major body of opinion in favour of the revocability of the *lex regia*. As they stood, the relevant texts in the *Corpus Iuris Civilis* could be read in the senses of either an irrevocable translation of power or a revocable concession.[121] Azo in the early thirteenth century maintained that the Roman people had conceded power to the emperor in such a way that it had not abdicated any power with the result that the Roman people of his day retained the capacity for general legislation, the emperor

---

[117] Ad C. Const., 'De novo codice componendo' (fol. 1v). For the emperor as officer and the sense in which he is *dominus* see below, pp. 86–8.

[118] Baldus ad D.V. Proem, ad v. 'Quoniam' (fol. 1v), where he refers to Guilelmus de Cuneo's view that the Donation was irrevocable (for Guilelmus' arguments in favour of the Donation's validity see his commentary ad D.V. Proem, ed. Brandi, pp. 106–7).

[119] Baldus ad X.2.24.33, n. 6 (fol. 315r).

[120] See, for instance, Gierke, *Political Theories*, pp. 43–6; Carlyle, *Medieval Political Theory*, v, 64–7; and Ullmann, *Medieval Idea of Law*, pp. 48–9.

[121] D. Const. 'Deo auctore'; D.1.11.1; and C.1.17.1, 7 refer to a 'translation' of power. Inst., 1.2, 6 and D.1.4.1 refer to a 'concession'. See also Kantorowicz, *King's Two Bodies*, p. 103.

being in this respect in no way superior to the people as a whole but only to individual members of it.[122] The full implications of this theory of concession were realized by the early French Commentator, Jacobus de Ravannis: he saw that the people's retention of power derived from its sovereignty over the emperor, whose jurisdiction it could therefore revoke.[123] This statement appears to mark the extreme expression of this view; his younger fellow-countryman, Guilelmus de Cuneo, for instance, was unwilling to go so far, but nevertheless held that the Roman people had never lost its power to make generally valid customary law, since it had only transferred the power of legislation to the emperor through the *lex regia*: the people's capacity to make *consuetudines* (customs) by the exercise of tacit consent remained intact, evidence of a growing recognition of the people's autonomous power to make law.[124]

A fundamental problem of interpretation is posed by the question of how wide the application of the term, *populus Romanus*, is meant to be in this discussion: it could possibly be as wide as Christendom[125] or as narrow as the inhabitants of the city of Rome. In the precise area of juristic opinion in which Baldus' view on the *lex regia* is located the *populus Romanus* in the context of the discussion is understood to be the inhabitants of Rome. In the fourteenth century the city of Rome had of course in practice no power to make generally valid law or to revoke the emperor's authority. Nevertheless there were attempts at forms of resurrection of the sovereignty which the geographical Roman people had once enjoyed. On 17 January 1328, Lewis IV went through a form of coronation 'by the Roman people'; and Cola di Rienzo informed Charles IV, as Arnold of Brescia had Frederick Barbarossa, that the Roman people was the source of his power. Here was no real resurrection, however: the popular election was merely convenient for

---

[122] See Azo, *Summa Codicis*, ad C.1.14 (ed. Pavia, 1484); id., *Lectura* ad C.1.14.11, n. 49–51 (p. 44), ad v. 'Soli imperatori'; and id., *Lectura* ad C.8.52.2, n. 2 (p. 671). For Hugolinus' role in the development of the theory of concession see Carlyle, *Medieval Political Theory*, II, 63–7, and Cortese, *Norma giuridica*, II, 175–6. Odofredus also held that the Roman people could still make law because it had only conceded authority to the emperor (ad D.1.4.1, n. 1, fol. 17v, and ad D.1.3.32, n. 6–7, fol. 15v). For the *dissensiones dominorum* on this point see Cynus ad C.1.14.12, n. 4 (fol. 29r).

[123] Ad C.1.14.12 (fol. 36v). The culmination of his argument is: 'Esto quod populus voluisset a se abdicare, non potuit, nam potestatem vel iurisdictionem sibi commissam non potest abdicare quis a se nisi in manu superioris, ut [D.1.18.20]; et populus non habet superiorem. Verum est quod imperator est superior quolibet de populo, sed non est superior populo' (for a discussion of the whole passage see Ullmann, *Medieval Idea of Law*, p. 48).

[124] See Bartolus ad C.8.52.2 (fol. 114r) for a report of Guilelmus' view.

[125] See Bartolus ad D.49.15.24, n. 6 (fol. 228r).

Lewis in his conflict with John XXII, and its significance was subsequently diminished by his coronation by his anti-pope, Nicholas V;[126] and Charles took no account of Cola's claims. Jacobus Butrigarius, one of Bartolus' teachers, accepted that the era of the people's sovereignty lay in the past, and that in his day ('hodie') the *respublica Romanorum* possessed not general legislative powers but the same local ones as any other municipality; but he still considered that the Roman people retained the power to revoke the *lex regia* and thus begin to issue generally valid laws again, his reason being that because the empire had been established by means of a law this could always be revoked.[127] In contrast the major fourteenth-century Commentators, Cynus, Bartolus and Baldus, concentrated on the political reality of the lack of power of the inhabitants of Rome, realising that the arguments for the people's capacity to revoke the *lex regia* and issue generally valid laws again were essentially an unrealistic view suggested by texts in the *Corpus Iuris Civilis*, and amounting to a purely juristic construction. Cynus' intellectual mentor, Petrus de Bellapertica, had clearly considered that the Roman people through transferring to the emperor its capacity to make general law had thereby lost this power which it had once enjoyed, and currently could only make municipal law of purely local effect, there being no suggestion of its regaining its former capability.[128] For Cynus himself the whole debate about whether the *populus Romanus* could legislate generally was in practical terms quite irrelevant: having given a lengthy exposition of the opposing views he says, 'Make what choice you like from these opinions because I do not care. For if the Roman people were in fact to make a law or custom, I know that it would not be observed outside the city [of Rome].'[129] Cynus did not envisage either real participation by the *populus Romanus* in the choice of individual emperors, or the revocation of the *lex regia*, the consequent abolition of the empire, and the re-establishment of the people's previous jurisdictional position: the empire was divinely sanctioned, and the princely electors had replaced the people as the human agency in the making of emperors.[130] According to Bartolus the relationship between the emperor and the people had changed since the *lex regia*: after this was passed the people had initially still retained the capacity to elect and depose the emperor, and consequently the

---

[126] See Ullmann, *Short History of the Papacy*, p. 285.
[127] Ad D.1.3.32, n. 3 (p. 10); id. ad C.1.14.12 (fol. 31v); and id. ad D.1.3.9 (p. 7). Although the people retains this residual power, Jacobus is clear that the era of popular rule lay in a previous age (ad D.1.18.6, 1, n. 5, p. 44).
[128] Ad Inst., 1.2, n. 14 (p. 74), n. 41 (pp. 92–3) and n. 48–9 (p. 97).
[129] Ad C.1.14.12, n. 4 (fol. 29r).   [130] See above, p. 33.

ability to legislate, whereas in his day, because the German princes elected and the pope deposed the emperor, the contemporary people had abdicated all its *imperium* and with it the right to legislate:[131] the *lex regia* had in short become irrevocable in time.

It is significant that Bartolus does not suggest that it is the will of the people which makes the *lex regia* irrevocable, but rather the actual supplanting of its role of appointing and deposing the emperor by the princes and the pope respectively. Indeed, in his most pro-papal work he develops this theme by giving to the origin of imperial power a hierocratic interpretation which transcends the whole concept of the *lex regia*,[132] a view also to be found, as we have seen, in Cynus' *Lectura* on the *Digestum vetus*.[133] In contrast, what makes Baldus' view quite distinctive is that he considers that it was the will of the people which made the *lex regia* an irrevocable transfer of power from the start: 'The efficient cause however was the Roman people which gave him [i.e. the emperor] the empire. And note the word, "gave": the people therefore lost it.'[134] Baldus realised that the people in establishing a monarchy to rule it had the choice of either revocably committing its jurisdiction and thus remaining the ultimate sovereign, or of irrevocably transferring that sovereignty to its ruler. In the case of the *lex regia* it was an irrevocable grant; but the question of revocability or irrevocability depended on the nature of the contract, the *pacte de gouvernement*, as it were.[135] It remains a perennial problem of political theory whether it is a contradiction in terms to maintain that a sovereign body can alienate its sovereignty; Jacobus de Ravannis, as we have just seen, had held that the Roman people could not abdicate its authority to the emperor precisely because it was sovereign, whereas Baldus expressly disagrees by holding that the Roman people could lose its sovereignty by choosing a superior, the emperor:

Again, note that the people's authority was given over to the emperor. Thus the word, 'formerly', means that such jurisdiction does not remain with the people. Thus it is one thing when the people entrusts its jurisdiction [to someone], but another when it transfers and abdicates it. If, therefore, someone who could do so sets up a superior for himself, he remains the inferior and the subject and loses sovereign authority. That word ['formerly'] therefore indicates that these days sovereignty does not lie in the hands of the Roman people.[136]

---

[131] Ad C.1.14.12, n. 3–4 (fol. 29r).
[133] See above, p. 34, n. 52.
[135] Baldus ad D.1.3.9 (fol. 14r).
[132] See above, p. 39, n. 72.
[134] Ad D.1.2.2, 11, n. 1–2 (fol. 13r).
[136] Ad C.8.47.2 (fol. 323r). The reference to 'formerly' ('olim') is explained shortly before: 'Ibi, "per populum romanum", dicit glossa immo fortius valet apud cesarem quam olim apud populum.'

The implications of this irrevocable loss of authority by the people are crucial in determining the nature and limitations of the emperor's power, and result especially in the lack of institutional controls over him.[137]

The reasons why Baldus holds the *lex regia* to have been irrevocable arc contained in his theory of imperial and papal jurisdiction. For him the *lex regia* was the necessary first stage in the process through which there was established Christendom's fundamental constitution whereby temporal authority was divided between the emperor and the pope: the *lex regia* was the human instrument which instituted the perpetual and universal empire sanctioned by divinity and then approved by Christ and later by the church, the law which served as the basis for the validity of the irrevocable Donation of Constantine, upon which papal temporal jurisdiction depended, and which placed the contemporary Roman people under papal rule – the people through the *lex regia* gave its general legislative power to the emperor whose successor, Constantine, gave it in turn to the pope: 'The question is whether these days the Roman people could legislate. It has to be said that it could not, because it has been denuded of its general power, since that has been transferred to the emperor, as in [C.1.14.8] above, and afterwards transferred by the emperor to the pope.'[138] Thus any undermining of the emperor's position by the suggestion that the *lex regia* was revocable could be seen as removing the major justification of the papal claim to temporal jurisdiction in the papal patrimony. Baldus' interpretation of the *lex regia* is, therefore, as much pro-papal as pro-imperial.

Baldus is not, however, perfectly consistent in his treatment of the *lex regia*, although he remains consistent in his use of the concept of *lex regia* as the source of the validity of papal temporal jurisdiction. As a major argument in favour of the Donation's validity he describes it as a new *lex regia*:

There is a contrary argument in favour of the Donation's validity: that it was made by Constantine together with the senate and the whole people. It is valid therefore as a result of the new *lex regia* which has been made concerning the empire, because it has not been the product of a less effective cause than the first *lex regia*, but of the same or greater force and power (see the end of [D.1.1.4,3] and the argument at [D.20.6.8,11] below). Thus what would not be valid on its own account is valid by the people's authority. Furthermore,

---

[137] See below, pp. 91–2.
[138] Ad C.1.14.12. (fol. 55r–55v). Cp. the immediate continuation of id. ad C.8.47.2 (above).

because the people never dies [D.5.1.76], the death of Constantine does not matter (this is proved in a similar case in [D.2.2.1,1] below), and thus the city of Rome belongs to the church not Caesar, as is noted in [D.1.12.1].[139]

Ultimately the transfer of *imperium* derives from the will of the people. By associating the people with the Donation Baldus circumvents the objection that the emperor thereby alienates what had been entrusted by the people to his predecessor.[140] The papacy thus derived its temporal jurisdiction both from the emperor and directly from the people rather than indirectly. He goes on to repeat his argument that this grant is perpetual and irrevocable because it is made to a superior.[141] The text of *Decr. Grat.*, D.96, c.14 invited the interpretation that Constantine had acted with the counsel of the senate and people of Rome, a view which could be reconciled with the idea that the original *lex regia* had been a transfer of power, whereas Baldus' opinion here that this new *lex regia* drew its efficacy partly from the authority, and thus the consent, of the people cannot be reconciled with his major argument that the original *lex regia* was irrevocable, because it suggests that the people retained authority up to the time of Constantine. Certainly Baldus considers here that the people's loss of authority in the patrimony was irrevocable from the time of the Donation: the perpetuity of the people serves as a guarantee of the everlastingness of the transfer rather than of the continuation of real popular power. For the question of the contemporary papacy's powers of jurisdiction the status of the Roman people between Augustus and Constantine is irrelevant; yet there is an intractable contradiction between Baldus' mutually exclusive views of the irrevocability of both the original and the new *lex regia*, and his auxiliary argument that the temporal subjects of the pope had *de iure gentium* elected him their ruler thereby providing him with a basis for the prescription of imperial jurisdiction: if the people had transferred its power it should not have been in a position to do this.[142] Nevertheless too much need not be made of these problems, because they occur in the context of Baldus' piling up of arguments to demonstrate cumulatively his fundamental position that the Roman people has lost its sovereign jurisdiction, and that the papacy possesses temporal authority both in the city of Rome itself and

[139] Ad D.V., Proem, ad v. 'Quoniam omnia' (fol. 1v).
[140] Cp. id. ad *Feud.*, 2.26 (fol. 52r), 'Constantinus quando donavit urbem beatro Silvestro fecit cum consensu populi ut patet in (*Decr. Grat.*, D.96, c. 14)'.
[141] Ad D.V. Proem, ad v. 'Quoniam omnia' (fol. 1v).
[142] This point applies specifically to the *populus Romanus* within the patrimony: those 'provinces and cities' mentioned by Baldus ad C. Const., 'De novo Codice componendo', fol. 1v (above, p. 54).

the patrimony as a whole (this is especially true in his commentaries on the Proem to the *Digestum vetus* and C. 'De novo Codice componendo'): the coherence of these arguments in relation to one another was not his primary concern. Certainly a major demonstration of the impotence of the contemporary *populus Romanus* is that it lacks the ability to depose the emperor which the pope now possesses:

Solution. The Roman people can depose him [i.e. the emperor]...The contrary appears to be the case: firstly, because the Roman people is subject to the pope, and thus this power resides in the pope, since he is the brain and head of the whole people; secondly, because the people cannot confirm the emperor, and therefore cannot depose him; and thirdly, because the emperor does not swear fealty to the people but to the lord pope. And this is the truth, although Cynus and Raynerius de Forlì would say that the people could depose him, which is not true, however, since it could neither elect nor confirm him, as in Auth. 'De defensoribus civitatum' [Coll.,3.2 = Nov.,15].[143]

Again one possible interpretation implied by the argument from the pope's headship of the people is that he operates powers of deposition which were part of the authority the people had possessed before the Donation. It is impossible to determine whether this interpretation should be pushed so far; but whatever the Roman people's authority in the distant past Baldus trenchantly says of any contemporary pretensions to depose the emperor, 'Formerly therefore it could; these days it cannot...And thus the Roman people should beware of vain opinions and thoughts.'[144]

In Baldus' political theory the *lex regia* explains the human origin of imperial power and the source of papal temporal jurisdiction, but does not provide a general model for the origin of governmental authority: for him the source of the jurisdiction of kings and city-regimes lies, as we shall see, elsewhere, that is in the *ius gentium*. Baldus' crucial but limited usage of the *lex regia* should caution us against employing it as any such general explanation in elucidating medieval political thought.[145] The application of the *lex regia* could be extended from the relationship between the emperor and the Roman people to that between any monarch and his people, and many medieval writers, including Bracton, did this;[146] but such an extension was a matter of choice, which was not taken up by Baldus and was expressly

---

[143] Baldus ad D.1.3.9 (fol. 14r).
[144] Ad *Feud.*, 1.26 (fol. 29v).
[145] I would therefore disagree with the interpretations of for instance Lewis (*Medieval Political Ideas*, I, 148), and Kantorowicz (*King's Two Bodies*, p. 298).
[146] See for instance Kantorowicz, *King's Two Bodies*, pp. 150–1.

rejected later by Bodin as an analogue for the origin of royal power in France.[147] For Baldus any such extension would have made no sense, because it had been the function of the *lex regia* to establish the universal imperial jurisdiction, divided now between the emperor and the pope, within the context of which all other forms of government in Christendom had their existence: the *lex regia* was for him a unique historical event, with the result that any explanation of the origins of the rule of kings and city-regimes would have to employ other concepts available in the *Corpus Iuris Civilis* and elsewhere. As we have seen, the *lex regia* could be interpreted in a manner which either retained or rejected ultimate popular sovereignty. Strictly speaking the *lex regia* can stand as a model for the origins of monarchical power. Problems arise, however, if modern historians, when considering popular or oligarchical regimes, see the *lex regia* as a model for the origins of government and the relationship between rulers and ruled. Here the arguments of both Bartolus and Baldus should again serve as a warning against any such general interpretation using the *lex regia* as a formula in a thesis of popular sovereignty.[148] Both jurists did indeed produce theses of the sovereignty of the people in the context of independent cities; but neither used the concept of the *lex regia* to achieve this – their proofs lay elsewhere. Indeed, since both considered the *lex regia* to be irrevocable, it was not suitable for this purpose; thus, as we shall see, if any interpretation in terms of the *lex regia* is placed on Bartolus' and Baldus' theories of popular sovereignty it is misleading. For Baldus the *lex regia* was an historical grant without contemporary political relevance for the forms of government in kingdoms and independent cities.[149] Moreover, in the works of the Commentators there develops no general thesis of popular sovereignty applicable to such diverse entities as the Roman people, kingdoms and city-republics. Any arguments they advance for popular sovereignty have to be seen as possessing relevance only within the context of the particular political entity to which they apply. Thus from Jacobus de Ravannis' concept of the Roman people's sovereignty enshrined in his theory of the revocability of the *lex regia* there is no progression to Bartolus' and

---

[147] *Les six livres de la république*, 6, 5 (pp. 986–7).

[148] I would thus disagree with Wilks' use of this interpretation (*Problem of Sovereignty*, pp. 184–8).

[149] Considering Bartolus' theory of popular sovereignty Ullmann in 'De Bartoli sententia', p. 713, supported this interpretation, but later maintained that the Bartolist formula, *civitas sibi princeps*, was a populist (or 'ascending') interpretation of the *lex regia* (*History of Political Thought*, pp. 214–16, and *Law and Politics*, pp. 109–10), a view also adopted by Skinner (*Foundations*, II, 130–1). For Baldus' theory of popular sovereignty and its relationship to that of Bartolus see below, pp. 93–127.

Baldus' conception of the sovereignty of the people in independent cities.[150] In short, great care should be taken by any modern historian before any medieval statement of the popular origin of government is seen in terms of an application of the *lex regia* concept: it may simply be a statement containing elements which are merely similar to those of the *lex regia* – it could for instance be another example of the operation of the *ius gentium* of which the *lex regia* itself is but a specific expression.[151]

The essentially secular nature of papal temporal jurisdiction as derived from the *lex regia* and the Donation of Constantine is clear; but so far the pope has been presented as sharing the exercise of imperial power, a view which does not totally represent Baldus' position. Being acutely aware that the pope as a temporal ruler in Italy appeared to be just like any secular monarch he describes him as a king possessing the same powers as any other: 'In sum, whatever a king can do in his kingdom, the pope can do in his ecclesiastical monarchy, and just as formerly everything was ruled by royal hand, as in [D.1.2.2,1], so also whatever pleases the king has the force of law.'[152] As a corollary the pope in his temporal government is, therefore, also subject to the same limitations as a secular monarch: the inalienability of the rights of the kingdom and the crown is a case in point:

> For the pope should be the preserver of the papal kingdom and crown, because he is bound to keep the honour of the crown unharmed, and even if he were to take an oath to the contrary it would not be valid. The same applies to a secular ruler, because the honour of the crown is not alienable, nor can it be conceded or transferred to another, although it can be passed on.[153]

Furthermore his subjects are freed from their allegiance if he acts tyrannically, a clear application of a feudal interpretation of kingship:

---

[150] For the contrary view see Ullmann, *Law and Politics*, p. 110, n. 1.

[151] I thus disagree on these grounds with Kantorowicz's interpretation of Baldus, *Cons.*, 3.159, n. 6, fol. 46r, ed. Venice, 1575 (*King's Two Bodies*, p. 298): for the text see below p. 211, n. 9.

[152] Ad X.2.1.12, n. 6 (fol. 189v). This view is unconnected with the Thomist one that the pope's sovereignty in the church is like that of a king in his kingdom: Aquinas, *Commentum in Sententias*, 4.20.4.3 ad 3, 'Papa habet plenitudinem potestatis pontificalis quasi rex in regno' (see the acute remarks of Hay on this passage: *Italian Renaissance*, p. 18). Whereas Aquinas so applies the originally papal *plenitudo potestatis* to kings that it in turn serves as a royal model for the sovereignty of the popes themselves, Baldus here adapts D.1.4.1 by substituting 'regi' for 'principi' (for the *rex–imperator* equation in Baldus see below, pp. 212–13).

[153] Baldus, *Cons.*, 3.274, fol. 82r, ed. Brescia, 1491 (= *Cons.*, 1.324, ed. Venice, 1575). The context of this passage is the creation of a new fief within the papal territories. For inalienability see below, pp. 219–20.

His subjects therefore have to obey the beneficiary of the Donation [i.e. the pope] except in so far as he were to use his jurisdiction in a savage and tyrannical manner, as above [D.1.1.3; D.1.2.2,3] and see what is noted by Bartolus [D.49.15.24], for if a lord does not give his subjects their due as demanded by his office, his subjects are not bound to serve him, above [D.1.4.1] at the phrase, 'ei et in eum', and note [D.1.6.2], § 'dominorum', that is so long as their due is not being given them.[154]

THE 'DE IURE – DE FACTO' DISTINCTION

It has been necessary to deal with imperial and papal jurisdiction at such length because for Baldus the basic context, within which he treats all other forms of government, is provided by the emperor's universal temporal sovereignty and the pope's sovereignty, which is universal in a spiritual sense and territorial as regards the government of the patrimony, but which also in specific circumstances exhibits an ultimate form of temporal superiority over the emperor. The problem remains of how to accommodate territorially sovereign cities, kings and lords within this overall view.

The solution lay to hand in juristic discourse: the application of the *de iure–de facto* distinction to the relationship between the emperor and lesser rulers. The first words of *l. Cunctos populos* (C.1.1.1) – 'All peoples whom the sovereign authority of our clemency rules' ('Cunctos populos quos clementie nostre regit imperium')[155] – provided a *locus classicus* for this discussion: was 'quos' to be taken *declarative*, thus signifying that all peoples were under the emperor's rule, or was it to be understood *restrictive*, indicating that only his subjects were? According to Baldus, *de iure* the emperor is indeed lord of the world, but *de facto* some peoples do not obey him; thus 'quos' can be interpreted in either a *de iure* or *de facto* sense: 'It cannot rightly be used restrictively with respect to the law, but with respect to facts it could be used restrictively according to Bartolus, and this statement is new, notable and well-said.'[156] The reference to Bartolus is odd both in that Baldus does not quite echo his view, and because Bartolus did not introduce the distinction. Although Bartolus indeed accepted that some peoples did not obey the emperor *de facto*, and that therefore 'quos' could be understood in a restrictive sense, he nevertheless maintained the emperor had intended 'quos' to possess a *de iure* declarative

---

[154] Baldus ad D.V., Proem, ad v. 'Quoniam omnia' (fol. 1v). For the limitations on monarchy see below, pp. 218–21.
[155] Ed. Venice, 1498 (cp. 'regit *temperamentum*', ed. Krueger).
[156] Ad C.1.1.1 (fol. 3r).

meaning. This was a reaction against the view of Petrus de Bellapertica and Cynus who held that, although the emperor was *de iure* lord of the world, he had intended 'quos' to be taken in a restrictive *de facto* sense so as to avoid making his laws a laughing-stock through trying to apply them to peoples not worthy to be ruled by them.[157] As Woolf pointed out, Bartolus was unwilling to restrict the validity of the universal Roman law to those territories where the emperor was obeyed.[158] Baldus, however, following the arguments of Petrus and Cynus accepts that the emperor voluntarily refrains from attempting to impose his laws on those who will not obey him,[159] although, as we shall see, he treats the Roman law as a *ius commune* in Italy applicable to cities and *signori* whether they obey the emperor or not.[160] As Baldus' political thought is unravelled it emerges that his use of the *de iure–de facto* distinction permits him to retain the *de iure* universal sovereignty of the emperor and the *de iure* territorial temporal sovereignty of the pope, while accepting the co-existence of other, *de facto*, sovereign bodies, be they kings, cities or *signori*. There is thus revealed a hierarchy of sovereign powers, and a complicated one at that. At one end of the scale there are peoples and lords below the level of sovereignty enjoying powers of jurisdiction *de iure*, but in a subordinate sense through imperial or papal concession: as we shall see, their position may be described as one of autonomy. Next, in Italy, either in the imperial lands or the papal patrimony, are cities and *signori* possessing *de facto* independence amounting to sovereignty, and also, parallel to these, other *signori* exercising through *de iure* concession sovereign powers without actually being themselves sovereign but still subordinate to their superior. Finally, there are the sovereign monarchies, such as those of France, the Iberian peninsula, England and Sicily which lie outside any claim to direct imperial rule but are within the empire understood in its widest sense. As will be seen, there are reasons for considering that Baldus felt that there existed certain differences between the sovereignty of Italian cities and *signori*, and that of kings. Throughout this whole scale the universal *de iure* sovereignty of the emperor is

---

[157] See Bartolus ad C.1.1.1, n. 1–2 (fol. 3v). Cp. Cynus, ibid., n. 3 (fol. 1v). The major immediate source for Cynus' view is clearly Petrus de Bellapertica, ibid., n. 3 (p. 8). See also Guilelmus de Cuneo, ibid., n. 1 (fol. 2r): '"quos" est positum post signum universale, "cunctos", et sic restringitur ad subiectos...Et ratio est quia par in parem non habet imperium...sed non subiecti videntur pares, et sic quod eis legem non possit facere imperator.' For the application of the *de iure–de facto* distinction to imperial authority see Wilks, *Problem of Sovereignty*, pp. 437–51.

[158] *Bartolus*, pp. 43–4.

[159] Ad C.1.1.1 (fol. 3r).   [160] See below, pp. 148–52.

retained, with all other truly sovereign powers (except papal temporal rulership) being essentially *de facto*, even that of the King of France, a position which Baldus sums up through a neat distinction:

I reply that all are subject [i.e. to the emperor] *de iure*, and rightly so; but not all are subject by custom, and they sin like the French and many other kings... And although the kingdom of France is not part of the Roman empire, it does not however follow that the empire is not therefore universal, for it is one thing to say, 'universal', and another, 'whole', as [D.50.16.25] notes.[161]

Custom of course is the pre-eminent expression of the creation of *de facto* legal rights; and the recognition that the empire is universal but not whole reflects the facts of the political situation produced by custom: that the existence of territorially sovereign entities produces gaps in the universal spread of the emperor's sovereignty. This whole view involves a medieval rather than a modern conception of sovereignty and envisages variously limited powers for any holder of sovereignty. The *de iure–de facto* solution to the problem of the co-existence of universal and territorially sovereign powers permits the modern historian to use the term 'sovereignty' in a useful fashion, so long as the sense in which it is used is clearly understood: universal *and* territorial sovereignty exist in a form of hierarchy with one kind not excluding the other.[162] Certainly Baldus' theory of independent cities, *signori* and kings will demand the application of forms of sovereignty to them.

The *de iure–de facto* distinction had been applied to the relationship between kings and the emperor since at least the beginning of the thirteenth century. Canonists, publicists and civilians debated whether monarchs were *de iure* or *de facto* independent of the emperor: their debate was mostly carried on with reference to the French and Neapolitan monarchies.[163] As we shall see, with the crucial exception of the Neapolitan civilians and Oldradus the canonists tended to be more willing to accord *de iure* sovereignty to a king than were their

---

[161] Ad *Feud.*, 2.53 (fol. 74r–74v).

[162] This is shown very clearly in the question of the authority of notaries: see Baldus ad *Specul.*, 2.2.7 (p. 375), 'Notarius creatus auctoritate pape, vel imperatoris, ubique locorum habet exercitium officii; secus in creato ab inferiore, puta a rege, vel habente auctoritatem a consuetudine, que non habet exercitium extra territorium'; and id. ad *Sext.*, 2.2 (fol. 8v).

[163] See especially Ullmann, 'Medieval idea of sovereignty'; Ercole, *Dal comune*; and Calasso, *I Glossatori*. Walther, *Imperiales Königtum*, pp. 135–59, provides a highly useful summary of the vast modern literature and a survey of relevant sources.

Roman law colleagues. The canonists were, however, not unanimous. Thus, for instance, Innocent IV and Bernard of Parma, when commenting on *Per venerabilem* (X.4.17.13), both attributed only *de facto* independence to the king of France; but whereas Bernard did so on the grounds that the king was subject *de iure* to the emperor, Innocent expressly denied this, maintaining that he was instead so subject to the pope.[164] Although it is arguable, but not totally clear, that the civilians, Johannes de Blanosco and Guilelmus de Cuneo, were willing to accord *de iure* sovereignty to the French king at least,[165] the major thirteenth-century French Commentators, Jacobus de Ravannis and Petrus de Bellapertica, still maintained that *de iure* sovereignty resided only with the emperor. Jacobus de Ravannis for instance says, 'Some say that France is exempted from the empire. This is impossible *de iure*. You have it in [C.1.27.2,3] that France is subject to the empire... If the king of France does not recognise this, I do not care.'[166] Use of the *de iure*–*de facto* distinction had, therefore, become in this context a fundamental part of juristic language. There was, however, something new and profound about the use Bartolus made of this basic distinction. Previously, whatever the point of view expressed, full legitimacy had been accorded only to the *de iure* power; indeed, the distinction had been used specifically as a means to locate such legitimacy. Bartolus took the crucial and innovatory step by realising that complete legitimacy in this question of sovereignty could be acquired both *de facto* and *de iure*. He developed this interpretation of *de facto*

---

[164] Innocent, n. 3, ad v. 'cum rex ipse superiorem in temporalibus minime recognoscat' (fol. 481r), 'De facto, nam de iure subest imperatori Romano, ut quidam dicunt, nos contra, imo pape' (all references to Innocent IV are to the Frankfurt, 1570, edition, unless otherwise stated); and Bernard of Parma, ibid., 'De facto, de iure tamen subest Romano imperio [*Decr. Grat.*, C.7, q.1, c. 41]' as quoted in Meijers, *Etudes*, IV, 213, n. 24).

[165] See Meijers, *Etudes*, III, 192–3, and especially Guilelmus ad D.1.11.1, fol. 11v (Bodl. MS. Can. Misc., 472): 'Omnes reges sunt hodie sub imperatore excepto rege Francie qui non habet superiorem.'

[166] Ad D.V. Proem, fol. 2r, MS, Leiden, d'Ablaing 2 (as quoted in Meijers, *Etudes*, III, 192). Cp. id. ad C. Rubr. 'De emendatione Iustiniani Codicis', ad v. 'Augustus' (fol. 1r), 'Non recognoscens de facto non prescribit dominio, nisi forte dicas immo a tempore a quo non extat memoria, sed nec ab illo forte prescribit, ut in [C.7.39.6]. Et hoc valet contra regem Yspanie et regem Francie qui non recognoscunt superiorem de facto. Tamen lex est expressa dicens quod ipsi sunt sub imperatore. Vnde de iure se non possunt tueri prescriptione, quia [C.1.27.2, 2] ibi dicit quod imperator misit quemdam ut preesset in Yspaniam et Franciam. Ergo de iure sunt subiecti imperio, quia semel fuerunt subiecti.' C.1.27.2, 2 provides the *locus classicus* for the argument that the French and Spanish kings are subject to the emperor. See Petrus de Bellapertica ad C.1.1.1, n. 3 (p. 8). Petrus himself, however, ad Inst., Rubr., n. 17, entertained the current French view that the French king should take over the empire (see Meijers, *Etudes*, III, 192–3).

sovereignty to account for the powers of the independent city-republics of north and central Italy;[167] Baldus adopted and developed Bartolus' argument in general, and applied it both to cities and kings. The implications of this view of *de facto* authority were enormous: it marked an acceptance of the facts of human political organisation and government as having full validity on their own account without being dependent upon those *de iure* powers which ultimately derived their authority from God. Most of Baldus' treatment of the government of cities and monarchies is a detailed development of this view, and we shall examine the various terms in which he expresses his argument. Certainly for Baldus *de facto* sovereignty is a genuine form, and is *not* mere power without legitimacy. He thus accepts a hierarchy of sovereign powers according full recognition both to the *de iure* ones which were ultimately sanctioned by divinity, and to the humanly created *de facto* ones.

THE NEAPOLITAN SOLUTION

Baldus' thesis forms a highly important contribution to the first solution to the problem posed by the claims of universal and territorial sovereign powers. There was, however, a second major juristic solution which Baldus in no way followed: it was the most radical view put forward by civilians in Italy, and amounted to an outright rejection of the universal sovereignty of the emperor. This opinion was especially prevalent in the works of Neapolitan jurists: in the thirteenth century it is to be found in the work of Marinus de Caramanico, and in the fourteenth in that of Andreas de Isernia.[168] It also appears in the work of Oldradus de Ponte, who taught at Padua (and possibly Bologna and Siena), and served the *curia* at Avignon. Oldradus provided a major statement of the pro-Neapolitan view in his famous *Consilium*, 69, in which he justified king Robert of Naples' rejection of imperial overlordship in the latter's dispute with Henry VII.[169] Oldradus denied that the Roman emperor was *de iure* lord of the world on the grounds that the Roman people, lacking themselves any just title to dominion over other nations, could not through the *lex regia* legally

---

[167] This theme runs throughout Woolf, *Bartolus*, but see especially pp. 195–6. Skinner, *Foundations*, I, 9–12, lays considerable stress on this aspect of Bartolus' achievement.

[168] See Calasso, *I Glossatori*; Ullmann, 'Medieval idea of sovereignty', pp. 19–33; Costa, *Iurisdictio*, pp. 333–41; and Paradisi, 'Il pensiero politico', pp. 57–76.

[169] See Will, *Die Gutachten des Oldradus*, pp. 51–62, and Meijer's review of this (*Etudes*, III, 195–6).

transfer any such authority to the emperor.[170] The *de iure* independence of kingdoms (and indeed cities) was based on the fundamental *ius gentium*, and was thus anterior to and stronger than any claims of the Roman emperors to rulership over them, because imperial jurisdiction was a product solely of the *ius civile* of the Romans, whereas other peoples were free in their *ius civile* to deny any subjection to the emperor.[171] The independence of the kingdom of Sicily was thus guaranteed by the *ius gentium*, and indeed like that of Spain was reinforced by the argument that its inhabitants had conquered it with their own blood.[172] This made all the arguments of Henry VII against Robert of Naples irrelevant. Similarly the king of France was subject to the emperor neither *de facto* nor *de iure*.[173] Furthermore Oldradus claimed that he could find no justification in the Old or New Testament for any divine origin of the empire, and rejected the papal *translatio imperii* considering that the church could not thereby create a right which did not previously exist.[174] Indeed, Marinus before him had given an ingenious twist to the general discussion in the thirteenth century by explaining that the Roman empire because it was founded on force itself existed 'de facto potius quam de iure'.[175] The image of the pro-Neapolitan view was that of a political world in which the emperor did not enjoy universal sovereignty but only territorial dominion over the areas where he could exercise actual political power; elsewhere the *ius gentium* provided the legal title for monarchies. The pro-Neapolitan *ius gentium* argument envisaged a world of a plurality of kingdoms where the empire was only one territorial body amongst several. Thus Andreas de Isernia did indeed maintain that a king in his kingdom possessed the same power as the emperor in the empire; he meant by this, however, not that the king had in his kingdom the same power of jurisdiction as the emperor enjoyed in the empire as a whole understood in any universalist sense, but rather that a kingdom and the empire were in essence the same kind of territorial body, and that

[170] See n. 7 (fol. 24v), and n. 12 (fol. 24v–25r). Oldradus was not consistent in his view: his *Cons.*, 180, accepts a universalist theocratic interpretation of the origin of imperial authority (n. 15, fol. 67v).

[171] n. 5–6 (fol. 24r–24v). For the *ius gentium* as a justification for the independence of kings (especially the king of Sicily) from the emperor see Marinus de Caramanico, *Super libro Constitutionum*, Proem, 3–7 (ed. Calasso, pp. 180–6).

[172] n. 8–9 (fol. 24v). See Meijers, *Etudes*, III, 193–4, for the Spanish juristic influence on Oldradus (notably that of Vincentius and Johannes de Deo).

[173] n. 12 (fol. 25r).   [174] n. 10 (fol. 24v).

[175] Ed. cit., 17 (pp. 196–7). Baldus faces the objection that the rule of the emperors was founded on violence, but then proceeds to deny this by affirming the divine origin of imperial authority (ad C.1.1.1, fol. 3r).

therefore the world had returned to its pristine condition before the conquests of Rome.[176] If the universal sovereignty of the emperor was rejected it could reasonably be asked why the Roman law should be accepted as valid in Sicily. To this Marinus produced the response which retained the kingdom's integrity: the Roman law had validity there because it was accepted by the custom of the kingdom.[177]

It is clear that the Neapolitan jurists' and Oldradus' rejection of the universal sovereignty of the emperor involved an approach to a modern state concept in that the empire being understood as those territories in which the emperor had actual political power was placed on the same level as other territorial states, whereas in the thought of Bartolus and Baldus the empire was not put on the same level as territorial cities, kingdoms and lordships: for them the empire was not one state among many. For this reason Bartolus and Baldus did not produce a modern theory of state-sovereignty which would require a plurality of territorially sovereign states. The extent to which Baldus did elaborate particular ideas of the state remains to be seen; but through retaining the validity of the universal sovereign powers of the emperor and the pope at the very foundation of his view of the world he remained very much within the Middle Ages, although this was a view which was to keep adherents certainly in the sixteenth and seventeenth centuries.

---

[176] Ad *Feud.*, 2.56, n. 2 (fol. 286r), 'Cum causa rex alius poterit in regno suo quod imperator potest in terra imperii, que hodie modica est. In Italia non habet nisi Lombardiam, et illam non totam, et partem Thuscie; et alia sunt ecclesie Romane, sicut et regnum Sicilie. Primi domini fuerunt reges, ut dicit Salustius, et patet [D.1.2.2, 3]...in Auth. 'Vt preponatur imperatoris nomen' [Coll., 5.3 = Nov., 47] in princ. Reddite ergo sunt provincie (que regem habent) forme pristine habendi reges, quod de facili fit [D.2.14.27]. Liberi reges tantum habent in regnis suis quantum imperator in imperio.' For the king as the emperor in his kingdom see below, pp. 212–13.

[177] Ed. cit., 19 (pp. 198–9).

Chapter 2

THE NATURE AND LIMITATIONS OF THE EMPEROR'S POWER

Before examining Baldus' theories of sovereign cities, kingdoms and *signori* it is logically necessary first to complete the picture of the nature and extent of the emperor's authority because of his fundamental *de iure* position, which results in his role as the model for sovereign power, directly in the case of monarchies, more subtly in that of cities. This is not to deny that some aspects of imperial authority are unique to the emperor; others, however, reappear in different contexts.

The fundamental structure of Baldus' political thought makes it necessary to distinguish between the emperor and other monarchs, a point of interpretation reinforced by the need to bear in mind the historical entities he is discussing, if his meaning is to be established. Thus it would misrepresent his theory of monarchy if it were discussed in blanket-terms, such as 'the ruler' or 'the monarch', without distinguishing between the emperor, the pope, kings and *signori*, who, while sharing common elements in their public power, each exhibit characteristics peculiar to themselves. Where Baldus employs the term *imperator*, he clearly means the emperor, except in those passages where he is specifically using it in the context of another ruler. It is with the term *princeps* that problems might appear to arise, because it features in his discussion of all forms of monarchy. Because of the nature of the juristic sources on which Baldus is commenting, the term *princeps* without qualification normally and primarily refers to the emperor; and it is usually made clear when it is applied in a secondary sense to other monarchs or, indeed, princes, as in the case of imperial electors. Thus to translate *princeps* as 'the prince' in the general sense of 'the ruler' would normally be misleading except in discussion of elements common to all forms of monarchy. A distinction should thus be drawn between three major ways in which Baldus employs the term *princeps*, together with relevant supporting texts: when it refers to the emperor uniquely; to the emperor, but in a manner which would permit a reader to extend Baldus' remarks to other rulers; and finally with explicit application to other rulers. Thus it is for instance normal for Baldus

71

in his commentary on the *Liber Decretalium*, when dealing with papal government of the church, to refer to the pope as *princeps*, and to apply to him relevant public law texts from the *Corpus Iuris Civilis* without obscuring (except in a few cases) that it is the pope he has in mind.

THE ABSOLUTE POWER OF THE EMPEROR

In order to express the sovereign power of the emperor Baldus habitually uses two traditional terms: *suprema potestas* and *plenitudo potestatis*. The concept of *plenitudo potestatis* developed by the medieval papacy and adopted by medieval emperors and kings played a crucial role in the development of the idea of sovereignty.[1] Baldus employs both terms interchangeably in discussing imperial sovereignty. His conception of the emperor's power is that it is essentially a positive law one, and is as such absolute, in that the emperor in the exercise of his will is unconstrained by human law: 'Nothing resists plenitude of power, for it overcomes all positive law and in the case of the emperor his will is reason enough.'[2] The definition he gives to this form of sovereignty leaves nothing to be desired: 'Plenitude of power however is the fullness of authority subject to no necessity and limited by no rules of public law.'[3] In seeing the emperor's will as being its own justification Baldus is following an old-established view: the formula, 'in principe pro ratione voluntas', was familiar to all jurists and underlay Accursius' statement, '*From some cause*. Great and just cause is his will.'[4] The emperor is, however, only *legibus solutus* in the limited sense that he is freed from human positive law, the *leges*, as Baldus makes clear when commenting on the statement, 'The emperor is freed from the laws' ('princeps legibus solutus est'): '[Note] that phrase, "from the laws": that is from the civil law not the natural or divine law.'[5] This is a distinctively medieval conception of the absolute

---

[1] See for instance Wilks, *Problem of Sovereignty*, p. 151, and Black, *Monarchy and Community*, p. 84. For Frederick II's usage see *M.G.H., Const.*, II, n. 156, p. 192, and for that of kings see Ullmann, *Principles*, pp. 205–6.

[2] Ad X.1.2.1, n. 30 (fol. 12r). For the emperor's plenitude of power see also id. ad X.1.2.13, n. 4 (fol. 28v), and ad C.7.62.6 (fol. 255r).

[3] Ad C.3.34.2 (fol. 190v).

[4] Gl. ad D.48.19.4, ad v. 'Ex aliqua causa' (fol. 246r). See the text of D.48.19.4: 'et nemo potest commeatum remeatumve dare exuli, nisi imperator, ex aliqua causa.' Cp. Bartolus, ibid., n. 4 (fol. 197r). The formula remained a common-place: see, for instance, the late fifteenth- and early sixteenth-century jurist, Philip Decius (*prima lectura* ad X.1.2. Rubr., n. 26, fol. 3r; and ad X.1.2.7, n. 132, fol. 27r).

[5] D.1.3.31, additio Baldi (fol. 21v). Cp. Accursius, ibid. (fol. 9r): '*Princeps legibus*. ab alio conditis... vel a seipso.'

power of the *princeps* leaving him subject, as we shall see, to higher norms.[6]

This absolute nature of imperial jurisdiction is for Baldus the product both of the people's irrevocable alienation of power to the *princeps* through the *lex regia*,[7] and of its theocratic origin through divine confirmation.[8] The emperor thus represents, in the sense of 'stands for', a people which has abdicated its sovereignty; he is not the chosen representative of one which retains its original authority.[9] In this hierarchical structure his subjects, being his inferiors, can have no control over him; as we have seen, only the pope can *in extremis* depose him: 'We jurists should say that the emperor is lord of the world even if he were to administer badly, because an inferior cannot correct his superior, although the pope can depose him for a very great cause.'[10] Walter Ullmann has shown that such a hierarchical relationship between ruler and ruled is necessary in a theocratic or hierocratic system.[11] Yet Aristotelian political conceptions were also available from the mid-thirteenth century to describe both political structures in which ultimate sovereignty remained with the people, and those where the people had no sovereignty but was subject to a monarch. Thus Baldus also claims Aristotle as a source for this hierarchical relationship between the emperor and his subjects: 'Any act which is above the law, however, is a sign of absolute power and it is not for subjects to complain, because as Aristotle says, nothing inferior participates in what is superior, but should obey it.'[12] Whereas the theocratic aspect of

---

[6] See, for instance, Wilks, *Problem of Sovereignty*, pp. 211–17.

[7] *Prima Rep.* ad D.2.1.3 (fol. 61v).

[8] Ad *Feud.*, 1.13 (fol. 23r).

[9] This is Baldus' meaning when he says of the emperor and the *populus Romanus*: 'Princeps representat illum populum, et ille populus imperium etiam mortuo principe' (ad C.10.1. Rubr., fol. 1v). This is located in a discussion of the effects of the transfer of power through the *lex regia*. There is no suggestion here that the people retains any real power during an imperial vacancy; but simply that it stands for the empire in such circumstances.

[10] Baldus, *Cons.*, 3.283, fol. 88r, ed. Brescia, 1491 (= *Cons.*, 1.333, ed. Venice, 1575).

[11] See for example *Individual and Society*, pp. 12–16.

[12] *Cons.*, 3.278, fol. 86r, ed.Brescia, 1491 (= *Cons.*, 1.328, ed. Venice, 1575). It is not clear which passage in Aristotle Baldus is referring to here. The nearest passage which I have found is, 'inferiora a superioribus reguntur', in a *florilegium* (Hamesse, *Les auctoritates Aristotelis*, p. 272). According to Hamesse this passage is derived from pseudo–Aristotle, *Secretum secretorum*, c. 61, which certainly uses the terms, *rex–subditus*, and *superior–inferior*, but in a theocratic rather than an Aristotelian sense. It cannot be shown that Baldus had this source in mind. There are, however, Aristotelian sources for the absolute rule of one man (*Pol.*, 1288a), and for the rule of a monarch over his subjects (*Eth. Nic.*, 1160a–b). See Rubinstein, 'Le dottrine politiche nel rinascimento', pp. 189–92, where he illustrates how Italian political thinkers from the thirteenth century used Aristotelian concepts to justify the claims of both monarchy and republicanism.

Baldus' concept of imperial power certainly explains his conception of the hierarchical relationship between the emperor and his subjects, in so far as he also claims to use Aristotelian argument, which has essentially no connection with theocratic conceptions, he neatly supports his interpretation of the role of the *lex regia*, whereby this hierarchical structure was originally established directly through human action with only the indirect involvement of divinity through the granting of permission. This is not to deny that the emperor can occasionally make errors of law or fact, and that his *scientia* (knowledge) or *voluntas* (will) in these individual cases can be questioned by his subjects; his power, however, cannot be brought into contention by them.[13] Indeed, it is sacrilege to disobey the emperor.[14]

THE EMPEROR AND THE POSITIVE LAW

This conception of the absolute power of the *princeps* does not exhaustively describe his relationship with the positive law, the *leges*. Although such law ultimately depends upon his will and could theoretically be swept away by him, its existence limits him in practical terms. Surely the emperor, whose power is a legal creation, should work through the law? Otherwise the whole legal system would be subject to imperial caprice; and an element of total unpredictability would enter if the emperor were to act *supra legem* in everything. It would appear to be self-contradictory for the emperor to create a body of law and then be unwilling to work though it. These are fundamental questions facing any advocate of absolutist government which claims to rule through the law, and thus distinguish itself from an arbitrary regime. The *Corpus Iuris Civilis* recognises the problem by maintaining both that the *princeps* is *legibus solutus*, and in *l. Digna vox* (C.1.14.4) that it is fitting for him to be bound by the *leges* specifically because his power derives from the law. The medieval civilians reached a consensus by maintaining that although the *princeps* was under no necessity to obey the *leges* he would nevertheless wish to do so:[15] thus in terms of positive law the emperor's will remained paramount – his will was both the constitutive element in law, and also determined whether he was

---

[13] Baldus ad D.1.4.1. (fol. 20v–21r).

[14] Baldus, *Cons.*, 2.271, n. 1, fol. 75v (ed. Venice, 1575).

[15] See Accursius, gl. ad D.1.3.31; Odofredus ad C.1.14.4, n. 1 (fol. 36r); id. ad D.1.3.31, n. 1 (fol. 14); Cynus ad C.1.14.4, n. 2–3 (fol. 25v–26r); Albericus de Rosciate ad D.1.3.31, n. 8 (fol. 33v); Bartolus ad C.1.14.4, n. 1 (fol. 27v); and for a later view, Bartholomaeus de Saliceto, ibid., n. 3 (fol. 35v).

bound by any such law. Baldus makes a refreshingly clear contribution to this well-worn discussion by introducing the concepts of the emperor's *potestas absoluta* and his *potestas ordinaria*:

> The emperor should live according to the laws because his authority depends on the law. Understand that this word, 'should', is interpreted as applying to the obligation of honesty which the emperor should possess to the highest degree. But this is not a precise interpretation because the supreme and absolute power of the emperor is not beneath the law. The law in question [i.e. C.1.14.4] therefore applies to his ordinary not his absolute power...Note that the emperor says he is bound by the laws and this is so out of his good will and not of necessity.[16]

The distinction between *potestas absoluta* and *potestas ordinaria* or *ordinata* had been used by Hostiensis in relation to papal plenitude of power and was also well-established in thirteenth- and fourteenth-century theological and political writing. In adopting this distinction Baldus seeks to differentiate that aspect of the emperor's power which appears in the ordinary day-to-day exercise of his jurisdiction (in which it would, indeed, be *honestum* for him to judge and legislate *secundum leges*), from the aspect of ultimate and absolute sovereignty which underlies his jurisdiction in positive law.[17] The emperor has the necessary freedom of action as the fount and source of law, but normally (ordinarily) for the sake of the stability of the legal system he works through the *leges* which he has made. His absolute power is the fundamental guarantee of the structure of positive law; but his ordinary power is that which his subjects normally experience.

Thus the emperor's power remains ultimately and in essence absolute. Certainly as the source of law he is not ultimately bound by those laws which he has personally made; but is he bound by those of his predecessors? Can he constrain his successors to observe his own? Baldus adheres to juristic tradition by holding that the emperor, being on a par with any previous or future incumbent of that office, cannot bind his successor: 'Note finally that no one can impose a law on a successor to his dignity, office or imperial authority. The reason is that

---

[16] Ad C.1.14.4 (fol. 50r–50v). Cp. id. ad C.1.14.8 (fol. 54v); id., *De pace Constantie*, ad v. 'Imperialis clementie' (fol. 88r); and id., *Cons.*, 2.16, fol. 7r, ed. Brescia, 1490 (= *Cons.*, 4.19, ed. Venice, 1575).

[17] Cp. id., *Cons.*, 4.436, fol. 103v, ed. Brescia, 1490 (= *Cons.*, 5.300, ed. Venice, 1575). Baldus does appear only to apply this distinction between absolute and ordinary power to the highest level of sovereignty, that possessed by the emperor and the pope. For the distinction between *potestas absoluta* and *potestas ordinaria* (or *ordinata*) in general see Wilks, *Problem of Sovereignty*, pp. 292, 294–5, 311, 319, 349 and 441.

equals have no authority over each other.'[18] This is a final sign of the emperor's sovereignty.

THE EMPEROR AND HIGHER NORMS

Although Baldus considers that the emperor's power exists essentially within the ambit of positive law, he does not understand imperial sovereignty according to a positive law theory in the modern sense, that is to say that the sovereign's will alone expressed in a duly constitutional form makes valid law. For Baldus the emperor's *potestas absoluta* exists within strict limits: if these are transgressed, his measures have no legal validity. The positive law power of the emperor operates within the context of a structure of higher norms, expressed in the traditional language of *ius naturale*, *ius gentium* and *ius divinum*. That Baldus should take this view is only to be expected because it was the universal orthodoxy of late medieval jurists, publicists, theologians and philosophers, with the possible and notorious exception of Marsilius of Padua:[19] for Baldus the constitutive element of law was not the ruler's command or the people's consent alone, but that will exercised in accordance with moral, religious and rational criteria. Thus Baldus considers that the *ius naturale*, *ius gentium* and *ius divinum* are so axiomatic that there can be no debate about whether the *princeps* can infringe them – if he does do so, his law is not valid, because otherwise he would be doing the impossible:

Note however that this authority, 'whatever pleases the emperor', should be understood to mean what is 'possible' and 'honest', for the emperor cannot do the impossible. The impossible however is that whose contrary is necessary. The divine law however is necessary as is the natural law... Thus the law of peoples cannot be abolished, as above [D.1.1.11; Inst., 1.2, 1]. And thus if what does not please God pleases the emperor, it does not have the force of law.[20]

---

18 Ad C.1.14.4, fol. 50v (in context this applies to the emperor). Cf. id., *De pace Constantie*, ad v. 'Hoc quod nos' (fol. 90r). For an earlier statement of this view see, for instance, Odofredus ad C.1.14.4, n. 2 (fol. 36r–36v); and id. ad D.1.3.31, n. 1 (fol. 14v).

19 Marsilius of Padua, the one fourteenth-century writer who produced a theory of law which can appear positivist, had no influence on late medieval juristic conceptions of law. Modern scholars disagree as to whether Marsilius was indeed a thorough-going positivist: for the interpretation that he was a positivist see, for instance, Gewirth, *Marsilius of Padua*, I, 134–6; and for criticism of Gewirth's interpretation see Quillet, *Philosophie politique*, pp. 135 and 139. Marsilius indeed considered only human positive law (understood as the product of coercive command) to be law properly speaking, but held that its content usually either had a moral quality or was morally indifferent, although he was willing to accept, if necessary, the validity of objectively unjust laws.

20 Ad D.1.4.1 (fol. 21r). Cp. id. ad Auth., 'Habita' (ad C.4.13.5), fol. 230v; and id. ad D.1.3.31, n. 1, fol. 21v (ed. Venice, 1616). For an earlier view see Odofredus ad D.1.4.1, n. 4 (fol. 17v–18r).

The power of the emperor, subject in positive law neither to dispute nor human regulation, is limited by such higher norms, and in this he serves as a model for monarchy as is made clear in a passage in which the *princeps* is the pope as temporal ruler in the patrimony: 'You should know however that there must be no dispute about the power of the prince because his supreme power is subject to no rule, except only the divine law and the natural, as [C.1.22.6] fully notes.'[21] These higher norms, however, provide only a general framework and Baldus adheres to the jurists' *communis opinio* whereby the emperor can in his measures go against the specific effects of these fundamental laws rather than the general principles, a process similar to casuistry in theological terms. Thus, for instance, the *ius divinum* forbids killing, but the emperor can introduce the death penalty for certain crimes. Some limitation still nevertheless remains on the emperor, because, whereas he can without showing any cause contravene *ius civile* being positive law, he can only infringe higher norms with cause by applying general principles to specific cases.[22]

The emperor is subject to these higher norms because of the divinely instituted order of the world. The natural world and man were created by God as first cause.[23] God created man a rational animal;[24] and it is reason which links the emperor as a human being, human positive law and the higher norms of *ius naturale*, *ius gentium* and *ius divinum* – in the exercise of his jurisdiction the emperor is subject to the rational higher norms which govern human actions:

By positive law the emperor is obliged by the dictates of reason, because he is a rational animal, and therefore the emperor is not freed from reason. For no authority whether of the emperor or the senate can make the emperor other than a rational and mortal animal, or free him from the law of nature or from the dictates of right reason or the eternal law [D.7.5.2].[25]

---

[21] Baldus ad X.2.1.12, n. 2–3 (fol. 189r).
[22] Details of Baldus' view emerge when he deals with specific cases; but for a general discussion of the *communis opinio* see his commentary on C.1.19.7 (fol. 62v–63r). His statement ad C.6.8.1 (fol. 20r), 'Licet [imperator] sit vicarius dei in temporalibus tamen contra legem divinam non potest dispensare nisi ex magna causa,' became well-known: see Philip Decius ad X.1.2.7, n. 79–80 (fol. 25r). See Cortese, *Norma giuridica*, I, III for Azo's important contribution to this process.
[23] Baldus ad X. Proem, ad v. 'Rex pacificus', n. 47 (fol. 6r); id. ad D.1.1.1, ad v. 'Ius naturale' (fol. 5v); id. ad X. Proem, n. 1(fol. 2r); id., *Consilium* on the Great Schism (ad C.6.34), fol. 96v; and id. ad D.1.1.Rubr. (fol. 4r).
[24] Baldus ad X.1.2.5, n. 3 (fol. 13v); id. ad X.2.24.26, n. 2 (fol. 302r); and id. ad C.4.2.Rubr. (fol. 213v).
[25] Baldus ad C.3.34.2 (fol. 190v). 'By positive law' may refer to D.7.5.2: 'Nec enim naturalis ratio auctoritate senatus commutari potuit.' See also id., *Rep.* ad D.4.4.38 (fol. 203r).

Baldus is clearly influenced here by the Thomist conception that the natural law, being a product of man's reason, is a partial revelation of the divine eternal law.[26] In purely Roman law terms also the identification of *ius naturale* with the *ius gentium* as a product of natural reason, propounded by Gaius and a common-place among medieval jurists, is frequently used by Baldus, although he also at times follows Ulpian's definition in distinguishing between these two forms of norm,[27] and indeed can refer to the natural law as that obtaining in man's state of innocence before the fall.[28] The fundamental significance of Baldus' view is that he considers that the positive law of the emperor should not simply be command, but the embodiment of reason: that it is the emperor's duty to exercise his supreme power in a rational manner, 'The emperor is a rational creature possessing supreme power, but insofar as he is rational he should obey reason, as is noted at the beginning of Auth. "De monachis" [Coll., 1.5 = Nov., 5].'[29] The emperor's plenitude of power is thus not arbitrary, but in its operation a force for good limited by the demands of reason:

The emperor could not give permission that someone could on his own authority expel a person enjoying just and legitimate possession, because such permission would be disgraceful [C.8.4.6]...Nor does the formula, 'by plenitude of power', provide any obstacle to this view, because that formula is understood to refer to good and praiseworthy plenitude of power not blameworthy or tyrannical, for the emperor is said to be able to do only that which he can do by law... There are two further reasons: natural and civil reason are more powerful than the emperor; and even the emperor is a rational and mortal animal.[30]

[26] *S.T.*, 1a 2ae, 91, 2.

[27] As ad D.1.1.1, 4 (see below, p. 105). Cp. D.1.1.1 (Ulpian) and D.1.1.9 (Gaius). For an identification between *ius naturale* and *ius gentium* see Baldus ad D.1.1.5 (fol. 7v): 'Dicitur hic quod dominia sunt distincta de iure gentium, contra immo de iure naturali, ut [Inst., 4.1] in princ. Solutio: hic ponitur ius naturale pro iure proprio nature humane id est pro iure gentium, vel pro lege Mosaica.' For Baldus' conceptions of *ius naturale* and *ius gentium* see Horn, *Aequitas*, pp. 65–76. For the origins of the Commentators' views in the theories of the Glossators and Decretists see Weigand, *Die Naturrechtslehre*, especially pp. 62–4.   [28] Ad X. Proem, n. 2 (fol. 2r).

[29] *Cons.*, 3.277, fol. 84r, ed. Brescia, 1491 (= *Cons.*, 1.327, ed. Venice, 1575). This is the same as *Cons.*, 1.456 (ed. Brescia, 1490), although I have normally followed the text of *Cons.*, 3.277, because it is in general less corrupt. In a profound sense the emperor's liberty of action in positive law is not infringed by his duty to obey reason: see Baldus' general statement, 'Quid si libertas queritur nulli rei servire, nulli necessitati, nullis casibus? Qui ergo vim patitur liber non est nisi vis inferatur a iure vel a ministro legis modo servato. Nam non minus est liber quia obediat rationi, et in frenis mens freno moderantie honestatis [D.1.5.3]. Immo summa libertas est rationi servire' (*Consilium* on the Great Schism, ad C.6.34, fol. 102v).

[30] Baldus, *Cons.*, 3.295, fol. 95r, ed. Brescia, 1491 (= *Cons.*, 1.345, ed. Venice, 1575). Cp. id., *Cons.*, 2.303, fol. 81r, ed. Brescia, 1490 (= *Cons.*, 5.178, ed. Venice, 1575), 'Est

Civilis ratio refers here to reason expressed through the civil law, and is not meant to suggest that the emperor is limited simply by positive law. The possible conflict between the command and reason aspects of the emperor's law is avoided since the emperor is presumed to will himself both what is objectively just and to be limited by the normative structure: 'Again note that nothing is presumed to please the emperor except what is just and true...And the emperor wishes all his actions to be ruled by divine and natural justice as well as human'[31] (human justice relates to his *potestas ordinaria*). This is completely different from maintaining that whatever the emperor wills is *ipso facto* just (a purely positive law conception in modern terms): as we have seen, Baldus considers that the emperor can will what is contrary to necessary higher norms, but that in such a case his measures would be invalid. For Baldus the valid exercise of the emperor's supreme power is a moral, just and rational one.

PRIVATE PROPERTY

This then is the general structure; but on the crucial question of the status of these higher norms in relation to the emperor's powers concerning the rights of others (*iura alterius*) major differences emerge between Baldus' treatment of private property and that which he accords to feudal rights, differences which have important implications for his conception of the extent of the emperor's sovereignty. Following juristic tradition Baldus considered that private property was the product of the *ius gentium* (or of *ius naturale* understood in the sense of *ius gentium*).[32] The question of the emperor's transfer or removal of his subjects' property rights was a common-place of juristic debate: that the emperor could so transfer these rights was not contested; what was at issue was whether he required a cause, without which he would infringe the *ius gentium* guaranteeing such rights. Baldus was faced with two lines of argument among the civilians. Confronted with political reality Petrus de Bellapertica accepted that *de iure* the *princeps* could not remove private property without cause, but indicated that in practice

---

contra rationem naturalem, quod ille qui non deliquit, puniatur, et ratio naturalis sicut ratio civilis immo fortius, quoniam civilis ratio restringit arbitrium potestatis etiam absolute, ut [D.26.7.40; D.29.1.15]'; and id., *Cons.*, 1.82, n.1, fol. 27v (ed. Venice, 1575).

[31] Baldus ad D.1.4.1 (fol. 21r). This passage is given special mention by Jason de Maino in his commentary, ibid. (fol. 25r) where he gives a useful conspectus of passages by Baldus concerning the nature and extent of the emperor's power.

[32] In addition to his commentary on D.1.1.5 (above, p. 78, n. 27) see that on Inst., 1.2, 1 (fol. 5r).

his absolute power was not subject to such a limitation.[33] Cynus clarified this distinction by maintaining that the emperor, although he had no *de iure* right to remove private property without cause, could do so *de facto*, in which case, however, he would still be committing a sin.[34] It was, however, Jacobus Butrigarius who went furthest by holding that the emperor could deprive someone of his private property without cause, that is by the exercise of the imperial will alone.[35] Clearly this view was radical in the extreme in that it ignored the normative structure, and accepted the arbitrary actions of the ruler: Cynus' distinction had become redundant in Jacobus' eyes. Bartolus, however, gave a magisterial statement of the opposing point of view. He expressly rejected Jacobus' opinion on the grounds that, whereas Jacobus was treating property rights and imperial power on the same positive law level, the emperor's jurisdiction in this matter as in others was hedged about by the requirements of justice, to achieve which God had instituted the imperial authority: a classic statement of the location of the emperor's supreme power within the structure of higher norms.[36]

In Baldus' works there is some evidence for the view that the emperor requires a cause to remove the property of others, as in this observation: 'Again, note that just as the emperor *should* not take away anyone's property without cause, neither should he remove their own jurisdiction, as in [D.1.5.20], but entrusted or precarial jurisdiction he can freely take away, as below [D.5.1.58]',[37] although here there is no mention of any necessity. Another statement, although it concerns the *princeps* and is supported by texts from the *Corpus Iuris Civilis*, in fact applies in context to the pope, and thus can only with some reservation be thought relevant to the position of the emperor:

Note that all fiscal rights belong to the prince and that he can concede them to anyone. But the rights of individuals do not belong to the prince, nor do

---

[33] Ad Inst., 1.2, n. 67 (p. 108).   [34] Ad C.1.19.7, n. 12 (fol. 36v).

[35] Ad C.7.37.2 (fol. 41v), 'Nota casum contra illos qui dicunt quod princeps per privilegium non potest rem meam alteri concedere et dominium mihi auferre; immo potest...Vnde quod princeps non possit mihi auferre dominium meum non est ex defectu potentie, sed quia non vult, et dicit quod si contingat eum facere non valet rescriptum, ut [C.1.19.2]; sed si velit et dicat, "non obstante tali lege," bene valet, et potest'; id. ad D.1.14.3, n.12 (p. 37), 'Item opponitur quod imperator non possit quem privare de dominio rei sue, ut [C.1.19.2]. Solutio: potest ex causa, ut hic favore publice utilitatis, sine causa non potest, ut ibi. Immo puto quod ubicunque princeps non errat in facto et refert ibi contra ius aliquid, quod valeat rescriptum, nam quod ipse non possit aliquem privare re sua non est ex defectu potestatis sue, sed ideo quia dixit se nolle hoc facere. Vbicunque ergo ipse vult, dummodo non sit error in facto, tenet rescriptum, et videtur tollere legem derogatoriam, que contra hoc est, cum scire omne presumatur'; and id. ad C.1.19.2 (fol. 36r).

[36] Ad C.1.22.6, n. 2 (fol. 35v).   [37] Ad D.1.4.1 (fol. 21r).

they come into his possession...unless the prince by his absolute power and for a reasonable cause should make other special provision [D.31.1.78, 3; D.40.11.3]. For he could concede rights to one person and deprive another of them for the public welfare of the church or the people, and again for the liberty of the church.[38]

The contrary view, however, clearly emerges as Baldus' main opinion: the emperor does not require a cause to deprive subjects of their property rights. In holding that the emperor's will is cause enough Baldus gives a classic definition of this exercise of absolute power:

Thirdly, the doctors ask whether the emperor can issue rescripts contrary to the law of peoples. The Gloss appears to maintain that he cannot, with the result that someone's property cannot without cause be taken away by the emperor's rescript, although it certainly can be with some kind of cause [D.40.11.3; D.21.2.11; D.31.1.78, 1; D.6.1.15]; and *whatever reason motivates the emperor himself is considered cause enough.*[39]

A justificatory cause other than his will is of course desirable; but it is not necessary.[40] It is thus no accident that Baldus does not mention the requirement of a cause when stating that the emperor can as a result of his plenitude of power transfer private property: 'For it is the privilege of the emperor alone to take away the rights of one person and give them to another by his plenitude of power.'[41] The implications of this view are very great indeed: it means that in respect of his subjects' private property the emperor's *potestas absoluta* has broken through the limitations of the structure of higher norms, and no longer appears as simply the restricted positive law power we have seen so far. The emperor's sovereignty in the sense of his power to command

---

[38] Ad X.2.26.13, n. 2 (fol. 329r).

[39] Ad C.1.19.7 (fol. 63r). Baldus' view became well-known: see Philip Decius' prominent inclusion of it in his discussion of this whole question (ad X.1.2.7, n. 98–9, fol. 26r).

[40] Baldus ad C.7.37.3 (fol. 201v), 'Bona vero singularium personarum non sunt principis...de his tamen imperator disponere potest ex potestate absoluta ut de propriis, ut supra dixi super lege proxima, et *maxime* causa subsistente' – a just cause is clearly not essential. He refers here to his commentary on C.7.37.2: 'In tex. ibi, "pariter privilegiis", hec est causa contra illos qui dicunt quod non potest imperator rem meam per privilegium alteri concedere et auferre mihi dominium, et subaudi etiam sine causa...Nec obstat supra [C.1.19.7] ubi rescripta et privilegia per que absorbetur ius alterius nihil valent et [C.1.19.2], quia concedo hoc nisi habeant clausulam derogatoriam, "non obstante lege", tunc ergo non tenent quia imperator non vult et presumitur nolle etiam concedendo rescriptum nisi addat clausulam...nisi imperator aut papa concederet motu proprio quia ista exprimuntur in rescripto, quia tunc nulla est necessaria alia clausula derogatoria.'

[41] Ad C.3.34.2 (fol. 190v) – this passage immediately precedes his definition of the emperor's *plenitudo potestatis* (above, p. 72). Ullmann, *Medieval Idea of Law*, p. 103, relates this passage to Baldus' highly developed conception of sovereignty.

is very considerably strengthened. If Baldus had adhered to a straightforward theocratic interpretation of imperial power, according to which property rights were conceded by the ruler to his subjects, there would have been no problem in his adopting this view.[42] But the juristic *communis opinio*, to which Baldus adhered and which derived from the view of the twelfth-century Glossator, Bulgarus, held that the emperor did not ultimately own the property of his subjects, but through his *dominium mundi* conserved and protected it.[43] Furthermore, the derivation of property rights from the *ius gentium* ruled out the *princeps* as their source. Indeed, the whole juristic discussion of the *princeps* and the property of his subjects arose because it became accepted that he was not the proprietor of these rights: if he had been, there would have been no point at issue. In Baldus' political thought, therefore, his treatment of private property provides a big exception to his overall view of a limited absolute power for the emperor. In taking this step he decisively parts company with Bartolus. Why he should adopt this view on property and leave the emperor limited in other important respects, appears unclear. Manifestly, on this question both he and Jacobus Butrigarius have a conception of absolute power more in tune with absolutist theories of the seventeenth century than with the views of their juristic contemporaries. For Baldus property rights are not sacrosanct.

FEUDAL RELATIONSHIPS

In his feudal relationships, however, the emperor is certainly limited by feudal custom which had become so deeply ingrained that Baldus represents it as an aspect of the *ius naturale* itself: the emperor is subject to feudal custom which amounts to nothing less than a day-to-day revelation of the natural law: 'For the emperor is subject to feudal customs as if they were latterly discovered natural law, because natural law is born every day.'[44] This is an aspect of the long-established juristic theme that custom is second nature (a derivation ultimately from

---

[42] For this theocratic view see Ullmann, *Principles*, p. 76, and *Individual and Society*, p. 39.

[43] This is clear from the passages quoted above from his commentaries on X.2.26.13 and C.7.37.3. In his famous dispute with Bulgarus, Martinus had maintained the theocratic view that the emperor owned all the property of his subjects. The *communis opinio* is to be found in commentaries on C.7.37.3. See also Baldus ad D.V. Const., 'Omnem', for an exposition of the opinions of Martinus and Bulgarus.

[44] Ad *Feud.*, 2.7 (fol. 36r). For the inclusion of feudal customs within natural law see Ullmann, *Individual and Society*, p. 83 (especially, n.43).

Aristotle and Cicero).[45] Baldus explains the introduction of feudal law, which of course was totally unknown to the *Corpus Iuris Civilis*, by seeing it as the product of nature itself, which being a force for change produces new forms of legal relationship for which new law is required.[46] This stress on the naturalness of feudal custom indicates that the emperor is not the source of its validity, but rather is bound by it. Thus the emperor in the exercise of his will as *dominus mundi* is limited to the area of legal activity open to him and cannot infringe the right of another when that is a feudal one, as distinct from another form of private property; otherwise the emperor would be acting in an unjust and unnatural manner, as Baldus makes clear in a *consilium* devoted to a feudal *dignitas*:

> I happily concede, however, that the emperor or pope can create and suppress dignities, as is noted in [X.1.2.8]. This is true, however, while the dignity is vacant and exists in the abstract; but if it has an incumbent he [i.e. the emperor or the pope] cannot suppress it without cause because he cannot suppress a right which another person has acquired, but insofar as the law permits he can certainly freely make such dispositions as he wishes...Again, the emperor can make perishable something which is permanent, but not to another's disadvantage, although he is lord of the world, because he is understood to be such only insofar as his rule is good and natural, lest the source of rights become the occasion of injuries, as in [C.8.4.6].[47]

In maintaining that feudal custom has its source in nature and is therefore justified by natural law, Baldus is seeking to express the profound point that this whole body of law emerged gradually as the legal expression of the natural development of this form of human relationship, that it was not, in his eyes, instituted by God or any ruler. Baldus like all jurists sees the feudal bond as being based preeminently upon the most fundamental legal relationship, contract, without which human intercourse and society would be impossible. The sanctity of contract, and the *fides* involved in keeping it, are so fundamental that they are seen as the product of *ius naturale* or *ius gentium*, and are prior to any positive law power possessed by the emperor, and limit him as well as anyone else.[48] Thus the divinely approved commission of power

---

[45] See Baldus ad *Sext.*, 2.2 (fol. 8v), 'Consuetudo est altera natura'; Aristotle, *Eth. Nic.*, 1152a; and Cicero, *De finibus bonorum et malorum*, 5.74. For the influence of the Aristotelian passage on medieval juristic thought see Kirshner, 'Between nature and culture', pp. 193–4, and for that of the Ciceronian see Cortese, *Norma giuridica*, II, 161–2.

[46] Ad C.1.14.8 (fol. 54v). Cp. id. ad D.1.3.10 (fol. 14r). Cp. D. Const., 'Tanta', and C.1.17.2,18: 'multas etenim formas edere natura novas deproperat.'

[47] *Cons.*, 3.277, fol. 84r, ed. Brescia, 1491 (= *Cons.*, 1.327, ed. Venice, 1575).

[48] Baldus, *Cons.*, 4.167, fol. 32r (ed. Brescia, 1490). For a trenchant later expression of the *communis opinio* see Paulus de Castro, *Cons.*, 1.318, n.5 (fol. 168r), 'Communiter

to the emperor does not include plenitude of power over contracts, and especially feudal ones, a limitation he shares, for instance, with the king of France – in feudal matters both must observe due process of feudal law:

Suppose that the emperor or the king of France creates someone a duke and invests him with a dukedom; or a marquess and invests him with a marquisate; or a count and invests him with a county; or a baron and invests him with a barony. Can he divest him of his fief at will? The answer is that he cannot, except on account of a conviction for a crime or felony. Furthermore nor could his successors to the empire or kingdom do this, as [X.2.1.13] notes. That the emperor has plenitude of power poses no problem for this view, because it is true that *God has subjected the laws to him, but has not subjected to him contracts* by which he is bound, as is noted and said in [C.1.14.4].[49]

There is thus no doubt that an emperor who makes a feudal contract is bound absolutely by it; and Baldus indicates here that his successor is also, a crucially important provision because the whole fabric of feudal relationships is at stake.[50] But this view contravenes his general rule that an emperor is not bound by his predecessors' contracts, there being no inheritance of obligations since the emperorship is elective. He does however make a crucial exception for feudal contracts on the

doctores tradunt quod ibi etiam princeps contractum initum cum subdito tenetur servare et non potest venire contra de iure, etiam ex suprema potestate, quia faceret contra ius naturale primevum, seu legem nature...tale ius gentium seu naturale princeps ex suprema etiam potestate non potest tollere.'

[49] Baldus ad *Feud.*, 1.7 (fol. 17v); this passage is also quoted by Ullmann in *Individual and Society*, p. 83, n. 43, and by Carlyle in *Medieval Political Theory*, VI, 21. Cp. Baldus ad D.1.4.1 (fol. 20v); and id., *Cons.*, 2.308, fol. 82r, ed. Brescia, 1490 (= *Cons.*, 5.182, ed. Venice, 1575). It is notable however that Baldus appears to permit the *princeps* to annul contracts between third parties for the public good, as emerges in a passage which treats in particular the temporal rulership of the pope, and which is neither concerned with feudal matters nor brings into issue any contract of the *princeps* or the pope himself (*Cons.*, 4.401, fol. 92r, ed. Venice, 1575).

[50] Ad X.2.19.1, n. 2 (fol. 238r). For the emperor's obligation *de iure naturali* to adhere to the *fides* of his predecessors concerning the granting of fiefs see also id., *Cons.*, 3.283, fol. 88r, ed. Brescia, 1491 (= *Cons.*, 1.333, ed. Venice, 1575); id., *Cons.*, 2.190, fol. 50v (ed. Brescia, 1490); and id., *Cons.*, 3.276, fol. 83v, ed. Brescia, 1491 (= *Cons.*, 1.326, ed. Venice, 1575). Cp. Cynus ad C.1.14.4, n. 7 (fol. 26r): 'Vltimo sciendum quod Guido de Suzaria formavit hic questionem utrum si imperator ineat aliqua pacta cum aliqua civitate vel barone teneat ea observare, tam ipse quam eius successor...Videtur quod sic, nam grave est fidem fallere, ut [D.13.5.1], et naturalia iura suadent pacta servari, et fides etiam hostibus est servanda.' Baldus, *Cons.*, 4.167 (above, n. 48), and ad D.1.4.1 (above n. 49) refers to this passage. Ullmann in *Individual and Society*, p. 83, n. 43, says of this passage, 'As far as I can ascertain the problem [i.e. of feudal custom's falling within the category of natural law] was first clearly perceived by the thirteenth-century jurist Guido de Suzaria as reported by Cynus.' See Cortese, *Norma giuridica*, I, 155–9, for the argument that the text of Guido de Suzaria's *quaestio* (establishing what was to become the juristic *communis opinio* on this question) can be reconstructed.

grounds that they are not of a purely personal (and therefore private) nature, but of that class made through the exercise of the imperial office:

> Although the emperor is not bound by positive law, he is bound by the law of contract, as is noted at [C.1.14.4] by Cynus and below [D.2.1.14]. He, I say, is bound and not his successor, because the emperor's contract does not pass on to his successor... because imperial rights do not pass on to his successor, but are created anew through election [X.3.5.25]... And this is true unless [the emperor] does things which relate to the nature of his office or are a customary part of it, such as infeudation, see the argument in Auth. 'Vt nulli iudicum liceat habere loci servatorem', § 'et hoc vere iubemus' [Coll., 9.9, 6 = Nov., 134, 6], and in Auth. 'Constitutio quae dignitatibus', § 'illud' [Coll., 6.9, 2 = Nov., 81, 2].[51]

This binding of successors is a clear limitation on imperial sovereignty which also suffers another major infringement. It is essentially the element of mutual consent in the feudal contract that limits the emperor: both he and his vassal thereby freely subject themselves to the requirements of feudal law. The contract is of its nature reciprocal; and the obligation to keep faith lies on both the emperor and his *fidelis*: 'Some however are under the emperor by reason of a fief alone, and these are in no way bound to anyone, save that they are bound to give fealty to the emperor himself, and likewise the emperor is bound to keep faith with them all and not violate it.'[52] Although this passage concerns those with only a feudal relationship with the emperor, rather than those who are in a direct sense otherwise subject to him (as in the *terrae imperii*), it does clearly emphasise that reciprocity which of course exists in feudal relationships between the emperor and those who are also his subjects.

The picture, therefore, begins to emerge of the dual aspects of imperial authority: the emperor possesses absolute sovereignty through the *lex regia* and divine approbation within the context of a higher normative structure; he is also a feudal ruler enmeshed in feudal relationships and thus limited by the nature of the feudal contract, which is itself protected by higher norms. Of course, feudal limitations only operate as regards those with whom the emperor has a feudal relationship, whereas his positive law *dominium mundi* is *de iure* universal. There is, however, a profound sense in which the emperor's absolute power is reconciled with the feudal aspect of his rulership. The feudal explanation of how the emperor was the source of the public authority

---

[51] Ad D.1.4.1 (fol. 20v).
[52] Baldus, *Cons.*, 3.277, fol. 85r, ed. Brescia, 1491 (= *Cons.*, 1.327, ed. Venice, 1575). Cp. id. ad D.1.3.31 (fol. 16r).

of important lesser rulers held great juristic attraction for any civilian, and was especially relevant in fourteenth-century Italy for describing the nature of the imperial vicariates of *signori*. Through granting public jurisdiction in fief the emperor did not alienate any part of the empire, and by definition retained his ultimate sovereignty: 'The emperor is called, "augustus". Why, I ask, is he called this? The Gloss gives as the reason that it should be his task to increase [the empire]... We must consider whether the right to alienate is binding in law... When the emperor concedes in fief, he can do so without doubt, precisely because in that case sovereign right remains with him.'[53] Furthermore the emperor was under no necessity to initiate fiefs: he voluntarily subjected himself to the requirements of feudal custom; but once an emperor had created a fief feudal law dictated all his and his successors' legal dealings over that fief –

Feudal custom says that the emperor could not deprive dukes [of their fiefs] unless they previously be deemed unworthy by their peers. Could an emperor issue a statute to the contrary and thus make dignities empty? I reply that he could not, as in [*Feud.*, 1.7], for custom which applies to the emperor himself is greater than the emperor unless such custom should lead to the actual or near destruction of the empire's existence.[54]

The general proviso that customs must not infringe the well-being of the empire is clearly not relevant to the accepted structure of feudal relationships, which would not be considered to do this.

THE EMPEROR'S OFFICE

There remains a final limitation inherent in the very nature of the emperorship itself. For Baldus, as for all jurists, it is an office established by the *lex regia* and confirmed by God for a purpose: to rule and conserve the empire. The emperor is not the outright proprietor of the empire: he cannot do with it what he will. He is not the *dominus* of the empire in the sense of absolute owner, but rather an officer whose function is to act in the empire's interests:

But the emperor cannot divest himself of or sell the property [of the empire], because he does not possess it in his own right but by right of the *lex regia*, and because it is not transferred to him and therefore cannot be alienated by

---

[53] Baldus ad C.Const., 'De novo Codice componendo' (fol. 1r).
[54] Baldus ad Auth., 'Omnes peregrini' (ad C.6.59.10), fol. 166r. Cf. id. ad *Feud.*, 1.1 (fol. 7v).

him. Indeed, the emperor is the main *procurator* of the empire: he is not, however, the empire's absolute owner, but rather an officer.[55]

In describing the emperor as a *procurator* he is using a term common in both Roman and canon law, and which had experienced developments in meaning in the writings of different jurists.[56] Baldus is not trying here to distinguish the precise sense in which the emperor represents the empire, but simply to stress his function as an officer with the duty of any proctor: that of not injuring the interests of his principal, although in this case the original principal, the *populus Romanus*, has lost any control over its proctor. This explains why the emperor has that duty of non-alienation of the empire which emerged in Baldus' discussion of the Donation of Constantine – any loss of authority on his part through alienation damages the empire itself: 'The emperor cannot however donate so much that his authority becomes worthless, as in Auth. "Quomodo oporteat episcopos" [Coll., 1.6 = Nov., 6], at the beginning of the gloss (and the argument is to be noted in [D.32.1.34, 1]), because he cannot defraud the empire by diminishing himself (see the argument in [D.37.14.16]).'[57] Indeed, if the emperor were to alienate part of the empire committed to his care he would be guilty of destroying his own *dignitas*, that is his office, and thus breaking his coronation oath:

The emperor could not however donate the keys of the empire just as he who holds the gate-keys is bound to hand them over to his successor, otherwise he can be called a traitor, as [C.7.32.12; D.31.1.77, 21] note. Again, he cannot eviscerate the empire, because he would be the murderer of his office...Again, nor can he concede one barony which could undermine the majesty of the empire, because he would be a perjurer.[58]

Thus the irrevocable commission of imperial power through the *lex regia* was even in positive law terms not of truly absolute power, but rather of power with a limiting and defining purpose, that is a specific office. The power of the emperor is absolute within the sphere allocated to him – what might appear his omnicompetence is limited by the overriding rights of the empire: 'The Roman emperor can by reason

---

[55] Baldus, *Cons.*, 3.277, fol. 84v, ed. Brescia, 1491 (= *Cons.*, 1.456, fol. 139v, ed. Brescia, 1490; and *Cons.*, 1.327, ed. Venice, 1575). See Ullmann, 'A note on inalienability in Gregory VII', p. 140, for the earlier history of this conception of rulership.

[56] See Tierney, *Foundations*, pp. 117–27.

[57] Ad *Specul.*, 2.2.7 (p. 376). Cp. id. ad C. Const., 'De novo Codice componendo' (fol. 1r).

[58] Baldus ad X.2.19.9, n. 7 (fol. 248r).

of his certain knowledge do anything, that is the emperor can in things temporal, always saving the majesty of his empire.'[59] The emperor's sovereignty therefore exists under a basic constitutional law and is of its nature far removed from arbitrary power.

The emperor is an officer of this kind because, as we have seen, the empire is a sempiternal entity:[60] precisely because it is undying and indestructible the emperor's function must be to conserve it. The individual emperor is mortal, but the empire and the office (*dignitas*), through the exercise of which he serves and acts for that empire, are immortal.[61] The human person is required because an abstraction such as the empire or the imperial office is of itself incapable of acting and willing.[62] This emphasis on the sempiternity of the empire has to be reconciled with Baldus' noted awareness of the changes which had occurred through time in its physical extent and the relationship between the emperorship and its various provinces. His solution is that the empire, in so far as its essential nature as a legal entity is concerned, is immutable: 'Nothing can increase or decrease contrary to its own nature or definition, as in the said [D.23.8.6, 1]. Thus the Roman empire cannot increase or decrease so far as the disposition of the law is concerned.'[63] The empire's physical disposition, however, like everything else in this world is subject to change.[64] Similarly the powers of the imperial office, because they exist to serve the empire as an immortal entity, remain the same for a contemporary emperor as they were for any previous one: 'The emperor could these days correct Auth. "Quas actiones" [ad. C.1.2.23] just as he corrected [C.1.2.23], for these days the emperor has no less power than he had then, because the empire never dies, as in Auth. "Quomodo oporteat episcopos" [Coll., 1,

---

[59] Baldus ad *Feud.*, Proem, ad v. 'Aliqua' (fol. 3r).

[60] See above, p. 27, and also for instance Baldus, *De pace Constantie*, ad v. 'Imperialis clementie' (fol. 1r), 'Imperium non moritur'.

[61] 'Imperator in persona mori potest, sed ipsa dignitas seu imperium immortalis est' (Baldus, *Cons.*, 1.359, fol. 109v, ed. Brescia, 1491 (= *Cons.*, 3.159, ed. Venice, 1575)) – see my discussion of this *consilium* below, pp. 215–17. Cf. id. ad X.2.24.33, n. 5 (fol. 315r), 'Imperator rei sue potest dare legem quam vult, et non obligatur homini sed deo et dignitati sue, que perpetua est.'

[62] See for instance Baldus ad C.10.1, Rubr.; and id. ad D. Const., 'Omnem', ad v. 'Hec autem tria' (fol. 3r).

[63] *Cons.*, 1.177, n. 4, fol. 51v (ed. Venice, 1575).

[64] See Baldus, *Cons.*, 3.278, fol. 86r, ed. Brescia, 1491 (= *Cons.*, 1.328, ed. Venice, 1575), 'Licet imperium semper sit, ut in Auth. "Quomodo oporteat episcopos" [Coll., 1.6 = Nov., 6], tamen non in eodem statu permanet, quia in continuo motu et perplexa tribulatione insistit; et hoc apparet immutatione quattuor principalium regnorum, inter que duo preclariora constituta sunt Assiriorum primum Romanorum postremum, ut ait Augustinus, li. x. c. viii. de civitate dei, quod debet durare usque ad finem huius seculi, et per imperatorem regi in temporalibus, per apostolicum regi in spiritualibus.'

6 = Nov., 6].'[65] This understanding of the function of the emperor and the nature of the empire fits in with a wider view which Baldus holds concerning the role of the ruler or government and the nature of the political entity which is governed. To anticipate somewhat, it will become clear that his conception of the empire as an undying abstract entity with a distinct legal identity, governed by an imperial *dignitas* of a matching sempiternal kind, a *dignitas* operated by an individual and mortal ruler, is in accordance with his theory of corporations which he applies to all forms of political organisation. Baldus, however, works out the political application of corporation theory in greatest detail in his treatment of city-republics and kingdoms; and it is in considering these that the full implications of his view will be discussed.

Baldus contributes of course to a long-standing juristic tradition of considering the empire and the imperial *dignitas* as immortal entities.[66] Likewise the crucial financial aspect of imperial authority, the fisc, had attracted lengthy and complicated debate among jurists,[67] which variety of views Baldus reflects notably in his commentary on the rubric to the title, *De iure fisci* (C.10.1). His commentary on the *Tres libri* is the most skimpy and least satisfactory of his works; and his treatment of fiscal questions there lacks the sense of application to contemporary reality which characterises the vast bulk of his work, and in consequence has a theoretical feel about it. Baldus' interesting, and at times original contributions to political aspects of fiscal powers are to be found in his discussions of kings, *signori* and independent city-republics, in whose territories fiscal questions were of immediate concern in the fourteenth century, whereas the imperial fisc did not operate directly in Italy, although it stood as the model for any other kind of fisc. As far as the empire is concerned, the fisc, being for Baldus its financial aspect, is itself an immortal entity distinct from the individual emperor, and for which he acts.[68] Yet the fisc can be said to be located in the emperor because he operates it, and for this reason can be figuratively identified with him.[69] Nevertheless, because the fisc is in essence differentiated

---

[65] Baldus, *Rep.* ad C.1.1.1, n. 85, p. 38 (ed. Meijers).

[66] See for instance, Kantorowicz, *King's Two Bodies*, pp. 291–302.

[67] Ibid., pp. 179–90.

[68] The fisc belongs not to the individual emperor, but to the immortal empire, and secondarily to the Roman people as the origin of the empire (ad C.10.1.Rubr., fol. 1v). Indeed, the immortal fisc outlives the mortal emperor, 'Quero mortuo imperatore ubi est iste fiscus cum sit mortuus ille qui erat fiscus? Responsum: fingitur non mortuus, donec alius creetur imperator, sed vice persone fungetur' (ibid.) – for the full implications of 'vice persone fungi' in corporation theory see below, pp. 189–93.

[69] Baldus ad C.10.1.Rubr. (fol.1v).

from the emperor, the fiscal possessions of the empire itself are distinct from the private possessions of the emperor: he owns neither the goods of his individual subjects, nor the fiscal rights of the empire.[70] The emperor's fiscal function and duties are the financial aspect of his imperial office, and are limited by the same considerations.

THE EMPEROR AND THE COMMON GOOD

The emperor's duty to conserve the empire is manifestly an expression of his responsibility to serve the common good, the *utilitas publica*, a basic requirement for any medieval ruler. Baldus is perfectly clear that the emperor's positive law liberty of action exists to achieve the good of his subjects:

Then it seems here that the emperor uses the word, 'should'. On the contrary he is bound by no necessity, for the emperor acts freely like God who is an entirely free agent, as in [D.1.4.1]. The solution is that the word, 'should', is explained as meaning 'opportune' or 'useful', that is to his subjects, as in [D.1.11.1].[71]

This is a profoundly orthodox view-point not requiring further comment. Baldus does, however, produce two statements which in a highly original way treat the emperor's duty to adhere to the *utilitas publica* in his dealings with the Italian city-republics, and illustrate further the limitations on his freedom of action. The first concerns the cities of both the *terrae ecclesiae* and the *terrae imperii*:

Innocent says, 'To whom does a city of the church belong?' The answer is that it belongs to the church, but more so to the citizens whose city it is. Bologna belongs to the church, but more so to the Bolognese, because the church possesses no authority there except as the republic whose likeness and name it bears. Again, the question is, 'To whom does the city of Siena belong?' My answer is, to Caesar, but more so to the Sienese, for 'republic', 'fisc' and 'princeps' are interchangeable terms meaning almost the same thing, as [C.6.1.7] notes. The republic is like the vital force of the senses. The fisc is the republic's stomach, purse and strength. In consequence the emperor

70 This is of course implied by what has already been discussed concerning his *dominium mundi*. If the emperor owned the fiscal rights of the empire, he could alienate them, which he cannot. His own patrimony belongs to him, but he can only be said to possess the *iura fisci* within the limitations of his office (Baldus ad C.7.37.3, fol. 201v). This view is common-place among the Commentators, although in one passage at least Petrus de Bellapertica appears not to adhere to it: 'Fiscalia sunt principis, et ecclesiastica sunt domini pape tanquam patrimonium proprium, et ea ad libitum alienat [C.7.37.3; & D.43.8.1]' (ad *Feud.*, ad v. 'Qui potest dare feudum', fol. 163r).
71 Ad C.Const., 'De novo Codice componendo', ad v. 'Hec que necessario' (fol. 1v).

would be like a tyrant if he did not conduct himself like a republic, and so too would many other kings who act for their own private advantage, because he who is zealous, not for the advantage of his master, but for his own, is a robber.[72]

This is an explanation of the relationship between the republican forms of government in the *terrae imperii* and the underlying ultimate authority of the emperor. Imperial authority is expressed through republican regimes: the emperor acts through republics to procure the common good, and is not at liberty to sweep them aside. Indeed, achievement of *utilitas publica* involves respect for republican institutions: if the emperor were to act unilaterally and for his private good alone, he would be a tyrant. In the second passage this view is taken further. Since the empire was originally founded for the purpose of achieving the common good, any attack on the republics by the emperor justifies resistance on their part:

It is to be noted therefore that the original intention in creating the empire was the public good and advantage rather than private, say that of the emperor Charles. If therefore the emperor were to turn his anger on the republics, to shake off his yoke of such servitude would not be contrary to natural reason.[73]

It is significant that Baldus supports a natural right of resistance which justified by reason breaks through the constitutional structure derived ultimately from the *lex regia*, which is thus revealed to have involved no total transfer of political rights. Subjects can in short judge their emperor. The resort to a naturalistic concept, as we shall see in the next chapter, reflects Baldus' explanation of how it is possible for certain Italian city-republics to enjoy practical sovereignty, while remaining under the emperor's ultimate sovereignty. Judgment by subjects illustrates the reciprocity existing between the emperor and those he rules – a conception which Baldus may have in part derived from feudal sources: 'Relatively speaking, the emperor is said to be like a father and just as his subjects are bound to obey him well, he is also bound to rule them well.'[74]

Baldus' views on the limitations of imperial power illustrate one of the major problems in the interpretation of medieval political thought. It is a commonplace to indicate that medieval monarchy, although it was essentially limited in nature, was not in general subject to effective

---

[72] Ad *Feud.*, 1.14 (fol. 23r). This passage is also quoted in Gierke, *Political Theories*, p. 163, n. 217.
[73] *Cons.*, 3.283, fol. 88r, ed. Brescia, 1491 (= *Cons.*, 1.333, ed. Venice, 1575).
[74] Ad D.1.8.Rubr. (fol. 36r).

institutional controls, a deficiency which could appear to render any theoretical limitations ineffective in practice: that there is, in short, a crucial distinction between limited and controlled monarchy. To press this point is to take an essentially non-medieval view: the defining limitations of rulership were taken very seriously by jurists, publicists, theologians and philosophers. This is clearly the case in Baldus' treatment of the emperor, the model in this respect for other rulers. It is anyway not true to maintain that he proposes no effective limitations on the emperor: the element of control over the emperor is provided by feudal law and, ultimately, papal deposition. It remains true however that he rejects any constitutional control by the electoral princes once papal coronation has taken place; thus below the level of papal intervention institutional controls are lacking. The extent of princely control over the *Rex Romanorum* is not specified. If, however, the emperor, especially through absence, fails to fulfil his obligation to provide effective rulership, then his subjects can take matters into their own hands, which is precisely what Baldus accepts has happened in the independent Italian city-republics.

Chapter 3

THE SOVEREIGNTY OF INDEPENDENT
CITY-REPUBLICS

In considering the independent Italian city-republics Baldus elaborates
a theory of the legal sovereignty of the city conceived as a whole, that
is as a *populus*. His thesis of popular sovereignty is no general theory
or blue-print, but is tailored to apply to this specific political context.
Within the overall structure of the sovereign city-*populus* he is able to
elaborate his theory of its membership, its form of government, and
the limitations on its authority. Baldus, recognising that contemporary
cities present a range of levels of jurisdiction from subordination to
sovereignty, finds for all levels a place in his political theory; but his
major contribution lies in his justification of the status of sovereign
city-republics through developing and deepening the *de facto* argument,
the result of his thorough-going acceptance of political reality. This is
not to deny that Baldus admits for many cities a parallel structure of
valid *de iure* jurisdictional rights derived from imperial or papal
privilege or concession. Certainly any sovereignty enjoyed by a city
is to some extent curtailed by Baldus' basic hierarchical view; yet the
aspect of direct subordination to a superior contained in *de iure*
concession means, as we shall see, that it is the *de facto* argument which
produces the highest level of sovereignty of which cities are capable.

The civilian background to Baldus' theory

The Bartolist argument for the sovereignty of independent city-*populi*
is the immediate context of Baldus' theory. It is especially notable that
a theory of the sovereignty of cities was formulated in specifically
civilian terms, because the *Corpus Iuris Civilis* would appear to place
almost overwhelming difficulties in the way of developing any such
thesis. Quite apart from the location of sovereign power in the person
of the emperor, the very position of cities in the *Corpus* offered on the

93

face of it no scope for the elaboration of the idea of their sovereignty: they enjoyed the status of *municipia*, licit corporations subject to imperial confirmation for their legal rights. Furthermore the *lex regia*, a major *locus* for possible popular sovereignty, did not apply to cities in general; and, in any case, for the reasons already noted,[1] was not used by Bartolus and Baldus in their theories of sovereign city-*populi*. The point remains that there are several strands in medieval juristic theory of the sovereignty of the people: that associated with interpretations of the *lex regia* is but one, and is quite distinct from Bartolus' and Baldus' theories of the sovereignty of a specific kind of people, that of the independent city.

In treating Italian cities the Glossators had not developed a theory of the sovereignty of independent city-*populi* with republican regimes. For them sovereignty remained with the cities' superior, the emperor. The cities' law-making in the form of custom and statute was seen essentially as custom subject for its validity to imperial consent in the form either of direct confirmation or tacit acquiescence: the Glossators had no idea of a truly autonomous law-creating capacity on the part of the cities.[2] Even when Azo, for instance, admitted custom as a source for the full powers of jurisdiction of some Lombard cities he retained imperial consent through acquiescence as the ultimate validation.[3] The Peace of Constance, the legal source for the liberties of so many Lombard cities, was itself a prime example of imperial concession. Amongst the early Commentators there was isolated recognition that some Italian cities recognised no superior, the fundamental requirement for a claim to sovereignty: by Jacobus de Ravannis[4] in the thirteenth century and by Oldradus[5] in the early fourteenth; and Petrus de Bellapertica and Cynus had referred generally, but without approbation, to *populi* who did not recognise the emperor's sovereignty.[6] But before Bartolus there was no articulated civilian theory of the sovereignty of independent city-*populi*. It might seem that canon law because it was not committed to imperial sovereignty might have provided greater flexibility in the treatment of these cities. Yet while the canonist

---

[1] Above, pp. 61–3.

[2] See for instance Woolf, *Bartolus*, pp. 112–14, and Michaud-Quantin, *Universitas*, pp. 248–9.

[3] *Quaestiones Azonis*, p. 67 (ed. Landsberg).

[4] Ad C.7.33.12 (fol. 344v): 'Hodie, vacante imperio, civitates regunt se ipsas; et una civitas regit se ipsam nec habet superiorem.'

[5] *Cons.*, 69, n. 6 (fol. 23v): 'Sed si ius cuiuslibet civitatis consideremus, de illo non est dubium, quia multe civitates et reges fecerunt leges et constitutiones quod non subessent imperatori.' [6] Above, p. 65.

tradition accorded considerable effectiveness to the law-making of cities,[7] it did not produce a theory of the sovereignty of cities to match its theory of the sovereignty of kings. Before the impact of Bartolus' theory the furthest that a canonist was prepared to go in accommodating the claims of independent cities is probably this statement by Hostiensis: 'These collegiate or corporate rights therefore also flourish in the cities, especially of Lombardy, and even if they have a lord, they do not however recognise him, as would befit a republic, just as neither does the king of France'[8] – a recognition but expressly not a justification of political fact.

Bartolus' achievement was within the civilian tradition to make the leap of justifying the sovereignty of independent city-*populi*.[9] He did this specifically in the context of the doctrine of the early Commentators by drawing the full implications from the element of consent in popular law-making in the form of statute and custom.[10] It was the virtue of the early Commentators to realise more clearly than had the Glossators the constitutive role of consent in the making of popular customs and statutes. For these Commentators the fundamental difference between custom and statute lay in the mode in which that consent was expressed: statute was express consent and custom tacit.[11] A major source for this idea was provided by a passage from the classical jurist, Julian (D.1.3.32), in which the people's custom and legislation are accorded the same force because of their common constitutive element of consent.[12] The early Commentators were in essence taking this

---

7 See Mochi Onory, *Fonti canonistiche*, pp. 248–9, and Michaud-Quantin, *Universitas*, pp. 249–50.

8 *Lectura* ad X.1.31.3, fol. 147r.

9 See Woolf, *Bartolus*, pp. 112–207; Ercole, 'Studi sulla dottrina politica'; id., *Dal comune*, pp. 257–60; id., *Da Bartolo all'Althusio*, pp. 70–104; Ullmann, *Principles*, pp. 279–87; and Skinner, *Foundations*, I, 8–12. For a recent survey of modern treatments of Bartolus see Walther, *Imperiales Königtum*, pp. 176–86.

10 See Ullmann, 'De Bartoli sententia', pp. 711–26.

11 For details of the Glossators' and Commentators' theories of customary and statute law Brie, *Gewohnheitsrecht*, pp. 96–164, is fundamental; see also Cortese, *Norma giuridica*, II, 101–67. For an early Commentator's treatment of tacit and express consent see for instance Jacobus de Ravannis ad C.8.52.1 (fol. 392v). For later expressions of this theme see for instance Cynus ad C.8.52.2, nn. 5 and 23 (fols. 521r and 524v); and Raynerius de Forlì, *Rep.* ad D.1.1.9, n. 42 (fol. 20r).

12 In this connection see the commentary of the post-Accursian jurist Odofredus ad D.1.3.32, n. 6 (fol. 15r) where he closely follows the text, 'Si leges scripte sunt [sint *ed. Lyon, 1550*] servande, quia iudicio populi sunt recepte, multo fortius consuetudo. Nam quid interest declaret [declarat *ed. cit.*] populus voluntatem suam verbis expressis an rebus et factis? Certe nihil, ut hic dicitur'; and Cynus ad C.8.52.2, n. 10 (fol. 522r), 'Nam consuetudo non differt a lege, nisi sicut tacitum et expressum, ideo etc., ut dicta [D.1.3.32].'

concept, applied by Julian to the *populus Romanus*, and applying its fundamental principle to the law-making of Italian cities. In giving such prominence to consent these jurists were adopting the most profound element in the Roman law's treatment of custom which was otherwise dominated by the superficial distinction between *ius scriptum* and *ius non scriptum* (written and unwritten law), one which merely stressed the form rather than the constitutive element of law-making. These early Commentators were thus able to reach a clear understanding that a city-statute, being the product of the people's will, was legislation rather than *consuetudo scripta* (written custom), as Accursius had termed it,[13] and that legislation was not therefore the monopoly of the superior, the emperor. They did not, however, develop this argument from consent so as to arrive at the idea of the legislative sovereignty of the city-*populi* with the supplanting of the superior which this would involve.

Bartolus saw with the greatest clarity that in law-making the consent of the people could act as a complete alternative to the will of the superior. Bartolus' well-known argument begins with customary law: because this is made by consent it does not require the authorisation of a superior. But the people's statutes being the product of their express consent are in consequence of the same force (*paris potentiae*) as their custom, their tacit consent: statutes also do not therefore require the authorisation of a superior.[14] Consent, however, as the constitutive element of the people's law leads beyond this to the non-recognition of a superior, the fundamental requirement for sovereignty. The *civitas quae superiorem non recognoscit* (the city which does not recognise a superior) is in the position of a *populus liber* (free people), a quite daring use of this term, because he is applying it to Italian cities, which for him are certainly within the empire, whereas in the *Corpus Iuris Civilis* it signifies an independent people outside the empire, but quite possibly in alliance with it. To indicate the complete independence of such a city Bartolus produces his juristic masterstroke by attributing to it within its territory the same powers of jurisdiction which the emperor enjoys in the empire as a whole: it is a *civitas sibi princeps* (city which

---

[13] See Brie, *Gewohnheitsrecht*, p. 98, n. 9.

[14] See Bartolus ad D.1.1.9, n. 4 (fol. 9v), 'Quando populus habet omnem iurisdictionem potest facere statutum non expectata superioris auctoritate...Et quod isto casu non expectetur superioris auctoritas patet exemplo consuetudinis, que inducitur ex tacito consensu populi et equiparatur statuto in quo constat quod non requiritur superioris auctoritas'; and id. ad D.1.3.32, n. 4 (fol. 17r), 'Tacitus et expressus consensus equiparantur et sunt paris potentie.'

is its own emperor).[15] This completes the argument because the emperor, in civilian terms the model for sovereignty, is thereby supplanted. Within the language of Roman law there is no clearer way of signifying the sovereignty of such city-*populi*. Through Bartolus' understanding of the power of consent the established formula for a sovereign king, *rex in regno suo est imperator regni sui* ('the king in his kingdom is the emperor of his kingdom': a straightforward transposition because sovereignty in both cases inheres in the person of the ruler), has mutated at his hands into a form applicable to a corporate entity, the city-*populus*, a far from obvious concept which it took a genius to see.[16] Bartolus' argument from consent is clearly a classic *de facto* theory: the law-making activities of the people, whatever the *de iure* claims of the emperor, break through to sovereignty. He provides a juristic justification for the legal sovereignty of the independent Italian cities as it actually existed.

[15] See, for instance, Bartolus ad D.4.4.3, n. 1 (fol 133r), 'Civitates tamen que principem non recognoscunt in dominum et sic earum populus liber est...possent hoc forte statuere, quia ipsamet civitas sibi princeps est.' For similar passages from Bartolus see Woolf, *Bartolus*, pp. 155–8. For the position of a *populus liber* see D.49.15.7.

[16] The modern literature on the formulae, *rex in regno suo est imperator regni sui*, and *superiorem non recognoscere*, as an expression of sovereignty is large: for surveys see Walther, *Imperiales Königtum*, pp. 65–111, and Paradisi, 'Il pensiero politico,' pp. 43–62 (bibliography, pp. 147–50). The formulae, used by both canonists and civilians, were in origin distinct, although they often came to be combined: 'non-recognition of a superior' indicates active non-subordination to the emperor, whereas the *rex–imperator* idea maintains that the king possesses within his territory the same powers which the emperor enjoys within the empire as a whole (see Ullmann, 'This realm of England is an empire', p. 188, n. 48, and Canning, 'Ideas of the state', p. 6). The *rex–imperator* idea emerged in canonist writings in the last decade of the twelfth century (see Mochi Onory, *Fonti canonistiche*, but also Tierney's criticisms of his approach in 'Some recent works', pp. 612–19), and also in a *quaestio* by Azo written at the beginning of the thirteenth century (for a recent contribution to the long-standing debate about the significance of this *quaestio* together with its text see Ullmann, 'Arthur's homage'). The juristic elaboration of the theme, *rex qui non recognoscit superiorem*, derives from a phrase in Innocent III's decretal, *Per venerabilem* (X.4.17.13), 'quum rex ipse [i.e. Francorum] superiorem in temporalibus minime recognoscat...', although Ullmann, 'Arthur's homage', p. 362, n.1, maintains that Innocent was there essentially reiterating phraseology used by Philip Augustus in his petition to the pope of 2 November 1201. See in particular Mochi Onory, *Fonti canonistiche*, pp. 271–88, for the significance of *Per venerabilem* in canonist treatments of the sovereignty of kings. Both the *rex–imperator* idea and the theme of the non-recognition of a superior were developed by French and Neapolitan civilians in the thirteenth century. Bartolus' achievement was to be the first jurist to take the concept of non-recognition of a superior and to apply it systematically, together with the equiparation of the free city and the emperor, in order to establish the sovereignty of independent cities. For Bartolus' use of these formulae see Costa, *Iurisdictio*, pp. 253–60.

Autonomy and sovereignty

Because of his basic view of a hierarchy of sovereignty Baldus discusses the independence of cities in terms of their relationship to a superior. Two levels of self-government emerge: local autonomy below the level of sovereignty and full independence or sovereignty itself. The arguments for autonomy are of the widest application because they both apply to cities recognising a direct superior and are relevant to sovereign ones, although in the latter case they do not, of course, fully describe such cities' jurisdictional claims. Baldus discusses local autonomy in terms of the capacity to legislate, the most important aspect of jurisdiction. He recognises that *populi* vary as to the amount of jurisdiction which they possess. There are for him three main grades of *populus* each possessing powers of jurisdiction with a related degree of legislative competence; and only the highest grade, the *populus* with *plena* or *omnis iurisdictio* (full or all jurisdiction), enjoys autonomy which is shown by its capacity to legislate without the confirmation or authorisation of a superior:

And the first question is whether every people is allowed to make statutes without the permission of a superior. And it seems that they are not, see the argument at [C.10.65.5], and Auth. 'De defensoribus civitatum' [Coll., 3.2 = Nov., 15] is relevant to this. Solution. You are to say this: either the people which wishes to make a statute has no jurisdiction, but is subject to some city, as are villages and fortified places in the *contado*; or it has full jurisdiction conceded by the emperor or prescribed by custom in temporal or civil matters and in criminal ones, and this can be the case, as in Auth. 'De defensoribus civitatum', § 'iusiurandum' [Coll., 3.2, 1 = Nov., 15, 1] at the end of the great gloss; or it has limited jurisdiction, for instance in civil matters only. If it has no jurisdiction, then either it wishes to make statutes about the distribution of money or something else which does not concern jurisdiction, in which case it can do so, as long as such a statute does not involve financial corruption, as in [D.50.9.4]; or it wishes to make statutes about the deciding and hearing of cases, and it cannot do this without the permission of a superior on account of the aforementioned rights, and [X.1.2.8 & 9] support this. And the reason is that making such statutes is part of jurisdiction, as is clear from the definition of jurisdiction put forward in the gloss on [D. 2.1.1], and since it does not have jurisdiction, it cannot therefore have what derives from jurisdiction, as is argued in [D.23.1.16]. If we ask about a people possessing jurisdiction, then it can do so [i.e. make statutes] without a superior's authorisation...as is clear in this § and in [D.1.1.9], at the word, 'populus', where permission to make statutes is given without distinction. This is proved by similarity, for custom and statute go together step by step, as

I shall say in [Inst., 1.2, 3], and custom is produced by tacit consent without the authorisation of a superior, as in [D.1.3.32], therefore statute is as well. And that this § should be understood to apply to a people possessing jurisdiction is clear because the law gives the examples of the Roman and Athenian peoples, who without doubt possessed jurisdiction. Or we are speaking about peoples possessing limited jurisdiction, and they can make statutes within the competence of their jurisdiction, but not otherwise.[17]

Clearly there is no originality in this statement: he follows very closely Bartolus' commentary on D.1.1.9 which is directly applicable because the relevant section of Inst., 1.2, 1 incorporates the whole of D.1.1.9.[18] Indeed, his endorsement of his master's argument is made explicit in a *consilium* in which Baldus to support his argument against some other jurists quotes at length the relevant section of Bartolus' commentary word for word with few verbal differences which do not change the sense.[19] The importance, however, of this part of Baldus' commentary on Inst., 1.2, 1 is that it forms a basis for discussing the major aspects of his thought concerning the legislation of city-*populi*, and for assessing the degree to which he elsewhere deepens Bartolus' argument and, indeed, innovates.

At this level of autonomy both jurists accept two parallel sources of validation of a people's jurisdiction: concession by the privilege of a *princeps*, who is the people's superior, and prescription through the people's custom. This view, a reflection of contemporary political reality in central and northern Italy, acknowledges two alternative sources for the jurisdiction of a people: either the will of the superior or the consent of the people itself expressed through custom[20] – a distinction which, as we shall see, corresponds to that between *de iure* and *de facto* powers. It is the possession of jurisdiction itself (by either means) which brings with it a freedom from the involvement of the superior in the law-making process. In the case of jurisdiction by the superior's concession there is no need for further recourse to his authority, and where custom is the source any superior is by-passed. Full jurisdiction permits autonomy from a superior in all internal civil

---

[17] Inst., 1.2, 1, fol. 2r (ed. Pavia, 1489).

[18] 'Omnes populi, qui legibus et moribus reguntur, partim suo proprio, partim communi hominum omnium iure utuntur. nam quod quisque populus ipse sibi ius constituit, id ipsius proprium civitatis est vocaturque ius civile, quasi ius proprium ipsius civitatis: quod vero naturalis ratio inter omnes homines constituit, id apud omnes gentes pereque custoditur vocaturque ius gentium, quasi quo iure omnes gentes utuntur' (D.1.1.9).

[19] *Cons.*, 4.497, fol. 122v, ed. Brescia, 1490 (= *Cons.*, 5.372, ed. Venice, 1575).

[20] For *omnis iurisdictio* acquired through custom see Baldus, *Cons.*, 2.377, fol. 95v, ed. Brescia, 1490 (= *Cons.*, 5.83, ed. Venice, 1575).

and criminal matters, while limited jurisdiction produces a more circumscribed autonomy. Clearly freedom from the need for a superior's confirmation of a people's law-making is widely disseminated amongst cities and does not indicate in itself whether such a city is sovereign.[21]

The role of consent

This acceptance of either a superior's concession or custom as the source of a people's jurisdiction creates a large problem of interpretation for the role of consent in Baldus' (and therefore) Bartolus' thought, for manifestly the argument, that the common element of consent in the people's customs and statutes removes the need for the authorisation of a superior, is applied to both kinds of people. What then is the effectiveness of consent? What modification is required of the Bartolist consent argument as so far presented?

Baldus consistently understands a people's law-making to be the product of consent. As regards customary law he directly benefits from the work of the earlier Commentators who had elaborated in detail their realisation that consent was the constitutive element of popular customs: the element which made them law. To express this he designates the tacit consent of the people as the immediate cause of custom.[22] Baldus makes this point elsewhere in different language: consent, which essentially creates customary law, is termed its substance; other factors are purely secondary – the lapse of time, for instance, serves not to make the custom, but to confirm the constitutive consent: 'Again, note that the people's tacit consent, that is confirmed by the lapse of time, is of the substance of custom...I say that the strength given by time is required not for introducing the custom but for formalising the consent'.[23] Similarly the function of the common usage of the people is to reveal consent: 'Secondly, the gloss asks whether one act on the people's part suffices for introducing a custom in such a way that law would result from it...The truth is that a plurality or frequency of acts is required because the people's consent is more clearly

---

[21] As is made plain in Baldus' consideration of the extent to which a commune subject to Arezzo would have the capacity to make statutes without the confirmation of its superior: Campitelli–Liotta, *Consilium*, 2, p. 404. Cp. Baldus, *Cons.*, 4.324, n. 1–2, fol. 73v (ed. Venice, 1575): 'Prima ratio est quod communitates possunt statuere super re peculiari ipsarum nec egent talia statuta alia singulari confirmatione, ut plene no. [D.2.2.1, 1] per Jacobum Butrigarium.'

[22] 'Tacitus consensus est immediata causa consuetudinis' (ad C.7.64.1, fol. 267r). Cp. Jacobus Butrigarius ad D.1.3.32, n. 7 (p. 12), and Albericus de Rosciate, ibid., n. 52 (fol. 38v).

[23] *Secunda lectura* ad D.1.3.32 (fol. 20r). Cf. id. ad X.2.19.2, n. 7 (fol. 240v).

revealed through a plurality and frequency of acts.'[24] Baldus then follows previous Commentators in taking the crucial step of identifying consent as the constitutive element, not only of custom, but of popular written law, of *statuta populi*, as well: whereas custom is made by tacit consent statute is created by express consent.[25] He understands, therefore, that the difference between popular custom and statute lies in the manner in which the constitutive consent is expressed. Statute is seen to be what it in fact is: written law made by the people's express consent. The writing down serves a function which is only subsidiary to the consent: 'In written law writing down is required for confirmation and not for consent'.[26] The essence of statute is consent, but consent with the strength of law: 'For although statute is the citizens' consent, it is nonetheless not simply consent, but consent fortified by law.'[27] Consent is the common element in custom and statute, whereas it is the form of that consent which distinguishes them: 'Custom and statute do not differ in their efficient cause and its efficacy, but they do differ in their mode and form.'[28] Indeed, so well-established has the consent argument become by Baldus' time that he is able to express it in the form that only a *populus* which can make statutes can also make custom:

Note...at 'Nam cum ipse' he makes a third addition of substance, namely the tacit consent of the people. Again, since in comparing statute and custom he makes statute his starting-point, a fourth substantial point is clear, namely that it is such a people as could make statutes. For unless it can make law in an express manner, it cannot do so in a tacit one, since in both cases an equally effective efficient cause is needed.[29]

[24] Id. ad C.8.52.Rubr. (fol. 326r). Cf. Albericus de Rosciate ad D.1.3.32, n. 2 (fol. 38v); and Bartolus, *Rep.* ad D.1.3.32, n. 10 (fol. 19r). For details of Bartolus' doctrine of customary law see Brie, *Gewohnheitsrecht*, pp. 128–64; Ullmann, 'Bartolus on customary law'; and id., 'De Bartoli sententia', pp. 711–12.

[25] See Baldus ad X.1.4.Rubr., n. 5 (fol. 64v).

[26] Id., *secunda lectura* ad D.1.3.32 (fol. 20r): *lex scripta* in this context refers to legislation by the people. This is the continuation of the passage quoted above. Cp. Cynus ad C.8.52.2, n. 3 (fol. 520v), 'Breviter istud concedi oportet, quod quantum ad essentiam scriptum non sit de esse legis, nec non scriptum de esse consuetudinis, sed expressum et tacitum, ut [D.1.3.32].'

[27] Baldus ad C.4.30.3 (fol. 279v).

[28] Id. ad C.8.52.2 (fol. 327r). Cf. also id. ad X.1.4.11, n. 24 (fol. 70r), 'Causa efficiens consuetudinis est consensus populi.' Because of this perceived connection between custom and statute Baldus applies to statute the Roman law description of customary law as a 'civium conventio' (D.1.3.35): '...cum statutum dicatur esse quedam civium conventio, ut [D.50.17.27]' (*Cons.*, 3.206, fol. 58v, ed. Brescia, 1491 = *Cons.*, 1.236, ed. Venice, 1575). For Bartolus' application of the description, 'quedam conventio civium', to statute see Ullmann, 'De Bartoli sententia', p. 714.

[29] Ad D.1.3.32 (fol. 16r). Baldus takes the comparison *from* statute *to* custom from the text of D.1.3.32. See however id. ad C.8.52.2 (fol 327r) for Placentinus as a source for

He goes so far as to say, 'It is of the substance of custom that those introducing custom should have the power to make statutes.'[30] Bartolus' achievement had been to establish the legislative autonomy of *populi* by arguing essentially *from* the independence involved in the formation of custom *to* independence in statute-making. Baldus writes when the full legislative power of the people has already been established. Thus so firmly fixed, for him, are the people's legislative power and the common element of consent in both custom and statute, that he can go so far in one passage as to say, 'Custom is a tacit statute'.[31] In the Gloss statute is *consuetudo scripta*; according to Baldus custom is *tacitum statutum*. This shows the distance that has been travelled from the Glossators' inclusion of statute under the heading of custom: the recognition of the common element of consent shared by custom and statute, permitting thereby the understanding of statute as legislation, has resulted in placing the primary emphasis on this aspect of the people's law-making.

According to Baldus peoples with jurisdiction whether by concession or by custom enjoy through the exercise of their consent an autonomous sphere of action in their law-making. The operation of their consent being fully valid removes the requirement for the involvement of any superior. This much is common to both kinds of people. Thus in the case of peoples with jurisdiction by concession the theme of consent applies not to the origin of this jurisdiction but only to the mode and effects of its operation. In the case, however, of those with jurisdiction by custom the potentialities of the argument from consent are much more fully explored. The will of the people appears throughout as the alternative to that of the superior: popular consent is the very source of jurisdiction, its expression and the reason why the superior's authorisation is not required. Baldus has not thereby enunciated a theory of popular sovereignty, but the basis has been laid.

The terminology however of Baldus' usage of custom at Inst., 1.2, 1 ('Or it has full jurisdiction...conceded by the emperor or prescribed

---

this interpretation of D.1.3.32. On occasion Bartolus argues in the same manner: cf. *Rep.* ad D.1.3.32, n. 10–11 (fol. 19r).

[30] Ad Auth., 'Omnes peregrini' (ad C.6.59.10), fol. 166r.

[31] Ad Auth., 'Et qui iurat' (ad C.7.72.9), fol. 281v. The canonist, Zabarella, takes up the idea (ad X.1.4.11, § 'Licet', n. 5, fol. 86v). See also Baldus ad C.6.61.2 (fol. 172v), 'Consuetudo idem est quod statutum,' an identification noted by Jason de Maino: 'Imo appellatione statuti venit etiam consuetudo quia consuetudo idem est quod statutum, ita singulariter dicit Baldus in [C.6.61.2]' (ad D.1.1.9, n. 6, fol. 13v); and see also id. ad D.1.3.32, n. 91 (fol. 25r).

by custom') raises the problem of the relationship between *consuetudo* and *praescriptio*. This is a very complicated question to which Baldus like other Commentators devotes a great deal of attention, notably in his commentaries on C.8.52 and D.1.3.32. Prescription will appear in our discussion of the origins of the jurisdiction of city-*populi*, but for the moment it is only necessary to consider a couple of aspects of the subject. Custom and prescription can, of course, be easily distinguished in that, as Baldus like the other Commentators maintains, custom creates rights (it is *ius disponens*), whereas prescription in Roman law terms is essentially the gaining of a right or a possession originally belonging to another.[32] Yet there is also clearly a common element in that prescription is the product of customary usage; thus prescription can in a sense be identified with custom.[33] The notion of 'jurisdiction prescribed by custom' suggests that such jurisdiction originally belonged to another, a superior.[34] The extent to which Baldus considers this to be true will shortly be considered; but certainly the idea of prescription through custom stresses the constitutive role of popular consent in establishing the people's jurisdiction. It is surely no accident that Baldus seeks to make this crystal-clear by inserting 'by custom' whereas Bartolus refers only to 'all jurisdiction conceded by the emperor or prescribed'. Of course the active custom of an inferior prescribing the right of a superior is matched by the equivalent negligence or complaisance of that superior, with the result that immemorial custom can be said to have the same force as an imperial privilege.[35] Certainly custom and prescription are for Baldus connected in another major sense in the concept of *consuetudo praescripta*; but he is understanding prescription here, not in the sense of the usurpation of the right of another, but of the consolidation of a customary right through time. This view of prescription is normally considered by modern scholars to have been produced by the canonists; and this is indeed how Baldus and other Commentators present it as well. As Ennio Cortese has pointed out, however, since the detailed attention to *praescriptio* in the *Corpus Iuris Civilis* was the only model for lapse of time available to both canonists and civilians, this temporal usage of prescription can be seen as being as much a civilian as a canonist one.[36] Thus for Baldus prescription as applied to custom can describe

---

[32] Baldus ad Auth., 'Et qui iurat' (fol. 281v).
[33] Baldus ad D.1.3.32 (fol. 16v).   [34] Id. ad C.8.52.Rubr (fol. 332r).
[35] Id., *Tractatus de tabellione*, n. 19, fol. 126r (ed. Lyon, 1549); and id. ad D.1.3.32 (fol. 16v).
[36] See Cortese, *Norma giuridica*, II, 142–6. Cp. Brie, *Gewohnheitsrecht*, pp. 78–95, and 194–9; and Köstler, 'Consuetudo legitime praescripta.'

the element of time necessary for revealing the efficient cause of consent; and it is this temporal element which partly differentiates statute and custom as regards their form and manner of coming into being.[37] The concept of *consuetudo praescripta* signifies the process of popular observance through time whereby custom gains its strength and force.[38]

Non-confirmation by a superior: Baldus' commentary on '*l. Omnes populi*' (D.1.1.9)

Baldus' discussion in his commentary on Inst., 1.2, 1, although it is not original, provides a basis for assessing the significance of his major treatment of the question whether a people can legislate without the authorisation of a superior: this is to be found towards the beginning of his commentary on D.1.1.9 itself. The interpretation of this part of his commentary has proved contentious among modern scholars; but it does contain Baldus' most original contribution.

The relevant part is divided essentially into three sections, and the problems of interpretation are caused by the difficulty in assessing the status of the arguments of the first section in the light of their position in the overall structure of Baldus' discussion.[39] The first section consists of proofs that a people's statutes do not require the authorisation of a superior. These proofs are in the nature of general statements justifying the capacity of *populi* to make law, thus reflecting the major characteristic of the text of D.1.1.9: that it attributes to *populi* in general the ability to create their own bodies of law. Baldus delves beneath the surface of the text to discover the fundamental reason why peoples have the power to legislate; and his answers amount to this: that such power is innate in a people. Since it is innate, no other human agency has a part in popular law-making; a people is not, in this respect, dependent on a superior:

Note therefore that peoples can make statutes for themselves...Now it remains to see whether the authority of a superior is required in such a statute. And it seems that it is not, because peoples are from the *ius gentium*, and therefore a people's government is from the *ius gentium*. But government

---

[37] See Baldus ad C.8.52.2 (fol. 327r) – as we have seen above, p.100, time and actions are on a different level of causation from consent. The canonist source of this conception of prescription is specifically mentioned by Baldus in his *secunda lectura* ad D.1.3.32 (fol. 20r).

[38] Id. ad X.1.4.Rubr., n. 1 (fol 64v). Cp. id. ad D.1.3.32 (fol. 16v).

[39] See Appendix I for the complete text of the relevant part of Baldus' commentary on D.1.1.9.

cannot exist without laws and statutes. A people, therefore, for the very reason that it has existence, consequently has governmental power as part of that existence, just as every animal is ruled by its own spirit and soul.

Baldus' arguments here are an ingenious combination of old elements in jurisprudence and innovation. In saying that a people gains its existence from the *ius gentium* he is stating nothing new, but is simply following the text of the *Digest* and the tradition of the Glossators and Commentators.[40] The *ius gentium* is for Baldus a fundamental norm of human organisation and law, and is both universal and necessary to all men. It is peculiar to man since it is apprehended by reason:

The *ius gentium* is what proceeds from the reason and understanding of peoples, and all peoples use it to an almost equal extent. It is always good and equitable, and mankind could not live without it, as here and below [D.1.1.9; D.1.1.11; Inst., 1.2, 1], and it differs from natural law as the brain of man differs from that of animals.[41]

The association of men in a *populus* is, therefore, a necessary ordering of life dictated by reason. The significance of attributing the source of a people's existence to the *ius gentium* is clear: for its coming into existence, at least, a people is dependent upon no other human agent, no superior: '[It speaks] here about peoples and towns or villages, for they exist by the *ius gentium* and can come into existence without the authorisation of a superior.'[42] But Baldus goes further than this in this passage from his commentary on D.1.1.9 by developing an argument which has not been articulated before by jurists. He understands that government (*regimen*) forms an integral part of a people's existence. A people is a governmental entity: it is impossible to separate, as regards the people, government from existence ('a people for the very reason that it has existence, consequently has governmental power as part of that existence'). *Regimen*, in short, is indigenous in the people – it is inherent. Baldus supports his argument with an analogy between a people's government and the soul of an animal ('just as every animal is ruled by its own spirit and soul'): both are the ruling part *within* the organism.[43] This power of government is innate in a

---

[40] See D.1.1.5 (above, p. 26, n. 32). Cp. for instance Bartolus ad D.47.22.4, n. 5 (fol. 148v), and ad D.50.16.2, n. 6–7 (fol. 245r–245v).
[41] Baldus ad D.1.1.1, 4 (fol. 5v).
[42] Baldus ad D.1.1.5 (fol. 7v).
[43] Baldus' comparison between *regimen* and *anima* draws, in the first place, on the medieval anthropomorphic view of government and society; and in the sense that *regimen* consists of law-making this comparison is a version of the medieval theme that *lex* is the *anima* of society. Baldus in specifically comparing the *populus* here with an animal, and its *regimen* with that animal's *spiritus* and *anima*, may be influenced by Aristotle,

people which depends upon no other human agency for its existence, but which is a product of the *ius gentium*. A people's government is, as a consequence, itself dependent on no one else, upon no superior: it too derives from the *ius gentium*. Self-government by the people (*regimen populi*)[44] is, therefore, a necessary and integral aspect of a people's existence. Because Baldus here understands popular government in terms of legislation ('government cannot exist without laws and statutes'), we may say that his particular juristic skill lies in using the familiar concept of the *ius gentium* in a new way: as the source of the legislative autonomy of *populi* from a superior. For Baldus a *populus* gains both existence and law-making capacity from the *ius gentium*: the ability to make law lies within the people.

Clearly this argument from the *ius gentium* could form the basis for a theory of true popular sovereignty; but at this stage Baldus is working at the level of autonomy: there is no proof here of the exclusion of a superior. Indeed the immediate continuation of his commentary retains the superior in the background: 'And if [a people] rules itself well its superior cannot stand in its way, because prohibitory laws were not made for those living good lives but for those who stray; for if they naturally do what the law demands, they are a law unto themselves. And the healthy need no medicine from without.'[45] Thus the people has a considerable measure of autonomy while its government is good. If it is bad, then the way is left open for the superior to intervene. The question remains: who is to decide whether the people rules itself well? This passage does not suggest that it is anyone other than the superior.

Baldus then proceeds to expand his point that a people is autonomous while it governs itself well: 'If therefore statutes are good ones bearing in mind the requirements of the place in question and the preservation of its public good, they do not need anyone else's direction, because they have been confirmed by their own natural justice.' The reference to *conservatio publica* is unremarkable: it is an expression of the fundamental medieval theme of the *utilitas publica, bonum publicum* or *bonum commune* as part of the aims of government. But Baldus then ingeniously elaborates the concept of *conservatio publica* in terms of the basic principle of self-conservation: 'Moreover in as much as anything

Pol., 1254a–b, 'Animal autem primum constat ex anima et corpore...manifestum est, quod secundum naturam et expediens corpori regi ab anima' (trans. William of Moerbeke, ed. Susemihl); cp. Aquinas ad *Pol.*, 1254a–b, pp. 19–20 (ed. Spiazzi).

[44] The context makes it clear that 'populi' is a possessive, not an objective genitive.

[45] Cp. Romans 2:14. Cf. Baldus ad C.4.6.3 (fol. 220v).

has an essential form it also has a capacity to act. But the people derives its form from itself, and therefore also the exercise of self-preservation as regards its existence and proper form. For it is natural and allowed that anything should strive after the conservation of its existence.' The relationship between *forma* and *esse* had given rise to many disputes in scholastic philosophy,[46] but Baldus' meaning is clear and straightforward: the origin of the *forma* of the people lies within itself, not outside it. Since the *forma essentialis* implies the capacity to act in order to maintain its existence, this *virtus activa* is itself derived from the people:[47] it is inherent in it. In the context of this first section of Baldus' commentary this capacity to act is understood as *regimen* in the sense of legislation. The people, therefore, has an indigenous law-making capability, an autonomous capacity for self-government in the interests of the common good. Nevertheless the superior still hovers in the background as Baldus' next words imply: 'Moreover peoples are forbidden to make illicit statutes, and therefore licit ones are permitted.'

Finally Baldus turns to the consent argument, and upholds the sufficiency of popular consent as a law-creating element, a view he takes to be the essence of D.1.3.32: 'Moreover we should not demand more than the law does, as below [D.2.2.2]...because we should be content with the stand the law takes. But the law is content with the consent of the people, and therefore we should be too, as below [D.1.3.32]. Nor can it be said that it speaks in that law only of the Roman people, and the reason for this is provided by the beginning of the law, where it speaks only of another people.' He then adopts the familiar Bartolist argument that it is the common element of consent in the people's customs and statutes which renders the authorisation of a superior unnecessary:

Moreover the people can introduce tacit law without the consent and knowledge of a superior, for it introduces custom without a superior knowing, as in [*Sext.*, 1.2.1,],[48] and therefore it can introduce express law, that is statute, because express and tacit law, where attention is given to the consent and not the form of the words, have the same effect, because they accord in cause,

---

[46] See Weisheipl, 'The interpretation of Aristotle's *Physics*', p. 524.

[47] It is impossible to establish the precise scholastic sources which Baldus is using in this passage, although resemblance to Thomist concepts is strong. For *virtus activa* see for example, *S.T.*, 1a 2ae, 41, 1. As a source for the idea of the instinct of self-preservation in animals Baldus ad D.1.1.1, 2 (fol. 4v) refers to Aristotle, *De anima*, 2, 'naturalissimum'. Cp. Aquinas, *S.T.*, 2a 2ae, 64, 5 & 7.

[48] See *Sext.*, 1.2.1: '[Romanus Pontifex] quia tamen locorum specialium et personarum singularium consuetudines et statuta, quum sint facti et in facto consistant, potest probabiliter ignorare: ipsis, dum tamen sint rationabilia, per constitutionem a se noviter editam, nisi expresse caveatur in ipsa, non intelligitur in aliquo derogare.'

origin and force, and therefore in effect. For thus argues the jurisconsult in the said [D.1.3.32].

Baldus is here, in effect, combining two crucial passages from Bartolus;[49] although, however, he does not add anything essentially new to the other's meaning, he does express with even greater clarity that it is the people's exercise of consent which rules out the need for the assent of a superior. Certainly he considers the Bartolist interpretation of D.1.3.32 to be correct.

The arguments of this first section of Baldus' commentary on D.1.1.9 are clearly very powerful. Indeed, both Francesco Calasso and Walter Ullmann considered Baldus' *ius gentium* argument to be a major juristic contribution to the development of the theory of popular government.[50] Yet the first section is immediately followed by the second which is a very lengthy *in contrarium* argument. For this reason Pietro Costa down-graded the significance of the *ius gentium* argument on the grounds that it forms part only of the 'thesis' as opposed to the 'antithesis' of Baldus' argument.[51] Can Baldus' arguments in the first section then truly represent his own position? Perhaps their content is such in relation to the *solutio* of the argument that they can be seen as part of the mainstream of Baldus' theory – a possibility not considered by Costa. Only further analysis of the argument will reveal this. For the moment it is sufficient to say that the consent argument, to which Baldus certainly adheres, by its very presence gives a strong indication that his real meaning is to be found in the first section.

The second section sets forth the objections which the *ius commune* poses to the people's ability to make statutes without the confirmation of a superior. By *ius commune* Baldus certainly means the Roman law here; but he also makes a number of references to canon law. The *populus* is presented as being subordinate to its magistrate because he is confirmed by the superior. The people cannot make legal dispositions concerning its magistrate without the confirmation of the superior; it cannot impose law on the magistrate; and without the participation of its magistrate it cannot exercise any aspect of jurisdiction including legislation: it cannot make statutes by itself.[52] Indeed, Baldus goes so far as to say, 'The people should be subject and not in charge since

---

[49] See above, p. 96, n. 14. Cp. Albericus de Rosciate ad D.1.3.32, n. 2 (fol. 34v), 'Hi duo consensus [i.e. expressus et tacitus] sunt pares; et nihil refert inter eos; ergo eorum effectus, id est iuris scripti et iuris consuetudinarii, est idem.'

[50] See Calasso, *Medio evo del diritto*, p. 501, and Ullmann, 'Juristic obstacles', p. 62, n. 65.   [51] *Iurisdictio*, p. 171, n. 118.

[52] Cp. Baldus, *Cons.*, 1.361, fol. 111r, ed. Brescia, 1490 (= *Cons.*, 3.161, ed. Venice, 1575).

the magistrate is its head.' He then introduces a stock argument against the people's capacity to manage its own affairs: 'Moreover no people seems to be of sound mind because the greater the number the less the understanding [D.49.1.12; D.40.9.17; D.50.12.6].' An equally stock interpretation of the *lex regia* then follows: 'Moreover the Roman people in whom lay the might and power of all peoples abdicated its supreme authority which did not therefore remain with its members.' Baldus then gives the conventional *de iure communi* treatment of whether a people's statutes are valid without the superior's confirmation through the medium of his magistrate, and comes to the conclusion that so long as the superior does not expressly forbid the statute it is valid unless it either derogates from the superior's jurisdiction or concerns matters reserved solely to him. There is thus for *populi* a restricted area of autonomy guaranteed by the *ius commune;* indeed Baldus sees this capability as being conceded by D.1.1.9 itself, a commonplace amongst jurists, as we shall shortly see.

In the third section Baldus admits the truth of these objections in terms of the *ius commune*, but maintains that they simply do not apply to cities whose magistrates are not confirmed by any superior:

And these things are true according to the common law, because a magistrate is confirmed by a superior. But if it is such a city (*civitas*) whose magistrate whether by law or custom is not confirmed by a superior, then such a city possesses full jurisdiction, as is noted at the end of the great gloss on Auth. 'De defensoribus civitatum', § 'nulla' [Coll., 3.2, 2 = Nov., 15, 2]. And jurisdiction is lordship, as below [D.1.5.20]. And just as a lord is ruler and arbiter, so is such a city, as is noted below [D.2.2.1, 1] in the ordinary gloss, and it can make statutes for its subjects on all matters; and in sum, it has as much authority to make statutes as it has jurisdiction, because the making of statutes is an aspect of jurisdiction, and if one is present so is the other, and if one is absent so is the other according to Bartolus.

Clearly there is a close connection here with Baldus' argument in his commentary on Inst., 1.2, 1: custom or *de iure* concession are the sources of such a city's autonomy. The emphasis is, however, somewhat different, because the lack of need for the superior's confirmation of the people's statutes is an implied conclusion, as is made clear by the explanation of *plena iurisdictio* in terms of an unlimited capacity to impose legislation on those subject to its laws. Manifestly far more is involved here than the narrower form of autonomy admitted by the *ius commune*. The power to confirm its magistrates and statutes lies within the people itself and does not belong to any external superior:

to such peoples does Baldus consider D.1.1.9 to apply.[53] Such a power of self-confirmation is crucial to the fully autonomous city, because a capacity to make statutes without the confirmation of a superior does not in itself necessarily indicate full autonomy: indeed, as we have seen, Baldus clearly considers that a manifestly subordinate city can have a measure of power to make statutes 'without any confirmation by some superior'.[54] What is crucial is the extent of a people's freedom so to act.

Furthermore it can come as no surprise that Baldus here presents *statuta condere* as an aspect of jurisdiction (the extent of the capacity to legislate matches the level of jurisdiction): this avowedly Bartolist conception runs through the section quoted from his commentary on Inst., 1.2, 1. The notion is to be found repeatedly in Baldus' works.[55] In so far as Bartolus and Baldus are arguing for the people's legislative function on the basis of custom the advantages of this view are clear: popular consent creates jurisdiction which can find expression through legislation. Yet there is a problem in that Baldus in the continuation of his commentary on D.1.1.9 expressly questions this Bartolist view, saying of it in words reminiscent of those of Raynerius of Forlì, 'That reasoning is undiscriminating' ('illa ratio est indiscreta'), and after posing objections in support of this contention comes to the conclusion: 'Others say many things which are of no concern to me. I say therefore that the making of statutes is not so much connected with jurisdiction as derived more from some permission given by the law.' That is to say, the prime cause of the people's capacity to legislate derives from texts in the *Corpus Iuris Civilis*, notably D.1.1.9 itself. Raynerius' fundamental disagreement with Bartolus on this point on the grounds that jurisdiction lay not with the people but with its superior was very well-known especially through Raynerius' lengthy *repetitio* on D.1.1.9; and indeed elsewhere Baldus appears expressly to support Raynerius' view:

[53] Cp. Baldus, *Cons.*, 1.143, n. 1, fol. 43r (ed. Venice, 1575); and id. ad X.1.6. Rubr., n. 11 (fol. 76r), 'Hec confirmatio [i.e. iurisdictionis] in magistratibus populi non pertinet ad populum de iure communi, quia apud populum non est iurisdictio plene formata. Potest tamen competere de consuetudine prescripta.' Baldus gives Florence as an example of the kind of city he has in mind: 'Commune Florentie est rei sue moderator et arbiter' (ad C.4.55.2, fol. 322r). For the city-*populus* as *dominus* of its subjects, see below, pp. 203–4.

[54] Above, p. 100, n. 21.

[55] See for instance, *Cons.*, 4.396, n. 1, fol. 90r (ed. Venice, 1575), and *Cons.*, 2.377, fol. 95v, ed. Brescia, 1490 (= *Cons.*, 5.83, ed. Venice, 1575). For both jurists' treatment of the relationship between *iurisdictio* and *statuta condere* see Costa, *Iurisdictio*, pp. 161–4 (Bartolus), and 167–73 (Baldus).

Bartolus says that making statutes is an aspect of jurisdiction. Master Raynerius de Forlì says the opposite, because a people makes a statute yet possesses no jurisdiction, as in Auth. 'De defensoribus civitatum', § 'interim' [Coll., 3.2, 1 = Nov., 15, 1], and as is noted by Innocent at [X.1.2.6]. As a result Master Raynerius says that the people does not make a statute as an aspect of its jurisdiction but by virtue of permission [D.1.1.9], which is the very truth.[56]

It was, of course the *communis opinio* (expressing the argument *de iure communi*) that D.1.1.9 conceded the right to make statutes within limits respecting the superior's authority.[57] Indeed, this view retained the sovereignty of the emperor, as Albericus for instance made clear.[58] Is there then a major contradiction in Baldus' approach on this fundamental matter?

In this third section Baldus is using D.1.1.9 as the source of the people's capacity to legislate, not in a context in which the people has an immediate superior overseeing its legislation, but in one in which a superior is not involved in its government. Indeed, its magistrates are bound to observe the people's statutes under the authority of the *ius commune*.[59] In these terms the use of D.1.1.9 serves to end the argument about whether the people has the autonomous power to legislate: Baldus, like Bartolus, realises the potential of D.1.1.9 as a source for the autonomy of the people. For Baldus the people's capacity to legislate is both an aspect of its jurisdiction and something permitted by D.1.1.9: it is 'derived *more* from some permission given by the law' for the immediate purposes of his argument, which is not to say that the fundamental connection with the people's jurisdiction is thereby denied. Both levels of argument retain their truth.

That Baldus is happy to use both arguments in parallel is shown in an important passage at the end of his commentary on X.1.2.6. The context is admittedly that of *populi* with only limited autonomy, but the lesson is the same:

[56] Ad D.2.1.1 (fol. 60r). See Raynerius de Forlì, *Rep.*, ad D.1.1.9, n. 23–6 (fols. 17r–17v) for his lengthy rejection of Bartolus' view. The reference to Innocent IV should surely be ad X.1.2.8, n. 2–3 (fol. 31r), 'Vniversitates autem que habent iurisdictionem possunt facere statuta super omnibus, que ad iurisdictionem suam pertinent, sicut et consuetudinem inducere possunt [D.1.3.32]. Et est notandum quod rectores assumpti ab universitatibus habent iurisdictionem, et non ipse universitates. Aliqui tamen dicunt quod ipse universitates deficientibus rectoribus possunt exercere iurisdictionem sicut rectores, quod non credo [X.5.31.14].'

[57] As Baldus says in *Cons.*, 2.407, n. 2, fol. 109v (ed. Venice, 1575). Cp. id., *Cons.*, 2.58, n.5, fol. 13v (ed. Venice, 1575).

[58] Ad D.1.1.9, n. 3 (fol. 15r).

[59] As he says at the end of the section: 'Idem dico quod magistratus tenetur sequi statutum sicut pactum, ar. [D.1.3.35], et si non servat facit litem suam, nec ligatur auctoritate statuentium sed auctoritate iuris communis approbantis statutum [C.1.17.1].'

Hostiensis says here that these days peoples, for instance very famous ones of the first rank, cannot make any statute unless the emperor expressly concedes this power to them or confirms it. And his proof is that the Roman people in which every people is included transferred all its sovereign authority to the emperor. But you are to say that jurisdiction and the power to make statutes are connected, and he who has the one also has the other to the same extent. And Hostiensis' reasoning has no validity because [D.1.1.9] was approved by Justinian and Caesar, and thus should be considered as an imperial constitution, especially because Justinian was after Caesar Augustus, as is noted at the end of [D.4.4.38]. And thus you should say that peoples' statutes are valid, unless their emperor expressly restrains them... Again, they thirst for jurisdiction as a stag longs for springs of water according to some.[60]

Here is a neat refutation of the *lex regia* argument as put forward in the second section above from Baldus' commentary on D.1.1.9, which law, like everything else in the *Corpus Iuris Civilis*, could be considered as an imperial constitution. This is an approach which Baldus wishes to stress for the purpose of his argument at this point, although the truly significant aspect of Baldus' treatment of D.1.1.9 is that he sees within the text the fundamental truth about a people's capacity for self-government through the medium of the law.

The overall meaning of the whole three-section part of Baldus' commentary on D.1.1.9 is as follows. The second, *in contrarium*, section does not infringe the general truth of the arguments of the first section. The capacity of peoples to govern themselves through the medium of law remains basic to the human race as rational creatures. The *ius gentium* which guarantees them this fundamental right is older than the *ius civile Romanorum* in the context of which the emperor's power operates. The objections of the second section only apply to those peoples directly subject to a superior *de iure communi*. In the third section those city-*populi* autonomous *de consuetudine* are enjoying the fundamental capacity possessed by peoples under the *ius gentium* to govern themselves by means of their own consent – they are outside the restrictions of the *ius commune*. Those autonomous *de iure* enjoy in practice something of the same freedom, but for the origin of their power remain within the hierarchical *ius commune* structure. The point is that, although Baldus is on occasion willing to employ the purely civil law argument that a text in the *Corpus Iuris Civilis* (D.1.1.9) accords to peoples the capacity to legislate, his fundamental achievement is to explore the implications of the recognition contained in

---

[60] n. 37–8 (fol. 16v). Cp. Hostiensis, *Summa aurea*, X.1.2, ad v. 'Quis possit constitutionem facere,' n. 9, col. 18.

D.1.1.9 that a people has in itself power of jurisdiction and specifically of legislation, an entirely different proposition. Baldus' overall opinion is, therefore, that peoples possess an autonomous capacity to legislate through the exercise of their own consent, which capacity is an aspect of their power of jurisdiction derived from the *ius gentium* itself; that this capacity can be obscured where the hierarchical structures of the *ius commune* are operative; but that wherever a people is freed from the restrictions of the *ius commune* its rights of self-government under the *ius gentium* re-emerge, partly when its autonomy exists *de iure*, fully when it exists *de consuetudine*. Clearly Baldus is on the verge at least of the concept of popular sovereignty, but we should hesitate to follow Walter Ullmann in saying that he does in this commentary on D.1.1.9 produce such a concept.[61] Baldus is dealing with non-confirmation by a superior. Sovereignty should properly speaking be reserved to the next stage: the non-recognition of a superior – the crucial step to sovereignty through the exercise of the popular will. This is the logical extension of the *ius gentium* argument.

Non-recognition of a superior and the replacement of the emperor

For Baldus a city (*civitas*) which has no practical or effective superior enjoys full liberty and complete self-government:

> In the case of cities I do not however think that they could act without the authority of a superior who possessed the actual power of one. But cities which live in their own liberty and enjoy absolute self-government do not require anybody else's assistance, because they use their own laws. The position is the same whether they act on the authority of a privilege or by virtue of prescribed custom.[62]

This is nothing other than Bartolus' *populus liber*,[63] and through the strongly-expressed exclusion of the superior Baldus suggests the contemporary republican theme of *libertà*, although it remains to be seen whether he advocates the other necessary aspect of that theme – a republican form of government. The form of liberty expressed here is certainly applicable to a sovereign city; but the passage in so far as it envisages the *auctoritas privilegii* as a source for this liberty rules out sovereignty because such a source recognises the direct higher authority of a superior, whereas liberty obtained *auctoritate consuetudinis praescriptae* can obviously be an expression of sovereignty.

---

[61] See 'Juristic obstacles', p. 62, n. 65.
[62] Ad C.7.46.2 (fol. 220r).   [63] See Bartolus ad C.10.65.5, n. 4 (fols. 26r–26v).

It is through his acceptance of the facts of contemporary Italian political life that Baldus is led to attribute sovereignty unambiguously to certain cities. He by no means abandons the emperor's *de iure* sovereign claims, but sees before him an Italy in which the emperor's sovereignty is in practice non-existent, because the cities simply do not obey him: 'These days the superior has in fact no power since the cities do not obey Caesar.'[64] Some autonomous *populi*, as also *signori*, enjoy full *de facto* liberty because there is in practical terms a lack of any effective superior over them, whether emperor or pope: '[A superior] may be said to be lacking, when he cannot take effective decisions, like the emperor and the pope as regards action against the tyrants of Lombardy and also against the peoples who live as by their own law in *de facto* liberty.'[65] In the absence of an effective superior the cities have to provide for themselves. Baldus does not see himself as hammering out a new political theory, but as simply reflecting contemporary political reality in legal terms. His attitude is most clearly summed up in the following passage:

But, as I said, cities which in reality do not recognise superiors and appropriate regalian rights for themselves do this by custom, and what they have always had as an established custom should not, it seems, be changed at all, as above [D.1.3.23]. Let us bear this with equanimity, because it is not of our doing. But it is agreed *de iure* that power reserved to the emperor alone is denied to cities [C.10.32.19 and C.4.62.2]... But formerly there was an emperor who looked after the authority and general good of the commonwealth; now, however, there is not the same bond of good faith between emperor and subjects, with the result that things have of necessity gone from one extreme to the other.[66]

---

[64] Ad C.9.12.7 (fol. 366r). Cp. Bartolus, *Tract. represal.*, qu. 2, n. 11–12 (fol. 123v), 'Queritur quomodo intelligatur quod superioris copia haberi non potest?...Quandoque potest haberi copia de iure sed non de facto. Exemplum: imperator est modo in Alemania, et de iure est superior, tamen de facto in partibus istis ei non paretur.' Cp. Baldus, *Rep.* ad C.8.4.1 (anno 1365), fol. 291v, concerning whether the Florentines may wage war on Pisa to regain long-lost fortified places: 'Debent adire superiorem, scilicet imperatorem, et si non esset imperator papam qui faciat eis ablata restitui [X.2.1.13], non autem incivili modo bellum movere [C.2.3.14]. Sed cum nec imperator nec papa timeatur in Tuscia credo quod tale bellum sit licitum ex causa non obstante lapsu temporis, quia illud procedit ubi iudice mediante potest ius suum consequi, sed hic nullus est iudex effectualiter.' Both Florence and Pisa were in the *terrae imperii*, and the emperor therefore was their *de iure* superior, but according to Baldus even in the *terrae imperii* the church may fill a jurisdictional vacuum when secular authority is lacking (see below, p. 147), and the pope may on occasion intervene *ratione peccati* in secular matters, for which *c. Novit ille* (X.2.1.13) is the *locus classicus* – the prevention of war would be a clear justification (see below, p. 157).

[65] Id. ad Auth., 'Sed omnino' (ad C.4.12.4), fol. 228r.

[66] Ad D.1.8.Rubr. (fol. 36r).

Baldus places the shift to sovereignty squarely within the *de facto* as opposed to the *de iure* order. The city through the exercise of the popular will rejects the superior on the level of political reality (*realiter = de facto*); and popular consent in the form of custom gains certain sovereign rights (*regalia*) which *de iure* belong only to the emperor.[67] Whereas he can accept that a city can enjoy autonomy through a *de iure* concession from a superior, he sees clearly that the non-recognition of a superior essential for sovereignty must be of its nature *de facto* because it cannot depend on the element of concession inherent in a *de iure* claim within the terms of Roman law. In taking this view he appears to be more rigorous than Bartolus or his brother, Angelus, who refer to cities which do not recognise a superior both *de iure* and *de facto*.[68] But what makes the passage truly memorable is the tone of its treatment of the emperor. As a civilian Baldus is happy not to be responsible for this diminution of imperial jurisdiction; he simply accepts it as a fact. This means that he is no missionary for popular sovereignty, just the lawyer who records political reality. What he clear-sightedly sees, however, is that the era of the emperor's personal overseeing of state interests and state affairs in Italy belongs to the past; that the contemporary situation has completely changed in that the previously existing bond of faith, as he puts it,[69] between the emperor and his subjects has been broken – on both sides, that is: by the emperor through his absence and impotence; and by the cities through their disobedience. But imperial jurisdictional claims even when rejected have to be taken seriously.

Baldus draws back, however, from Bartolus' conclusion that an independent city-republic not recognising a superior is a *civitas sibi princeps*. Strictly speaking Bartolus' formula is not fully logical: the

---

[67] This crucial element of the active exercise of the popular will as a requirement for gaining sovereignty is absent from Jacobus de Ravannis ad C.7.33.12 (above, p. 94, n. 4) – he stresses the absence of imperial power – but present in Oldradus, *Cons.*, 69 (above, p. 94, n. 5) and Hostiensis, *Lectura* ad X.1.31.3 (above, p. 95).

[68] See Bartolus ad D.5.3.20, 7, n. 2, fol. 167v (below, p. 120); and Angelus de Ubaldis ad C.10.10.1, n. 5, fol. 36v.

[69] Baldus certainly considered that the Peace of Constance had created a bond of *fidelitas* between the emperor and the cities of Lombardy, a bond which provided an argument against the legality of the institution of doges at Venice and Genoa (ad C.1.2.16, ed. Quaglioni, p. 80). But in that commentary Baldus previously justifies these doges' jurisdiction (see below, p. 119, n.83). Cp. id., *De pace Constantie*, ad v. 'Vasalli nostri' (fol. 91r), where he says of those covered by the bond of fidelity, 'Vasalli tanquam vasalli et ceteri omnes tanquam subditi iurare debent fidelitatem principi...vasalli recipiunt ergo hi investituram tanquam vasalli et iurabunt tanquam vasalli...ceteri autem iurabunt tanquam cives.' Baldus' remarks here ad D.1.8.Rubr. have application however far beyond Lombardy.

expression is elliptical because the city or *populus liber* is not actually the emperor, the *princeps*. Baldus is, probably for this reason, a little more circumspect, as he shows in the following passage concerning the age requirement for a judicial appointment: 'My reply is this: when he is chosen by the emperor, any age suffices...and the same applies if he is chosen by a people in the emperor's *place* because it is the emperor in its own territory.'[70] He says of independent Italian cities exercising originally imperial rights that they are peoples which 'therefore have the *place* and *image* of the emperor';[71] that 'a city free from superiors can concede a franchise to its inferiors, because in its dominion it takes the *place* of the emperor';[72] and that cities with fiscal or regalian rights 'fill in their territory the *place* of the emperor'.[73] Baldus is not seeking to convey that the cities are imperial vicars, but that in the gaps caused by the absence of effective imperial jurisdiction in the fourteenth century the cities have had to take the law into their own hands. In a universal and normative sense the emperor is the bearer of sovereign power; but where his power is not operative the city wields sovereign power in the emperor's stead: the city *replaces* the emperor as the bearer of sovereignty. If, however, the emperor should be physically present in the city's territory, then the gap would be closed up, and Baldus is perfectly clear that any city statutes would then require imperial confirmation:[74] in this sense the emperor remains the ultimate sovereign. But in normal circumstances this argument is totally irrelevant, because the whole precondition for the sovereignty of the cities is the practical weakness and absence of the emperor. The situation is, therefore, that there is a hierarchy of sovereignty with the cities not possessing the ultimate grade, enjoyed by the emperor: indeed, Baldus deliberately does not accord to sovereign cities that *potestas suprema* which is possessed by the emperor and the pope.[75] Although Baldus accepts that the *populus Romanus* possessed *potestas suprema* before the *lex regia*,[76] he maintains that contemporary *populi* do not enjoy that supreme jurisdiction which he identifies with plenitude of power itself: 'The emperor is not

---

[70] Ad X.1.29.41, n. 3 (fol. 143r).
[71] *Cons.*, 2.49, fol. 14r, ed. Brescia, 1490 (= *Cons.*, 4.52, ed. Venice, 1575).
[72] *Cons.*, 5.406, n. 6, fol. 107r (ed. Venice, 1575).
[73] Ad X.1.2.13, n. 3 (fol. 28v). For the fiscal rights of cities see below, pp. 120–1.
[74] Ad C.1.14.8 (fol. 54v). Jason de Maino thought this passage especially notable (ad D.1.1.9, n. 27, fol. 14r).
[75] In addition to the relevant passages above p. 24 (emperor) and p. 31 (pope), see id. ad D.1.4.1 (fol. 21r); id. ad C.Const., 'De novo Codice componendo' (fol. 1v); and ad C.7.50.3 (fol. 233v).   [76] Ad D.1.3.9 (fol. 14r).

accustomed to legitimise except in the form reserved for this, that is with the formula, "previous legislation not withstanding," added. But a people, which has less authority, cannot attach that formula of derogation, because that formula is an aspect of supreme jurisdiction which is called plenitude of power and which does not belong to peoples.'[77] Baldus only applies supreme power or jurisdiction, together with plenitude of power, to personal sovereigns, that is monarchs: the emperor, the pope and kings.[78] The implication is that in the hierarchy of sovereignty independent city-*populi* are below sovereign kings. The reason for this is, perhaps, that although kings are in the empire in the widest sense of Christendom, they (unlike the Italian cities) are not in the *terrae imperii* in Italy, where the emperor could claim a more direct jurisdiction, nor, with the exception of Sicily, in the lands of the church. In modern terms the external sovereignty of such cities, precisely because it exists within this hierarchy, would appear to be impaired with the result that true sovereignty would seem to be denied them. Yet the cities' non-recognition of a superior and their replacement of the emperor suggest that the attribution of sovereignty to them is reasonable. It is, however, a late medieval form of sovereignty within an overall hierarchical structure. Baldus' view is very similar to that of Bartolus who accepts both that *populi liberi* are sovereign, being within their territories legally identified with the *princeps*, and that they are subject to imperial jurisdiction in that they continue to use Roman law and recognise that the emperor is *dominus mundi*, a claim which nevertheless leaves their practical sovereignty unimpaired.[79]

It is in the context of this replacement of the emperor that it is easiest to understand Baldus' occasionally expressed view that such cities have prescribed imperial jurisdiction. Given his theory of the nature, sources and extent of imperial authority it is simple to comprehend how these cities' gaining of jurisdiction can be presented as prescription of this kind. Any supposed conflict with Baldus' argument for the sovereignty of such city-*populi* is more apparent than real, because the emergence of such sovereign cities is both an expression of their inherent right to self-government through consent, and necessarily, in the gaps so formed in the universal empire, a prescription of imperial rights: in asserting their own rights the cities have prescribed the emperor's. There is no

---

[77] Ad X.1.2.1, n. 24 (fol. 11v).
[78] Ad D.1.2.2 (fol. 12v), 'Nota quod omnes reges habent supremam potestatem, ut dicitur [X.2.22.15] per Inn.' Cp. Innocent IV ad X.2.22.15, n. 3 (fol. 280r), where he refers to 'reges qui habent supremum et merum imperium.'
[79] See Bartolus ad D.49.15.24, n. 3–4 (fol. 228r).

doubt, as we have seen, that cities can through custom obtain imperial sovereign rights. This process is, however, to be viewed in the light of the fundamental *de iure–de facto* distinction. Whenever Baldus maintains that imperial sovereign rights cannot be prescribed he is presenting what is essentially the *de iure* position.[80] The real problem of interpretation arises through his statement that peoples in prescribing their liberty, which involves prescription of the sovereign rights of the *princeps*, do so through the knowledge and acquiescence of the *princeps*, which is thus tantamount to his concession:

> I say that, although there is no prescription against the empire and the church of Rome over those things which have been reserved as a sign of special preference and preeminence, as Johannes Andreae notes in [*Sext.*, 1.6.1], there is perhaps however prescription over a space of a hundred years. Through such prescription the Roman people gained its liberty, and [D.49.15.24] is relevant, where it speaks of free peoples. A further reason is that there is no doubt that the emperor could concede liberty to the Roman people through his privilege and rescript and also all regalian rights and jurisdiction in public matters, as in [*Feud.*, 2.56], and Frederick made such a concession to the Lombards in the Peace of Constance (in the *Decima collatio*) and you have it also in Auth. 'De defensoribus civitatum', § 'et iudicare' [Coll., 3.2, 3 = Nov., 15, 3]. In the same way therefore he could confer these through acquiescence, because the acquiescence of the mind confirmed through length of time does not have less effect than concession.[81]

Certainly custom with the presumed or express consent of the *princeps* can confer rights reserved to him; and such custom if it exists from time immemorial has the force of an imperial privilege.[82]

---

[80] Ad C.1.2.24 (fol. 25v), 'Tu dic quod suprema iurisdictio domini pape non potest prescribi…sic non potest prescribi contra imperium. Alioquin imperium posset desinere propter prescriptionem subditorum, quod est falsum, quia imperium semper est [semper est *ed. Venice, 1474;* superest *ed. cit.*], ut in Auth., "Quomodo oporteat episcopos" [Coll., 1.6 = Nov., 6] in fine…Ex his apparet quod non potest prescribi quod non appelletur ad principem quia hoc pertinet ad summam iurisdictionem.' The right of appeal to the emperor could only have effect when the emperor retained real power: thus the *de iure* possibility of such an appeal does not infringe the cities' *de facto* sovereignty which exists in the context of imperial powerlessness. In any case, the emperor's theoretical right to act as the supreme judge of appeal in the *terrae imperii* is an aspect of supreme jurisdiction which is not possessed by cities.

[81] Ad C.7.38.1 (fol. 202r). Cp. id. ad C.8.52.2 (fol. 327r), 'Italici qui prescripserunt merum imperium presumuntur prescripsisse de scientia principis, ut not. in Auth., "De defensoribus civitatum" [Coll., 3.2 = Nov., 15] in fine magne glo. ubi omnino vide.' *Merum imperium* signified full powers of jurisdiction in public matters, including (where relevant) the power to make statutes and criminal jurisdiction: see in particular Woolf, *Bartolus*, p. 407, for a tabular presentation of Bartolus' definitions of *merum imperium*, *mixtum imperium* and *iurisdictio*; see also Gilmore, *Argument from Roman Law*, pp. 37–43.

[82] Baldus, *Tractatus de tabellione*, n. 18 (fol. 126r); see also id., ibid., n. 19 (above p. 103).

Does this mean that the whole *de facto* consent argument for the sovereignty of the people is undermined so that the emperor through his concession of power is seen as the ultimate source of the people's jurisdiction? Prescription of sovereign rights with the knowledge and acquiescence of the emperor fits in with the cities' place in the hierarchy of sovereignty. The emperor, as we have seen, voluntarily refrains from trying to impose his authority on those who will not obey him, 'lest his laws be a laughing-stock.' Thus the gaps in imperial jurisdiction emerge with the emperor's *patientia*, *scientia* and *consensus*. It is precisely through the emperor's absence, impotence and hence neglect of his rights and duties that the opportunity is given to the cities to assert their *de facto* jurisdictional claims,[83] an example of the operation of custom which through *diligentia* prescribes the rights of another lost through *negligentia*. This accurately reflects the way in which effective imperial jurisdiction had in fact receded in Italy; the emperor, in a legal sense, did *know* about such developments in Italy, but was unable or unwilling, after the expeditions of Henry VII and Lewis IV, to do anything about them. After all, Charles IV's grants of liberties to cities were essentially fund-raising exercises. Baldus is not dealing with a situation in which cities exercise independence in the face of imperial opposition. Thus the acquiescence of the *princeps* in the cities' prescription of sovereign rights accords with Baldus' overall theory of the *de facto* sovereignty of independent cities in the context of his respect for *de iure* imperial jurisdictional claims. In Roman law terms he is seeking to reconcile both the real authority of the emperor and the real independence of such cities. In addition it could well be that in according to such prescription the same weight as imperial concession Baldus is primarily concentrating on the point that they are of equal validity. Thus Baldus' view that such cities validly prescribe these powers of jurisdiction must be contrasted with the opinion of those Commentators who, through maintaining that sovereignty lay only with the *princeps*, held that, whenever cities exercised jurisdiction without imperial privilege, this amounted to mere usurpation.[84]

---

[83] As in the case, for instance, of Venice and Genoa: 'Sed nunquid populus propter absentiam imperatoris potest eligere sibi ducem, sicut faciunt Veneti et Ianuenses? Respondeo quod non de iure, quia non est confirmatus a superiore...sed de consuetudine, ex quo imperator scit et tolerat propter bonum regimen eorum, dico quod ipsi iuste dominantur...Item quia illi duces non sunt precise domini, sed habent consilia populi vel maiorum, unde habent potius quandam preeminentiam dignitatis quam dominium, ut ita servatur' (Baldus ad C.1.2.16, ed. Quaglioni, pp. 79–80).

[84] See for instance Albericus de Rosciate ad C.3.13.7, n. 1 (fol. 145r); and Jacobus de Belvisio ad Auth., 'De defensoribus civitatum', ad v. 'iusiurandum' (fol. 22v). Nevertheless Jacobus de Belvisio, ibid., also expresses a note of realism: 'Queritur quinto an

The possession of fiscal rights is, as we have seen, an important aspect of the sovereignty of these cities. In civilian theory outside the Bartolist tradition the fisc was understood to belong properly only to the emperor, or to have belonged to the *respublica Romana* before it transferred its powers to the emperor by means of the *lex regia:* any cities claiming fiscal rights otherwise than through imperial concession did so merely by *de facto* usurpation.[85] Bartolus, however, unambiguously accorded the fisc to those cities which did not recognise a superior and which were thus *populi liberi*:

> Note the gloss which says that goods without an owner become the property of the fisc and not of any other city. And this is a true statement in the case of cities which recognise a superior, but in the case of those which do not recognise a superior *de iure* or *de facto*, like the cities of Tuscany, the city itself is the fisc. For it is called a free people as is mentioned in [D.49.15.24]...But in those cities which do not recognise anyone as lord, statements concerning the fisc are understood to apply to their commune.[86]

Baldus follows him: 'Do cities have their own fisc? I say that they do not, except certain ones which do not recognise a superior and which have the rights of the fisc through their own statutes and customs.'[87] What is noticeable here is that the possession of the fisc as an aspect of sovereignty is established, as we would expect in Baldus' case, by the exercise of the people's will (through custom and statute). Such cities in prescribing the fisc share with the emperor 'proper' possession of

semper cum universitas electionem facit et dat iurisdictionem aliquam vel potestatem sit necessaria confirmatio superioris...Tu dic necessariam esse...Sed de consuetudine contrarium observatur in civitate Bononiensi.' See also Jacobus Butrigarius ad D.5.1.2, 2, n. 4–6 (p. 318), 'Et ideo solet dubitari an civitas possit merum imperium concedere, et videtur quod non...Quomodo ergo fit in Italia? Respondeo, fuit concessum ex pace Constantie merum imperium et ius faciendi monetam, et dato quod non esset concessum ex pace Constantie nos allegaremus [allogaremus *ed.* Rome, *1606*] concessionem factam, et probaremus per consuetudinem, argu. [D.22.1.6]': this approaches the *de facto* argument, but of course to rely on custom to support the claim that there actually was such a concession is not the same as maintaining that custom has the force of an imperial concession.

85 See for instance Jacobus de Ravannis ad C.1.2.23 (fol. 14v), and Jacobus Butrigarius ad C.7.49.1 (fol. 50v) for the transfer of fiscal rights through the *lex regia*. Albericus de Rosciate, *De statutis*, 3, qu. 19, n. 3–4 (fol. 57v), accepts imperial concession as a source of fiscal rights, but concludes concerning the fiscal right of *publicatio bonorum*, 'De facto tamen usurpatum est in omnibus civitatibus, quia hodie civitates, maxime Italie, utuntur iure provincie, ut no. in gl. [C.7.33.12].'

86 Ad D.5.3.30, 7, n. 2 (fol. 167v). Cf. id. ad D.49.14.2, n. 2 (fol. 221v). For Bartolus' attribution of the fisc to such cities see Woolf, *Bartolus*, pp. 119–22. Cp. Angelus de Ubaldis ad C.10.10.1, n. 5 (fol. 36v).

87 Ad D.1.8.Rubr. (fol. 36v). Cf. id. ad C.10.10.1 (fol. 18v) where he gives Perugia as an example of such a city.

it: 'No purse is called fiscal properly speaking except the purse of the emperor or the Roman republic, as in [D.39.4.6 and D.50.16.16], except for those cities which have prescribed fiscal rights.'[88] As we have seen, in their territories they replace the emperor in the enjoyment of fiscal rights;[89] but theirs is a *fiscus singularis* as opposed to the *fiscus universalis* of the emperor.[90] This is not to deny that the emperor can also concede fiscal rights to cities through privileges;[91] but this, for Baldus, would be essentially an aspect of autonomous status rather than sovereignty. Indeed, in one *consilium* Baldus presents imperial concession as the only valid source of fiscal rights for cities.[92] The point is that the nature of fiscal powers possessed by a city is related to its position in the hierarchy of sovereignty. Thus Baldus is also capable of referring to the fisc of a city clearly subordinate to a direct superior,[93] meaning thereby its common purse and not imperial fiscal powers, a usage reflecting that· aspect of contemporary civilian language which had debased the original meaning of the term. That 'any city in its territory takes the place of the fisc'[94] is indeed true; but in order to determine the extent of such power it is first necessary to know whether the city is sovereign, autonomous or subordinate.

There remains, however, a further unambiguous sign of sovereignty. In terms of Roman law *laesa maiestas* is committed against either the *princeps* or the *respublica Romana*. In the case of the *princeps* this was a hierarchical conception: *laesa maiestas* was committed against the superior by a subject who was his inferior.[95] But Baldus also maintains that the crime of *laesa maiestas* can be committed against the *populus* of

---

[88] Baldus ad C.4.39.1 (fol. 307r). Cf. id. ad C.4.31.7 (fol. 285r).

[89] Above, p. 116.

[90] Baldus, *Cons.*, 4.462, fol. 111v, ed. Brescia, 1490 (= *Cons.*, 5.336, ed. Venice, 1575). Cp. id. ad *Feud.*, 2.54 (fol. 79v).

[91] Id. ad C.6.62.1 (fol. 174r). Cf. id., *Margarita*, ad v. 'Civitas potest confiscare' (fol. 6v); and id. ad *Feud.*, 2.27 (fol. 53r).

[92] *Cons.*, 3.313, fol. 102r, ed. Brescia, 1491 (=*Cons.*, 1.363, ed. Venice, 1575).

[93] For instance, in his *in contrarium* argument in his commentary on D.1.1.9 as discussed above, pp. 108–9, in the context of cities specifically subordinate to a superior he says, 'Sed Inno. dicit quod in constitutione non requiritur consensus nec scientia superioris, secus in consuetudine [X.2.22.15] per Inno., sed nihil allegat. Idem tenet Jacobus Bu. [D.2.2.1, 1]. Sed puto verum in his que non tangunt aliquo modo ius vel interesse superioris, unde civitates habentes suum fiscum possunt facere penalia statuta, quia de iure suo licitum est eis statuere sed non in alienum falcem mittere [C.3.39.4].' Such cities have a 'quasi fiscus' (id. ad C.4.31.7, fol. 285r). This usage of 'fiscus' goes back to the early Glossators: see, for instance, Placentinus ad C.4.31.3, ad v. 'Reipublice', 'id est fisco, vel rei publice romane, vel etiam cuiuslibet civitatis ut dicunt quidam' (Pescatore, *Miscellen*, p. 67).

[94] Baldus, *Rep.* ad C.1.1.1, n. 98 (ed. Meijers, p. 44).

[95] See, for instance, Oldradus, *Cons.*, 43, n. 8–9, fol. 15v (discussed in Ullmann, *Individual and Society*, p. 27).

an Italian city: 'It is the duty of the *podestà* to guard against those who try to incite the people to disorder, as in Auth., "De mandatis principum" [Coll., 3.4, 17 = Nov., 17, 17], and to seek information, question and punish. Thus anyone who tries to change the people's form of government through force of arms is punished by death, because it is the crime of treason.'[96] He makes the same point in discussing the penalty for forging money (a crime of *laesa maiestas* in Roman law): 'In the case of that city I should say that it would be a crime similar to treason, if any subject of that city were to forge its money. Thus I say a subject, because a non-subject does not fall into the crime of treason, as Paulus notes on [*Clem.*, 2.11.2]. Therefore anyone who wants to betray the people falls into the crime of treason. This is true of a subject but not of a non-subject.'[97] In the context of Baldus' overall treatment of Italian cities these statements apply to sovereign cities which have filled the place of the emperor, who in his turn had been given through the *lex regia* that *maiestas* originally possessed by the Roman people. It must be admitted however that Baldus is not completely consistent, because in *Cons.*, 1.58–9 (ed. Venice, 1575) he denies that *laesa maiestas* can be committed against a city such as Florence on the grounds that such a crime can only be committed against the *princeps* or the *respublica Romana* and not against a city which as a mere *municipium* is the object only of *seditio*.[98] As we have seen this statement is totally unrepresentative of his normal view of the status of such cities; indeed, *Cons.*, 3.264 (ed. Venice, 1575) is concerned with aspects of *laesa maiestas* against the city of Florence understood as a

---

96 Ad X.1.32.Rubr., n. 1 (fol. 155v). Cf. id. ad C.9.41.16 (fol. 373r), 'Nota casum quod si potestas istius civitatis torquet aliquem de prioribus durante officio punitur pena capitis excepto crimine maiestatis vel proditionis populi que connumeratur inter crimen lese maiestatis.'

97 Ad C.9.24.2 (fol. 370v). Cf. id. ad D.4.5.5, 1 (fol. 204r) concerning a rebel against his own city, 'Nota quod proprie dicitur rebellis qui primo erat civis vel subditus, ut in glo. parva, et iste proprie incidit in crimen lese maiestatis.'

98 The very lengthy *Cons.*, 1.58 (fols. 18v–20v) after setting out the facts of the cases in question and the relevant Florentine statute law ends with *pro* and *contra* arguments as to whether *laesa maiestas* can be committed against a city like Florence: the *contra* argument (n.3) maintains that *laesa maiestas* can only be committed against the *princeps* or the *respublica Romanorum*, and addressing the reported Florentine statute which accorded to Florence the legal status of the *respublica Romanorum*, rejects any suggestion that by virtue of this claim *laesa maiestas* can be committed against the city of Florence. *Cons.*, 1.59 appears to be the *solutio* of *Cons.*, 1.58 – see especially n. 2 (fol. 20v) where this conclusion is reached: 'In primo sit ergo conclusum, quod titulus criminis istius non est proprie lese maiestatis titulus, sed est crimen seditionis, et posito quod esset lese maiestatis, est ex capite speciali seditionis.' Baldus' opinion here is expressed strictly 'loquendo de iure communi'; this is clear because he derives the authority of Florence's magistracy and governmental powers from imperial concession.

respublica,[99] and he also views treason against Perugia in the same way.[100] Under the Roman Republic *maiestas* belonged to the *populus Romanus*. Vestiges of this view remain in the *Corpus Iuris Civilis*.[101] In applying the concept of the *respublica* to such sovereign city-*populi* Baldus is able to reactivate the idea of the *maiestas* of the *populus* (or the *respublica*) and therewith that of treason against it. Thus *laesa maiestas* can be committed against the sovereign city both because it replaces the *princeps* and because it thereby ultimately enjoys (within its territory) that sovereignty which the Roman people had once enjoyed but had transferred to the emperor.

It is, of course, to be expected that Baldus would term cities *respublicae*. This usage, however, could imply a great deal or very little. *Respublica* had become in fact a devalued term among the Glossators and Commentators. In the *Corpus Iuris Civilis* it applies to the *respublica Romanorum*, except in the few cases in which the word, *respublica*, is applied to the inhabitants of another specific city.[102] Yet Azo, for example, feels able to apply the term, *respublica*, to any city,[103] and Accursius too does not reserve it for the *respublica Romanorum*.[104] A question at issue among the post-Accursian jurists and early Commentators was whether the term, *respublica*, was properly or improperly applied to cities generally, with a common opinion being that it was done so improperly.[105] Bartolus, however, consistently applies the term, *respublica*, to cities in general,[106] but distinguishes between grades of *respublica*: the empire as a whole, the *respublica Romanorum*, any city and any *municipium*.[107] Baldus largely follows this grading, but, crucially, does not apply the term to a *municipium*:

Note that the term, *respublica*, is used in three ways: firstly, for the whole congregation of the faithful of the empire, or for the whole empire; secondly, for the *respublica* of the city of Rome; and thirdly, for any city (*pro qualibet*

---

[99] n. 1–4 (fol. 74v).
[100] Ad X.1.29.1, n. 7 (fol. 121v).
[101] See D.48.4.1, 1; and for instance Jolowicz, *Historical Introduction*, p. 323.
[102] A case much commented on by jurists occurs at C.8.17.4.
[103] *Summa Codicis*, C.11.30, fol. 252v (ed. Lyon, 1557).
[104] See gl. ad C.11.30.3, ad v. 'rempublicam' (fol. 135r); id., gl. ad C.1.50.1, ad v. 'In causa' (fol. 35r); and id., gl. ad C.11.29.Rubr. for a list of occasions on which the *Corpus Iuris Civilis* applies the term, *respublica*, to cities other than Rome.
[105] See, for instance, Odofredus ad D.V. Const., 'Omnem', n. 4 (fol. 2v); id. ad D.3.4.2, n. 2 (fol. 123r); and Jacobus Butrigarius ad C.2.53.4 (fol. 82r).
[106] See Woolf, *Bartolus*, pp. 116–18.
[107] Ad C.10.1.Rubr., n. 4 (fol. 2r). In this he has Accursius' grading in mind although the latter considers cities and *municipia* to be termed *respublicae* improperly (gl. ad Auth., 'De heredibus et falcidia', ad v. 'Reipublice' (Coll.1, 1 = Nov., 1, 1), fol. 2r).

civitate). And thus *respublica* sometimes stands for the head and members together, sometimes for the head alone, that is for the city of Rome, and sometimes for the other members.[108]

This treatment of other cities as *membra* of the empire fits in admirably with Baldus' overall view of the hierarchy of sovereignty; likewise the definition of the empire as a *congregatio fidelium* stresses the bond of faith we have already seen between the emperor and his subjects, and with the erosion of which bond Baldus is particularly concerned in the case of Italian cities. The crucial point is however that, quite apart from any devaluation of the use of the term, *respublica*, it is essential that cities should be classified as *respublicae* if they are to be considered as being sovereign, because they are thus seen as being covered by public law (the proper dimension for sovereign entities) rather than private law, under which they were placed by any Roman law theory denying them sovereignty:[109] Baldus, in short, quite deliberately distinguishes between cities as *respublicae* and mere *municipia*. Thus he considers that the fisc belongs to a *respublica* (together with the emperor and kings) but not to a *municipium*: 'The fisc is the same as the purse of Caesar or a king or a *respublica*, as is noted in [C.12.49.4], for *municipia* do not properly have the fisc, as in [C.10.10.1], although they have a common purse, as in [D.3.4.1, 1].'[110] In his commentary on C.7.49.1, in a context in which the term, *respublica*, is applied to a city other than Rome, he maintains that the fisc belongs to a city-community understood specifically as a *respublica*: 'You are to say that "respublica" signifies a corporation; "fisc" however signifies something belonging to the corporation itself.'[111] The level of independence of a city-*respublica* would vary between autonomy and sovereignty (as in the case of fiscal powers), but only as a *respublica* can a city be sovereign as he makes clear in a discussion of the right to levy tolls: 'Those rights to tolls are specially reserved for the superior as a sign of his sovereignty (*in signum superioritatis*), as in [C.7.39.6]; however, according to the custom of Italy those very cities which govern themselves are the sovereign (*superior autem secundum consuetudinem Italie sunt ipse civitates*

---

[108] Ad D.V., Const. 'Omnem' (fol. 2r). Cp. id. ad D.1.1.1, 2 (fol. 5r), 'Status civitatum et castrorum pertinet ad statum reipublice, id est ditionis Romane, quoniam sunt eius membra.'

[109] See D.50.16.15, 'Bona civitatis abusive "publica" dicta sunt: sola enim ea publica sunt, que populi Romani sunt'; D.50.16.16, 'Civitates enim privatorum loco habentur'; Baldus, *Cons.*, 1.59, n. 2, fol. 20v (ed. Venice, 1575); and Costa, *Iurisdictio*, p. 232.

[110] Ad C.7.73.Rubr. (fol. 283r). Bartholomaeus de Saliceto considered that this passage merited special mention (ibid., n. 2, fol. 93v).

[111] Fol. 226v. For the city as a corporation see below, pp. 185–97.

que per se reguntur), as in [D.49.15.7 and 24], for they are called *respublicae*, not fortified places or villages.'[112] Etymologically, the modern term, 'sovereignty', is derived from *superioritas*, an expression of sovereign power in an ultimately monarchical and hierarchical sense. Baldus' usage here, in which he develops Bartolus' bracketing of the *superior populus* with the *princeps*,[113] might appear out-of-place in being applied to cities which have, as he says, obtained their sovereignty through the exercise of their own consent in the form of custom, an essentially populist conception: this might well be an example of the poverty of the language available whereby *superioritas* comes to be attributed to a city-people in order to indicate its possession of sovereignty. There is much to be said for this view, but Baldus' usage need cause no surprise if it is seen in the overall context of his vision of the hierarchy of sovereignty in which the sovereign city as *respublica* replaces the *princeps*, the ultimate superior. Thus the concept of the sovereignty of cities is taken yet one stage further: the city which does not recognise a superior itself enjoys *superioritas*. Certainly, the connection between the status of a sovereign city as a *respublica* and the full and proper possession of fiscal rights becomes well established as Baldus' pupil, Paulus de Castro, very clearly shows, although in a combination of the Bartolist and the pre-Bartolist view he would only accord the status of *respublica* properly to a city not recognising a superior.[114]

The occasional references which Baldus makes to cities as *provinciae*, and to their chief magistrates as *praesides provinciae*, might seem to contradict his treatment of cities as *respublicae*, in that the *provincia* is on a lower level. This is in fact typical of the civilian tradition which applied both terms to cities. In terming cities *provinciae* civilians were seeking to account for them as territorial entities enjoying jurisdiction (including *merum imperium*) within the context of the empire as a whole. The Commentators took their lead from Accursius' famous gloss on

---

[112] Baldus, *Cons.*, 2.369, fol. 94v (ed. Brescia, 1490). But for a loose application of the term, *respublica*, to *castra* see id., *Cons.*, 1.72, n. 1, fols. 25r–25v (ed. Venice, 1575). Paulus de Castro reports Baldus' view of the city-*populus* which is *superior*, but does so in his commentary on D.1.1.9 (n. 6, fol. 8v), thus drawing from Baldus' argument in the third section of his commentary (quoted above, p. 109) an implication which Baldus himself does not develop at that point: 'Sed an requiratur auctoritas potestatis illius loci, quando populus condit statuta? Dic quod sic si potestas non imponebatur ab ipso populo, sed a superiore, ut in hac civitate Padue, ut ita no. in [D.2.2.1]; secus si ponebatur ab eo, quia tunc populus est superior, et non indiget auctoritate illius secundum Baldum.'

[113] See Bartolus ad Auth., 'Sacramenta' (ad C.2.27.1), fol. 85v, 'Cum ergo superior populus vel princeps hoc precipiat, si quis facit contra legem peccat mortaliter.'

[114] Ad D.3.4.1, 1, n. 1 (fol. 103r). See also id. ad D.1.1.1, 2, n. 2–3 (fol. 2v).

'Id est in una provincia' at C.7.33.12: 'And note that [in this text] "one place" is defined as "one province." These days, however, this does not seem to apply: they should rather be in the same city, since individual cities have their own governments just as individual provinces had formerly.'[115] The immediate implication drawn was that the city's supreme judicial magistrate, the *podestà*, was thus in the position of the *praeses provinciae*, who exercised *merum imperium*, rather than, as previously thought, in that of a mere *defensor civitatis*, who did not enjoy such jurisdiction.[116] Cities possessed the level of jurisdiction of a *provincia* either properly through imperial concession or improperly by *de facto* usurpation.[117] The long-term importance of Accursius' statement is that it was one of the major advances which ultimately led to a realisation of the sovereignty of cities and the full jurisdiction of their chief magistrates. Indeed, Jacobus de Ravannis in the immediate continuation of the passage already noted from his commentary on C.7.33.12 takes this very step with specific reference to this self-same gloss by Accursius.[118] Baldus expressly interprets this gloss of Accursius in the light of his own *de iure–de facto* distinction:

Note the words, 'since individual cities', in the gloss which begins, 'in una provincia.' This gloss is unique in the law and does not have another like it according to Accursius: namely that any city (*unaqueque civitas*) which has its own distinct government and is not subject *de facto* to the jurisdiction of a superior is called a province. Take the examples of Florence, Perugia and the city of Siena: they are considered to occupy the position of a province. Therefore those who exercise authority in them have the position of a *praeses provinciae*. Finally, you must see here which place should be called a province: follow Cynus' view here because his remarks are clear.[119]

---

[115] Fol. 239r. 'They' refers to 'the claimant and the possessor' (the question is one of prescription of ownership).

[116] See Costa, *Iurisdictio*, pp. 212–14.

[117] As Albericus de Rosciate made clear (above, p. 120, n. 85).

[118] 'Vnde dicit glossa et bene, quod unum regimen unius [unus *ed. cit.*] districtus reputatur pro una provincia.' See above, p. 94, n. 4.

[119] Ad C.7.33.12 (fol. 200v). Cp. id., *De pace Constantie*, ad v. 'Imperialis clementie' (fol. 89r), 'Preterea merum imperium competit in provincia soli presidi provincie, ut [D.1.18.4, 6 & 8]. Sed potest dici secundum Accursium quod hoc iure cavetur; sed consuetudine non habetur in civitatibus que populariter reguntur, nam potestas eligitur ab eis, et de consuetudine investitur et alium presidem non habent; unde merum et mixtum imperium et omnimoda iurisdictio apud eum est, quia loco presidis habetur respectu illius civitatis, ut no. in Auth. "De defensoribus civitatum", § "nulla" [Coll., 3.2, 2 = Nov., 15, 2] . . . et [C.7.33.12]. Idem in castris seu terris que alterius iurisdictioni non subsunt sicut in insulis multa sunt.' For the *de iure communi* position see Baldus, *Cons.*, 4.499, n. 1–2, fol. 116v (ed. Venice, 1575), 'Sciendum est quod civitates nedum castra de iure communi non habent gladii potestatem. Et ideo potestates civitatum vel castrorum de iure communi non habent gladii imperium, sed soli presides provinci-

126

There is no doubt that Baldus considers as *provinciae* cities which in their government are not subject to a superior either *de facto* or by *de iure* concession;[120] it is thus a term which covers both sovereign and autonomous cities. In this context the employment of the term should really be seen as parallel to that of *respublica* rather than a contradiction of it: there is in short no implication which undermines Baldus' overall view of the self-government of cities. This usage of *provincia* certainly fits in with the thesis of the hierarchy of sovereignty.

Territorial sovereignty

The territorial aspect, stressed by the description of a city as a *provincia*, clearly informs Baldus' whole treatment of cities. Within his overall *de iure–de facto* hierarchical structure the sovereignty or autonomy of cities is seen as being essentially territorial. The sovereign city replaces the emperor within its territory. Territory defines as much as it limits a city's sovereignty. In the gaps left by the effective retreat of universal imperial authority in northern and central Italy there has emerged a plurality of powers whose sovereignty or autonomy must by definition be territorial. In the case of cities this situation is further illustrated by two crucial questions which Baldus also considers: banishment and extradition.

Banishment itself (a form of penalty peculiarly prevalent in fourteenth-century Italy) reveals the territorial limits of the city-community's jurisdiction. According to Baldus the effect of banishment is limited to the territory whence the person is banished, because the jurisdiction upon which the sentence of banishment depends is limited to that territory:

arum, et non inferiores eis.' See Cynus ad C.7.33.12, n. 5 (fol. 444v): 'Glo. dicit hic, quod quantum ad tractatum huius legis hodie quelibet civitas est provincia; quod forte verum est in Italia, ubi de facto non preest dominus generalis.'

[120] Ad D.1.18.6, 8 (fol. 58r); id. ad Auth., 'Sed omnino' (ad C.4.12.4), fol. 228r; and id., *Cons.*, 3.284, n. 3–4, fol. 79r (ed. Venice, 1575). Cp. Bartolus ad Const., 'Qui sint rebelles' ad v. 'Lombardie' (fol. 6v). See also Paulus de Castro, *Rep.* ad D.1.1.5, n. 13 (fol. 6r). *Provincia* can, of course, have a wider meaning: see, for instance, Baldus, *Rep.*, ad D.12.2.2 (fol. 38v), 'Dico quod interdum contractus est simpliciter promissus, et tunc si fit cum principe vel civitate, que principatum teneat in sua provincia sicut est civitas Florentie et similes civitates, et tunc dico quod obtinet vim legis' (clearly an obvious meaning here is that such cities are the most important in their province, but Baldus could be understanding them as enjoying jurisdiction *vice principis*); and id. ad Auth., 'Sed omnino' (fols. 228r–229v), where he includes Perugia in the province of Tuscany: see Rubinstein, 'Florence and the despots', p. 31, n. 5, for the Florentine inclusion of Perugia within Tuscany on the ideological grounds that it was Tuscan in that it had a republican form of government.

Banishment does not affect a person except in the territory from which he is banished. This, therefore, is a penalty applying to a person in a particular place and not to a person simply, for jurisdiction which is limited as to place does not extend outside that place, as in [D.1.16.1 & 2; D.1.12.1, 4 and D.2.1.20], for jurisdiction adheres to a territory, as in [C.2.26.3], but a territory has its own boundaries...And thus, so to speak, such outlaws are banished from a particular part, namely the territory of the person banishing them, and are not outlawed as regards another part, namely in other places in which they have free domicile.[121]

This is in contrast to penalties of exile which have universal application, because the power imposing them has universal jurisdiction. Thus as regards the geographical extent of its effect banishment by a city is not similar to imperial *deportatio* or excommunication,[122] compared with both of which the contemporary form of banishment is a recent development.[123] Since banishment does not apply outside a city's territory, such an outlaw only loses those rights stemming from the city's legal authority, and not those he enjoys under the *ius commune*, the Roman law itself (which an imperial *deportatus* would forfeit): '[An outlaw] may have his abode anywhere in the whole world except the land from which he is exiled...Although [outlaws] lose their rights and property in their own city, they do not however lose the common rights of Roman citizens.'[124] There is nothing new in Baldus' position on banishment: it accords with the ideas of, for instance, Jacobus Butrigarius and Bartolus.[125] Albericus de Rosciate considers that banishment from one city would only have effect in others either if they were in confederation, or if they were subject to the same lord or in the same kingdom.[126] The treatment of banishment in the *communis opinio* of the Commentators illustrates their territorial conception of the jurisdiction of cities, but with Bartolus and Baldus can become an attribute of territorial sovereignty itself.

Baldus further represents it as being the general custom of con-

---

[121] Ad C.6.24.1 (fol. 57r). The context of Baldus' remarks is a discussion of banishment from a city-community.
[122] See Baldus, ibid.
[123] Id., ibid., 'Apparet igitur ex predictis bannitos nostri temporis non habere propriam et totalem similitudinem nec cum deportatis, nec cum excommunicatis, sed esse novum genus.' [124] Id., ibid.
[125] See Jacobus Butrigarius ad Auth. 'Item nulla' (ad C.1.3.2), fol. 16v; Bartolus ad D.4.5.5, 1, n. 1–2 (fol. 141r); and id. ad C.6.24.1, n. 3, fol. 18v (referred to in Baldus, *Cons.*, 2.24, fol. 9r, ed. Brescia, 1490 (= *Cons.*, 4.27, ed. Venice, 1575)). See also Jacobus de Arena ad D.36.1.18, n. 5–6 (fol. 127v). Cp. Bartholomaeus de Saliceto ad C.6.24.1, n. 16–17 (fols. 106v–107r).
[126] Ad D.49.15.7, n. 1–2 (fol. 214r).

temporary Italy that there is no extradition between self-governing cities not subject to any *princeps generalis*:

Guilelmus raises the following question here. The judge in the place of domicile starts proceedings and the judge in the place where the offence was committed seeks extradition. Should the extradition take place? Guilelmus decides that it should. It is thus to be noted that even he who can punish on his own account should extradite...These days, however, we do not use these extraditions except in lands which are subject to one general ruler, and not however in lands which are not subject to the rule of anyone else. And this is the content of the custom which must be observed because it is general and of long standing. We therefore see that outlaws from the city of Pisa can stay here in security: they do not however fear extradition because it is not the practice that it should apply between equals.[127]

The lack of extradition is a crucial aspect of territorial sovereignty because it clearly shows that a city's jurisdiction is strictly contained within its territorial limits. The territorial element is important here especially as Baldus discusses these cities in terms of self-governing *terrae*. Furthermore, as Baldus plainly sees, territorial sovereignty involves an essential equality between these independent territorial entities, a clear application of the basic juristic principle that 'equals do not have authority over each other'.[128] Baldus is in no sense innovating: he is expressing, as he says, the general custom of Italy which Bartolus himself had already recognised.[129] Insofar as territorial sovereignty is at issue the stress on custom here as the origin of this state of affairs fits in with Baldus' conception of the *de facto* source of the cities' sovereignty. Although Bartolus and Baldus are united in their view on extradition, later juristic tradition is nevertheless divided, as the fifteenth-century canonist and civilian, Johannes de Imola, makes clear: a specific sign that the thesis of the sovereignty of cities was by no means universally accepted.[130]

---

[127] Ad D.1.18.3 (fol. 58r).

[128] 'Par in parem imperium non habet.' In medieval juristic writings this phrase was often derived from D.36.1.13,1.

[129] See Baldus, *Cons.*, 1.72, fols. 28v–29r, ed. Brescia, 1490 (= *Cons.*, 2.209, ed. Venice, 1575); and Bartolus ad D.47.12.6, n. 3 (fol. 146r). Cp. Baldus ad C.6.1.2 (fol. 2v), 'Remissiones de consuetudine non fiunt nisi in terris que sunt sub eodem principatu, ut no. in [*Clem.*, 2.11.2]' – the reference to *Pastoralis cura* is notable in the light of that decretal's fundamental contribution to the development of the theme of territorial sovereignty (see above, p. 22).

[130] Ad *Clem.*, 2.11.2, n. 64 (fol. 71r), 'Secundum hoc ergo, ut dicit hic Panormitanus, sequitur quod materia remissionis vana est, quia hodie quelibet civitas dicit se habere merum imperium et quasi suum regimen sicut olim habebant provincie...Contrarium...putat verius dominus Antonius [de Butrio], scilicet quod sive sint loca sub eodem, sive sub diversis debeat fieri remissio de necessitate, et ad hoc compelli debeat

Baldus, however, goes beyond simply holding that a sovereign city-*populus* enjoys jurisdiction which is territorially confined. In a notable passage he would appear to consider that a city-*populus* is nothing less than a territorial entity; that its territorial aspect forms part of what constitutes such a *populus*:

A further question is whether those inside [the city] can make statutes against those who have been expelled. And it seems that they can because those inside comprise the people not those who are dispersed and wandering through the world, as Innocent says [X.5.32.2]...On the contrary...because of the fact that they have been expelled they have ceased to belong to that corporation and body [D.4.5.5, 1], and therefore as outsiders they are not subject to statute. You are to say that if they have indeed been expelled for just cause, the statute is valid, because their offence should not gain them exemption, as in the said [D.4.5.5, 1; D.50.12.8; D.42.4.13]. And I concede that jurisdiction remains in the hands of those inside the city because it adheres to the territory, and those inside possess the territory. Again, those inside are a corporate body, and those expelled are separate individuals.[131]

Baldus thus defines the *populus* as being composed of those living within the territory. Furthermore, he appears to consider that the people's living within a territory is one of the factors which make it into a corporation – the people is a territorial, corporate entity. The implication is that the people through inhabiting a defined area becomes a unity which is corporate.[132] This passage admittedly has a general application, but it is certainly relevant to sovereign city-*populi*. His words here are also important for the further information which they provide concerning the relationship between the people's jurisdiction and the territory within which it operates. Baldus maintains that the people possesses jurisdiction because it possesses the territory; and that the reason for this is that jurisdiction adheres to the territory.[133] This view gives a strong emphasis to the territorial aspect of the people's jurisdiction: that jurisdiction is clearly located in a particular territory.

per superiorem; et si de facto pretendant se liberos, tamen adhuc de iure fieri debet et illam facere debeant, quia ius eos necessitat, et peccant, si non faciant, quia ius quod est supra omnes iubet hoc fieri per verbum "iubemus". Est tamen verum quod si volunt contradicere de facto servatur opinio Panormitani, quia non est superior qui compellat, sed male faciunt.'

[131] Ad D.1.1.9 (fol. 9v).

[132] See below, p. 208, for the significance of the concept of the people as a territorial corporation.

[133] Baldus gives detailed attention to the juristic commonplace, 'iurisdictio coheret territorio': see his commentaries on C.9.1.11 (fol. 347v); D.1.12.1, 4 (fol. 43r); *Feud.*, 2.54 (fol. 79v); and C.7.63.4 (fol. 269v). See also Bartolus ad D.2.1.1, n. 15 (fol. 47r). For Bartolus' view see Vaccari, 'Vtrum jurisdictio cohaereat territorio.'

Baldus' theory of the sovereignty of cities is thus ultimately a territorial one in which the possession of a territory limits the extent of a people's power, but more importantly forms part of the definition of what such a city-*populus* is. His whole theory of city-sovereignty must be seen as a major component of what ranks as one of the most important contributions which medieval jurisprudence made to political thought: the elaboration of the concept of territorial sovereignty, an idea fashioned first in the context of kingship, given impetus by papal support, most notably through *Pastoralis cura*, and applied to cities by Bartolus and Baldus. Nevertheless for both jurists this plurality of sovereign entities, together with autonomous ones, exists within the overall structure of a hierarchy of sovereignty in which the imperial authority is not just one territorial power amongst many.

II: THE LIMITATIONS ON TERRITORIAL SOVEREIGNTY

There remain, however, two major questions which have to be considered in order to complete the picture of a city's territorial sovereignty: the extent to which the existence of competing jurisdictions and bodies of law within the city's territory may or may not limit its internal sovereignty; and the limitations imposed on its jurisdiction by that same structure of higher norms which we have seen confining the exercise of imperial authority. Baldus was faced with a situation in which a city's own customs, statutes and law-courts existed within its territory side-by-side with the whole apparatus of ecclesiastical law and jurisdiction, the statutes of guilds and the Guelph and Ghibelline parties, and the *ius commune*, the Roman law itself, which was applied in the city's courts. It emerges in his treatment that whereas ecclesiastical jurisdiction, like the overall normative structure, does indeed limit the sovereignty of a city's secular authorities in the legislative, judicial and governmental spheres, the status of the *ius commune* within its territory and the subordination of the jurisdiction of guilds and parties tend only to reinforce a city's territorial sovereignty. The independent city is shown to enjoy internally a limited sovereignty, a term which may appear self-contradictory, and at least paradoxical, but which, as we shall see, is demanded by the sources.

Ecclesiastical jurisdiction and the position of the clergy

A consistent theme throughout Baldus' works is the acceptance of ecclesiastical jurisdiction autonomous on its own terms, and the

accompanying respect for the privileges of the clergy. This should cause
no surprise not only because Baldus was a canonist, but also because
the general trend of fourteenth-century civilian thought was to accept
the autonomy of ecclesiastical jurisdiction and legal claims, despite
differences of attitude by individual jurists on particular points. In taking
this position the Commentators were doing no more than accepting
the position of canon law in contemporary legal reality. This is not
to deny, however, that Baldus' discussions, like those of other jurists,
also reflect attempts by Italian cities from the thirteenth century to limit
the privileges of the clergy. There was nevertheless no uniformity on
this point among cities; and it could well be said that as regards Italy
this general attitude of the Commentators with its respect for the rights
of ecclesiastical jurisdiction reflected those city-statutes which protected
the *libertas ecclesiae* (such as the vulgar statutes of Perugia of 1342,[134]
and the statutes of Milan of 1351),[135] rather than those which
consciously infringed it (such as the communal legislation of Padua
between 1270 and 1290, and the Florentine Statutes of the Captain of
the People of 1322).[136]

Baldus' arguments about the relationship between secular and
ecclesiastical jurisdiction within cities are expressed in terms which have
general application. It is necessary, however, to bear in mind his
fundamental distinction between the *terrae imperii* and the *terrae ecclesiae*,
because in a couple of important respects that relationship is different
in each. In expressly rejecting Accursius' view that Roman law must
give place to canon in cases of conflict between them[137] Baldus follows
Bartolus in maintaining that within the *terrae ecclesiae* canon law applies
to both secular and spiritual matters, whereas in the *terrae imperii* secular
and ecclesiastical law apply in their respective fields:

Thirdly, note that where Roman law is contrary to a canon, the canon should
be observed and not the civil law. You are to say concerning this that either

---

[134] See degli Azzi (ed.), *Statuti di Perugia dell'anno MCCCXLII*, II, 451 (Lib. 4, cap. 157).
But see Bartolus ad Auth., 'Cassa et irrita' (ad C.1.2.12), n. 5–6 (fol. 14v), 'Quero,
in volumine statutorum reperitur quoddam statutum contra libertatem ecclesie, in fine
voluminis apponitur unum aliud statutum, quod si qua sunt statuta contra libertatem
ecclesie sint cassa et irrita ipso iure; an propter statutum istud ultimum statuentes sint
liberati a pena huius legis et illius [X.5.39.49]? Certe non, quia textus non solum precipit
annullari verbo, sed etiam aboleri et cancellari de volumine statutorum de facto... quod
tene menti ad multa, que vidi semel in civitate Pisarum.' The Perugian statute referred
to does, indeed, come at the end of the volume; but there is no suggestion that Bartolus
also had Perugia in mind.
[135] See Prosdocimi, *Diritto ecclesiastico*, pp. 24–5.
[136] See Rubinstein, 'Marsilius of Padua', pp. 47–8.
[137] Gl. ad C.1.2.12,1, ad v. 'ambitionis': 'succumbit ergo lex canoni, ubi est ei contraria'
(fol. 86v).

we are speaking about matters spiritual and belonging to the faith, and then we stand by the canon, as here in the gloss, and the same is true as regards ecclesiastical possessions and other ecclesiastical rights, as in [X.1.2.10]; or we are speaking about purely temporal matters, and then either in the lands of the church, in which case we observe the canons in matters of both civil and ecclesiastical jurisdiction, or in the lands of the empire, and then in civil matters we observe Roman law unless such observance were to lead us to sin, as in [X.4.17.13], but in the bishop's field of jurisdiction we stand rather by the canons.[138]

Although the secular law discussed here is the Roman law itself, this passage can be taken as a general statement about secular law, because Baldus has no doubts that the same principle applies to the statutes of cities in the *terrae imperii* and indeed to fiefs other than strictly ecclesiastical ones: 'And through the text of this chapter I say that in the cities of the Roman empire city-statutes prevail over the sacred canons of the popes on account of this chapter, because, if there can be no appeal to the pope, they [i.e. the cities] do not have a superior jurisdiction above them. Therefore in feudal matters the constitutions of princes and lords should be observed rather than those of bishops unless the fief is an ecclesiastical one, as in [*Sext.*, 2.15.3].'[139] Thus in cities in the *terrae imperii* the city's secular jurisdiction and that of the local bishop coexist in parallel each with, as it were, his own distinct legal territory,[140] whereas in the *terrae ecclesiae* the fundamental distinction between secular and ecclesiastical jurisdiction is blurred ('note that temporal jurisdiction is in every way separate from the church's jurisdiction, except in the lands of the church')[141] – there, because the church has secular jurisdiction, canon law applies to secular matters and secular city-statutes are subject to ecclesiastical confirmation.[142] Thus in the *terrae ecclesiae*, although the canons and secular statutes coexist, canon law has secular application and overall supremacy. Baldus' arguments, therefore, for the liberty of the church and the

---

[138] Baldus ad C.1.2.12 (fol. 13v). Cp. Bartolus, ibid., n. 2 (fol. 14r). For Bartolus' and Baldus' treatment of the relationship between Roman and canon law see Wolter, *Ius canonicum in iure civili*, pp. 43–50.

[139] X.2.28.7, n. 5 (fol. 349r). This statement is subject to those restrictions which according to Baldus ecclesiastical jurisdiction imposed on secular.

[140] See Baldus ad X.1.2.1, n. 11 (fol. 10v).

[141] Id. ad X.2.18.7, n. 1 (fol. 349r).

[142] See Baldus ad X.2.24.19, n. 4 (fol. 303v); id. ad D.1.1.9, fol. 9r (in the *in contrarium* argument), 'Item ibi [i.e. X.1.2.8] notat Compostellanus quod nulla universitas potest facere constitutionem absque magistratu; et hec opinio severa est et [et est *ed.* [*Lyon*], *1498*] tenaciter servatur in terris ecclesie, adeo ut si tota provincia Marchie vel ducatus faceret statutum non admitteretur per ecclesiam, nisi esset approbatum'; and Bartolus, ibid., n. 4 (fol. 9v). See Ermini, 'Diritto Romano comune', pp. 58–63.

privileges of the clergy apply most directly to cities in the *terrae imperii* or to those cities formally within the papal patrimony, but which, like Perugia and Bologna, from time to time made claims to independence with varying success:[143] where the church was in temporal control in the patrimony its liberty and privileges were assured.

In his treatment of the privileges of the clergy and the liberty of the church in general Baldus adheres to the orthodoxy of canon law. For him the separation of secular and ecclesiastical jurisdiction and the accompanying freedom of the clergy from lay control was willed by God: 'Note here that no ecclesiastical person can be brought for trial before a secular judge, and all the old laws permitting the contrary have been corrected. The canonists say that this is not a new law but an abandoning of the error of the old laws, because clerics never came under the temporal jurisdiction of lay judges. And this is the very truth, because from the beginning God made these jurisdictions distinct, as in [*Decr. Grat.*, D.96, c. 6] and Auth. "Quomodo oporteat episcopos" [Coll., 1.6 = Nov., 6].'[144] The laity are simply incompetent to extend their jurisdiction over clerics and spiritual matters.[145] It goes without saying that laymen cannot legislate against the liberty of the church, but (following Innocent III's decretal, *Ecclesia sancte Marie*, X.1.2.10) they cannot even make statutes directly in the church's favour unless the papacy approves.[146] The great exception was of course the imperial legislation in favour of the church contained in the *Codex* and the *Authenticum* (Frederick II's decrees at his imperial coronation in 1220, including *Cassa et irrita* and *Statuimus*, did not infringe X.1.2.10 because they were confirmed by the papacy): 'What statutes, however, would be said to be against the liberty of the church? Innocent says all those which are against the privileges conceded to the universal church, whether by God, God's vicar or the emperors, as is noted by him at [X.5.39.49]. Cynus refers to this in his commentary on "Cassa et irrita"

---

[143] See Ercole, *Dal comune*, pp. 331–54.

[144] Ad Auth., 'Statuimus' (ad C.1.3.32), fol. 37v. Cp. id. ad Auth., 'Clericus quoque' (ad C.1.3.32), fol. 36v, 'Hodie per Auth., "Statuimus", nec civiliter nec criminaliter potest [clericus] conveniri nisi sub episcopo'; and id. ad X.2.1.Rubr., n. 7 (fol. 175v), 'Item episcopi possunt mandare potestati ne se intromittat de causis ecclesiasticis [D.33.2.12], quia potestas debet ei obedire.' But see also id. ad X.1.2.7, n. 1 (fol. 17r), 'Libertas ecclesiarum est de iure naturali, et pena que est comes peccati inde originem trahit.'

[145] Id ad Auth., 'Sacramenta' (ad C.2.27.1), fol. 127v; id. ad D.1.9.11 (Add.), n. 4 (ed. Lyon, 1585); and id., *Rep.* ad C.1.1.1, n. 93, p. 41 (ed. Meijers). Usury is a case in point: id. ad X.2.30.1, n. 15 (fol. 376r).

[146] See id. ad X.1.2.10, n. 1–5 (fol. 25r). For the invalidity of statutes against the liberty of the church see also id., *Rep.* ad C.1.1.1, n. 7, p. 3 (ed. cit.); id., *Cons.*, 3.367, n. 1, fol. 104r (ed. Venice, 1575); and id. ad Auth., 'Cassa et irrita' (ad C.1.2.12), fol. 14r.

[ad C.1.2.12].'[147] The point about cities, however, is that Baldus is quite specific that a city-*populus* cannot extend its jurisdiction over ecclesiastical persons or property, or over cases which should be heard by church courts.[148] Even the capacity to legislate according to the legislator's own free will does not impart the power to make statutes against the liberty of the church.[149] Clerics are simply *non subditi* to a city's legislation.[150] Thus a local church, although it is in the territory of a city, is exempt from its jurisdiction.[151]

The object of clerical privilege is clearly meant to be to a cleric's advantage. What then is the status of lay statutes which would seek to penalise clerics for declining lay jurisdiction, a common ploy by cities seeking to extend their control over their clergy? Baldus supports the canon law position that it is simply not in an individual cleric's power to renounce a privilege of clergy with general effect: he has no choice but to decline secular jurisdiction.[152] In this situation the city's duty to continue to protect the cleric remains in force, although he is not subject to its jurisdiction.[153] Clerics cannot therefore be prevented by secular authorities from declining lay jurisdiction nor be punished for contempt of court for so doing.[154] Any statute which goes so far

---

[147] Baldus ad Auth., 'Statuimus' (ad C.1.3.32), fol. 38r: this is a quotation from Cynus ad Auth., 'Cassa et irrita' (Add.), n. 5 (fol. 6r). See Bartolus ad Auth., 'Cassa et irrita', n. 1–3 (fols. 14r–14v), 'Ista est constitutio domini Federici imperatoris, qui postea fuit damnatus ut hereticus per ecclesiam; tamen constitutiones facte favore ecclesie fuerunt per papam confirmate...Quero, que dicuntur statuta contra libertatem ecclesie et ecclesiasticarum personarum? Inn. in d. [X.5.39.49], cuius dicta hic retulit Cynus et addidit lecture sue veteri, dicit quod ista dicuntur statuta contra libertatem ecclesie, que sunt contra privilegia concessa ecclesiis, seu ecclesiasticis personis per principem seu papam. Et hoc probat per istum tex. ibi "adversus canonicas vel imperiales sanctiones." Istud satis placet.' Cp. Innocent IV ad X.5.39.49, n. 2 (fol. 213r), 'Nobis videtur quod in hac excommunicatione incidant qui veniunt contra libertatem vel privilegium dei vel imperii vel imperatoris super temporalibus vel pape super spiritualibus, libertas enim data est ecclesie universali non singulari.' For Frederick's decrees of 1220 see de Vergottini, *Studi sulla legislazione*, and *M.G.H., Const.* II, 85, pp. 106–9.
[148] Ad X.1.2.7, n. 1 (fol. 17r). In *Cons.*, 1.299, n. 2, fol. 91v (ed. Venice, 1575), however, Baldus appears to apply the principle of double effect to this question: 'Dico quod res publica preferendo suam publicam utilitatem utilitati ecclesie non dicitur statuere contra libertatem ecclesie, nam principaliter intendit propriam utilitatem, licet incidenter tangat ecclesie damnositatem.'
[149] Id. ad D.2.2.3,1 (fol. 71v).
[150] See for instance Baldus, *Cons.*, 4.496, n. 4, fol. 116v (ed. Venice, 1575).
[151] Id. ad D.2.4.19 (Add. Baldi), n. 1, fol. 95r (ed. Lyon, 1585).
[152] Ad C.2.3.29 (fol. 94v); and id. ad C.6.40.1 (fol. 114v).
[153] This protective function of secular authorities was the normal juristic view: see, for instance, Cynus ad C.1.3.10, n. 1 (fol. 14r).
[154] See Baldus ad C.6.40.1 (fol. 114v).

as to make a cleric an outlaw through placing him outside the protection of the commune, if he so declines secular jurisdiction, is of its nature invalid on the grounds that it is against the general privilege of the clergy.[155]

The extent to which Baldus is willing to go to protect clerical privilege is also shown in his treatment of an aspect of the taxation of the clergy: this concerns the vexed contemporary question of whether clergy are liable to a city's *collectae*, the occasional taxes imposed on the basis of real estate owned. Baldus' general principle is that clergy are not liable to such *collectae*: 'Communities have no power over the church or ecclesiastical persons, nor can they impose *collectae* on them.'[156] It was, however, a *locus communis* among the Commentators to discuss as linked questions whether clergy were liable if they inherited or otherwise obtained estates already subject to *collectae*, or whether new *collectae* imposed on all property-owners also applied to clergy who had obtained their property before such new measures came into effect. The civilian tradition, including Baldus, did not doubt that the clergy were liable to *collectae* attached to the property before they acquired it, but not to *collectae* imposed after acquisition by them.[157] The problem was that current practice in Italy made clergy liable in both cases. Although in places Bartolus did follow the normal civilian opinion[158] he also, notoriously, produced the argument that clergy were liable like laymen to new *collectae*, levied after their acquisition of the property, on the grounds that all estates were pledged or mortgaged to the commune. This was clearly an attempt to justify what the cities were in fact doing. Baldus stringently rejects this argument of Bartolus in favour of the traditional opinion as represented by Jacobus Butrigarius:

And the opinion of Bartolus is followed in practice for the sake of the public benefit and public necessity. Otherwise the whole world would stand condemned. But Jacobus Butrigarius in his lecture on the said Auth., 'Item nulla communitas' [ad C.1.3.2], does not confirm this, but gives us sufficiently to understand that before the imposition of a *collecta* property would not be mortgaged (as if this were impossible), and thus on first acquisition

---

[155] See Baldus ad Auth., 'Cassa et irrita' (fol. 14r), and ad Auth., 'Statuimus' (fol. 38r).

[156] Ad Auth., 'Item nulla' (ad C.1.3.2), fol. 26r. See also id., *Rep.* ad C.1.1.1, n. 11–13, pp. 5–6 (ed. Meijers).

[157] See for instance Petrus de Bellapertica ad Inst., 1.2, n. 46–7, p. 96 (see also Meijers' transcription from the Lyon, 1536, ed.: *Etudes*, III, 146); and Jacobus Butrigarius ad Auth., 'Item nulla', fol. 16v. Cp. Baldus ad C.4.47.3 (fol. 314r).

[158] Ad C.1.2.5, n. 35–7 (fol. 12v); id., *Cons.*, 1.180 (fols. 44v–45r); and also id. ad C.10.64.1, n. 29 (fol. 24v).

ownership of it will be free and unaffected. It at once follows from this that clerics are not bound by new *collectae*, because their estates, as far as this is concerned, do not seem to belong to the territory or sphere of laymen. And this is the safer opinion, because it is dangerous in these matters to speak against the church and clerics. Bartolus' opinion, however, is in fact followed, unless there is another way whereby, through the obligations of their predecessors, rich clerics on account of their patrimonies could together with their fellow citizens be bound to contribute to those things which are to the republic's advantage, and through which the prosperity and safety of all are taken care of.[159]

Baldus then continues and concludes the discussion of new *collectae* by giving his own solution: the clergy should come to the aid of the commune in cases of necessity, but have only a moral, not a legal obligation to do so, 'And certainly in cases of necessity they [i.e. clerics] should offer themselves so that what affects all should be felt by all. I am not, however, thereby saying that laymen may make statutes which they would not otherwise make except out of hatred of clerics; for I would believe that something then done to the detriment of ecclesiastical liberty would not be valid.' The point is that the new *collectae*, if they were applied to clergy, would be the product of lay statutes taxing *res ecclesiasticae*, something forbidden both by canon law and the *authentica*, 'Item nulla'. Baldus does not, however, leave communes totally defenceless against the clergy: he admits that cities could validly make statutes forbidding the alienation of taxable property to clergy, so that the common good would be served by preventing loss of revenue (this would result presumably from the clergy's predictable refusal to pay new *collectae* on such property in the future).[160] There is a clear difference between lay legislation being

---

[159] *Cons.*, 1.148, fol. 49r, ed. Brescia, 1490 (= *Cons.*, 2.280, ed. Venice, 1575). Cp. Baldus, *Cons.*, 2.112, n. 6–7, fol. 26v (ed. Venice, 1575). See Jacobus Butrigarius ad Auth., 'Item nulla' (fol. 16v), and Bartolus ad D.50.4.6, 3, n. 3–5 (fol. 236v), and id. ad C.10.19.8, n. 1–4 (fol. 13v). But ad X.2.15.3, n. 6 (fol. 230r) Baldus may be approaching Bartolus' opinion: 'Si statuto cavetur quod clerici qui non solvunt munera pro patrimonialibus, pro quibus debentur collecte loco tributorum ex hypotheca descendente ab estimo communi, non audiantur, istud statutum valet, quia est laudabile propter bonum publicum; de hoc tamen alibi aliter scripsi.' Baldus also refers there to the practice in France, where, he says, in property matters the clergy are subject to the customs of the kingdom, and mentions Guilelmus de Cuneo's statement to this effect (see Guilelmus ad Auth., 'Clericus', ad C.1.3.32, n. 2, fol. 16v, where he says that privilege of clergy does not apply in cases concerning property).

[160] Ad X.1.2.7, n. 8 (fol. 17v); and id. ad X.2.1.8, n. 2–3 (fol. 187v). But for a contrary opinion see Baldus, *Cons.*, 3.132, n. 1, fol. 37v (ed. Venice, 1575), where he maintains that *pia loca* are not affected by secular statutes forbidding alienation of property to those not paying taxes.

applied to ecclesiastical property, and such legislation designed to prevent secular property becoming ecclesiastical.

Given the privileges of the clergy and the autonomy of ecclesiastical jurisdiction, the question arises of the political status of the clergy: are the clergy in any sense part of the civil community, or are there in effect two parallel societies within the same territory? In the works of the Commentators two superficially opposed lines of argument coexist. On the one hand their consistent opinion is that clergy and laity constitute two distinct groups within any community with the clergy being superior to the laity in that laymen cannot validly make law for clergy. Even Cynus, who in his commentary on the *Codex* clearly opposes himself to the overextension of ecclesiastical jurisdiction, nevertheless in his commentary on C.8.52.2 has to admit the validity of separate clerical jurisdiction:

The question is whether the people's custom binds clerics. And we say that it does not for two reasons. Firstly, because there are two peoples, which is clear because there are two judges, therefore etc., as in [D.1.22.3]. Therefore the clergy have nothing in common with the public acts of lay people, as in [C.1.3.17]. Secondly, because clerics are greater than laymen...But the statutes of inferiors do not bind superiors...therefore etc., unless the clerics shall have so wished it.[161]

Albericus de Rosciate also, for instance, adopts the same view on this topic.[162] The idea that clergy and laity constitute *duo populi* (expressed about 1160 by the canonist, Stephen of Tournai)[163] for these jurists derives directly from the statement, 'duo sunt genera Christianorum' ('there are two kinds of Christian'), attributed to St Jerome in Gratian's *Decretum* (C.12.q.1, c. 7). Yet it could not be denied that the *Corpus Iuris Civilis* clearly treats the clergy as part of the civil community through maintaining that sacred persons and property are covered by the *ius publicum* (public law)[164] and by including imperial decrees concerning the church. Further, the *Corpus Iuris Civilis* clearly thereby provides the concept of the subjection of the clergy to state authority. All civilians accepted that the church came under *ius publicum*, and that the condition of the church, because it existed in a public dimension,

---

[161] n. 27 (fol. 525v).
[162] Ad D.1.3.32, n. 138 (fol. 43v); and id., *De statutis*, 2, qu. 2, ad v. 'Ex predictis oritur', n. 16–17 (fol. 28v).
[163] See von Schulte, *Die Summa des Stephanus Tornacensis*, Introductio, p.1.
[164] D.1.1.1, 2: 'publicum ius in sacris, in sacerdotibus, in magistratibus consistit.'

was a matter of concern to the *respublica*.[165] Yet because they also accepted the privileges of the clergy they manifestly did not draw the conclusion of the subordination of the clergy to lay authority: there was thus a somewhat uneasy acceptance of apparently conflicting ideas.

Baldus in producing his solution shows that the tension between these two lines of thought is more apparent than real. There is no doubt that he considers clergy to be part of the civil community: 'Could or should a priest be reckoned to be part of the corporation of the citizens? You are to say that he is [D.35.1.33, 1; X.2.2.17], just as churches too are part of the body of the city according to Oldradus.'[166] The privileges of the clergy, however, and their capacity to use lay legislation when this is to their advantage[167] (although laymen themselves cannot directly legislate for clergy) give them a special membership of the civil *populus*: 'Clerics are part of the people insofar as this is to their advantage, but not insofar as it is to the church's detriment.'[168] Clergy are in short privileged citizens: they have the advantages of citizens ('Statutes made by the common law in favour of clerics are extended to cover clerics...and as a result clerics enjoy the privileges and advantages of citizens, and see on this [*Decr. Grat.*, C.12, q. 1, c. 7]');[169] they do not have the disadvantages, like a full liability to taxation. The point is that their privileges do not remove the clergy from the citizen-body. This view grew out of the civilian tradition. It was to be found in Bartolus,[170] and was to have a future as Baldus' pupil, Paulus de Castro, shows in a notable passage:

Again, do clerics enjoy the benefits which the laity do? You are to say that they do, because they are part of the people and together with laymen

---

[165] Out of a host of possible examples see for instance Azo, *Summa Inst.*, 1.1 (fol. 294v); Odofredus ad D.1.1.1, 2, n. 11 (fol. 6r); Cynus ad D.1.1.1, n. 16, fol. 3v (ed. Frankfurt, 1578); and Albericus de Rosciate ad D.1.1.1, 2, n. 2 (fol. 10v).

[166] Ad *Feud.*, 2.21 (fol. 42v); and as we have seen in *Cons.*, 1.148 above, clerics are by implication *concives* of lay citizens.

[167] Baldus, *Cons.*, 3.30, fol. 10v, ed. Brescia, 1491 (= *Cons.*, 1.30, ed. Venice, 1575). Cp. id., *Cons.*, 1.227, n. 4, fol. 66v (ed. Venice, 1575). Thus statutes which might disadvantage clerics are not to be understood to include them: id., *Cons.*, 2.5, n. 1–2, fol. 2v (ed. Venice, 1575).

[168] Id. ad X.1.2.7, n. 7 (fols. 17r–17v).

[169] Id., *Cons.*, 1.243, fol. 76r, ed. Brescia, 1490 (= *Cons.*, 3.45, ed. Venice, 1575).

[170] Ad D.50.1.1, n. 11 (fol. 230v), 'Primo an civis huius civitatis qui efficitur monachus vel aliter religiosus desinat esse civis?...Per monachationem non desinit esse civis; et licet non teneatur ad munera realia vel personalia, non minus propter hoc dicitur civis...sed nunc est enim civis privilegiatus.' For a relevant general principle see id. ad D.49.15.24, n. 5 (fol. 228r), 'Iurisdictio in clericos est concessa totaliter pape; desinuntne propter hoc clerici esse cives Romani? Certe non, quod apparet, quia retinent ius succedendi [C.1.3.54].'

constitute one republic...although they are exempt from the burdens of laymen; but this does not make them any the less part of the people or less able to enjoy the benefits of statutes, because many other laymen have exemptions and privileges, and nonetheless enjoy such benefits, because their privilege should not be harmful to them.[171]

Clearly, if a cleric is understood as a privileged citizen, the difficulties involved in treating the clergy under *ius publicum* begin to recede. Indeed, Albericus himself had already been willing to entertain the opinion that the privileged position of the clergy did not clash with their status under *ius publicum*,[172] although in context his view is only a line of argument and contradicts his main theme in accordance with which he expressly denies to the clergy the capacity to use lay legislation even to their advantage.[173] As a civilian Baldus certainly accepts that the clergy in their ministry and church affairs come under *ius publicum*; this appears, as would be expected, in his commentary on D.1.1.1, 2:

Then note that public law consists of things, that is sacred things; it also consists of human acts, that is sacrifices, as below [D.1.1.2]. It also directly consists of persons, that is of priests on account of their priesthood, which is a public ministry, and of magistrates on account of their public office...The priest who presides over souls, and the magistrate who presides over trials, were not instituted on account of particular individuals but of unspecified people and cases, and as a result, whoever is to be the person exercising priesthood or magistracy is of no concern, but the *respublica* takes heed that it should be ruled rightly. And take note here concerning public law. But I ask on the contrary about injury: that is, which would be called a public one? I reply, that which happens to all for equal reason...Again, because the law shall have deemed it to be public...on account of the office of the public person, because it is inflicted on a magistrate or priest who represents the *respublica*.[174]

On the face of it this passage can appear as a rather traditional explanation bound closely to the text, yet its argument conforms with Baldus' conception of clergy as privileged citizens. The point however is that the *respublica* consists of both clergy and laity with the *ius publicum* covering the public jurisdictional office of lay magistrates and the public spiritual ministry of priests: indeed, elsewhere Baldus considers the bishop of a city to have a civil or political role meriting

171 Ad D.1.1.9, n. 8 (fol. 8v).
172 Ad D.3.4.1, n. 6–7 (fol. 228v): full text in Canning, 'Ideas of the state', p. 21, n. 71.
173 Ad D.1.3.32, n. 138 (fol. 43v).
174 Fol. 5r. Cp. id. ad C.1.3.10 (fol. 28v), 'Item no. quod quando offenditur ecclesia vel clericus est publicum crimen.'

a similar juxtaposition with that of its *podestà*.[175] The public status and function of the clergy within the *respublica* mean therefore that the *respublica* is concerned that the clergy should be effective, and that the clergy, because their function is a public one, in their own field represent the *respublica*. The crucial question, however, is this: given the position of clergy as privileged citizens, in what does this *ius publicum* consist? It can neither be composed of the city's own secular legislation nor can it imply the subordination of the clergy to lay authority. Only one answer is possible: it consists of the relevant parts of canon law and the imperial decrees accepted by jurists as applying to the clergy. Thus the clergy are public ministers of the *respublica*, but because of their privileges are exempted from the control of the lay magistrates of that *respublica*. There exist, therefore, two parallel forms of public authority within the same *respublica*, a situation which clearly weakens the power of the secular authorities because the clergy are not subject to them on the basis of privileges which derive from legitimising sources outside the city itself. The parallel relationship of these two jurisdictions has become apparent already, but the crucial point that now emerges is that these are not two totally separate jurisdictional communities inhabiting the same territory, a divisive arrangement, but rather that these two communities are brought into a unity insofar as they together comprise the *respublica* which is itself one territorial and political community composed of both clergy and laity who nevertheless both enjoy different jurisdictional statuses: there is in short no simple division between citizens and clergy since the clergy are privileged citizens. Indeed, in the continuation of his commentary on D.1.1.1, 2 Baldus treats the bishop of Perugia's court as essentially a territorially Perugian court – the ecclesiastical one: 'Further note the argument that priests are part of the *respublica* and belong to the city's territory, as Johannes Andreae notes on [X.1.3.43] in his *Novella*, and this is relevant to the statute that no one may take anyone to court outside Perugia, with the result that it does not include those taking someone to the bishop's court; for this also is said to be a Perugian one, just as the church is said to be Perugian [X.2.12.3].' Furthermore, the fraternal relationship between a city's secular and ecclesiastical courts

---

[175] Ad C.7.53.5 (fol. 236r), 'Tertio modo potest considerari [i.e. homo] prout est quoddam corpus civile seu politicum sicut est episcopus civitatis et potestas, et hoc si consideretur in preeminentia'; but see below, pp. 159–61, for the crucial importance of the whole section from which this passage is extracted. Cp. id. ad C.3.11.3 (fol. 156v), 'Constitutio episcopi est ius pretorium cum episcopus sit de maioribus magistratibus, quod apparet quia habet merum et mixtum imperium, unde est preses sue civitatis et dyocesis, ut [D.1.18.6, 8].'

is illustrated by the common juristic opinion (accepted by Baldus) that the bishop of a city cannot dispense justice to someone already outlawed by the secular authorities of that city.[176] Clearly, Baldus' treatment of the relationship between clergy and laity in a city involves a mixture of territorial and personal conceptions of law: the jurisdiction of both secular and ecclesiastical authorities spreads throughout the city's territory, but different persons, according to their lay or clerical status, have different relationships to both.

In sum Baldus' moderate view combining clerical membership of the civil community with a retention of clerical privileges and the whole apparatus of ecclesiastical jurisdiction constitutes a *via media* between an extreme hierocratic position involving a complete separation between clergy and laity, and a Marsilian interpretation whereby the clergy are as men simply citizens subject to secular authority and as priests no more than ministers with a purely spiritual function, with ecclesiastical jurisdiction and privileges having no legal reality.[177] Two major conclusions ensue: for Baldus the civil community is a universal society including both clergy and laity; but since the coexistence of secular and ecclesiastical jurisdiction within the public domain limits the power of the city's secular legislative, judicial and governmental authorities, there is no one *locus* of sovereign power within the city. Thus although the city composed of its lay and clerical citizens possesses external sovereignty, there is no one authority within it enjoying internal sovereignty over all its members. This medieval pluralist view is in sharp contrast with that of Marsilius who maintains that, if the clergy are not subject to the internal secular sovereign, there would result a plurality of governments leading to the dissolution of the polity.[178] Clearly Baldus' views on the location of authority within a civil community are far from a more modern conception of internal sovereignty which Marsilius approaches. What Baldus and Marsilius have in common is that they do not consider religion to be a purely private matter; but while Baldus for this reason accepts that the priestly ministry and ecclesiastical matters come under the *ius publicum*, he does not approach Marsilius' interpretation whereby the whole of a city's people, clergy and laity, determine public ecclesiastical matters because they are a concern for the whole community.[179] Baldus does indeed

---

[176] Baldus ad D.3.1.9 (Add.), fol. 145v, where he adds, 'Item si statutum dicit quod non solvens collectam non audiatur, iste debet repelli tam in curia seculari quam in curia episcopi, si tamen est persona subiecta.'

[177] See Marsilius, *Def. pac.*, 2.5.10 (p. 197), and 2.8.7 (p. 226).

[178] *Def. pac.*, 2.8.9 (p. 230). Cp. ibid. (pp. 227–8).

[179] See for instance, *Def. pac.*, 2.17.14 (pp. 368–70).

admit that ecclesiastical issues involve the whole *respublica*, but he retains the canonical view that only clerics have control over them. There is no evidence that Baldus knew the works of Marsilius; nevertheless the comparison is instructive for illustrating the range of possibilities in fourteenth-century thought. One reason for the difference of approach between the two is that Marsilius, because he is consciously writing political theory, is free to speculate on the position of the clergy, whereas Baldus, because he is producing primarily juristic works, has to remain within the civilian and canonist tradition and fashion a jurisprudence reflecting the contemporary legal position of the clergy who indeed in Italy were in civil communities but jurisdictionally not entirely of them.

There is, however, a post-script to Baldus' treatment: towards the end of his life he gave approval to Giangaleazzo Visconti's partial extension of secular control over the clergy in his state, and accepted that prince's legislation in favour of his clerical subjects. This appears in *Cons.*, 1.442, ed. Brescia, 1490 (= *Cons.*, 3.241, ed. Venice, 1575) where he is discussing two *capitula* of Giangaleazzo, the first of which refers to his 'subjects of both parts, the clerical as well as the lay,' and is favourable to all his subjects, while the second refers solely to his 'subjects':

Now the question is whether that *capitulum*, which does not mention clerics, has to restrict the first one, which does mention clerics. And briefly it must be said that whatever the prince ordains in favour of clerics or churches is never understood to have been revoked by any other princely decree, unless it mentions clerics by name, for which the text is [C.1.2.12]. And thus the first *capitulum* composed about clerics is to be observed. It is also relevant that the [words] of the said most serene prince call even clerics subjects in this matter which concerns protection [*Decr. Grat.*, D.10.7].[180]

The clear implication is that the clergy are members of the civil community ruled by Giangaleazzo; and this is precisely what Baldus goes on to say: 'Again clerics are also part of the city, and indeed its most honourable component, and are not if at all distinct from the corporate body [of the city], because their honour is increased [D.35.1.33, 1].' It is possible, but by no means certain, that Baldus feels able to adopt this attitude to Giangaleazzo's legislation, because he rules, as we shall see, *vice principis* (in the emperor's place), and therefore may imitate the imperial function of legislating for the church (hence the

---

[180] Fol. 134v.

reference to C.1.2.12).[181] It is notable, however, that Baldus makes no mention of papal approval of such legislation, and thus ignores here Innocent III's prohibition against independent lay legislation in favour of the clergy. Baldus accepts that clergy are in this case subjects of the lay ruler; but the extension of lay jurisdiction over the clergy is limited precisely because he is concerned here only with legislation favourable to the clergy. In any case this legislation may not have been unwelcome to the clergy of Giangaleazzo's state, because, as Luigi Prosdocimi has shown, Giangaleazzo's decrees developed earlier and far less extensive Viscontean measures which had been undertaken in response to requests from the clergy of Milan to enjoy certain legal advantages as subjects of the state rather than remain in the category of non-subjects.[182] Admittedly these remarks by Baldus apply to a *signoria*; but the principles involved have general relevance to the status of clergy in cities.

Finally, although Baldus' general position is that ecclesiastical jurisdiction being autonomous within a civil community exists in parallel with secular jurisdiction, he does not consider the status of both to be equal. In attributing a certain superiority to ecclesiastical jurisdiction he is simply following the juristic tradition. Thus he says of the fraternal relationship between the two: 'And note that the secular and ecclesiastical powers should give each other mutual aid, because they fraternise, although in this fraternal relationship the church is greater and freer, as in Auth., "De non alienandis ecclesiasticis rebus" [Coll., 2.1 = Nov., 7].'[183] Indeed the bishop's jurisdiction is superior to that of the *podestà*: 'In the self-same city the principal court is the one beneath which the others are. Therefore ... the bishop's court is greater than that of the *podestà*, because the *podestà* is sometimes beneath the bishop and not the contrary, as [D.3.1.9] notes.'[184] Thus the limitations on the scope of secular jurisdiction are reinforced, although Baldus is

---

[181] See below, p. 221, for Giangaleazzo's imperial vicariate. It can be speculated that Baldus considers that Giangaleazzo can so act, because as imperial vicar he legislates directly in the emperor's place, whereas a sovereign city, being *vice principis* solely by juristic construction (in the sense already noted), cannot do so, because it has no direct delegation of authority to this effect. This view would clearly accord with the conception of a hierarchy of sovereignty. According to Baldus' report, the first *capitulum* refers to Giangaleazzo as 'imperialis vicarius generalis', and there is no reference in either *capitulum* or in the body of the *consilium* to his dukedom.

[182] *Diritto ecclesiastico*. pp. 28–9 and 288–96.

[183] Ad X.2.28.7, n. 4 (fol. 349r).

[184] Id. ad C.6.33.3 (fol. 96r). Cp. id. ad D.3.1.9 (fol. 145v); and id. ad D.3.1.9 (Add.), fol. 145v, 'Episcopus in his que pertinent ad suum officium potest inhibere potestati tanquam inferiori et eum excommunicare.'

very careful to respect the autonomy of lay jurisdiction within its own field: 'Just as laymen cannot remove clerical liberty, neither can clerics remove the liberty of laymen and their jurisdiction over their lay subjects.'[185]

Two questions illustrate this superiority of ecclesiastical jurisdiction. Firstly, if a case has both a spiritual and a secular aspect then a lay judge cannot interfere in it because of his incompetence in spiritual matters; the bishop must hear it even if the case is primarily temporal because of the hierarchical relationship between spiritual and temporal cases. In taking this position Baldus follows canon law and rejects the complaint of Cynus that the canonists are thereby seeking to infringe secular jurisdiction:

According to canon law a spiritual case impinging upon a civil one is not heard by a civil, that is a secular judge; but on the contrary, if a case for a civil court impinges upon a spiritual case, it belongs to the spiritual judge, that is to the bishop, as in [X.4.20.3]. But according to Cynus this is what the canonists say, because they strive to annex jurisdiction to themselves and to make it all their own out of ambitious desire for jurisdiction. But he is wrong. For we must consider that there are some cases belonging to two different principal jurisdictions, for example civil and secular on the one hand, and ecclesiastical and spiritual on the other; then a secular judge could not hear them even if he were the emperor, because such jurisdiction has been kept away from him by divine law, and he therefore has no capacity for this jurisdiction through any human law or reason, as in the said [X.2.10.3]. It does not matter that a bishop on the contrary hears a temporal case impinging on a spiritual or ecclesiastical one: for this is so because the latter cases are worthier and thus attract the less worthy to themselves according to the dictates of natural reason.[186]

Thus spiritual jurisdiction is distinct from secular and superior to it: lay judges are competent in their own field so long as no ecclesiastical interest is involved. Secondly, although the bishop may forbid the *podestà* to interfere in ecclesiastical cases,[187] the bishop in contrast may intervene in secular cases if a question of flagrant injustice, and therefore sin, is involved: that is to say, the episcopal court is a court of appeal against unjust lay statutes or judges: 'On account of the alleged injustice of a statute recourse is had to an ecclesiastical court...It is agreed therefore that by reason of injustice and sin, which cannot be hidden

---

[185] *Cons.*, 4.496, n. 3, 116r (ed. Venice, 1575).
[186] Ad C.3.1.3 (fol. 145r). For Cynus' complaint see his commentary, ibid., n. 1 (fol. 128r), where he also maintains that canonists make what laws they like.
[187] Baldus ad X.2.1.Rubr., n. 7 (fol. 175v).

by any subterfuge, an approach is made to the church to aid laymen,
but this would not be the case if it were not a sin properly speaking or
could not be proved to be such.'[188] This is, of course, a straightforward
acceptance of the position according to canon law,[189] and had long been
an established view in civilian jurisprudence.[190] In the continuation of
this passage Baldus justifies the episcopal intervention through well-tried
arguments for the superiority of ecclesiastical over secular jurisdiction:

Concerning the courts of the bishop and the *podestà* it is agreed that they are
distinct by virtue of the principal distinction which exists between the empire
and the church of which they are members. The sun however is superior to
the moon...The one however should not trespass on the office of the other,
except to the extent that the sacred canons should have the same validity as
civil law, as in Auth. 'Quomodo oporteat episcopos', § ii [Coll., 1.6, 2 = Nov.,
6, 2], indeed, not only have the same but even more validity, because the civil
law does not disdain to imitate the sacred canons, as in Auth. 'Vt clerici apud
proprios episcopos' [Coll., 6.11 = Nov., 83].

Nevertheless Baldus' fundamental respect for the distinct role of secular
jurisdiction is also clearly present here; and it is this respect which leads
him elsewhere to be very circumspect in applying the principle of
reason of sin to justify recourse to ecclesiastical courts.[191] He is well
aware that the principle is of infinite extension because it is up to the
clergy to determine what is sin: he must have thought there was some
substance in Cynus' well-known fears on this point.[192] Normally the
fundamentally distinct spheres of secular and ecclesiastical jurisdiction
remain in force except that in one extreme case the inherent superiority
of spiritual jurisdiction is again shown: if secular jurisdiction simply

[188] Id., *Cons.*, 2.310, fols. 83r–83v, ed. Brescia, 1490 (= *Cons.*, 5.184, ed. Venice, 1575).
Cf. id. ad D.46.8.25, 1 (fol. 46r).
[189] See X.2.1.10, 11 and 13.
[190] See for instance Petrus de Bellapertica, *Tractatus de feudis*, ad v. 'Quis sit iudex in causa
feudi' (fols. 179r–179v) for the related case of appeal to an ecclesiastical court on the
grounds of denial of justice in a lay court.
[191] Ad Auth., 'Ad hec' (ad C.4.32.16), fol. 228v, 'Generaliter quero nunquid quelibet causa
ratione peccati pertineat ad forum ecclesiasticum. Et videtur quod non nisi cause
speciales ecclesiastice sint, et nisi in quibusdam aliis casibus expressis in iure, ut
[X.2.2.8]...Si indistincte ratione peccati posset ad ecclesiam recurri sequeretur quod
ecclesia posset absorbere totum iudicium seculare quod est falsum, ut in [X.1.6.34].'
Cf. id. ad *Feud.*, 2.26 (fol. 49r), 'Concludo quod recursus ad ecclesiam nunquam habet
locum nisi quando iuris civilis observantia habet in se peccatum de iure naturali et non
in penarum executionibus vel odiosis [D.4.4.37; D12.6.19]. Item iste recursus nunquam
habet locum si per diffinitivam iudex secularis decidat negocium, ut in [Sext., 2.12.2],
nisi esset causa ecclesiastica.'
[192] See Cynus ad Auth., 'Clericus' (ad C.1.3.33), n. 1–2 (fol. 18v), 'Ecclesia sibi usurpavit
ratione peccati totam iurisdictionem.' Cf. Gierke, *Genossenschaftsrecht*, III, 354, n. 2.

does not exist in a territory, ecclesiastical authority may fill the vacuum;[193] but no jurist could suggest the reverse, if it were ecclesiastical jurisdiction that was lacking.

Furthermore Baldus follows the civilian and canonist tradition in maintaining that ecclesiastical courts also have a direct and dominating effect on the temporal sphere in cases of heresy and excommunication, clearly imposing thereby severe limitations on secular jurisdiction. The secular judge does not have a free hand in matters of heresy – he must execute the decisions of the bishop who in this matter is his superior: 'When however a bishop hands a heretic over to a secular judge, the secular judge is bound to stand by the actions of the bishop, because this handing over is as from a superior to an inferior. The inferior, therefore, only has to carry out the sentence not investigate the crime, as Bartolus says on this matter...and Jacobus Butrigarius on this law.'[194] It is the church which decides who is heretical and imposes its decision. Likewise the ecclesiastical penalty of excommunication has a debilitating effect in secular matters, because it can strike at the very heart of temporal jurisdiction: excommunicates cannot make statutes, and the sentence of a publicly excommunicate judge is invalid.[195]

There is in addition a whole range of secular disabilities incurred by an excommunicate.[196] The point is that secular authorities do not control the effects of excommunication in the secular field: for Baldus the superiority of the ecclesiastical judge is manifest in that such a penalty imposed by that judge can radically impede (and indeed prevent) the exercise of secular jurisdiction and affect secular legal relationships. If secular authorities were to possess true internal sovereignty, then either excommunication must be considered as being a purely private and internal church matter, or if it remained a public concern the secular government (or the *populus* as a whole in a city-republic) would have to control it. Marsilius had, of course, seen

---

[193] Baldus ad X.1.5.4, n. 26 (fol. 75r), where he concludes, 'Nec est hoc irrationabile, quia iurisdictio temporalis sumpsit originem ab ecclesiastica, et ei ab origine iurisdictionum fuit associata, ut no. Innocentius in [X.2.2.10].' This of course is not Baldus' normal view about the origins of secular and spiritual jurisdiction (for which see above, pp. 24–41), and the relationship between them: it is rather an argument to support the point he is making. Cp. Innocent IV ad X.2.2.10, n. 3 (fol. 77r), 'Et tempore Noe cepit deus creaturas suas regere per ministros quorum primus fuit Noe, de quo quod fuerit rector populi ex eo apparet quod sibi dominus gubernationem arche per quam ecclesia significatur commisit.'

[194] Baldus ad Auth., 'Clericus quoque' (ad C.1.3.32), fol. 37r. See also id. ad D.2.1.12 (fol. 67v).

[195] Id. ad D.1.3.32 (fol. 17v); and id. ad X.2.27.24, n. 1 (fol. 344v). Cp. Bartolus ad D.1.1.9, n. 13 (fol. 10r).

[196] See Baldus ad C.1.18.1 (fol. 56r).

this threat to the power of secular government, and had placed the sentence of excommunication in the hands of a judge appointed by the people, precisely because it was a matter entailing such public effects.[197] Admittedly Baldus' remarks exist at the level of legal theory without reference to the partial loss of effectiveness which excommunication had suffered as a penalty in contemporary Italy; but the point remains that according to Baldus there is no secular redress against excommunication, which theoretically at least opens up the possibility of immense clerical inroads into secular affairs.

The Roman law, guilds and Guelph and Ghibelline parties

On the level of secular jurisdiction the picture is completely different: overall, those jurisdictions and bodies of law which could possibly compete with that of the city do not in practice infringe the internal sovereignty of the city as expressed through its governmental, legislative and judicial institutions. Within its territory the city's courts are supreme, applying city-statutes and customs (in certain cases the statutes and customs of other cities), and the Roman law as *ius commune*.[198] The detailed problems concerning the treatment of foreigners and legal responsibilities and relationships undertaken by citizens abroad are essentially matters for the immensely complicated subject of private international law, to which Baldus made major contributions: it is in this area that the effect of personal statutes outside the city's territory (*extra territorium*), and the related question of which city's laws are to be applied in specific cases, belong.[199] As far as sovereign cities are concerned, their jurisdiction within their territories is not infringed by that of any other city or *signore*; the territorial limits of any city's jurisdiction reflect the plurality of sovereign powers. The possible threats to a city's internal sovereignty might rather derive from two other sources: given the overall hierarchy of sovereignty, from the application of Roman law and the connected jurisdiction of the

---

[197] See *Def. pac.*, 2.6.12 (p. 211).
[198] The jurisdiction of a city's judges is, however, territorially confined thus reflecting the territorial nature of a city's authority: the general point is contained in Baldus' treatment of the case of Padua (ad C.6.1.2, fol. 2v) – he directly applies the Roman law maxim concerning the territorial nature of a judge's jurisdiction: 'Extra territorium ius dicenti impune non paretur' (D.2.1.20).
[199] For Baldus see Meijers, *Tractatus duo*, above, p. 8, n. 32 (his important introduction there is reprinted in id., *Etudes*, IV, 132–41). For Bartolus' theory of statutes see Breschi, 'Alcune osservazioni' (especially, p. 55), where he takes issue with Calasso's view that it was Bartolus who introduced the distinction between real and personal statutes (*Medio evo del diritto*, pp. 576–7).

emperor; and from the legislation of corporations within the commune – guilds and Guelph and Ghibelline parties.

Baldus, following the contemporary civilian view of Roman law as a common law, considers that Roman law both supplements the provisions of local customs and statutes and provides a generally acceptable standard of law for their interpretation.[200] The validity of Roman law as a living law applicable in city-courts would only diminish the city's own rights of jurisdiction if it were thought of as being superior to the city's laws. For Baldus this is not the case: he holds that city-customs and statutes can revoke the provisions of Roman law in their own territory, a clear contrast with their status as regards canon law. He frequently and consistently puts forward two supporting arguments: 'For the common law is like the genus and municipal like the species; and if the municipal were to be contrary to the common law, it revokes it, both because it is later in time, and because species modifies genus.'[201] This is a terse statement of a view widely held by civilians that a special custom or statute (that is a local one) rescinds the *ius commune* on two grounds, firstly because it is special in application as opposed to the general effect of a provision of the *ius commune*, and secondly if it is made after the imperial law in question.[202] Given therefore that the Roman law was the common law of the *terrae imperii*, there clearly lie in this civilian view seeds for the development of the idea of the independence of cities from the emperor. Baldus applies this view generally to the law-making of city-*populi*; but it finds fullest expression in his theory of sovereign cities. There was, however, some dissent among contemporary Commentators on the grounds that

---

[200] See Baldus ad D.12.1.2, 3 (fol. 5r); id., *Cons.*, 5.24, fol. 8r (ed. Brescia, 1491), 'Nam extraneus a iure communi intellectus non cadit in statutis que possunt sane interpretari secundum ius commune quod est regula generalis directiva omnis actus humani, ut [C.3.41.2]'; and id., *Cons.*, 2.389, fol. 98r, ed. Brescia, 1490 (= *Cons.*, 5.95, ed. Venice, 1575).

[201] Ad D.24.3.1 (fol. 2v). Similar passages in Baldus' works are plentiful: see for example ad C.5.9.6 (fol. 359v); id. ad C.9.1.ꞙ1 (fol. 347v). At times Baldus presents the *ius commune* as a collection of mutable human enactments, which can therefore be revoked by local custom and statute, e.g. ad Inst., 1.2, 1, n. 19 (fol. 3v): 'Aut est [i.e. statutum] contra ius civile, et tunc potest, quia ius civile mutabile est.' Elsewhere, however, Baldus does admit that there are also immutable elements in the *ius commune*: 'Considera: aut ius commune est ius necessarium ita quod non posset tolli per ius municipale in loco municipii...aut continet ius voluntarium et derogabile per statutum...Conclude ergo quod aut statutum potest derogare iuri communi et est statutum, aut non et tunc non est statutum...Tunc autem ius commune est ius necessarium quando est immutabile, sed si mere positivum, tunc bene potest mutari' (ad C.7.9.1, fol. 181r).

[202] See for instance Odofredus ad D.1.3.32, n. 9 (fol. 15v); Jacobus de Arena ad C.8.52.2, n. 12 (fol. 251v–252r); and Bartolus ad C.8.52.2, n. 45 (fol. 117r).

such revocation would infringe the authority of the emperor, the cities' superior:[203] needless to say, Baldus does not entertain this view. For according to him the universal validity of Roman law remains undiminished by a city's revocation of part of it: its application is merely suspended in that territory, as he explains in the case of custom,

I say that local custom prevails there over the usage, that is the observance of Roman law; I do not however say that it would fundamentally eradicate the Roman law from that place, for these are two different things. For if it were completely to eradicate the Roman law from that place, and then, let us suppose, a statute were made annulling the custom, that place would be left without any law [D.1.2.2, 1]. But because the Roman law has not been abolished, but only the effect of that law, when the custom has been annulled we remain within the common law, and this matter reverts to its natural state, because the law was not completely destroyed, only hidden.[204]

At the level of sovereignty this is an aspect of the way in which the *populus* replaces the emperor in its territory without thereby destroying the universality of the empire and of the imperial dignity.

Indeed, the validity of imperial jurisdiction is crucial to Baldus' view of the world. The above passages concern the revocation of the *ius civile* as it existed. What however would be the case, if an emperor were directly to revoke a custom by a new imperial law? Then, according to Baldus, the custom would cease to have any effect:

There is a third objection: it seems that a custom does not revoke a law but is revoked by a law, because imperial constitutions should prevail everywhere [D.47.12.3, 5]. Solution: either the custom has been introduced after the law, and then the custom prevails, as here, or to the contrary the constitution has been made after the custom, and then, in this opposite case, the custom is revoked by the constitution. Fourthly, there is an objection to this solution: that a special custom is not revoked by a subsequent general law, as in [*Sext.*, 1.2.1]. Solution: either there is agreement about the legislator's intention, namely that he wishes to revoke the custom, and then one stands by the law

---

[203] For this reason Albericus de Rosciate (ad D.47.22.4, n. 1, fol. 159v), and Raynerius de Forlì (*Rep.*, ad D.1.1.9, n. 4–5, fol. 17r) denounce as error the common juristic opinion and deny the validity of such revocation. Such a hierarchical argument is not accepted by Jacobus Butrigarius ad C.8.52.3 (fol. 94r), 'Item op. quod consuetudo non vincat legem, ut [D.1.3.14]. Solutio: dicunt quidam quod consuetudo sine ratione non corrigit legem, sed si est rationabilis sic, ut hic. Sed quomodo hoc quia etiam legem duram et sine ratione servamus, ut [D.40.9.12]; ergo idem debet esse in consuetudine cum sit paris effectus quia procedunt a pari potentia, quia a consensu populi vel principis, ut [D.1.3.32].' The civilians' discussions of customs and statutes *secundum, praeter et contra legem* are lengthy and complicated: see for instance Brie, *Gewohnheitsrecht*, pp. 118–25, and 156–60; and Cortese, *Norma giuridica*, II, 115–38.

[204] Ad D.1.3.32 (fol. 16v).

as by a superior; or the opposite is agreed, and then one stands by the custom in its locality; or there is doubt, and then there are two possibilities. One is that what the custom permits, the new constitution deems to be an offence or against the public good and penalises it; in this case the law prevails, for where the law believes there is an offence, a custom could not come newly into being, nor therefore last for the future, as in the said [D.47.12.3, 5], and add what is noted in [*Clem.*, 1.3.7]. The second is that the law does not judge what has been introduced by an earlier custom to be an offence; in this case the custom of a specific place is not revoked by a general law, because a species is always exempt from its genus, and because the emperor is not believed to will what he does not know, for will is the act of a knowing intellect, and therefore no one is said to will what he has not thought in his mind, as below [D.33.10.7].[205]

Baldus thus clearly sets out the conditions under which a subsequent imperial *lex* revokes a custom: either it must be the particular intention of the legislator, the *princeps*, to revoke that custom, or the subsequent imperial constitution makes penal that for which the custom provides.[206] Otherwise the subsequent *lex generalis* does not revoke the custom. It is noteworthy that Baldus interprets the question of the emperor's knowledge in ways favourable to the people: thus here, where prohibition of a custom is involved, direct knowledge and express will on the emperor's part are required (so long as a new penalty is not at issue), whereas in a people's prescription of the emperor's sovereign rights his knowledge (and thus his permission) can either be express or assumed.[207] This passage is clearly a general statement in accordance with the *communis opinio* of the Commentators.[208] How does this view fit in with Baldus' conception of cities sovereign within their territories? The answer is to be found in his theory of the hierarchy of sovereignty. Just as the gap in imperial jurisdiction is closed up if the emperor is physically present in a city's territory with the result that any statutes it may make at that time have to be confirmed by him to be valid, similarly in theory the emperor can directly will the revocation of a people's customs. But in practice such a power of revocation is purely notional because, as we have seen, the sovereignty of city-*populi* in Italy is for Baldus the result of precisely the emperor's absence, impotence and negligence.

[205] Ibid.
[206] A custom leading to immorality and crime is also invalid (Baldus, *Cons.*, 5.349, n. 3, fol. 87v, ed. Venice, 1575).
[207] See above, p. 118.
[208] Cp. Bartolus, *Rep.* ad D.1.3.32, n. 5 (fols. 18v–19r); and Lucas de Penna ad C.10.28.1, n. 10 (p. 123).

Baldus' treatment of the revocation of Roman law is an aspect of his profound realisation of the power of popular consent to break through the restrictions of the *ius commune* to establish new laws in the form of custom or statute. Just how acutely he appreciates the implications of consent, is shown most clearly in his discussion of *consuetudines contra legem* made in error as regards the content of the particular *lex* in question. Whereas the *communis opinio* among the Commentators is that such a custom is invalid,[209] Baldus maintains that the question of such an error is made irrelevant, because the essential ingredient of the people's consent is in operation here:

Others say that either the custom was introduced against the law with certain knowledge or in error as to the content of the law... My reply to your remarks about error is that it is not true that consent disappears in this case, for error in cause or reason does not make consent absent or lacking... Note from this that, although error prevents the extension of jurisdiction by an individual, it is otherwise, however, in the case of such extension of jurisdiction by a corporation or people, for by such acts there is made custom which has a capacity suited to creating new jurisdiction.[210]

According to Baldus the jurisdiction of guilds and political parties does not undermine the internal sovereignty of the city because these are corporations subordinate in a hierarchical relationship to the city-authorities. Thus although guilds have their own judges and officers they and their members are subject to their jurisdictional superior, the *podestà*: 'Note that approved guilds can have their own judges and officers... Further note that guilds and guild-members, although they have their own judges, can nevertheless be brought before the *podestà*, and that the *podestà* is called the superior not only of the guilds but also of the guild-members and their officers too.'[211] The jurisdiction of guilds is autonomous within strictly defined limits. Thus because their statutes are essentially private law, any of their provisions contrary to the laws of the city apply only to guild-members, their heirs and professional matters concerning the activities of the guild, and cannot harm non-members:

The question here is whether guilds, for example the wool merchants, can make amongst themselves special statutes contrary to the general statutes of

[209] See Brie, *Gewohnheitsrecht*, pp. 152–4. Cf. Bartolus ad C.8.52.2, n. 45 (fol. 117r).
[210] Ad C.8.52.2 (fol. 327r). For a possible source for this attitude see Jacobus Butrigarius ad D.1.14.3, n. 16–17 (p. 38), 'Communis error presupponit veritatem, nam populus errando etiam disponit in eo, in quo errat, ut [D.33.10.3 & 7]; nam communis error pro consensu habetur, et id, quod est in errore omnium, habetur pro vero.'
[211] Baldus ad C.3.13.7 (fol. 158r).

that city. And it seems that they can, for in that the guild is approved it is able to make statutes among its sworn members [C.4.18.2]...Solution: amongst themselves they can have their own statutes which differ from the general law and which have been made concerning the affairs of that guild or profession, but not about other things, for example inheritances...These statutes however do not harm anyone but themselves and their heirs, for such statutes are called conventions, as below [D.1.3.25], and do not therefore harm others.[212]

On the subject of Guelph and Ghibelline factions within the city Baldus does not have much to say, unlike Bartolus who wrote a tract, *De Guelphis et Gebellinis*.[213] Baldus clearly has a poor opinion of adherence to Guelph or Ghibelline parties, seeing the origin of it in passion rather than reason: 'Guelph and Ghibelline are passions and attachments of the heart like love and hate, and thus the truth of the matter is that they are not those innate passions which, speaking rationally, derive from principles of reason.'[214] These factions, being in general subordinate to the city-community as a whole, are subject to superior authority (in a city this would typically be that of the *podestà*), and thus their statutes can be annulled when they are harmful to others, most notably when they discriminate against the opposing party out of hatred: 'And note that bad local statutes are to be condemned by the superior ([D.50.9.4] is relevant here), and especially when they smack of monopoly or illicit actions, as sometimes happens in the statutes of Guelphs against Ghibellines and the other way round; for what derives from a fount of irrational hatred is to be extirpated, because it is evil intent.'[215] Baldus does, however, face the possibility that a party may through political dominance gain control of the organs of the state, a reflection of contemporary Italian conditions. He maintains that if a party becomes the *maior pars* in the city-community, then it ceases to be a sect, and therefore loses its subordinate status with the result that it can take measures binding the whole city. Furthermore this holds true even in the theoretically conceivable case where such a party has been expelled from the territory. These views become apparent in his

---

[212] Id. ad D.1.1.9 (fol. 10r). There is of course a sense in which city-statutes are private law: although they fulfil the function of public law within the city, they can be seen as being private to the *populus* of that city (that is with reference to outsiders): see id. ad C.9.1.Rubr. (fol. 342v).

[213] For a discussion of this tract and of Bartolus' treatment of the factions within the city see Woolf, *Bartolus*, pp. 189–95; see also Quaglioni, 'Alcune osservazioni', and his critical edition in *Politica e diritto*, pp. 130–46.

[214] Ad C.9.21.1 (fol. 369r).

[215] Baldus ad X.2.19.2, n. 6 (fol. 240v). Cp. id. ad X.1.2.8, n. 11 (fol. 21r).

discussion of Raynerius of Forlì's opinion that the subjection of Todi to the Roman church by the exiled Guelph party was invalid: 'This is the very truth concerning the *respublica* unless perchance the major part of the city were expelled, because then it would make a licit corporation under the name of the majority and not that of a sect.'[216] Here Baldus also parts company with Bartolus who, being convinced of the subordination of these parties to the commune, had maintained that, when one party had been exiled, neither could act on its own for the whole city-community, but only both in concert: 'Bartolus says that if there are two parties in one city, one within (*intrinseca*), and the other without (*extrinseca*), because, for example, it has been expelled, then if these parties surrender the city separately, this is not valid. But you are to say that it is valid if it is done by the majority, as in [X.5.32.2], that is to the prejudice of those making the surrender but not of their superior.'[217] On the face of it this might appear to violate Baldus' view of the city-*populus* as essentially a territorial corporation. He is, however, concerned here with a theoretically conceivable exception to the normal situation in which the people's possession of the territory would be vital. Of its nature the exile would be temporary, and his objection in D.1.1.9 that exiles are *singuli* would not apply here,[218] because the decisions of the *maior pars* bind the city-corporation as a whole. The *maior pars* prevails, whether its members are the *intrinseci* or the *extrinseci*, because it is no longer a private corporation but a public one representing the city as a whole.

Higher norms

Where, however, there is a clear limitation on the jurisdiction of a city-*populus* is in an area of a completely different kind: the normative structure within which all human jurisdiction operates. We have already seen this in the case of the emperor; and the city-*populus* is subject to essentially the same constraints. As is to be expected, Baldus does not take a positive law view: the will of the people expressed through its consent is not the sole constitutive element of its law, because this must conform to higher norms.

There is a very large number of passages in which Baldus considers

---

[216] Ad D.3.4.1 (fol. 172v). For the capacity of the *maior pars* to act for the whole city-community see below, p. 199.

[217] Baldus ad D.30.1.32, 2 (fol. 6r). Cp. Bartolus, ibid., n. 3 (fol. 10v). Clearly if a city does have a direct superior it has no right to submit itself to another lord at the expense of its existing superior.   [218] See above, |p. 130.

the relationship between positive law and higher norms, both in general and with particular reference to city-*populi*. The content of such norms and the details of this relationship belong properly to a study of Baldus' theory of the nature of law:[219] the sole concern here is to demonstrate that for him a people's law-making is subject to these norms. His fundamental position is the traditional one among jurists: the people's laws must adhere to the general principles of these higher norms which provide no more than overall guide-lines; but in the detailed application of these general principles to specific cases, a people's customs and statutes may severely modify the general provisions which are of their nature expressed in very broad terms. Thus because of the basic principle that 'the natural law cannot be abrogated by the civil law'[220] statutes contrary to natural law are invalid,[221] although civil law can remove the particular effects of natural law.[222] Similarly in general terms a statute cannot destroy natural justice[223] nor infringe the demands of reason which, as we have seen, is embodied in natural law.[224] Likewise, Baldus treating the *ius gentium* as a general rule considers statutes against it to be invalid,[225] although he does not thereby deny that civil law (including the law of cities) can in particular cases, such as in the technicalities surrounding the making of a will, infringe the simple precepts of the *ius gentium*.[226] Furthermore customs and statutes contrary to the *ius divinum* are also invalid (those permitting usury being a case in point).[227] Indeed, any customs and statutes which lead men to sin have no legal force.[228] As we have already noticed in the case of the emperor, Baldus is influenced by the Thomist view of the connection between divine law, natural law and human positive law: thus human law is not rational if it does not conform to the will

---

[219] See Horn, *Aequitas*, and Ullmann, 'Baldus's conception of law'.

[220] 'Ius naturale tolli non potest per ius civile' (Baldus ad C.7.39.3, fol. 198r). Cp. id. ad D.12.2.Rubr. (fol. 271).

[221] See id. ad C.6.23.9 (fol. 50v).   [222] See id. ad C.7.39.4 (fol. 198v).

[223] See id. ad X.1.2.7, n. 16 (fol. 17v).

[224] Above, p. 78. See also Baldus ad D.1.3.32 (fol. 18v) for a difference between popular custom and statute in this respect: 'Si autem consuetudo videtur excedere rationem, tunc ratio videtur arctare consuetudinem...certe istud in statutis verum est; sed in consuetudinibus, si factum excedit rationem, ratio nil operatur, quia non potest infringere factum prescriptum, nam mens cadit factis, quia potentiora sunt facta quam mens [X.1.2.9].' A place is still left, of course, for legal fiction and presumption: 'Licet per ius civile non possit tolli ratio naturalis, potest tamen fingi et presumi cum ius civile ex presumptionibus sepe statuat contra veritatem quam non permittit probari' (id. ad C.6.23.9, fol. 50v).

[225] Ad Inst., 1.2, 1 (fol. 3v); id. ad D.24.3.47 (fol. 17v); and id. ad X.1.2.7, n. 3 (fol. 17r).

[226] Id. ad C.4.35.10 (fol. 295v); and id. ad D.17.1.29, 4 (Add.), fol. 111v.

[227] Id. ad D.12.1.11, 1 (fol. 12r).

[228] Id. ad D.1.3.32 (fol. 16v); and id. ad D.1.1.1, 3 (fol. 5v). Cp. above, p. 151, n. 206.

of God,[229] 'for divine law is the natural law of created nature'.[230] Nevertheless human law can modify the application of *ius divinum* in particular cases.[231] Human law cannot abolish the precepts of natural law, the *ius gentium*, and the divine law: these remain immutable as standards according to which mutable human laws are to be judged and interpreted,[232] but which in practical application may be subjected to rational distinctions according to particular circumstances. Similarly Baldus also accepts equity as a universal standard to which customs and statutes must conform, although he does admit some exception to this rule.[233] There is, however, one important exception to be made to Baldus' general scheme of a normative structure for customs and statutes. Some human positive law can be morally indifferent, in which case the authoritative will of the law-makers is its sole constitutive element: being at a mutable lower level it is not necessary that positive law should always be informed by those immutable and eternal moral or rational qualities which are the hall-mark of higher norms.[234] In this case, however, higher norms are not infringed; they simply do not apply.

Thus city-*populi* and the emperor are both in general constrained by a normative structure. According to Baldus, however, in one crucial area their capacities diverge. The emperor's power to deprive subjects of their property without cause but at will applies to him alone: city-*populi* do not enjoy a similar right over their citizens and subjects. Thus the passage quoted above from Baldus' commentary on C.1.19.7,

---

[229] Id. ad Auth., 'Ad hec' (ad C.4.32.16), fol. 288v. See above, p. 78.

[230] Id. ad C.9.1.Rubr. (fol. 342v).

[231] Id. ad X.1.2.8, n. 2 (fol. 20r).

[232] Id. ad C.9.1.Rubr. (fol. 342v), and ad Inst., 1.2, 1 (fol. 3v).

[233] Ad C.4.59.2 (fol. 325r), 'Nota iniqua statuta vel pacta non valere' (cp. id., *Cons.*, 1.218, fol. 70v, ed. Brescia, 1490 (= *Cons.*, 3.21, ed. Venice, 1575)). See Horn, *Aequitas*, pp. 80–2, and 84–6, for a discussion of the relationship between statute and custom and *aequitas* in Baldus' works. But see also Baldus, *De pace Constantie*, ad v. 'Imperialis clementie' (fols. 89r–89v), 'Quero utrum statutum iniquum teneat? Respondeo sic, si sit solemniter factum donec corrigatur per superiorem, secus si sit impossibile, ut no. in [*Sext.*, 2.15.12].' Cf. Horn (ibid., p. 81) on this passage: 'Baldus war sich bewußt, daß seine These von der Unwirksamkeit der Statuten bei Verletzung der *aequitas* sehr weit ging und weder mit der praktischen Autorität der Statuten noch mit der übrigen Lehre in Einklang stand.'

[234] Baldus ad C.6.58.14 (fol. 170r), 'Et ideo cum omne ius civile sit mutabile...sufficit quod statutum habeat aliquid motivum licet non contineat equitatem sed statuentium voluntatem et auctoritatem. Porro ubi de nullius preiudicio tractaretur omne statutum valet, sive habeat in se rationes sive non.' Similarly (in addition to n. 224 above) custom can be beyond reason: 'Dico quod ratio non est de substantia consuetudinis, nam tunc consuetudo tenet preter rationem ex sola auctoritate constituentium' (id. ad D.1.3.32, fol. 18v) – there exists, that is, an area in which rational criteria do not apply as far as custom is concerned.

where he discusses this imperial power,[235] immediately continues: 'It is otherwise with a statute of the people, because this should not contain such motivation as its cause, but rather a cause which is credible and suitable; otherwise it is not valid, as in [D.40.9.17].'[236] This means that in this respect the emperor's sovereignty is more far-reaching than that of city-*populi*, another illustration of his superior position in the hierarchy of sovereignty.

The problem remains, however, of whether this normative structure imposed an effective limitation on the cities' jurisdiction. In the case of a subordinate city the superior could of course intervene on such grounds. If, however, the city recognised no superior, who was there to enforce the invalidation of city-laws which infringed these higher norms? Certainly it would not be the emperor, because his impotence and absence were the precondition of such cities' sovereignty. The crucial distinction between limited and controlled power is at issue, as we have seen before, when considering the limitations on the emperor's jurisdiction.[237] Baldus does not really suggest any mechanism for enforcing the normative structure, but is simply concerned to place the operation of all jurisdiction within a moral context. Unjust and immoral customs or statutes are invalid whether they can be suppressed or not. There is however one authority to whom he does accord a universal competence to judge the morality of the exercise of power in Christendom: the pope. According to Baldus, the pope has the capacity to annul any secular legislation *ratione peccati*:

Secondly note that by reason of sin the pope can annul the laws of emperors, kings and peoples; therefore statutes permitting homicide are not valid, because he who lacks the legal power of the sword, and yet commits homicide, sins mortally. I say that a statute licensing sin is not valid, because it is impossible that to sin mortally be lawful... An objection is that the pope could not interfere in matters concerning laymen since he is an incompetent judge in their cases... Solution: he happens to be able to do so in this case by reason of sin.[238]

It is important, however, not to press this point too far. Outside the *terrae ecclesiae* the pope's jurisdiction is essentially spiritual. Any such action would be an occasional event and of its nature a spiritual one, justified according to the precise sense in which Baldus considers the pope to be at the apex of the hierarchy of sovereignty.[239] Baldus is

---

[235] See above, p. 81.
[236] Philip Decius thought Baldus' distinction worthy of notice (ad X.1.2.7, n. 98–9, fol. 26r).   [237] See above, pp. 91–2.
[238] Ad X.2.26.20, n. 1–2 (fols. 333v–334r). The case in point is prescription in bad faith.
[239] See above, pp. 43–4.

saying that the pope *can* act in such a way. He is not putting forward a hierocratic point of view, nor is he by any means suggesting that there is ordinarily any mechanism for controlling the unjust and immoral legislation of sovereign cities. Thus the normative structure does not usually provide either a practical limitation on the sovereignty of cities, or justify a continual papal intervention in the secular jurisdiction of cities in the *terrae imperii*; it does, however, according to Baldus and other jurists provide valid standards against which to weigh the validity of human positive law and where necessary find such law wanting.

III: SUMMARY

For Baldus city-*populi* exist at two levels within the fundamental hierarchy of sovereignty: those of autonomy and sovereignty. Such sovereignty is the product of *de facto* popular consent, a capability deriving from the *ius gentium*, itself a product of human reason. Furthermore this sovereignty is essentially territorial, and limited in the ways described. The *de iure* structure, whereby jurisdiction is derived from direct imperial or papal concession, remains in force side-by-side with the *de facto*. What is important is that so far Baldus' argument has been expressed solely in juristic terms. The Roman law in its public dimension provided for the late Middle Ages a rich mine for state concepts, and these were manipulated by Baldus to elaborate his theory of the sovereign city-state, which not recognising a superior replaces the emperor within its territory. It is crucial that the city-state should be treated both as a *populus*, which could then have its own *ius civile*, and as a *respublica*, which located it within the *ius publicum*: only in such a context could it be considered sovereign. Baldus' approach is essentially this-worldly being an attempt to provide a juristic account of contemporary political reality: in this he faithfully reflects both the noted this-worldly orientation of civilian jurisprudence, and also the canonist tradition of accepting developing political structures.[240] As Baldus' treatment of cities unfolds further his idea of the state becomes more articulated, and the sense in which it can truly be termed such becomes clearer. Certainly, given Baldus' notions of hierarchy of sovereignty and limited sovereignty, it cannot be a modern idea of the state, but since the idea of the state is historically fluid, we shall find that his state-concept is nonetheless a valid one. The next question to consider is the membership of such city-states; and it is here that Baldus shows his true mettle by breaking new juristic ground.

[240] See above, p. 6, and Canning, 'Ideas of the state', p. 2.

Chapter 4

MEMBERSHIP OF THE CITY-COMMUNITY: POLITICAL MAN AND CITIZENSHIP

POLITICAL MAN

In fourteenth-century terms there existed another language to describe the this-worldly and down-to-earth dimension of man's life in ordered and governed communities – the overtly political form of discourse deriving ultimately from Aristotelian conceptions made current from the mid-thirteenth century. Baldus dips into the broad stream of contemporary *scientia politica*, and uses the concept of natural man who becomes political in community. This in itself might appear thoroughly unremarkable if considered in isolation, because the idea that man is by nature a political animal was, of course, the common-coin of political theory; but Baldus' introduction of this concept into jurisprudence is revealed as a highly creative innovation when it is seen in the context of his whole *de facto* argument, and in comparison with the use which previous and contemporary jurists made of the term, 'political'.

Baldus introduces this concept of natural, political man in a passage of great importance. He has been discussing the definition of the *populus*, and continues,

You are to say, incidentally, that man can be considered in three ways. Firstly, insofar as he is in himself an individual naturally composed of soul and body, as in [D.21.2.56, 2]. Secondly, he can be considered insofar as he is an economic body, that is, the head of a family, as in [D.50.16.195, 1], like a *paterfamilias* and the abbot of a monastery. Thirdly, *he can be considered insofar as he is a civil or political body*, like the bishop of a city and the *podestà*, and this is the case if he were to be considered as being in a position of pre-eminence. But *if he is considered in congregation then natural man would be made political, and a people is created out of many men come together*, as in [D.41.3.30]. This people is sometimes girt by walls and inhabits a city, and as such is properly called political from 'polis' which is 'city'. There is another people which is rural and which lives in fortified places and villages, and there has its domicile, as above [C.6.23.31].[1]

---

[1] Ad C.7.53.5 (fol. 236r).

A wealth of meaning is compressed into this passage. The fundamental point is that Baldus locates the political dimension of human life in a specifically natural and this-worldly context, and adopts an essentially Aristotelian division of the aspects of the life of natural man. The different aspects of life can be considered according to different categories, and, as he says elsewhere, all are the concern of legal science: 'The final cause [of our art] is three-fold, namely within man, in relation to man, and in relation to the *respublica*. Within man, so that he may be good; and this belongs to ethics. In relation to man, so that someone may rule his family well; and this belongs to economics. In relation to the *respublica*, so that it may be ruled healthily; and this belongs to politics, as above in [D.Const., "Omnem", 11].'[2] Man enters this political dimension in a certain kind of community: generally expressed, this would be at the level of a *respublica*, more specifically in Italian conditions it would be a city. Baldus, therefore, illustrates the way in which the Aristotelian conception of political life as life in the πόλις was directly applicable to fourteenth-century Italian city-states. Indeed, the exclusion of country-dwellers (an aspect of the *contado*'s subjection to the city itself) mirrors Aristotle's exclusion of farmers from political life.[3] The political dimension is specifically concerned with the government of such communities, which is the reason why Baldus also follows Aristotle in considering that the concept of political man can be more narrowly applied to man as ruler, thus introducing the notion of grades of citizen (the ruler is considered 'in preeminentia').[4] In the urban context of north and central Italy such

---

[2] Ad D.1.1.Rubr. (fol. 4r). Cp. also Baldus ad Auth., 'Habita' (ad C.4.13.5), fols. 230r–230v.

[3] See, for instance, *Pol.* 1268a and 1328b–1329b.

[4] Cp. Aquinas ad *Eth. Nic.*, 3.8.474, 'Nec etiam politicus, id est rector civitatis.' For the connection between politics and government see also Baldus, *Cons.*, 4.482, ed. Brescia, 1490, fol. 102r (= *Cons.*, 5.537, ed. Venice, 1575), where he discusses Giangaleazzo Visconti's grant of the city of Asti with all its possessions: 'Modo sequitur in littera contractus tertia particula "que tenet et possidet"...prout autem respicit politicum regimen intelligitur "que tenet et possidet", id est que regit et gubernat seu nomine suo gubernentur.' For an ecclesiastical application see id. ad D.1.1.Rubr. (fol. 4r): 'Et nota quod regimen abbatis in monachos est yconomicum, sed regimen episcopi in subditos est politicum.' Baldus was familiar with the category of the *virtutes politicae* deriving ultimately from Plotinus *via* Macrobius' commentary on Cicero's *Somnium Scipionis*: 'Hic diffinitur iustitia prout est virtus politica, dicta a polis, quod est civitas, et icos, quod est scientia, quasi scientia de regimine civitatis. Et ponitur in diffinitione constans et perpetua ad denotandum, quod ita est impossibile civitates sine iustitia regi, que est virtus politica, sicut est impossibile montes de uno loco ad alium transferri. Et quod iste intellectus est verus, probatur, quia virtutes politice sunt quattuor: iustitia, temperantia, fortitudo et prudentia' (ad Inst., 1.1.1, n. 2–4, ed. Venice, 1615). Baldus, ibid. n.4, appears to credit Jacobus Butrigarius with this application of the *virtutes*

political men are citizens who in congregation compose the city-*populus*.[5] This fundamentally Aristotelian categorisation of man's life according to forms of activity means that Baldus maintains that natural man by virtue of his membership of the political *populus* is imbued with political characteristics which he would lack when considered as an isolated individual.

Previous and contemporary civilians had paved the way for Baldus' use of the concept of natural, political man. Since jurisprudence as a scholastic discipline employed Aristotelian methods of argument, it can cause no surprise that the overtly Aristotelian concept of man living in a political dimension had made some appearance in the works of the early Commentators. Although the concept of the political is lacking in the *littera Bononiensis* text of the *Corpus Iuris Civilis* used by the Commentators, the entry of such overtly political concepts into the technical language of jurisprudence was facilitated by the community of terms, such as *civis*, *civitas* and *civilis*, existing between civilian jurisprudence (*scientia civilis*) and Aristotelian-style *scientia politica*. William of Moerbeke, for instance, when translating Aristotle's *Politics* was constrained in trying to render Greek concepts by the concepts and terms available to him in Latin. Apart from transliterations, like *politia* and *politicus*, William in translating such terms as πόλις, πολίτης and πολιτικός also used the only Latin terms available, namely *civitas*, *civis* and *civilis*. Thus *civis* and its associated terms came to bear Aristotelian connotations. Aquinas in his commentary on Aristotle's *Politics* exemplifies the same process: 'Since therefore this whole which is the city must be subjected to the judgment of reason, it was necessary to complement philosophy by propounding a discipline which concerns the city and which is called political, that is civil, science.'[6] Guilelmus de Cuneo in a very prominent place, his commentary on the Proem to the *Digestum vetus*, describes political man as the subject-matter of legal science:

The question is, what is the subject-matter of this science?...It says elsewhere that the subject-matter of civil justice is political man, insofar as he is fitted to the government of the *respublica*...Is political man, therefore, the subject-matter? I say here that he is, because he is principally treated in the law as a man, since all laws were made for the sake of men, as below [D.1.5.2]. I say however concerning this that the subject-matter should be ruled well,

politicae. The tradition of the *virtutes politicae* in itself had nothing to do with the Aristotelian conception of 'political', and by *virtus politica* Baldus here means simply a virtue relevant to the government of a city.
[5] See Baldus ad *Sext.*, 1.6 (fol. 3r): 'populus dicitur a polis.'
[6] *Pol.*, Proem, 5 (ed. Spiazzi), p. 1.

because man living in a civil community can be said to be the subject-matter...Again, if the civil actions of man are considered, they can be called the subject-matter; as a result, it does not seem to matter at all whether we are to say that political man, that is one living in a civil community, or human actions are called the subject-matter, see the argument below [D.34.5.19].[7]

The similarities are striking between parts of this passage and Cynus' commentary on the Proem in his manuscript *Lectura* on the *Digestum vetus*;[8] and furthermore Albericus de Rosciate in the same place in his commentary expressly utilises Guilelmus' words.[9] Both Cynus and Albericus make more explicit the reference to Aristotle contained in Guilelmus' passage. The interplay between the legal and political senses of 'civil' is manifest, and the purpose of legal science as the government of man in a political society is established for Baldus to adopt.[10] Thus the political dimension possesses a legal expression and *vice versa*. But beyond this it is not clear whether there is any deeper meaning behind

[7] Ed. Brandi, pp. 111–12. The text of Bodleian MS, Can. Misc. 472 (fol. 1v) contains considerable variations (see Appendix I). Both texts are clearly corrupt.

[8] 'Alii dicunt quod humane operationes sunt subiectum huius scientie quia de illis principaliter agitur in iure...Et intellige operationes quando bene et civiliter[...]per homines. Vnde dicit philosophus in civili iusticia est homo politicus [policitus *MS*] prout aptatur ad regimen rei publice...Sed prout [pro hut *MS*] homo civilis adaptatur ad regnum rei [dei *MS*] publice est subiectus...Quid dicemus?...Item operationes humane possunt dici subiectum inspecto homine prout operatur civiliter, unde nichil differt ponere hominem politicum [policitum *MS*] sicut ponit per hunc vel operationes humanas civiles esse subiectum scientie legalis,' ad v. 'Iustiniani' (MS. Sav.22, fol. 11v); and cp. ibid.(MS. Vat. Urb. Lat., 172, fol. 8r) for a variant text.

[9] n. 11–12 (fol. 2v): 'Sed si queratur quod sit subiectum in ista scientia, de quo principaliter tractatur, dixerunt quidam quod bonum et equum, ut infra [D.1.1.1, 1]. Alii dixerunt quod operationes humane, quia de illis in iure principaliter agitur, ut in Auth. "Hec constitutio innovat" [Coll., 8.7 = Nov., 111] in prin. Philosophus, 3. Politicorum, dicit, quod iustitie civilis est subiectum homo politicus prout aptatur ad regimen reipublice...Concedo quod homo politicus sit subiectum quia de eo principaliter tractatur in iure, ut bene regatur, cum gratia hominum omnia iura facta sunt, ut infra [D.1.5.2]...Item operationes humane possunt dici subiectum inspecto homine prout operatur civiliter; unde nihil videtur interesse utrum dicamus hominem politicum, id est viventem civiliter, esse subiectum, an operationes humanas, argu. infra [D.34.5.19].'

[10] It is significant that his statement (above, n.2) is located just after the *Proem*, and thus forms part of this practice of introducing the term 'political' towards the beginning of the commentary on the *Digest*. For a similar treatment not making use of the concept of the political see the earlier jurist, Petrus de Bellapertica ad Inst., Rubr., 'In nomine domini Iesu Christi', n. 27–8 (pp. 22–3): 'Dicunt [moderni] quod idem est in scientia nostra subiectum et in ethica...Quare dicunt quod in ethica et in ista scientia homo est subiectum, sed quod homo est pars civitatis secundum quod contrahit et delinquit probatur...Dico imo erit [?] de homine tractatur secundum quod est pars civitatis.' The community of the term 'civil' in legal and political discourse makes it difficult to determine whether Raynerius de Forlì possesses the germ of the conception of political man living in a political community: '[Homines silvestres] faciunt populum silvestrem, sicut homines civiles populum civilem' (*Rep.* ad D.1.1.9, n. 10, fol. 17v).

the concept of political man as used by Guilelmus, Cynus and Albericus. Nevertheless, the point remains that *scientia politica* and *scientia civilis*, precisely because they are understood to concentrate on man's existence in political society in this world, appear as parallel disciplines with essentially the same subject-matter. Indeed, the Commentators universally define jurisprudence as a subdivision of moral philosophy, constantly referring back to the Glossator Azo's statement in relation to the *Codex*, 'It belongs to ethics, because it deals with morals, just like all the books of legal science also do.'[11] Guilelmus, Cynus and Albericus thus perceive with even greater clarity that their study shares with political science the same Aristotelian category of human knowledge.[12] For them jurisprudence, being concerned with mundane matters, is essentially different from theology, but in no way inferior to it for that.[13]

Overtly political terms had thus entered into the language of the Commentators, and had in this sense become part of civilian discourse. For instance, Lucas de Penna, who was Baldus' contemporary but appears to have worked completely separately from him, on occasion uses these terms.[14] But there also remained hesitation about the use of Aristotelian political terms in juristic works. The prime case was Bartolus himself. He was, of course, well aware of Aristotelian political concepts, and indeed begins his tract, *De regimine civitatis*, with the Aristotelian tri-partite division of forms of government, describing the first form of government thus: 'Aristotle calls this form of government, *politia*, or political. We however call it government by the people.'[15]

[11] *Summa Codicis*, ad v. 'Incipit materia ad codicem', fol. 25r (ed. Speyer, 1482).
[12] The ground was thus prepared for Baldus' statement: 'Nota autoritatem moralis philosophi pro lege servari, et in causis allegari. Et est ratio, quia scientia nostra supponitur morali philosophie, ut supra not. in rubr. proemii. Sic in materia naturali allegatur Hippocrates et Aristoteles [D.1.5.12; et D.46.3.36]. Et per hoc redditur philosophie debitus honor' (ad X.1.2.6, n. 37, fol. 16v). See also id. ad D.1.1.1 (Additio Baldi), n.7, fol. 8r (ed. Lyon, 1585): 'Subiectum est homo, qui per scientiam acquirit politicam id est moralem qualitatem seu philosophiam per quam perfecte cognoscit, separat iustum a contrario, quia indicat quod iustum est'; and id. ad X.Proem, ad v. 'Gregorius', fol. 4r: 'Quanto bonum est communius tanto divinius. Commune bonum dicitur quod debet esse subiectum in qualibet consideratione politica et morali, ut no. [D.1.3.2].'
[13] See Guilelmus de Cuneo ad D.V., Proem, Bodleian MS, Can. Misc. 472 (fol. 1v); Cynus, ibid., fol. 11v (MS. Sav. 22); and Albericus, ibid., n.12 (fol. 2v).
[14] See Lucas ad C.11.59.7, n.8 (p. 563): 'Inter principem et rempublicam matrimonium morale contrahitur et politicum'; ibid. (p. 564): 'Moraliter et politice homines coniunguntur reipublice, que corpus est, cuius caput est princeps'; and ad C.12.43.3, n.12, p. 897 (reference to Aristotle, *Pol.*, 4).
[15] Ed. Quaglioni, *Politica e diritto*, p. 150. For Bartolus' use of Aristotle in this tract see Quaglioni, 'Alcune osservazioni', pp. 6–13.

However, in his ensuing description of Giles of Rome's views he expressly eschews Aristotelian political terms on the grounds that they are not to the taste of jurists, for whom the tract is intended, and adheres to a strictly juristic exposition (*per iura*).[16] Nor can it be an accident that in his commentaries on the *Corpus Iuris Civilis* Bartolus appears not to use the term 'political' except in that on C.12.1.1.[17]

Clearly what distinguishes Baldus' approach from that of these other jurists is that he takes the simple but crucial step of overtly treating political man as existing within a specifically natural, that is this-worldly context. Whereas their use of the term, 'political', had been essentially piecemeal, and eclectic, Baldus adopts as his own the ultimately Aristotelian view that man's political existence properly forms part of the life of man conceived as a purely natural phenomenon: that man's existence as simply a natural animal is logically prior to his life as a political one.[18] Thus Baldus reveals a philosophical grasp which is unusual amongst jurists,[19] and which, as we shall see, endows his use of the concept of political man with meaning and important implications. In point of fact the concept of man as a natural political animal was waiting to be rediscovered in the *Corpus Iuris Civilis* itself. The second part of D.1.3.2 (*l. Nam et Demosthenes*) consists of a

---

16 'Ipsius itaque opinionem ponam et eius rationes faciam; verbis autem suis vel Aristotelis non utar: illa enim iuriste quibus loquor non saperent. Vtar autem rationibus suis et ipsas per iura probabo; postea quid michi videtur describam' (ed. cit., p. 153). See also Quaglioni's remarks, 'Alcune osservazioni', pp. 7–8.

17 See Basel, 1589, ed.: 'nobilitas politica' (n. 24, p. 118); 'nobilitas est politica seu civilis prout differt nobilis a plebeio' (n. 28); and n. 69 (p. 121). He also refers to *Pol.*, 1 (nn.14 & 26) and *Pol.*, 5 (nn.14 & 57). The commentary, ibid. (ed. Turin, 1577) is not by Bartolus: it contains references to Bartolus and Baldus in the text and has the *punctum* 'Alex.' at the end. The passage from Bartolus (n. 28, above) is, however, incorporated in the text at n.61 (fol. 47r). Despite this there seems to be no good reason for doubting the authenticity of the Basel text on internal grounds. Woolf (*Bartolus*, pp. 385–7) mentions finding only two references to Aristotle's *Politics* in Bartolus' commentaries. The commentary on D.1.14.3 (ed. Turin, 1577) referring to *Pol.*, 1 is in fact by Baldus.

18 The Aristotelian conception that political life is the perfection of man's natural life appears to lie behind Baldus' telescoped meaning in his *additio* ad D.1.1.1, 3, n.1 (ed. Lyon, 1585): 'Nota quod iurisconsultus principia iuris incipit et trahit a principiis nature...et quale unumquodque est in generatione perfecta hanc dicimus esse naturam, id est politicam.' He immediately continues to indicate natural man as the subject-matter of jurisprudence: 'De natura possumus naturaliter loqui. Vno modo de natura id est de intentione nature, et hoc est minus generale. Nam et inanimata sunt perita huius iuris naturalis. Alio modo de natura, id est de naturalibus motibus anime sensitive. Tertio modo de natura, id est naturalibus motibus anime intellective. De primo modo naturalis intentionis non est sermo legistis, sed naturalibus philosophis. De secundo modo est tractandum nobis prout est applicabilis humane societati. De tertio modo principaliter per se oportet nos considerare, quia subiectum in legibus est homo.'

19 For Baldus' fame as the most philosophical of the medieval jurists see Horn, 'Baldus philosophus', pp. 104–49.

quotation from the Stoic philosopher, Chrysippus, containing these words: 'Law should be the rule of the just and the unjust and of those by nature political animals.'[20] The translation in the *littera Bononiensis*, however, obscures the original sense: 'Law is the rule of the just and the unjust and of those things which are by nature civil.'[21] Thus Accursius, for instance, writing in any case before the general reintroduction of Aristotelian political concepts, when glossing this passage cannot recognise its political import: '*Are by nature civil, that is by the genius of natural man.*'[22] Nevertheless the reference here to 'natural man' does seem a movement towards the kind of natural dimension in which political conceptions could develop. In a stroke of juristic genius Baldus exploits the community of the term, 'civil', in contemporary legal and political discourse to resurrect the natural, political man hibernating in D.1.3.2: 'Note at those words, "things natural and civil," that man is naturally a civil animal: and law should be similar to a well-composed and civil man.'[23] Baldus is following William of Moerbeke's translation of Aristotle's famous phrase,[24] and thus understands the *littera Bononiensis* text in an avowedly Aristotelian sense. Either he directly realises despite the textual obscurities that an ultimately Aristotelian meaning lies behind the Stoic philosopher's words, or the text itself suggests an Aristotelian interpretation: in either case the result is the same. The use of 'civil' in a strictly legal sense, and as a synonym for 'political' (as in his commentary on C.7.53.5) permits him here a play on words: law should be *similis* to a 'civil man', that is one existing both within a political dimension and that of *ius civile*, the enacted law of a people.[25] The suggestion is that human law exists within a political dimension as he has already stated in the context of the third and public aim of legal science. This same play on the meanings of 'civil' also appears in a complicated passage: 'But where there is a tribunal there must be some political rule which can be called civil law, that is the law for living under some kind of civil order (*sub quadam specie civilitatis*).'[26] *Civilitas* is a term which in Baldus' works

---

[20] 'δεῖ δὲ αὐτὸν [i.e. νόμον]...κανόνα τε εἶναι δικαίων καὶ ἀδίκων καὶ τῶν φύσει πολιτικῶν ζῴων.'

[21] 'Lex...regula est iustorum et iniustorum et eorum que natura civilia sunt' (fol. 8r, ed. Venice, 1498).

[22] '*Natura sunt civilia*. id est, naturalis hominis ingenio' (ibid.).

[23] 'Nota ibi, "naturalia et civilia", quod homo naturaliter est animal civile; et lex similis debet esse homini bene composito et civili' (fol. 13v).

[24] 'ὁ ἄνθρωπος φύσει πολιτικὸν ζῷον'(1253a) is translated by William as 'homo natura civile animal est' (ed. Susemihl).

[25] From the immediate context of Baldus' statement it is clear that he is not discussing a particular *lex*, but *lex* in the sense of human enacted law in general.

[26] *Feud.*, 1.8 (Additio), fol. 19v.

usually signifies citizenship; here it appears to mean something like 'civil order' with both legal and political connotations. Thus *ius civile* signifies the law according to which one lives in a civil or political order or system. In all Baldus considers that law provides a structure for the political life of natural man, a view which is essentially a creative development of the juristic commonplace (deriving from Cicero) that law is the bond of civil society.[27]

Baldus' concept of man as a civil or political animal forms part of his wider view of man as a social animal: political man in the sense of a member of a citizen-body is a particular kind of social man. Thus law itself exists not just within the political structure of individual cities but within the framework of the human need for association: 'Because man is a social animal, as in the First Book of the *Politics*, the laws of society and his own city apply to him.'[28] This reflects the late medieval view which, unlike that of Aristotle, was unwilling to identify society totally with the state: human society was seen as something wider than any particular state organisation.[29] Although Baldus gives as his source the First Book of Aristotle's *Politics*, the concept of man as a social animal is not to be found there, either in the Greek text or in William of Moerbeke's translation. The obvious source of the concept is Aquinas who added it to the definition of man as a political animal and quoted as his source *Politics*, Book I, thus putting his own gloss on Aristotle: 'Man is by nature a political and social animal, as is proved in Book One of the *Politics*.'[30] Aquinas' definition and his attribution of it to Aristotle were extremely well-known and easily accessible to Baldus. It is also perfectly possible that Baldus obtained the concept from Aquinas' commentary on Book I of the *Politics* itself. Upon this text in William of Moerbeke's translation: 'It is therefore clear from this that the city is one of those things which exist by nature, and that man is by nature a civil animal,'[31] Aquinas comments: 'Then when he says, "therefore from this," he shows that man is by nature a civil animal. Firstly, he comes to this conclusion because of the naturalness of the city. Secondly, he proves this through the activity proper to man in those words, "from which it is clear that he is a social animal etc."'[32]

[27] Cp. Baldus ad Inst., Proem, ad v. 'Quoniam', fol. 2r (ed. Pavia, 1489): 'Scientia civilis...que tante mirabilitatis existit quod ea pretermissa humane societatis nullum est vinculum, sic nec civitatis consistit vocabulum.' Cf. Cicero, *De republica*, 1.32.49.

[28] Baldus ad D.1.1.1, 1 (Additio), n.4 (ed. Venice, 1616). Cf. also id. ad X.2.1.10, n. 2, fol. 157v (ed. Venice, 1595).

[29] See Lewis, *Medieval Political Ideas*, 1, 149–50.

[30] *S.T.*, 1a 2ae, qu. 72, art. 4 (ed. J. Fearon, London, 1969). Cf. also *S.T.*, 1a 2ae, qu. 95, art. 4 (ed. T. Gilby, London, 1966).

[31] Ed. cit., p.7.   [32] *Pol.*, 1, *lectio* 1, n. 34 (ed. Spiazzi), p. 11

Again Aquinas introduces his own interpretation of the words of Aristotle. This is not to deny, however, that there were other possible sources available to Baldus for the concept of man as a social animal: Seneca, Augustine and Albert the Great for example.[33]

Baldus' conception of natural man who becomes political is fundamental to his view of man's existence in organised society: man's political nature and tendency underlie all political structures. Most important, the concept of natural, political man provides a philosophical justification for the *de facto* argument. The practical autonomy and sovereignty of cities is an expression of man's political nature: his natural political capabilities are not superseded by the imposition of the *de iure* structure and reassert themselves with the retreat of imperial power. Baldus' adoption of the ultimately Aristotelian conception of natural, political man explains *why* men retain this capability. Man, understood as a this-worldly and natural phenomenon, possesses an inbuilt urge towards political society, a tendency which exists quite apart from any divinely sanctioned structure of authority. Thus the *ius gentium*, being a product of human natural reason, in that it underwrites both the existence and the sovereignty of city-states, is an expression of man's political nature. Baldus is thus exploring that fundamental level which lies behind the *ius gentium*, and which the *ius gentium* articulates. Furthermore the Bartolist justification of city-sovereignty on the basis of the efficacy of popular consent, an argument which rested on the acceptance of legal facts, is given an ultimate philosophical foundation beyond the *ius gentium*, in that such consent is the practical expression of man's political nature. Insofar as the *de iure* structure is a product of the divine will it exists on a level quite apart from man's natural tendency towards political association and superimposed upon it, yet it also finds a place in the natural, political dimension insofar as it is derived from an original grant of authority by the people in the form of the *lex regia* or the Donation of Constantine, which, as we have seen, Baldus considers to derive its validity in one sense from that law.

In itself the adoption of the natural, political dimension does not prescribe any one form of government: it is essentially neutral since it encompasses all forms of political association and organisation, so long as these are conceived in this-worldly terms. In this it is distinct from

---

[33] See Lucas de Penna ad C.10.38.1, n. 5–6 (p. 221): 'Et homo sociale animal communi bono genitus est, dicit Seneca, lib. de clementia'; and Augustine, *De civitate dei*, 19.5 & 21. Albert the Great also attributes the term 'social' to Aristotle: *Quaestiones de animalibus*, 1, qu. 8, p. 85 (ed. Filthaut).

theocratic theories of government advocating a divinely sanctioned or appointed monarch. The natural, political dimension's very openness to all possibilities is of crucial significance in Baldus' thought: it means that the whole range of contemporary political structures can be accepted. In the context of Italian city-states specifically the whole spectrum from republican regimes (whether autonomous or sovereign) to signorial ones can be accommodated. Most important, the idea of the sovereign city-*populus* composed of citizens actively governing themselves through the exercise of their own consent receives at his hands a firm philosophical base: where such cities with such citizens exist they do so ultimately as an expression of man's political nature. The theme of active citizenship is not made necessary by the adoption of the concept of natural, political man, but it is made possible.

Baldus' natural, political man may certainly be termed a citizen because he is a *corpus civile*, and because in Italian cities (which he has in the forefront of his mind) members of the political community were by definition *cives*. It would, however, be misleading to try and understand Baldus' theory of citizenship in terms of Walter Ullmann's sharp distinction between the natural citizen who governs himself through his own consent, and the subject subordinated to a theocratic superior.[34] For Baldus the theocratic dimension only exists externally to the city, that is in the divinely sanctioned aspect of imperial or papal power within the *de iure* structure: thus, for instance, those living in the *terrae imperii* are citizens in relation to their cities but subjects of the emperor (insofar as they recognise his authority).[35] Certainly within the confines of the city Baldus is not thinking in theocratic terms: for his political man as citizen there exists in purely natural terms a wide spectrum of possible political relationships with the rulers or governing body of his community. Thus at one extreme of this range active citizenship is an expression of sovereign republicanism; whereas at the other the citizen of a signorial regime is subject to his lord. There is in Baldus' mind no contradiction in seeing a citizen as the subject of his city, its laws and its government, a reflection, although he does not mention it, of the Aristotelian theme of the citizen as both ruler and ruled.[36] There are in any case grades of citizens with varying

---

[34] Out of a host of examples see, for instance, *Individual and Society*, pp. 122–24.

[35] See *Cons.*, 3.277, fol. 85r, ed. Brescia, 1491 (= *Cons.*, 1.327, n. 10, fol. 101v, ed. Venice, 1575): 'Quidam sunt subditi imperii duplici de causa, scilicet tanquam cives de terris imperii omni feudo circumscripto, et nihilominus ratione feudi; et isti tenentur obedire imperatori salvo feudo, et iurare tanquam cives meri.'

[36] For some relevant passages see below, pp. 178–9 and p. 204, and above, p. 122. Note also the remarks on Baldus' and other jurists' treatment of *civis* as *subditus* in Riesenberg, 'Citizenship at law', pp. 339–40.

political and legal rights; and certainly at the everyday level the status of the citizen as political man is translated into the dimension of legal rights and duties. Thus while a valid distinction can be made between natural, political man and the theocratic subject on the grounds that they indicate the status of the individual within completely different systems of thought concerning human society and its government, on the other hand within the natural, political dimension the terms 'citizen' and 'subject' are both perfectly at home, whereas within the theocratic structure the *civis* can be the subject of his superior.[37] What, therefore, is important is the distinction between political man, termed either a citizen or a subject, or both, and the theocratic subject (who may also be termed a citizen), not that between a citizen and a subject without further explanation. Furthermore a crucial difference is that political man may or may not enjoy the full potentialities of active citizenship, whereas a theocratic subject never can. The content and implications of citizenship emerge in Baldus' treatment of the corporate nature, organisation and structure of government of city-communities whether under republican or signorial regimes. The details of his treatment are couched in purely juristic terms which on that level can be understood solely within their own frame of reference. The whole juristic structure of his treatment of city-communities nevertheless rests upon the philosophical foundation of his use of natural, political man, and can only be fully understood if this is appreciated.

CREATED CITIZENSHIP

Baldus does, however, devote extensive and overt attention to citizenship as such in one particular area: the problem of citizenship created by legal enactment. This was a question to which late medieval Italian civilians gave a lot of consideration: their *consilia* above all reveal that problems concerning the status of created citizens were common. Indeed, their theories concerning the legal status of the created citizen were of far more than academic interest, because in practical terms so many of the legal rights and duties of the created citizen depended upon the interpretation which the courts, in the light of the opinion of jurists,

---

[37] In his review of Ullmann, *Individual and Society* (*Speculum*, XLIII, 1968, 389), Gaines Post criticised Ullmann's citizen–subject dichotomy making special reference to Accursius' gloss on D.1.6.3 ('Cives Romanos dicas omnes subiectos imperio', fol. 12r, ed. Venice, 1498); but Post missed the point because it was Ullmann's contention that the term, *civis*, could be employed in a theocratic context, but that with the Aristotelian-inspired revolution in medieval political thought new meaning was infused into the term.

placed upon the content of acquired citizen status. Through considering the qualifications for citizenship Baldus is led to refine his concept of *civilitas* itself.[38]

The juristic question was whether citizenship could truly be created by the law or whether native citizenship was the only kind with full validity. The problem was made critical by contemporary city-legislation which saw the citizen by birth as the model for citizenship and applied to the created citizen such formulae as 'let him be regarded as a true and original citizen' ('habeatur pro cive vero et originario') and 'let him be considered a true and original citizen and be one' ('intelligatur et sit civis verus et originarius'). Was the created citizen the same as or only similar to the original citizens? Could a created citizen be considered a true original citizen or was the original citizen the only true kind?

Bartolus had maintained the full validity of created citizenship. He considered that there were two species of citizen, original and non-original,[39] but did not hold that the original citizen (being but one species) was the model for citizenship as a whole. Thus the question he was concerned with was whether the created citizen was a true citizen, not whether he was a true original citizen. In his important discussion at D.41.3.15 the formula, therefore, which he discussed was 'habeatur pro cive'. Bartolus concluded that the extent of the citizen rights acquired was the only point at issue. Thus someone created a citizen 'in every respect' ('quoad omnia') was truly and properly a citizen. This formula, which at first sight might suggest fiction in the sense of an improper use of the term, citizen, conveyed truth if the reality of full citizen rights was to be enjoyed by the created citizen. True citizenship was not, therefore, a monopoly of the citizen born.[40]

---

[38] Baldus' ideas on created citizenship have already attracted some interest: see Rummer, 'A fourteenth-century legal opinion'; Kirshner, 'Ars imitatur naturam'; and id., 'Between nature and culture'. For other jurists' theories of created citizenship see Kirshner, 'Paolo di Castro on *cives ex privilegio*'; and id., 'Civitas sibi faciat civem'. For the general importance of ideas of citizenship in fourteenth- and fifteenth-century Italy (including discussions of created citizenship) see Riesenberg, 'Civism and Roman law'; and id., 'Citizenship and equality.' Still very useful as a general treatment is Bizzari, 'Diritto di cittadinanza'.

[39] Ad C.10.40.7, n.2, fol. 21v. The text of this law gives some assistance towards the development of a theory in terms of Roman law to account for the various sources of citizenship: 'Cives quidem origo facit manumissio allectio vel adoptio.'

[40] 'Premitto aliud, scilicet quod civitates possunt sibi facere statuta per quem modum illi qui non sunt cives efficiuntur cives...Pone ergo statuit civitas, quod nullus possit effici civis nisi de voluntate maioris consilii ipse presens in consilio recipiatur, ut alii cives... Et tunc aut dicit quod habeatur pro cive quoad quedam tantum, et est civis secundum fictionem, arg. d. [D.14.6.2], aut dixit quod habeatur pro cive quoad omnia, et tunc erit civis secundum veritatem, argu. eorum que supra dicta sunt. Et si opponis mihi

Bartolus revealed in *Cons.*, 1.62 the fundamental reason behind his view. All citizenship he considered to be a legal status created by the civil law: it was the product not of nature but of convention. Thus both birth and legal enactment were on a par as qualifications for citizenship: both when accepted by the civil law of the city produced true citizenship. The two species, original and created, were differentiated by the qualification for citizenship (birth or another cause), and had in common the constitutive element of citizenship – the enactment of the civil law:

The point is this. Someone has been made a citizen of some city by statute or decree. The question is whether he is truly or improperly called a citizen. In the said question it must be realised that for someone to be a citizen is not a natural condition but one pertaining to the civil law. This is clear, firstly from the name itself, because 'citizen' is derived from 'city'; and secondly, because according to natural law there was no city and no one was made a citizen through being born. It is therefore a constitution of the civil law which makes someone a citizen on account of his origin, merit or adoption, as in [C.10.40.7]. We must not say therefore that some are citizens naturally and some civilly. We must rather say that all are citizens civilly: some however on account of their natural origin, others by reason of some other cause. Therefore, if a city makes a statute that whoever has a house there is a citizen, he will truly be a citizen, as is noted in [D.50.16.139; D.50.16.190; and D.1.5.17]. And whoever is accepted for undertaking the burdens of citizenship is truly and properly a citizen. But this man has been so received, and is therefore truly and properly a citizen, as in [D.50.1.1] at the words, 'proprie quidem' etc. Therefore, he should be treated as a citizen of that city which has made him a citizen.⁴¹

It is not surprising that Bartolus, arguing within a juristic frame of reference, came to this conclusion. Furthermore, since for him citizenship was a legal status created by human positive law, a *civitas quae superiorem non recognoscit* would demonstrate its sovereignty in an essential way by determining the membership of its own citizen-body.

Baldus in contrast does not consider that citizenship is a purely legal status: indeed, he does not refer to Bartolus, *Cons.*, 1.62. Baldus' view is that citizenship can be produced equally well by nature (through birth) and by law: 'The name "citizen" is equally well a civil as a

quod ista oratio, "habeatur pro cive etc.", denotat fictionem, ut supra [D.35.1.24] et supra dixi, respondeo quod denotantia fictionem et improprietatem si apponantur in lege iuxta id quod potest esse verum secundum veritatem et proprietatem magis dicuntur verba proprietatis et veritatis expressiva quam improprietatis vel fictionis significativa, ut dicimus de verbo, "quasi"' (n. 34–6, fol. 104v). See also Kirshner's discussion of this commentary: 'Ars imitatur naturam', p. 310.

⁴¹ Kirshner's text: 'Civitas sibi faciat civem', p. 713.

natural one, and thus can be truly introduced by statute and privilege.'[42] Indeed, he says of a citizen created by legal privilege that he is 'a true citizen not by nature but by art, because citizenship is something which can be made and is not only produced by birth but is created.'[43] Both forms are fully citizenship. He constructs this model: citizenship itself is the genus (*civilitas in genere*) of which both *civilitas naturalis* or *originaria* and *civilitas civilis* are species – a more abstract expression of Bartolus' use of the species of citizen. But because Baldus does not consider all citizenship to be simply a construction of the law, he has to discuss the relationship between original and created citizenship: he cannot by-pass it like Bartolus. Thus exploring this question not considered by Bartolus he maintains that created citizenship is true citizenship in that as species it is contained within its genus, but that it can only fictively be thought of as the other species (original citizenship):

This is relevant to the statute that inhabitants of the *contado* should be regarded as city-folk. For these words 'city-folk' are used in a natural sense; and right of origin cannot be changed except through fiction, as in [D.50.1.6 and C.10.40.9]. But Bartolus says that such a statute makes its dispositions in truth not in fiction [D.41.3.15]. But you are to say that citizenship is two-fold, that is original, and as far as this is concerned it is a fiction; and citizenship in general, and as far as this is concerned it is truth, because this citizenship is predicated of many species, and thus a species contained within a genus is truly present in the genus because of the latter's own nature.[44]

The neatest expression of his argument is to be found in a passage dealing with citizenship created by legal prescription: 'Doubt is expressed whether someone can prescribe citizenship and citizen privileges of some place. It seems that he can, with the exception of origin which cannot be prescribed. But the advantages of origin can certainly be prescribed, and he will then be at one and the same time a true citizen and a fictive original one, that is as regards that form of citizenship which is by birth or in a citizen born, and he will be a true one as regards the true right of citizenship in a general sense according to Bartolus on [D.41.3.15].'[45] Thus a created citizen may

---

[42] Ad C.6.23.9 (fol. 50v).
[43] *Cons.*, 5.409, n. 1, fol. 107v (ed. Venice, 1575) – the *consilium* concerning Ser Orlando. The version of the whole *consilium* in MS. Vat. Lat. 14094 (ed. Kirshner, 'Ars imitatur naturam', pp. 325–30) is fuller than in the printed edition; but see Appendix I for the text of this passage. For discussion of this passage see also Riesenberg, 'Civism and Roman law', pp. 243–4. Cp. Baldus ad D.1.7.44 (fol. 35v): 'Nota quod filius alius nature iure alius iure legis; et sicut in patre ita in patria, nam alium recipit iure nature ut naturales cives, alium iure legis, id est per statutum.'
[44] Baldus ad C.6.8.2 (fol. 20v). [45] Baldus ad X.2.26.Rubr., n.23 (fol. 325r).

have the legal benefits of original citizenship, but such creational formulae as 'intelligatur et sit originarius civis', in identifying him with the original citizens, can only thereby denote fiction.[46]

Baldus goes yet further in isolating an abstract essence of citizenship distinct from the means by which it is obtained. He calls this core of citizenship *pura* or *mera civilitas* – citizenship pure and simple. It is this which is the common element of both original and created citizenship and which makes both forms of citizen equal in respect of being citizens: 'And the argument is relevant to foreigners who are received into original citizenship, because this is through fiction; for pure citizenship can in truth be introduced but original cannot, as in [D.50.1.6]; these forms of citizenship will therefore be equal in every respect.'[47] Thus the formula, 'habeatur pro cive', indicates true citizenship as regards *mera civilitas* but fiction as regards origin:

When the phrase, 'let him be regarded' (*habeatur*), is used about something which is true, it signifies truth, but if it is used about something which is fictive, it signifies fiction. And this is relevant to the question of the statute saying that foreign merchants should be regarded as citizens, because it denotes similarity not identity, because a mode of expression produced against nature introduces fiction... If therefore you were to consider their people of origin, that is their place of birth, it is fiction; if you were to consider pure citizenship, it can be the truth, as here and as is noted by Bartolus on [D.41.3.15].[48]

Clearly as the repeated references in these passages show, it is Bartolus' argument at D.41.3.15 which is seminal for Baldus. What Baldus has done in developing his conception of the created citizen as

---

[46] This point is clearly made in Baldus ad D.3.2.6, 1 (fol. 148r): 'Et nota quod ista verba "intelligantur esse et sit [sic *ed.* [*Lyon*], *1498*]" quotidie apponuntur in reformationibus et statutis terrarum. Et istud verbum, "sit" [si sic *ed.* [*Lyon*], *1498*], est aptum ad veritatem denotandum, verbum autem [aut *ed.* [*Lyon*], *1498*], "intelligitur", est aptum ad fictionem. Bartolus tamen in [D.41.3.15] dicit quod omne verbum importat veritatem si per legalem dispositionem potest introduci veritas, si autem non potest introduci veritas tunc denotatur fictio, et ad hoc facit iste...infra [D.28.2.23]. Verbi gratia, si statutum dicit quod aliquis intelligatur esse civis importat veritatem quoad civilitatem civilem, sed non quoad [quo *ed.* [*Lyon*], *1498*] civilitatem originis que requirit verum naturale principium, ut infra [D.50.1.6]. Vnde dato quod statutum diceret ita quod intelligatur esse et sit originarius civis, tamen quoad naturalem et originalem civilitatem ista verba non important nisi fictionem quia non habet tantam potestatem lex vel statutum quod possit tollere facti veritatem, ut infra [D.49.15.12, 2]. Vbi ergo verba possunt adaptari ad veritatem important veritatem, ubi non possunt adaptari ad veritatem important fictionem.' It should be noted, however, that whereas the point is made about fictive original citizenship, the argument here is limited to demonstrating that the created citizen is a true 'civil citizen' rather than a 'true citizen' *tout court*.

[47] Baldus ad D.12.1.14 (fol. 13v).

[48] Baldus ad X.1.6.6, n.4 (fol. 77v). Cp. also Baldus ad C.4.24.6 (fol. 268r).

a true citizen but a fictive original one is to apply Bartolus' thesis that truth applies where truth can and fiction where fiction. Thus precisely because Baldus retains the distinction between citizenship created by nature and by law, he arrives at a somewhat different conclusion from that which Bartolus had reached through the application of the concepts of *fictio* and *veritas*. In his commentary on C.6.8.2 he clearly considers Bartolus to have made only a limited use of the argument; yet the passages quoted from his commentaries on X.2.26.Rubr. and X.1.6.6 can be read in two ways: Bartolus on D.41.3.15 is there the acknowledged source either for the view that the created citizen is a true citizen but a fictive original or for the idea that he is a true citizen without further elaboration. The first possible interpretation would on the face of it attribute more to Bartolus than is justified, but it would indicate that Baldus felt a debt to his mentor here.

Julius Kirshner, in considering the question of created citizenship raised in the *consilium* concerning the case of Ser Orlando, does not mention Baldus' concept of the created citizen as true citizen but fictive original, but instead concentrates solely on the fictive element in such citizenship. He thus considers that Baldus rejects Bartolus' argument at D.41.3.15 and holds such citizens to be essentially fictive ones.[49] In support of his view Kirshner refers to five texts directly concerned with citizenship in Baldus' commentaries: D.V., Const., 'Omnem'; D.3.2.5; D.3.5.3; D.2.4.8 and C.4.19.16. Kirshner maintains that the following major statement at D.V., Const., 'Omnem' means only that created citizens are fictive original ones:

Just as it is one thing to be a natural and original citizen of Padua, and another to share citizen rights, as is noted in [D.50.16.66], so it is one thing to be naturally legitimate and another to be civilly legitimised, although both forms of legitimacy entail rights of inheritance. What, however, is the result if those words are joined together, namely, 'let him be regarded as and be'? My reply is that they signify truth if they can, as below [D.2.2.1, 2] where the text speaks on that matter when it says, 'quoniam pro nullo habetur'; and this is so, because we have accommodated the meaning of the law to the truth. And

49 See 'Ars imitatur naturam', pp. 309–15. The relevant part of the *consilium* is: 'Et primo quod dictus Ser Orlandus fuerit verus civis effectus a principio non venit in dubium. Nam vera civilitas, licet extraordinaria, conferri potest per cives forensibus, ut not. in [D.50.16.139] et [C.10.40.7], et per Bartolum [D.41.3.15]. Vnde dictus Ser Orlandus in numero et vera essentia civium est redactus. Nam cuicunque competit veritas diffinitionis, illud est vere tale, quia diffinitio substantiam demonstrat, circumlocutiones autem demonstrant accidentia, licet et illa magnam partem conferant ad cognoscendum quid est hoc [D.12.1.2, 2]. Sed huic competit vera diffinitio civis. Ergo est...' (ed. Kirshner, p. 326) – the passage quoted above, p. 172, is the immediate continuation and conclusion of this section.

note that what is not simply said to be something is similar to it rather than identical, because their condition is the same but their substance or nature is different. No problem is posed by Bartolus' comments on [D.41.3.15], where he says that those words, 'let them be regarded as citizens', would truly make a citizen, because as far as citizenship in a general sense is concerned it is true citizenship, because one species of that is the adventitious kind, but as regards the other species of citizenship, that is when it is viewed in relation to original citizenship, it is not true but fictive citizenship, because something which is adventitious cannot be true but can be similar or considered the same through fiction. For no art or ingenuity of man will in the case of someone lacking native origin be able to make him a truly original citizen, but will be well able to produce in him the fictive likeness of such a citizen, as is fully noted in [C.6.8.2] which is relevant as are [D.1.7.1; D.1.7.38; D.1.5.17; D.50.16.139 and D.41.3.2] below.[50]

In point of fact this passage is a prime example of Baldus' argument that the created citizen is both a true citizen and a fictive original, because it considers the fictive element in created citizenship to emerge when it is viewed expressly *in relation to* original citizenship ('civilitas in specie id est relatione facta ad originalem civilitatem non est vera sed ficta').[51] Furthermore Kirshner maintains that at D.3.2.5 Baldus considers the formula, 'habeatur et intelligatur', to signify fiction. Baldus is however applying there the Bartolist argument that it only signifies fiction *when* it cannot signify truth (otherwise, if it is possible, it signifies truth, as he says above at D.V., Const., 'Omnem').[52] On the other hand the passage at D.3.5.3 can, indeed, bear the interpretation that Baldus rejects Bartolus' argument and considers creative citizenship to be fictive. The passage is, however, somewhat indirectly expressed, and to interpret it in the way Kirshner does would be to attach to it a greater weight than it can perhaps carry, if it is to be the basis for a denial of the whole trend of Baldus' thought on this subject. It is

---

[50] Fol. 2v.
[51] Kirshner's translation of this passage is misleading: 'Citizenship "in specie", that is, when it is made to correspond to original citizenship, is not true but fictitious' (p. 312). For 'accidental citizenship' see below, p. 181.
[52] Ad D.3.2.5 (fol. 146r), 'Sexto nota hic de verbo, "intelligatur", quod significat paritatem, unde si statutum dicit quicunque civis non solverit collectam, intelligatur esse de comitatu, tantum est dicere quantum in isto casu civis et comitatensis equiparentur, et sic ammodo omnes leges loquentes de comitatense intelligentur de isto non solvente collectam, ut infra [D.35.2.1, 1], nam cum procedat per eandem rationem quod de uno dicitur ad alterum trahitur, ut [C.1.23.1]. Posses etiam allegare ex isto textu quod verbum, "habeatur et intelligatur", significat [significat *ed. Venice, 1616*; significat *ed.* [*Lyon*], *1498*] fictionem, quando ratione materie non potest designari veritas, et facit infra [D. 49.14.29].' Kirshner supports his argument with the reading, '*quoniam* ratione...' (ed. Venice, 1586) – p.311, n. 57 – whereas both the [Lyon], 1498, and the Venice, 1616, edns contain 'quando': see also, ibid., p. 314, n. 68.

of course possible that Kirshner is right here, and that this is therefore an inconsistency on Baldus' part. On the other hand the passage can be understood within the context of Baldus' theory of fictive original citizenship.[53] Overall the essence of Kirshner's interpretation is that Baldus, through retaining two distinct kinds of citizenship (that produced by nature and that created by law), could only view in terms of fiction the so-called original citizen created by law. Baldus' thesis is however more subtle than this, because for him citizenship created by law reveals its true or fictive aspect according to whether it is viewed in relation to the abstract common core of citizenship or to the physical fact of origin by birth. In his *consilium* concerning Ser Orlando, however, Baldus is concerned only to show that created citizenship is a true form – hence his reference to Bartolus on D.41.3.15 in support of his view.

Baldus' complex view raises a fundamental question about the juristic use of the concepts of truth and fiction. For Baldus, as for other medieval jurists, fictions of the law have the positive function of creating legal entities, relations and capacities which do not exist in reality outside the law: thus a fiction can be deemed to signify truth in purely legal terms.[54] Legal enactment could through the use of fiction create true and fully valid citizenship, which is how Kirshner

---

[53] 'Item si statutum dicit siquis offenderit civem intelligitur loqui de vero et naturali cive, non de eo qui ad civilitatem receptus est per privilegium sicut sunt iudei in civitate ista nisi in eorum privilegio exprimeretur quod omnia statuta loquentia de civibus vendicarent sibi locum in personis iudeorum, arg. infra [D.35.2.1, 1]. D. Bartolus in hoc sentit contrarium quia ipse dicit quod vera civilitas ita potest induci per statutum sicut per originem, cum civilitas habeat sub se plures species et omnis species vera sit vera species, ut [C.10.40.7]. Vnde non est verum quod isti sint cives ficti, immo sunt cives veri quia quotiens lex potest aliquid introducere per veritatem intelligitur vere non ficte secundum Bartolum, qui ita no., infra [D.41.3.15]. Preterea posito quod isti essent ficti cives privilegium vel reformationes eorum recipiunt interpretationem passivam ut leges que de civilibus loquuntur porrigantur ad eos tam ad favorem quam ad odium, ut d. [D.35.2.1, 1], quod credo verius licet sit ar. contra [C.2.44.4]' (fol. 175v). See Kirshner, 'Ars imitatur naturam', pp. 311–12. Similar considerations apply in interpreting Baldus' commentaries on D.2.4.8: 'Et est ille textus validum arg. quod statutum loquens de cive intelligitur de quocunque qui habetur pro cive, puta de scholari, licet aliud sit esse civem, aliud haberi pro cive, ut in [D.50.16.207]' (ad D.2.4.8, 1, fol. 74v); 'In "patrimonium" not. quod lex que loquitur de patrono intelligitur de omni eo qui habetur pro patrono; et sic lex que loquitur de cive intelligitur de omni eo qui habet iura civium, licet vere civis non sit' (ad D.2.4.8, Additio Baldi, fol. 81r, ed. Lyon, 1562); and 'Not. quod lex que loquitur de patrono habet locum in omni eo, qui habetur pro patrono, et facit quod omnis ille, qui habetur pro cive, comprehendatur appellatione civis, quod no.' (ad D.2.4.8, 1, Secunda Additio, fol. 89r, ed. Venice, 1616). Kirshner, ibid., p. 314, n. 68, mentions these two *additiones*.

[54] See Baldus ad C.4.19.16 (fol. 244v). Cp. id. ad C.9.2.7 (fol. 356r). For this juristic use of fictions see Kirshner, 'Ars imitatur naturam', pp. 313–15.

interprets Baldus' *consilium* concerning Ser Orlando. But, as we have seen, Baldus' view is not as simple as that. He is concerned above all with what is actually the case. He sees that as far as citizenship itself is at issue there is in the case of all created citizenship no need to call on fiction at all: it is simply a true and valid form of citizenship. Legal fiction can, however, impute to a created citizen a fully valid original citizenship. What Baldus is concerned to do is to demonstrate the full validity of created citizenship (whether or not it is termed original, which for him it clearly does not have to be) and to respect at the same time that the fact of origin cannot be changed. It could be argued that in purely legal terms the efficacy of created citizenship would be the same whether it was considered to be the product either of truth or of fiction, and that therefore this whole question is of no great significance. This is, however, clearly not Baldus' view since his concern is to explore the problem more profoundly and thereby through such detailed attention determine the precise role of truth and fiction in this matter. Furthermore, since the question of created citizenship was of such public concern, Baldus would be well aware that the jurists' use of fictions could be very misleading to the layman; it is highly likely therefore that he was seeking to answer affirmatively and unequivocally the basic layman's question of whether the created citizen was a *civis verus*.

Baldus' theory has to be understood against the background of contemporary Italian practice according to which there were many kinds and grades of created citizen. Indeed several different kinds of such citizenship have appeared in the passages quoted above: those resulting from privileges granted to individuals, general statutes covering *cives comitatenses* (citizens from the *contado*), general statutes concerning foreign merchants and joint agreements between cities to treat each other's citizens as their own. Clearly the amount of citizen rights conferred and obligations imposed would vary from case to case, but the essential point is that all such citizens, understood in the sense meant in each case, are according to Baldus to be treated in law as true citizens.

Given that in practice the generality of created citizens, even when termed original citizens, possessed a diminished citizenship in comparison with that enjoyed by original ones by birth,[55] the crucial question remains: does Baldus consider that a created original citizen can ever possess the full legal and political rights available to those born

---

[55] See, for instance, Bizzari, 'Diritto di cittadinanza', pp. 43–5, and Kirshner, 'Ars imitatur naturam', pp. 291–303.

original citizens? The first requirement is for a created citizen to be subject to the *munera* (obligations) which his adoptive city imposes on its citizens and to participate in public *honores*:

It says here, 'of your native place.' My question is whether your native place is said to be that in which you are an adoptive citizen and not one by birth? And it seems that it is, if you enjoy public honours there like the original citizens, for citizens are known by their obligations and honours, as below [C.10.40.7]. Those, however, who do not participate in public honours are not properly called citizens, because they are not treated as citizens in that which is the supreme and greatest proof of citizenship.[56]

Jurists agreed that a citizen was identified by the *munera* to which he was liable and, indeed, a *civis civitatis* (urban citizen) was distinguished from a *civis comitatensis* largely by the heavier *munera* which the latter had to pay.[57] It was the essence of the citizen's status that he was *subditus* (subject) to the city's authority and thus the obligations it imposed. Baldus considers therefore that any created citizen through accepting the contract of citizenship binds himself to subjection of this kind:

I argue that citizenship entails obligations both ways... for a mutual bond is contracted on both sides; for just as they are to be protected as duty requires, so also they are bound to obey and submit to the bond of our citizenship... Therefore it is not possible for its advantages to be accepted and its disadvantages rejected... Since therefore he has consented he has been made a citizen truly and fully, as in [D.41.3.15] according to Bartolus, and has therefore been placed under our jurisdiction; for he has been made a citizen of our choosing not with any reservations but with full effect, as in [C.10.40.7], where these three are equal: origin, domicile and being chosen. And thus he comes under the jurisdiction of our courts... When he was made a citizen... this involved submission and not a simple extension of jurisdiction... For such an extension properly speaking does not make someone a subject, but citizenship does, in respect to that with which this question is concerned.[58]

---

56 Baldus ad C.6.23.9 (fol. 50r). See also id., *Cons.*, 2.111, fol. 29v, ed. Brescia, 1490 (= *Cons.*, 4.445, n. 5–6, fol. 101v, ed. Venice, 1575) where he discusses a grant of citizenship not entailing subjection to *munera*: 'Civilitas potest considerari tribus modis. Primo modo ad favores; secundo quoad onera de iure communi imminentia; tertio quoad onera accidentalia contra ius commune, et quoad ista non videtur extendi, arg. [C.1.14.6], et ita in proposito. Preterea cum non teneantur ad munera non sunt mere et vere subditi [D.50.1.1] etiam si ibi habeant larem et domicilium, et ista est ipsa veritas.'

57 See Kirshner, 'Civitas sibi faciat civem', p. 704 for urban and rural citizens; Bowsky, '*Cives silvestres*'; and Bizzari, 'Diritto di cittadinanza', p. 66. See, for instance, Bartolus ad D.50.1.1, n.4 (fol. 230v); Baldus, *Cons.*, 4.294, n.1, fol. 64r (ed. Venice, 1575); and id. ad D.24.3.66, 5 (fol. 231r), where he refers to rural citizenship as 'civilitas qualificata'.

58 *Cons.*, Lucca, 358 (ed. Bonolis), pp. 152–4 (the case concerns the liability of a merchant of Florentine origin under an agreement between Florence and Perugia to treat each

On the basis of this voluntary subjection to obligation the created citizen wins access to the advantages (*favores*) of citizenship and participation in public honours. Yet, as Baldus points out, contemporary custom provided for such a citizen only limited access to such honours.[59] Precisely because, however, such restrictions were purely customary they could be set aside. Thus Baldus does envisage a category of created citizen who is in every respect identical with native citizens as regards his rights and standing as a citizen: 'And in sum, if native citizenship can increase his rights and standing in any way, he is not simply called a citizen. If, however, the effect of his citizenship could not be increased by native status, because he has been made a citizen in every respect and without reservation (*in omnibus et per omnia*), he is then called a citizen, as is argued at [D.28.2.29, 5, and above, C.1.3.54], and add what is noted by Bartolus at [D.48.5.4 and D.41.3.15].'[60] This overtly applies Bartolus' view at D.41.3.15 that citizens created *per omnia* are true ones. Yet it is not clear what Bartolus means by *per omnia*. It could have a very limited application solely to those with rights and status identical to those of natural citizens, an interpretation which is certainly what the text suggests, but which would make this statement by Bartolus inapplicable to the bulk of created citizens. It is doubtful, however, that Bartolus meant this, because he sets forth his argument in his solution to the status of citizens created by a mutual arrangement between cities.[61] Baldus, as we have seen, is willing to consider a wide range and gradation of created citizens as *cives veri*; at the end of this range are those received into the fullest form of citizenship (*plenissima*

other's citizens as their own). Cp. Bartolus ad D.50.1.1, n. 16 (fol. 231r): 'No. quod aliqui possunt recipi in civitate ut munera nobiscum faciant, et sic receptione contrahitur civilitas.' For Bartolus' doctrine of contractual citizenship see Kirshner, 'Civitas sibi faciat civem', pp. 707–8. For a citizen as subject see Baldus, *Cons.*, 3.299, fol. 97v, ed. Brescia, 1491 (= *Cons.*, 1.349, n.8, fol. 113v, ed. Venice, 1575), 'Solutio: si verba statuti incipiunt a persona subiecta, quia diriguntur ei, puta nullus civis placentie possit alienare in parmensem, unde valet statutum'; cp. id. ad X.2.22.15, n. 11 (fol. 292v), 'lex municipalis et consuetudo potest de rebus subditorum disponere.' As we have seen the status of citizen–clergy formed an exception in that they were not subject to the burdens of citizenship (above, p.139). It was also possible for a foreigner to be given certain privileges of citizenship without becoming a *subditus*: see, for instance, Angelus de Ubaldis, *Cons.*, 351, n.4 (fol. 151r). For a loose usage see Lucas de Penna ad C.10.40.7, n. 1 (p. 225): 'Et nota quod civis potest largo sumpto vocabulo dici quis etiam si munera in civitate non subeat [D.50.1.1] post prin.'

59 Ad D.1.5.17 (fol. 25v): 'Nota quod cives effecti ex constitutione habent ius civium ex origine quia sunt veri cives...Istum tamen adoptivum civem non admittari ad honores ad quos non consuevere admitti nisi cives naturales quia consuetudo restringit privilegium.'

60 Ad C.6.23.9 (fol. 50v). This distinction between simple and qualified citizenship is also to be found in Angelus de Ubaldis, *Cons.*, 351, n. 3 (fol. 151r).

61 See above, p. 170. Bartolus shows at n. 35 that he is concerned with such citizens.

civilitas) and who enjoy all the advantages of citizenship being considered to be citizens both actively and passively.[62] Certainly the created original citizen is identical to the citizen born in the crucial aspect that he passes on his new citizenship to his children (including those already born before the grant of citizenship) and his descendants.[63] Yet the formulation, 'active et passive habetur pro cive', raises the question of the political involvement of a person with the fullest form of created citizenship. On the face of it the passages quoted from Baldus' commentary on C.6.23.9 and *Cons.*, 1.460 suggest that a created citizen could enjoy full political involvement and office-bearing. This is in fact Baldus' view, because he considers that a created citizen can hold the political office of prior:

> But suppose it is forbidden by statute that anyone could be one of the priors unless he is an original citizen. Now Titius has been received into citizenship with the formula that he be regarded as an original one in every respect. The question is whether he will be able to be one of the priors. And it seems that he will not, because in his case he is the same [as an original citizen] through fiction not truth... The contrary view is supported below by [D.45.1.132 and D.27.1.44]. For since he is thus regarded as if he were born there, his species [of citizenship] tempers the genus [i.e. original citizenship], that is modifies the genus, and because it is expressly ordained that he be such and be considered as such, he should be deemed to possess equal rights.[64]

The crucial point is, therefore, that Baldus maintains that a created original citizen can enjoy the full legal and political rights and capabilities of a citizen born: a very progressive view in terms of fourteenth-century Italy.

Baldus' use of the long-established description of the created citizen as an adoptive one is very apt. Adoption as a grounds for gaining citizenship was familiar from C.10.40.7; but the application of the concept to created citizenship in general accurately indicates both the act of choosing and making on the part of the city and the giving and acquiring of a new shared status. The citizen-body, understood as a corporation (*universitas*), adopts created citizens into both active and

---

62 See Baldus, *Cons.*, 1.460, n. 2–3, fol. 147v (ed. Venice, 1575) for these forms of created citizen: 'pactionatus civis, et perpetuo alligatus civitati per pactum'; 'cives honorarii'; '[cives] honorarii recepti ut munera [publica] subeant'; 'civis effectus quoad munera publica' but without rights of inheritance; and 'quis receptus ad plenissimam civitatem', in which case 'iste consequitur omnes favores civium, et active et passsive habetur pro cive, ut [D.35.2.1, 1] et no. per Bartolum [D.41.3.15].'

63 See Baldus, *Cons.*, Lucca, 95 (ed. Bonolis), p. 147. Cp. Bartolus ad D.50.1.17, p. 649 (ed. Basel, 1589), where he maintains that created citizenship is passed on to children; ad D.50.1.6, n.3, he puts forward arguments on both sides of this question without a solution.   64 Ad D.1.1.9 (fol. 11v).

passive participation in its own number; their status is thereby changed and they are rendered distinct from *extranei*:

Anyone who on account of his merit is made a citizen by statute fully obtains the freedom even of native citizens, because he now belongs to the society of citizens, and is one of their number and an addition to it, and of the same citizen-body and corporation actively and passively, as in [D.29.1.20]; for since such people have obtained citizen rights, they could not be regarded as outsiders.[65]

Citizenship is thus an exclusive status differentiated from that of the foreigner – the outsider. Likewise the created citizen is termed a *civis accidentalis* because his adoption as a citizen results from a contingent act external to himself: whereas native citizenship is inherent, the created citizen acquires his citizenship from a source outside himself – it is something which happens to him.[66]

It is logical for Baldus to adopt the position which he does concerning the relationship between created and original citizenship. Clearly birth is an expression of the naturalness of citizenship, and in the case of sovereign cities through its very naturalness excludes any superior from determining the city's membership – a fundamental requirement for sovereignty. Yet there is for Baldus no reason why membership of a particular citizen body should be determined solely by birth: he also sees that citizenship created by human legal enactment can equally well reflect the natural, political condition of man, creating for an individual a new particular citizenship which permits the expression of his political nature. Furthermore this act of choosing its new members can also be an expression of sovereignty. This is not to deny, of course, that in non-sovereign cities the creation of citizens can lie with city-officials subject to the ultimate consent of a *princeps*,[67] for instance a *signore*, or indeed with the *princeps* himself.[68] Baldus' theory of created citizenship is certainly compatible with his *de facto* argument,

---

65 Baldus, *Cons.*, 3.299, fol. 97r, ed. Brescia, 1491 (= *Cons.*, 1.349, ed. Venice, 1575); see Ullmann, 'De Bartoli sententia', pp. 725–6, for Baldus' application here of corporation concepts in his theory of created citizenship.

66 See Baldus ad C.8.47.10, 4 (fols. 323v–324r): 'Hic dicit quod ordo succedendi que est inter naturales est inter adoptivos. Est argumentum quod in officiis idem sit ordo inter cives adoptivos, id est factos per statutum, et cives naturales, ut quemadmodum naturales inter se preferuntur ita isti accidentales cives tractentur et habeantur.' Cp. id ad D.2.1.19 (fol. 69r).

67 See Baldus, *Cons.*, 3.299, fol. 97v, ed. Brescia, 1491 (= *Cons.*, 1.349, ed. Venice, 1575) for the case of Piacenza.

68 See *Cons.*, 3.123, fol. 35r–35v, ed. Brescia, 1491 (= *Cons.*, 1.138, ed. Venice, 1575), where Baldus considers grants of the citizenship of Brescia made by Bernabò and Giangaleazzo Visconti.

yet the extent to which a *signore* may have *de iure* powers raises the question of the operation of such powers in the essentially *de facto* context of citizenship, although in such a case there is no suggestion by Baldus that the nature of citizenship is thereby changed.[69]

Baldus' perception is that being a citizen is a condition or state which is essentially political with a legal expression, and which is determined by the following: that a person lives in the city, acts as a citizen, is accepted by the community as such,[70] enjoys the rights and duties of a citizen and can pass his citizenship on to his heirs. Citizenship in itself, therefore, is a status divorced from the means by which it is obtained: being a citizen is an existential state recognisable from the possession of the attributes of a citizen. Different conceptions of nature lie behind Bartolus' and Baldus' approaches. Whereas Bartolus, through thinking of 'natural' as pertaining either to man's original condition before civil society or to the process of birth, can therefore in *Cons*, 1.62 only conceive of citizenship as a legal not a natural condition, Baldus, on the other hand, with his Aristotelian view, considers that man's political nature is put into effect through actually being a citizen, however this status is obtained.

There remain however two important areas of ambiguity in Baldus' theory of created citizenship. The first concerns the status of a woman who marries a foreigner and is thus through her marriage created a citizen of her husband's city. Is such a woman truly or fictively an original citizen of her new city? Baldus produces two completely different answers. According to the first the marriage bond is such that it changes the *origo* of the wife to that of the husband because they become one flesh; indeed, in this process in which the stronger element (the man) attracts to itself the less worthy (the woman) man and wife become 'one substance in two persons'. This change occurs in truth not in fiction because it is the product of divine law, and would therefore appear as a unique infringement of Baldus' general theory of created citizenship:

For marriage is of such a strength and nature that it transforms the wife's origin into that of her husband...This is also proved by the strength of the union in which the more powerful attracts to itself the less worthy...But there is no greater union than the conjugal through which man and wife are made

---

[69] For the complex question of the *de iure* and *de facto* aspects of the rule of *signori* see below, pp. 223–5.

[70] See *Cons*., Lucca, 249. For discussion of the significance of this *consilium* see Kirshner, 'Between nature and culture' (text, p. 206: based on this MS and MS 6, Joseph Regenstein Library, University of Chicago). See also *Cons*., 1.456, n. 5–6, fol. 146v (ed. Venice, 1575).

one flesh: it is also one substance in two persons... And thus the said lady Agnes should be regarded as a native and original citizen of the said territory of Castiglione, since by divine law there is one flesh, and divine law consists of truth and not fiction. It follows that the wife has been properly made her husband's fellow-citizen, and this is what the gloss holds at [C.10.40.7] as does Bartolus at [D.50.1.38, 1].[71]

Accursius, in his gloss on C.10.40.7, does indeed maintain that the wife becomes a citizen of her husband's city;[72] but in his gloss on this passage in the *Codex*, 'It is clear that no one can of his own free will be released from his origin',[73] he goes further, '*From his origin*, as also at the beginning of [D.50.1.6]: this however ceases to be the case through marriage, as in [C.10.64.1 and D.50.1.38, 1]',[74] which statement Baldus interprets as supporting his view that the wife becomes an original citizen of her husband's city.[75] Furthermore, Bartolus in his commentary on D.50.1.38, 1, where he certainly maintains that the wife becomes a citizen of her husband's city, also understands this gloss by Accursius as supporting the view that the woman has changed her *origo*.

Although Baldus thus has strong juristic precedent for this first answer, he was clearly not consistently convinced that the woman had lost her first original citizenship, because elsewhere he reverts to his general theory of citizenship maintaining that whereas such a woman through legal enactment truly becomes a citizen of her husband's city, she nevertheless retains her original citizenship as being a fact of nature, and can thus only become a fictive original citizen of her husband's city.[76] This means that she retains her original citizen rights and privileges.

The second area of ambiguity in Baldus' treatment of created citizenship concerns reprisals. Can these be granted against created citizens in the same way as they are against native ones or can created citizens benefit from them? If any distinction were made in this respect it would mean that there was an important difference between the two

---

[71] *Cons.*, 2.394, fol. 99r, ed. Brescia, 1490 (= *Cons.*, 5.100, ed. Venice, 1575). See Ullmann's discussion of this passage: 'De Bartoli sententia', p. 726. Cp. Baldus, *Cons.*, 4.439, n.4, fol. 99v (ed. Venice, 1575). [72] Fol. 121r.
[73] C.10.39.4. [74] Fol. 121r.
[75] *Cons.*, 1.456, n.5, fol. 146v (ed. Venice, 1575).
[76] *Cons.*, 2.433, fol. 109v, ed. Brescia, 1490 (= *Cons.*, 5.139, ed. Venice, 1575). In this *consilium* he expressly rejects the view he propounds in *Cons.*, 2.394, ed. Brescia, 1490 (= *Cons.*, 5.100, ed. Venice, 1575). Even if it were accepted that a married woman changed her *origo*, she would nevertheless retain her original domicile as regards property which she held in her native territory (*Cons.*, 3.310, n.7, fol. 86v, ed. Venice, 1575) – see Kirshner's remarks on such a woman's liability to property taxes in that territory ('Between nature and culture', p. 183).

forms of citizenship. Bartolus on the grounds of the full equality of created and native citizenship held that created citizens were as liable to reprisals as citizens born, and also that created citizens could benefit from reprisals declared against their city of origin.[77] In one passage Baldus appears to agree with Bartolus as regards those created citizens who share the common *munera* of citizens,[78] yet elsewhere he seems not to include in reprisals those with acquired citizenship.[79]

[77] See *Tract. represaliarum*, n. 7–9, fol. 124v, and Kirshner's discussion of this passage ('Civitas sibi faciat civem', p. 710).

[78] Ad Auth., 'Sed omnino' (post C.4.12.4), fol. 228v. Certainly those who do not pay *munera* cannot benefit from reprisals: id., ibid. (fol. 228v); and of someone made a citizen without the obligation of paying *munera* Baldus says, 'Patet igitur hunc sub represaliis non includi, ideo nec molestari posse in persona vel rebus', *Cons.*, 2.111, fol. 29v, ed. Brescia, 1490 (= *Cons.*, 4.445, n.7, fol. 101v, ed. Venice, 1575) – see above, p. 178, n. 56.

[79] Ad C.7.62.11 (fol. 265r).

Chapter 5

THE CITY-*POPULUS* AS A SELF-GOVERNING CORPORATION

THE 'POPULUS' AS A CORPORATE LEGAL PERSON

Baldus' theory of city-*populi* possesses a further dimension which completes it: he applies juristic corporation theory to all citizen-bodies, as would any fourteenth-century civilian or canonist. What is distinctive about Baldus' treatment, however, is the way in which his conception of the city-*populus* as a corporation, when coupled with his idea of a territorially sovereign citizen-body composed of natural political men, produces an innovative contribution to the development of the idea of the state.

It should, however, be noted (and has, indeed, probably become apparent already) that there is some imprecision in Baldus' use of terms to represent the citizen-body, the community of citizens. The most common, and indeed the major term employed by him to designate the citizen-body is *populus*; and it appears therefore most apposite to follow this usage by describing his theory of self-government by the corporation of citizens as government by the people. Other terms, however, such as *civitas* itself, *commune*, *communitas* and *corpus* (*civitatis* or *civium*) are used interchangeably and somewhat indifferently for *populus*. It is usually made clear when *universitas*, the generic term for a juristic corporation, is applied to the citizen-body. Further the term *populus* itself can convey several meanings: the corporation of citizens;[1] all the inhabitants of a particular place including resident aliens and foreigners;[2] and that part of the community which is distinguished from the *nobiles*. In this last case Baldus makes it clear that the *populus* only corresponds with the city-community as a whole when the *populus* holds governmental power. Properly speaking, for the *populus* to be in this position it must constitute the unified body of the citizens.[3] This

---

[1] See Baldus ad C.7.53.5 (above p. 159).
[2] See Baldus ad X.1.3.35, n. 2 (fol. 46r); and also id. ad D.3.5.3, 1 (fol. 175v).
[3] See id. ad *Feud.*, 1.5 (fol. 14v), 'Pone civitas Perusina habuit feudum ab ecclesia. Deinde dividitur civitas in nobiles et populum. Nobiles committunt feloniam. An civitas privetur? Respondeo non, quia neutri per se sunt communitas integra...Et nec

185

view fits in perfectly well with Baldus' overall thesis of popular government; and, as we shall shortly see, the concept of the *populus* as the unity of the citizens is fundamental to his thinking. The *populus* in this last passage may very well correspond to the *popolo* of fourteenth-century Italy. The hint at the idea of a restricted citizen-body (*sanior civium unitas*) suggests the familiar medieval principle of the *sanior vel melior pars*, the implication being that membership of the *populus* would depend upon some qualitative criterion, a suggestion not followed up by Baldus elsewhere. Indeed, apart from those considerations we have seen in his treatment of birth and legal enactment as the sources of citizenship, Baldus does not tell us anything about the composition of the citizen-body, or discuss qualifications for membership of it; neither does he give any indication of possible sizes of the citizen-body in relation to the whole of the population. In the light of the restricted citizen-bodies of fourteenth-century Italy this might well seem a strange omission. The most likely answer is that Baldus is interested in discussing popular government in general terms without exploring the details of the size and composition of the citizen-body which would vary from city to city. A certain level of vagueness as regards Baldus' use of terms to indicate the citizen-body has to be accepted. Thus in the majority of cases he employs *populus* as a term of general application meaning simply 'the people' without further defining it.

The context for Baldus' conception of the people as a corporation is provided by the advances which the Commentators had made in corporation theory. They considered that a corporation was both a body composed of a plurality of human beings and an abstract unitary entity perceptible only by the intellect and thus distinct from its human members.[4] Their source for this idea was to be found in Decretalist works certainly from Innocent IV onwards, although they were to develop this view in a way that was different from any canonist approach.[5] The Glossators, in contrast, had almost universally identified the corporation with its members, as, for instance, Accursius' famous formulation reveals: 'The corporation is nothing other than the men who are there.'[6] The Commentators, however, saw these human

contrahendo nec delinquendo potest civitas per unam partem obligari...Sed populus regens bene obligatur. Tamen proprie ille populus non dicitur civitas qui non est sanior civium unitas, quia non habet significationem universitatis sed partialitatis.'

[4] See Canning, 'Corporation', pp. 12–13.
[5] For the modern disputes concerning the interpretation of Innocent IV in this respect see below, pp. 191–2.
[6] Gl. ad D.3.4.7 (fol. 63v). But see Paradisi, 'Pensiero politico', pp. 118–19, for his discussion of whether Hugolinus may have initiated the beginnings of this distinction between the abstract unity and its physical components.

components not as mere isolated individuals (*singuli*), but as corporate men (*universi*), that is, men seen specifically as united in a corporate whole, a view anticipated to some extent by Johannes Bassianus, Azo and, indeed, Accursius himself.[7]

Baldus, in his definition of the *populus*, gives a superbly subtle solution to the difficult problem of how to explain precisely the relationship between the *populus* as an abstract entity and its physical members. He takes up Accursius' definition of the corporation mentioned above and expressly develops it by maintaining that the *populus* cannot simply be equated with the individual human beings who compose it, but is rather a collection of men into a unity:

And it does not matter that the gloss on [D.3.4.7] says that the people is nothing other than men, because that should be understood as meaning men taken collectively. Therefore separate individuals do not make up the people, and thus properly speaking the people is not men, but a collection of men into a body which is mystical and taken as abstract, and the significance of which has been discovered by the intellect.[8]

Baldus employs here the phrase, *corpus misticum*, which is of canonistic and ultimately Pauline origin,[9] in order to distinguish the *populus* in its abstract aspect as a corporational unity understandable only by the intellect from the bodies of its members which are real in the sense of apprehensible by the senses. This abstract entity (it is *unum corpus*) has a material substratum of real human beings. Baldus is, therefore, careful to define the *populus* as a collection of men *into* a *corpus misticum*. Elsewhere he expresses these two aspects of an *universitas* in terms of the relationship between *materia* and *forma*:

[7] For Johannes Bassianus see Ullmann, 'Delictal responsibility', pp. 80–1. See Azo, *Summa Codicis* ad C.3.13, n. 7, fol. 47r (Lyon, 1557). For Accursius see Paradisi, 'Pensiero politico', pp. 118–19. For examples from early Commentators see, for instance, Petrus de Bellapertica, *Quaestio*, 349 (fol. 97r); and Jacobus Butrigarius ad D.3.4.1, n. 5 (p. 228).

[8] Ad C.7.53.5 (fol. 236r). Baldus can, however, on occasions concentrate on the sense in which the *populus* is a unified collection of men in a purely physical sense: 'Collectivum enim nomen est illud quod in singulari numero multitudinem significat. Et dicunt auctores quod nomina collectiva sunt singularia voce sed pluralia intellectu, quia in singulari numero conveniunt plures [pluribus *ed. cit.*] simul, ut verbi gratia hoc nomen populus. Nam populus non est unus homo sed multi homines uno tamen intellectu comprehensi, ut no. [D.3.4.7, 2]. Et ideo omnis numerus facientium populum ad unum et quasi singularem intellectum refertur' (ad C.6.26.11); and 'Predicatur...populus de corporibus in unum collectis' (ad D.6.1.23, 2, fol. 234r).

[9] See Roberti, 'Corpus mysticum'; Kantorowicz, *King's Two Bodies*, pp. 207–32; and Ullmann, *Individual and Society*, p. 7. Cp. Baldus ad C.9.2.3 (fol. 351r), 'Tertium caput dicitur civitas et civilitas; unde qui perdit civitatem per hoc separatur ab ipso corpore mistico sue civitatis.'

Every corporation is called a body, because it is something compound and collective in which the bodies [of men] are like the material. The corporation is however said to be the form, that is the formal condition [D.8.2.11]. A college, therefore, is an image which is perceived more by the intellect than the senses [D.41.3.30; D.4.2.9, 1; and X.5.39.53].[10]

Baldus' definition of the *populus* is crucial for his treatment of the fundamental question of whether and how it can act and will — whether, in short, it can give effective consent, which in the case of a sovereign city it must be able to do if it is to be self-governing and fully independent. The conception that the *populus* is an abstraction might appear to rule out any possibility that it can truly act and will. Baldus with his definition, however, solves this problem with his particularly subtle demonstration that the *populus* is *at the same time* both real men and an abstract entity distinct from its human members. As we have seen, it is perfectly clear from his treatment of popular government that he considers that the city-*populus*, whether sovereign or autonomous, can in fact give effective consent: it can legislate; it can govern itself. Baldus never maintains that the *populus* as a conceptualisation can perform these legislative and governmental functions. In his treatment of the structure of popular government Baldus considers that the abstract entity and the real members are but two aspects of the same thing: the corporation of the *populus*. The *populus* acts and wills in that its members act and will as a unity, that is (as we shall shortly see) either in assembly (unanimously or through majority-voting) or through elected representative councils or magistrates.[11] In short the members are the physical expression of the abstract entity of the corporation

---

[10] Ad X.1.31.3, n. 7 (fol. 116r). Cp. id., *Margarita*, ad v. 'Vniversitas', fol. 35v (ed. Lyon, 1525), 'Est enim universitas singuli, et sic est quid naturale, et habet corpus quod videtur et tangitur; et est universitas universi, tunc est nomen, non res naturalis sed intellectualis; additur enim quedam significatio singularis que ex universo sumitur ex intellectu conservante [D.41.3.30]. Sic debet intelligi illud quod dicit et [D.3.4.7, 2], non est aliud quam homines qui in eo sunt, scilicet cum addito iuris [iure *ed. cit.*] intellectu et addita significatione que ex universo sumitur'; and id. ad D.3.2.6 (Additio Baldi), n. 2, fol. 183v (ed. Lyon, 1585), 'Vniversitas potest secundum doctores considerari duobus modis: aut in abstracto, et est inanimata...aut in concreto, et tunc sumitur pro singularibus in universitate contentis.' In referring to *singuli* in these two passages Baldus clearly wishes to stress the sense in which a corporation in its material aspect is composed of human beings, but does not mean that in a corporation such people are merely isolated individuals.

[11] Below, pp. 198–206. For a general statement about how a corporation exercises consent through its members see Baldus ad D.29.2.25, 1 (fol. 96r), 'Verum est quod universitas non potest consentire antequam congregetur, sed postquam congregatur bene consentit. Ita dicit Iacobus de Arena. Et sic corpus civile consentit sicut naturale corpus quia per naturalia instrumenta consentit, cum nihil aliud sit collegium quam homines qui in collegio sunt, et sic per homines ipsos collegium consentit, ut no. in [D.3.4.7].'

which acts through the instrumentality of these members who thus express not the wills of separate individuals but that of the corporation as a whole. Thus the *populus* acts and wills in its corporeal aspect, but that consent and action is imputed to it as an abstraction.

Baldus considers the *populus* as an abstract entity to be, legally speaking, one person:

Every collection of people, corresponding to one man, is to be regarded as a single person, as in [D.35.1.56]. It is also a corporate person which is understood as one person, but consists of many bodies, like the people, as in [D.46.1.22]; and this person similarly is regarded as corresponding to one man and is considered to be an individual body...[D.4.2.9, 1] is relevant to this. It is clear therefore that this word, 'person', is sometimes used for an individual, sometimes for a corporation and sometimes for the head or prelate, as in [X.3.5.28].[12]

The dual nature of the *populus* as a corporational unity composed of its corporeal members is thus neatly expressed in the phrase, *persona universalis* – the person which an *universitas* is: one person composed of many. This abstract person is distinct from the human persons who compose it as is clear from a crucial attribute which it possesses but which they conspicuously lack: it is immortal. The city-community is sempiternal precisely because it is universal (that is because it is a corporation): 'My question is whether a city, continuing to exist through new citizens who are adventitious rather than native ones, is said to be the same city. My answer is that it is...because a universal cannot die just as mankind does not die.'[13] Thus the city-community as a corporation is not only a *persona universalis*; it is as such also a *persona perpetua*.[14] The perpetuity of the *populus* was a commonplace among the Commentators, and emerged in their common opinion that the people can initiate measures with perpetual effect, as regards for instance legislation and banishment.[15]

[12] Ad C.6.26.2 (fol. 65r).
[13] Baldus, *De pace Constantie*, ad v. 'Imperialis clementie' (fol. 1v). On the sempiternity of the city-community see Kantorowicz, *King's Two Bodies*, pp. 291–313 (for this passage see pp. 300, n. 61, and 304). See also Gierke, *Genossenschaftsrecht*, III, 364–5 and 430. [14] See Baldus ad D.1.4.3 (fol. 21v).
[15] See for instance Baldus ad X.1.2.11, n.12 (fol. 26v) and id. ad C.6.24.1 (fol. 56r); Bartolus ad D.1.1.9, n.52 (fol. 12v); and Raynerius de Forlì, *Rep.* ad D.1.1.9, n. 80–1 (fol. 23r). There is in D.5.1.76 a passage which was taken by the Glossators and Commentators to indicate the sempiternity of the people, '...et populum eundem hoc tempore putari qui abhinc centum annis fuissent, cum ex illis nemo nunc viveret.' D.5.1.76 itself has no connection with corporation theory. See Baldus, ibid. (fol. 221r), 'Populus tamen nunquam moritur, ut hic dicit textus.' The *populus* is perpetual retrospectively and prospectively: see id. ad D.3.4.9 (fol. 174v); and id. ad X.1.2.6, n.10 (fol. 11r).

In describing the *populus* as a *persona* Baldus is overtly treating it as possessing a legal personality distinct from that of the individual persons who compose it. In the *Corpus Iuris Civilis* the term, *persona*, denotes a human being not a legal person. It was thirteenth-century jurists who invented the concept of the legal person by being the first to apply the term, *persona*, to the corporation,[16] although their usage was anticipated to some extent in theological terms by the Augustinian identification of Christ as the *persona ecclesiae*.[17] Baldus identifies the *populus* as a corporation with a *persona* through a constructive use of fiction to create a legal entity with legal capabilities and a purely legal existence.[18] It is crucial to understand the sense in which Baldus is treating the *populus* as a *persona ficta*. He is not thereby adhering to a modern fiction theory, in the sense that Gierke, for instance, understood it: it is misleading to try and force the corporation theory of thirteenth- and fourteenth-century jurists into either modern fiction or realist theories.[19] According to the realist theory which Gierke favoured, a corporation as a unitary entity has a real existence and can truly act and will: in Gierke's terms it has a real personality distinct from those of its individual members. The fiction theory attributes to the corporation only a fictive personality. According to that theory the corporation as a fictive person is a mere abstraction and fiction of the law: nothing corresponds with it in reality. Because it exists only in the mind it is represented by real people, whether its corporeal members or its ruler: it is thus a fictive and represented person. As a result the corporation itself can neither truly act nor will. Such a fiction theory

---

16 Duff, *Personality*, pp. 48–50 explains the usage of *persona* in the *Corpus Iuris Civilis*, which contains certain texts appearing to give some support to the application of the term, *persona*, to the corporation. These were referred to as supporting this interpretation by medieval jurists. Nevertheless it is clear that the original sense of these passages does not support the medieval interpretation, which was thus creative and innovatory. The texts in question are D.46.1.22; D.4.2.9, 1; and D.35.1.56 (see Duff, ibid., pp. 20–1).

17 See Wilks, *Problem of Sovereignty*, p. 24; and id., 'Corporation and representation', p. 258.

18 See id. ad D.1.1.9 (fol. 11v), 'Quando statutum loquitur de persona non intelligitur de persona ficta, nisi statutum nominatim se ad fictam personam extendat, infra [D.3.5.3, 1]. Hac ratione non comprehendit civitates et castra, quia proprie non sunt persone, sed vice persone, infra [D.46.1.22].'

19 For agreement on this point see especially Brian Tierney's discussion in *Foundations*, pp. 98–103. See Canning, 'Corporation', pp. 15–19, for the problems which Gierke's seminal interpretation of medieval corporation theory raised for subsequent scholarship. For criticism of Gierke's thesis see E. Lewis, 'Organic tendencies', and Duff, *Personality*, pp. 206–36. For a full-length study of Gierke's theory see J. D. Lewis, *Genossenschaft-Theory*. A useful discussion of fiction theory may also be found in Michaud-Quantin, *Universitas*, pp. 206–11.

would envisage the corporation as a legal person with its very existence conceded by a superior authority which creates it. Baldus' view is clearly very different: the *populus*, being the product not of human artifice (as the fiction theory would demand) but of man's political nature, in no sense derives its existence from any superior but from the *ius gentium* itself;[20] and furthermore the capacity of the *populus* to act and will results, when it is sovereign, in the non-recognition of a superior. Nor is Baldus' concept of the fictive person that which Gillet attributed to the Decretalists, including Innocent IV: namely that the corporation was not as a fictive person a distinct subject of rights, but that the physical members of the corporation were the subjects of rights, and that these members were only treated as if they were one person when this was required for specific legal purposes.[21] Baldus' approach is however certainly that of the Commentators: that the corporational entity is a legal person and as such a subject of rights distinct from its members. Bartolus expressed this view classically, pointing out that this was a specifically juristic way of thinking and different from that of philosophers who, he maintained, identified any group with its physical members. Bartolus was not denying the philosophical validity of a moderate realist or indeed nominalist position in extra-legal discussion but was stressing the validity of the purely legal concept of the fictive person strictly within the bounds of juristic discourse.[22] According to both Bartolus and Baldus the *populus* as a fictive person acts through the instrumentality of its members who represent it. Bartolus also maintains in this passage that the civilian approach is different from that of *all* the canonists who, he holds, share the view of philosophers on

[20] Baldus admits fiction in the sense of artifice in the case of a *collegium*, which would indeed be created by legal enactment: 'Item nota argumentum ad statutum quod loquitur de multitudine hominum, intellige singulorum. Sed universitas et collegium loco unius persone funguntur, ut [D.46.1.22; D.4.2.9, 1]. Tamen quantum ad presentem tractatum non puto quod in clausula, "quidam alii", intelligantur collegia, sed tantum singulares persone. Nam cum vera predicatio sit de rebus naturalibus et non fictis, et collegium non natura sed artificio hominum constat, merito non continetur appellatione persone, nisi per interpretationem extensivam' (ad X.1.3.15, n. 6, fol. 42r). This is not to say that Baldus even here is using the concept of the fictive person in the sense meant by Gierke.

[21] See Gillet, *Personnalité juridique*, pp. 163–8. For a similar interpretation of Innocent IV see Rodriguez, 'Innocent IV' (especially pp. 312 and 316–17). Rodriguez demonstrates with good documentation that Innocent did not uphold a fiction theory in the modern sense.

[22] See Bartolus ad D.48.19.16, 10, n. 3–4 (fol. 200r). Ockham, for instance, expressly rejected the juristic *persona ficta* concept: see his *Tractatus contra Benedictum*, c. 8 (ed. Sikes, Bennett and Offler), p. 189. Whereas I agree with Evans, 'Idea of the *populus*', pp. 36–63, that the Commentators were not nominalists in their corporation theory, I cannot accept her view that they were realists.

this point. This statement would certainly appear to support Gillet's interpretation of the views of the Decretalists. The role of Innocent IV, however, in the development of the concept of the fictive person has been hotly contested by modern scholars. Whereas one can support Gillet, Tierney, Feenstra[23] and Rodriguez in rejecting any idea that Innocent IV espoused a modern fiction theory (as Ullmann for instance continued to believe),[24] there seems very good reason to consider with Paradisi that Innocent was important in the development of the concept of the fictive person as a distinct subject of rights with a substratum of physical members.[25] After all Baldus makes constant reference to Innocent as an authority for the idea of the corporation as an abstract entity distinct from its members.[26]

There remains, however, a juristic problem which might appear to make it difficult to attribute to the *populus* as a fictive corporate person an imputed capacity to act and will. Baldus agrees with other jurists that when compared with human beings the *populus* as a fictive person lacks a soul. Those wishing to interpret medieval corporation theory in terms of a modern fiction theory would see this lack as precluding the *populus* from being able to act and will in general. This is however to take the argument too far. Baldus only refers to the lack of a soul on the part of the *populus* in two contexts: the taking of an oath for a city in a court case involving it; and the question of whether a city can be excommunicated. He maintains that the city, being a *nomen iuris*, and thus lacking a soul, cannot take an oath, but that its representatives must swear instead on the souls of its members.[27] From a theological point of view an oath can only be taken by a human being. No jurist could maintain that a corporation had a soul in the sense required for

---

[23] See Feenstra, 'Histoire des fondations', especially pp. 412–13.
[24] See 'Juristic obstacles', p. 59. In an earlier article, however, Ullmann was willing to criticise Gierke's thesis: 'Delictal responsibility', pp. 78–96.
[25] See Paradisi, 'Pensiero politico', pp. 120–1, and Canning, 'The corporation', p. 17.
[26] See, for instance, Baldus ad D.3.4.7 (Additio Baldi), fol. 205v (ed. Venice, 1616); and id. ad D.3.2.6 (fol. 148r). In both passages he refers to Innocent IV ad X.5.39.53, 'Vniversitas autem non potest excommunicari quia impossibile est quod universitas delinquat, quia universitas, sicut est capitulum, populus, gens et huiusmodi nomina sunt iuris et non personarum, ideo non cadit in eam excommunicatio' (n. 1, fol. 559r, ed. Frankfurt, 1570).
[27] See Baldus ad Auth. 'Principalis', § 'Hoc etiam' (ad C.2.58.2), fol. 144r. Cf. id., *De pace Constantie*, ad v. 'Si qui e parte nostra' (fol. 94r); id. ad C.9.2.3 (fol. 353r); and id. ad D.3.4.2 (fol. 173v). Baldus is not however always consistent: see id. ad Auth. 'Ad hec' (ad C.4.32.16), fol. 289v, 'Licet universitas ut universitas non habeat animam intellectivam, ut no. Innocentius in [X.5.39.53], et est manifestum, tamen propter singulares personas dicitur delinquere et in animam iurare, tamen iuratur in animam universitatis, ut [Sextus, 2.10.2] facit [D.4.2.6, & D.4.3.15 & D.46.1.22].'

taking an oath. Similarly Baldus holds that a city-community, lacking a soul, cannot be excommunicated – only its rulers can be.[28] Again, this shows no more than that he denies that the community possesses a soul in a theological sense: it would be in his mind that only a baptised human being could be excommunicated.[29] No corporation had, of course, ever been baptised. In both these cases, therefore, the lack of a soul applies in a literal and theological sense. Thus these passages are not good evidence for a general interpretation of the legal capacity of the city-*populus* in terms of a modern fiction theory. The point is that in its aspect as an abstract fictive person the *populus* indeed lacks such a soul and cannot act and will in a literal sense; but that in matters concerning government and politics it is deemed to act and will through the medium of its ensouled physical members or the rulers chosen by them.

A more important problem, however, is posed by the identification of the city-*populus*, understood as a *respublica*, with a minor under age. Walter Ullmann in particular focused attention on this aspect of medieval corporation theory.[30] Two of the major sources for this view are a couple of passages in the *Corpus Iuris Civilis* itself[31] where in addition *civitates* are placed on a par with madmen and infants because of their inability to express a legally valid will.[32] The implications contained in these passages for the government of the community were developed by medieval jurists. A minor in Roman law requires a *tutor* to act for him. It thus became current in juristic writings for the community to be identified with a minor and its ruler with a tutor on the grounds that the community does not rule itself but is ruled by others. Indeed, the jurists' equation of the public community with a minor is so universal that Walter Ullmann was able to say in this connection: 'I have not found one jurist who expressed a different standpoint.'[33] If one looks at the sources it is perfectly true that the comparison of the community with a minor is a common theme, being applied initially to the *respublica Romanorum* and then under Accursius'

[28] Ad X.2.7.4, n.6 (fol. 199v).
[29] For a similar interpretation applied to Innocent IV ad X.5.39.53 see Duff, *Personality*, pp. 223–4. For Innocent IV's view on the excommunication of a corporation see also Eschmann, 'Studies on the notion of society'.
[30] For a discussion of the place of this minority-concept in medieval jurisprudence see Ullmann, 'Juristic obstacles', pp. 48–64. Cp. Gierke, *Genossenschaftsrecht*, III, 397–400, 484–5 and 488.
[31] C.2.53.4 and C.11.30.3.
[32] D.4.6.22, 2.   [33] 'Juristic obstacles', p. 54.

influence to other cities.[34] The jurists were in fact giving precision to governmental concepts long established in medieval political thought.[35]

As regards the capacity of the city-*populus* to act and will, the significant implications of the minority-thesis are these: that the *populus*, being in the position of a mere minor, lacks a legally valid will; and that its ruler, whether he is styled the *rector*, the *podestà*, or by some other term, since he enjoys the position of a tutor, acts on its behalf, that is to say in its interests.[36] For these reasons Walter Ullmann maintained that there is a connection between the concept of the *respublica* as a minor and the idea that the public body as a corporation is a *persona ficta*: neither the minor nor the fictive person can truly will, an interpretation made possible, as we have seen, by Ullmann's application of an essentially modern fiction theory.[37]

Clearly there is a fundamental conflict between the minority-thesis and Bartolus' and Baldus' theories of popular sovereignty which of necessity involve the capacity of the *populus* to act and will in a legally valid sense. It is true that Bartolus in some passages designates the city-community as a minor,[38] and that there is some trace of this idea in Baldus' works. The point however is that neither jurist permits this concept to interfere with his major thesis of the sovereign and self-governing city-*populus*. In the cases of Bartolus and Baldus the comparison of the city-community with a minor was retained because the *respublica* was identified with a minor in the *Corpus Iuris Civilis*: they were not at liberty simply to ignore these texts. For both jurists

---

[34] See Accursius ad C.2.53.4, ad v. 'Respublica' & 'Solet', fol. 63r (here he is only thinking in terms of the *Respublica Romanorum*). In his gloss on C.11.30.3 (fol. 135r), however, he extends the term, *respublica*, to other cities. Jacobus de Ravannis (ad C.2.53.4, fol. 116r) tells us that Accursius' opinion that a city other than Rome can benefit from *restitutio in integrum*, the minor's remedy, became the generally accepted one (he refers to Accursius' remarks in a disputation, with supporting reference to the gloss on C.11.30.3). There was, in fact, disagreement among the Commentators as to whether *restitutio in integrum* could properly be extended to cities other than Rome (see also below, p. 195, n. 40). In the light of the discussion amongst the early Commentators as to whether cities other than Rome are properly or improperly termed *respublicae* (see above, p. 123) see Cynus, ibid., n. 3–4 (fol. 115r) for arguments against such extended application of *restitutio in integrum*. The jurists did, however, admit that the similarity between the republic and a minor was not close in every respect: see, for instance, Bartolus ad C.11.30.3, n. 4 (fol. 35v). Cp. id. ad D.3.4.1, 2, n. 1 (fol. 113v); Accursius, ibid., ad v. 'Proconsul' (fol. 63r); Jacobus de Arena ad D.40.3.3 (fol. 158r); Lucas de Penna ad C.11.30.1 (p. 433); and Innocent IV ad X.1.41.1, n. 1 (fol. 175v).

[35] See below, p. 220, n. 48.

[36] See Ullmann, 'Juristic obstacles', p. 55.

[37] Ibid., pp. 59–60.

[38] As in his commentary on C.11.30.3, n. 1–2 (fol. 35v).

the likening of the city-community to a minor does not involve the wholesale adoption of the minority-thesis as enunciated by Walter Ullmann.

The likening of a city-community to a minor makes its most prominent appearance in Baldus' works in his commentary on C.2.53.4 itself ('The *respublica* is accustomed to enjoy the rights of a minor and thus can seek the remedy of restitution'). The context of his remarks is the equation of the public body (*respublica*) with a minor, and its consequent enjoyment of *restitutio in integrum*, the minor's legal remedy.[39] Baldus is here employing a minority-concept expressly within the context of the city as a corporation. He rejects the opinion of Jacobus Butrigarius that the large corporation has the status of a minor and is therefore restituted, whereas the small corporation (including the small city) is not in this position:

But Jacobus Butrigarius says to the contrary that large fortified places and big villages which are ruled by others are equivalent to minors and enjoy complete restitution of rights, but that it is otherwise in the case of small fortified places or villages, and also of a small city, as in France (see the *lectura* of Jacobus Butrigarius) and Bartolus maintains the same. I believe that the opinion of Jacobus de Arena is the truer one for if the legate of a town enjoys restitution of rights, the town itself has therefore a much stronger claim to this... And the distinction between the small city and the large corporation has no support in law or reason, because, whether it is small or large, neither true consent nor true negligence is to be found there but only fictive, since there are many in the corporation who cannot truly consent, and there are many wards and minors there for whose sake the corporation of the city, fortified place or village earns the benefit of restitution, because these minors are part of the self-same body of the corporation itself. And this is my view too.[40]

---

[39] He here sums up the content of C.2.53.4 thus: 'Respublica equiparatur minori, et ideo habet beneficium restitutionis in integrum. h.d.' (fol. 136v).

[40] Fol. 137v. See Jacobus Butrigarius ad C.2.53.4 (fol. 82r), where he argues that large corporations are restituted because it is difficult for everyone to express their knowledge and consent, but that this is not the case in small ones (cp. id. ad D.4.6.15, 3, n. 17, p. 292). He maintains however that such restitution does not derive from the right of the *respublica* to *restitutio in integrum* but from a general formula of 'just cause', because cities other than Rome are not identified with the *respublica*. Cp. Bartolus ad C.2.53.4, n. 2 (fol. 92r), where he maintains that this law can be extended to any city because like a minor it is ruled by others, but continues, 'Iacobus Butrigarius dicebat iudicio meo satis bene, posito quod civitates non restituantur [restituentur *ed. cit.*] vigore huius legis, quia proprie non est respublica, tamen restituerentur ex clausula generali, "si qua mihi iusta causa esse videbitur"; et hoc puto esse verum.' In his commentary on C.11.30.3, n. 1–2 (fol. 35v) Bartolus follows Accursius' gloss there and understands *respublica* to apply to any city. See Jacobus de Arena ad C.2.53.4 (fol. 11r), 'Sed certe respublica dicitur municipium [D.39.4.13, 1; D.47.2.31]...et civitas restituitur...Certe illud intelligitur in qualibet civitate, idem ergo in quolibet municipio.'

The context of this passage is crucial. Baldus is discussing not cities which might be sovereign, but whether *castra* and *villae* can be restituted. He is clearly concerned with corporations on this relatively small scale. Furthermore this passage could not apply to a *populus* in the sense of a sovereign citizen-body, because the members of such a body would have the capacity to give genuine consent. Rather he is clearly envisaging a community in its widest sense as including all those who do not have the capacity for a legally valid consent.[41] The passage means that in a corporation, in which not all can consent, it is a fiction to attribute to all its members taken as a whole the capacity to consent – to do so would be to acknowledge a form of constructive consent. It does not mean that the members of any citizen-body taken as a whole can only give fictive consent, nor does it apply to the abstract aspect of the *populus* as a fictive person: it is concerned only with the human members of the corporation. Thus Ullmann's interpretation of this passage seeing it as evidence for his linking of the minority-thesis and a modern fiction theory seems inapplicable.[42] Furthermore Baldus gives only a very limited reason for justifying restitution: the presence of minors in such a corporation – there is no suggestion that restitution is justified because of any corporation's overall incapacity to consent.

In his commentary on D.4.6.8 Baldus reiterates the common juristic reason justifying a corporation's right to restitution – that it is ruled by others:

Note the argument that any city, fortified place or village can enjoy complete restitution of rights against prescription, because, if this is conceded to its legate, then its own claim to it is so much stronger...We commonly hold that corporations enjoy the rights of a minor and can benefit from restitution...And there is a reason for this, because they are always under the protection and government of administrators, and thus they are equivalent to churches and minors.[43]

Such restitution is a protection for the powerless against those who rule them. Baldus cannot have sovereign cities in mind because they, as we

---

41 Corporate bodies composed of men of sense are in a different position. See Baldus ad D.46.8.9 (fol. 44v); id. ad *Specul.*, 1.3.1, p. 194; id. ad C.1.14.8 (fol. 54v); and id. ad D.3.4.1, 2 (fol. 172v).

42 See 'Juristic obstacles', pp. 59–60.

43 Fol. 204v. It was however a common juristic opinion that the *universitas* was not restituted for past alienations: see for example Cynus ad C.2.53.4, n. 4 (fol. 115r), 'Et quod dicitur quod respublica equiparatur minori, verum est quantum ad lesiones futuras. Sed quantum ad lesionem preteritam equiparatur minori facto maiori. Et idem in ecclesia. Hoc credo verius'; and Albericus de Rosciate, ibid., n. 5 (fol. 118r), where he adds, 'Si enim aliter diceretur, non inveniretur qui vellet contrahere cum ecclesia vel republica, et sic in eorum lesionem redundaret.'

shall see, appoint their own rulers and administrators and can call them to account. Indeed, Baldus considers that wherever a *respublica* appoints its rulers they are comparable to tutors precisely in that they are accountable to the community for the way in which they exercise their office.[44] But there is no suggestion in this that such a community is in the position of a minor in this relationship – rather it is the authority appointing the tutor. The officer's tutorial function expresses his role of protection and responsibility. It is thus possible to employ the tutorial concept without implying the minority-thesis in the sense expounded by Walter Ullmann.

Such then are the significant appearances of the concept of the community as a minor in Baldus' treatment of cities. The equation of the *respublica* with a minor, which might on the face of it appear as an awkward legacy from the *Corpus Iuris Civilis*, is clearly not perceived as such by Baldus, and in no way impedes his major thesis of the capacity of the autonomous or sovereign city-corporation to act and will through its human members and officers.

THE GOVERNMENT OF THE 'POPULUS'

Baldus makes a unique contribution to political thought by combining this corporational view of the city-*populus* with the ultimately Aristotelian conception of natural, political man. This is clear from his commentary on C.7.53.5 where his definition of the *populus* in corporational terms[45] is followed immediately by the passage in which the concept of natural, political man is introduced.[46] Natural men become political not simply in congregation but through being members of the corporation of the *populus*. Insofar as they are members of the *populus* these men cease to be considered as isolated individuals (*homines separati*) but are seen as corporate men (*ut universi*) through being endowed with the characteristics of the physical members of a corporation. In the case of a city-*populus* this specific corporational characteristic is a political one. In short, to be a political man, a citizen, is to be a member of this corporation.

For Baldus the full potentialities of citizenship are realised in sovereign cities where the body of citizens is the origin of governmental power and jurisdiction which are exercised through a structure of general assembly, councils representative of the people and officers deriving their power from and representing the people. Thus citizenship

---

[44] Ad X.2.19.11, n. 58 (fol. 192v). Cp. Bartolus ad D.12.2.34, n.1 (fol. 35v).
[45] See above, p. 187. [46] See above, p. 159.

is exercised both through direct participation and by the establishing of representatives. A similar structure of government, but subject to the confirmation of a superior, is also to be found in non-sovereign cities as the treatments of other jurists not producing theses of popular sovereignty bear witness.[47] For Baldus, as far as such a citizen-body is concerned, this would be but a partial expression of man's natural political capacity, in contrast to its full realisation in a sovereign city.

The model which Bartolus produced for the structure of popular government is as follows: the general assembly of the people, which has no superior, elects the council which acts as the governing body of the city and in turn elects the city's executive and judicial officers.[48] This council is thus an elected body whose representative character is memorably expressed in the famous words: 'the council represents the mind of the people' ('concilium representat mentem populi').[49] The advantage of Bartolus' structure is that it provides a clear and simple general model for the government of a sovereign people. In itself, though, this model gives no indication about how oligarchical such a popular regime might be. The general assembly elects the council 'ab initio', which could mean either that the assembly elects each council or that it sets up the original conciliar constitution. Furthermore this structure is applicable both to the *populus* 'in primo gradu magnitudinis' (that is, the smallest size), which should be governed by the multitude, and to that 'in secundo gradu magnitudinis', for which government by the few would be suitable.[50]

In contrast Baldus produces no clear general model of a structure of popular representative self-government. This might well appear as a deficiency when compared with Bartolus' approach. On the other hand if one considers the sheer variety of constitutional structures in fourteenth-century Italian cities Bartolus' model appears too simple: it does not, for instance, reflect the multiplicity of councils in such cities nor does it tally with the conciliar structure of a guild-republic like Bartolus' own adoptive city, Perugia, in which guild-members, not a general assembly, elected directly or indirectly the councils by which

---

[47] See, for instance, Raynerius de Forlì, *Rep.* ad D.1.1.9, n. 29 (fol. 19r); and Albericus de Rosciate ad C.8.53.Rubr., n. 16 (fol. 169r).

[48] The best modern discussion is in Ullmann, 'De Bartoli sententia', pp. 716–23.

[49] Ad D.1.3.32, n. 10 (fol. 17v). See also id. ad C.10.32.2, n. 8, p. 37 (ed. Basel, 1588).

[50] For Bartolus' theory that the form of government should vary according to the size of the *populus* see his tract, *De regimine civitatis* (pp. 162–8, ed. Quaglioni, *Politica e diritto*), where he also considers that for one 'in tertio gradu magnitudinis' monarchy is most suitable.

the city was governed.[51] It may well be that Baldus precisely because of this variety was unwilling to set forth a simple model which must to some degree be removed from the complications of reality. Baldus' treatment of the structure of popular government is in fact very variable in quality: he gives deep attention to certain crucial points while totally ignoring others or treating them inadequately.

Baldus assumes a conciliar structure of government for cities. Although the *populus* still has the power to legislate in general assembly, councils acting for the people have grown up where the size of cities makes such assembly difficult.[52] He gives hardly any information, however, about these councils. He certainly envisages the role which a council representative of the people plays in the legislative process, but in his description of the making of city-statutes he makes no innovation whatsoever. Either the whole citizen-body is summoned in general assembly or the council representing it is convened. Both are treated as corporations and the ordinary rules of corporation procedure apply: a *quorum* consists of two-thirds of the members and voting is by simple numerical majority of those present to express thereby the will of the corporation as a whole. In the case of a general assembly members of the council participate in the debating of measures. Two possible forms of procedure are envisaged: either the assembly as a whole can hammer out its own proposals or it votes on a specific proposal put to it.[53] This legislative procedure could clearly apply equally well to sovereign and non-sovereign cities and is indeed substantially the same as that described by Raynerius of Forlì who emphatically did not favour a doctrine of popular sovereignty, taking issue with Bartolus on this point.[54] Whether such a legislative structure is an expression of sovereignty depends upon whether the city in question recognises a superior. Other councils also exist: those of the officers of the commune, termed *decuriones* by Baldus, a category including priors, *antiani*, *camerarii*, rectors and consuls according to the nomenclature employed in different cities.[55] Clearly Baldus differs from

---

[51] See Blanshei, *Perugia*, pp. 55–9; and degli Azzi (ed.), *Statuti di Perugia dell' anno MCCCXLII*, I, 136–44 (lib. I, cap. 47), for details of elections to councils.

[52] See Baldus ad D.1.2.2, 9 (fol. 13r).

[53] See Baldus ad Inst., 1.2, 1, fol. 2v (ed. Pavia, 1489). For majority-voting see id. ad D.8.3.11 (fol. 245v); and id. ad C.10.32.45. See Gierke, *Genossenschaftsrecht*, III, 392–4, and 466–76, for an extensive treatment of the views of the Commentators on majority-voting.

[54] See Raynerius de Forlì, *Rep.* ad D.1.1.9, n. 37–8, fol. 19v (legislative procedure), and n. 22–7 (denial of Bartolus' argument for popular legislative sovereignty, ibid.).

[55] Ad C.10.32.Rubr. (fol. 29v); and id. ad C.10.32.30 (fol. 33v). Sometimes it is not possible to determine who exactly the *decuriones* are: see id. ad C.7.45.10 (fol. 216v).

Bartolus who employs the title, *decuriones*, for the members of the council which represents the people and which appoints the people's officers.[56] For Baldus a council of *decuriones* does not have as much power as a legislative council possessing the same authority as the people as a whole, unless, of course, the people gives them such power.[57]

Such a structure of self-government is the mode by which the potentialities of citizenship are put into effect, so much so that a *populus* of this kind can be seen as a citizen writ large. Baldus overtly articulates this idea later in his commentary on C.7.53.5 than the passages already quoted: he says of the corporation of citizens, 'If it has congregated, it will be cited personally, because that congregation is, as it were, a political person.'[58] Clearly Baldus' remarks here have a somewhat restricted meaning because he is only considering the corporation of citizens in its corporeal form in congregation, and also manifestly has a non-sovereign city in mind, one that can be cited in law. Nevertheless the point is made: the *persona* with which the *populus* as a corporate body corresponds is a political man, a citizen. The implications of this vary, of course, according to whether the city is sovereign or not. Baldus is not here concerned with the *populus* as a person in the sense of a corporation in its abstract aspect, but as being as it were one person in its physical aspect. His somewhat tentative language reflects the fact that the congregated people is not literally one human being: thus some element of abstraction is involved even when the people in its corporeal aspect is termed one person. As we have seen, to identify the *populus* with a person is to endow it with legal existence and capability; yet the question does remain of what precisely are the capabilities of this human being, this *persona*, with which it is identified. On the corporeal

---

[56] See Bartolus, *Alia lectura* ad C.4.32.5, n. 2–3 (fol. 158r).

[57] Ad X.2.9.5, n. 8 (fol. 204v). See also his remarks on the Perugian constitution, 'Dic quod statuta dicuntur ea, que fiunt causa perpetue iurisdictionis; reformationes vero dicuntur fieri prout res incidit. In civitate Perusii sunt duo concilia, unum maius, aliud minus. In maiori fiunt statuta, que debent redigi in volumine statutorum... Aliud est concilium decurionum, cui non intervenit magistratus, sed soli decuriones; et illud, quod statuitur per eos, vocatur reformatio, que non potest derogare plebiscito; unde dicunt doctores, quod reformationes non derogant statutis, nisi decuriones habeant arbitrium a populo [D.50.9.4]' (ad X.2.27.19, n.3, fol. 342v); and cp. id., *Cons.*, 3.400, n. 2, fol. 113r (ed. Venice, 1575), 'Item consules mercantie habent iurisdictionem a communi Perusii, et ideo non potest eis auferri per minus consilium, scilicet priorum [prioris *ed. cit.*] et camerariorum.' For Perugia's conciliar structure see also *Archivio di Stato di Perugia: Archivio Storico del Comune di Perugia – Inventario*, pp. vii–xxxviii.

[58] Fol. 236r. Gierke, *Genossenschaftsrecht*, III, 426, n. 26, refers to the phrase, *persona politica* (in this passage), but does not explore its implications for the themes of citizenship and government by the people.

level, that at which the *populus* acts and wills through its structure of self-government, it is identified with a citizen. Baldus does not overtly describe the *populus* in its abstract aspect as a *persona politica*; but because he imputes the actions of its corporeal citizens to the people as an abstract entity the city-*populus* in both its abstract and corporeal aspects may be seen as a citizen writ large. What is certain is that there is no evidence in Baldus' thought for Walter Ullmann's argument that the jurists, including Baldus, through considering the *populus* to be a *persona ficta* in a modern fictionist sense identified it with a mere *subditus* on the grounds that both lacked a truly autonomous capacity to act and will:[59] the case is quite the reverse.

Baldus gives his most detailed treatment to the relationship between the people and its governing and judicial officers. His theme is that the city's officers have their power conceded to them by the people which they thus represent. The actions of these representatives in their official capacities are identified with those of the people itself. These officers are thus exercising authority which is ultimately possessed by the people. This jurisdictional structure, which is clearly an expression of citizen self-government through representation, is manifestly suited to sovereign citizen-bodies; it applies also to non-sovereign ones as an expression of their limited capacity for autonomy, but in their case their officers must be confirmed by a superior. Such a superior would have to be an immediate one because in normal circumstances imperial confirmation of city-officers had become a dead letter as in the case, for instance, of the cities of Lombardy.[60]

Baldus' treatment of city-officers reflects the dominance of the *popolo* in republican regimes and is heavily influenced by the rule of the *Raspanti* in Perugia itself.[61] In such republics Baldus attributes supreme governmental power to the officers of the *popolo*, whether they are termed *antiani* or priors, or (in the case of Perugia) *camerarii* as well.[62] Ultimate authority lies however with the *populus* itself: it concedes to the *antiani* or priors such authority as they possess within a specific time-limit.[63] They thus represent the whole city-corporation[64] and

[59] See 'Juristic obstacles', pp. 60–2.
[60] See Baldus ad *Feud.*, 2.28 (fol. 57r). Cp. id. ad *Feud.*, 2.53 (fol. 76r).
[61] See Martines, *Power and Imagination*, p. 153 and Heywood, *History of Perugia*, pp. 240–8, 269 and 283.
[62] For these *camerarii* (*camerlenghi*) see Blanshei, *Perugia*, pp. 58–9.
[63] See Baldus, *Cons.*, 1.40, fol. 17r, ed. Brescia, 1490 (= *Cons.*, 2.177, ed. Venice, 1575); id. ad C.6.21.15 (fol. 46r); id. ad D.12.1.33 (fol. 21v); id. ad C.9.26.1 (fol. 371r); and id., *Cons.*, 5.275, n. 3, fol. 69v (ed. Venice, 1575).
[64] See Baldus ad X.2.27.26, n. 14 (fol. 346r).

when they, like other officers, act in their official capacity the corporation itself is understood to act.[65] Indeed Baldus reaches a clearer understanding of this relationship than had Bartolus. The question arises whether the statutes of *antiani* are merely *ius praetorium* (as might be suggested by Bartolus' comparison of the *antiani* with the Roman magistracy, the curule aediles), or whether they enjoy the same status as statutes of the people itself, and are thus *ius civile*. Bartolus considered that the statutes of the *antiani* were ordinarily *ius praetorium* because they enacted them by virtue of their office, but that these statutes would be *ius civile* if the people either through the general assembly or general council specially mandated the *antiani* to act in its name and thus acted through the medium of its officers.[66] Baldus in contrast takes a more rigorous view of the representative role of the *antiani*: namely that in making statutes they act for the people in the strict sense that their statutes derive their legal force from the people's will which they articulate and not from the official status of their makers.[67] Nevertheless the statutes of the people are of greater weight than those of its *decuriones* precisely because the people is the source of their jurisdiction. Indeed Baldus describes the people as the superior of its *decuriones*, who cannot in consequence exercise the very power the people has given them, to revoke the people's own statutes, unless they have been endowed with specific authority to this effect.[68]

Baldus treats the *podestà* as the city's supreme judicial magistrate and, as we have seen, identifies him with the *praeses provinciae* in the case of sovereign or autonomous cities.[69] The *podestà* exercises juridical authority which other city magistrates including *decuriones* ordinarily lack.[70] The *podestà* derives his authority from the people and, in essence, performs jurisdictional functions which the people as a whole in practice cannot. Innocent IV had maintained that secular corporations could create their own rectors, but that jurisdiction remained with those rectors, who were confirmed by a superior, and not with the

---

65 See Baldus, *De pace Constantie*, ad v. 'Damna' (fol. 92r). This was a familiar view: see Albericus de Rosciate ad D.1.3.32, n. 45–6 (fols. 37r–37v). But the people's officers are not literally the people: see Baldus ad C.7.53.5 (fol. 236r), 'Modo ergo queritur qualiter contra populum fit executio, et dicendum est, quod aut loquimur de executione personali, et fit hoc modo, quia consules populi capiuntur qui quadam fictione sunt populus, arg. [D.11.7.8].'

66 Ad D.45.1.5, n. 4 (fol. 10r).

67 Ad D.1.1.9 (fol. 10r). Cp. id. ad C.6.9.Rubr. (fol. 21v).

68 *Cons.*, 2.335, fol. 88v, ed. Brescia, 1490 (= *Cons.*, 5.210, ed. Venice, 1575). This view coincides with his description of the Perugian constitution (above, p. 200, n. 57).

69 See above, p. 126, n. 119.

70 Id. ad Auth., 'Sed omnino' (ad C.4.12.4), fol. 228r.

corporation itself: thus when rectors were lacking, the corporation could not exercise jurisdiction.[71] Commenting on this well-known view Baldus reaches a different conclusion, namely that the people continues to possess potentially (*in habitu*) that jurisdiction which it concedes to its rector, the *podestà*, in order for him to put it into action. The point is that the people taken as a whole is unsuited to exercising jurisdictional in the sense of judicial functions, but that this unsuitability does not preclude it from being the ultimate possessor of that jurisdiction.[72] His statement elsewhere that the people does not possess the *imperium* which it concedes to its *podestà* should also be understood in this manner.[73] In his use of the scholastic terms, *actus* and *habitus*, Baldus acknowledges some debt to Johannes Monachus,[74] but his particularly neat application of this distinction to explain how the people possesses jurisdiction, which it does not actually exercise, appears to be his own. The distinction appears elsewhere in Baldus' works as an explanation of the relationship between the magistrate and the jurisdiction he puts into effect.[75] Certainly the *podestà* remains in essence

[71] Ad X.1.2.8, n. 2–3 (fol. 4r). Innocent's view was not generally accepted: see, for instance, Hostiensis, *Lectura*, ibid. (fol. 6v), and Tierney, *Foundations*, pp. 106–8.

[72] See Baldus, ibid., n. 10 (fol. 20v), 'Habet igitur populus iurisdictionem habitu in conferendo, sed non exercendo per se. At si populus est suorum civium princeps et dominus potest sibi potestatem eligere. Si autem alius ei principatur, immediate talis electio indiget confirmatione. Illud certum est quod iurisdictio, nisi prius habeatur in habitu, id est in virtute, non potest excitari ad actum suum, ut notat Ioannes Monachus in [*Sextus*, 1.3.11].' The people is unsuitable because it is unruly, of varying intelligence, quick to sink to the lowest level and incapable of mature deliberation. In the immediately preceding section of Baldus' commentary there is a statement which is difficult to interpret because it is embedded in his exposition of Innocent's argument, but which does correspond with his own view: 'Populus vel universitas civitatis eligunt sibi rectorem et rector habet iurisdictionem per commune, ergo ipsi sunt maiores, quia maior est causa quam effectus; et prima potentia est in causis.'

[73] *Cons.*, 'Rummer', ll. 139–42.

[74] See Johannes Monachus ad *Sext.*, 1.3.11, n. 12–13 (fol. 36r), 'Potestas prius nascitur quam excitetur ad actum...Et notandum est quod iurisditio ut est in termino a quo et in dante est iudicis dandi potestas. Sed prout est in termino ad quem, id est in dato iudice, est iuris dicendi potestas que postmodum reducitur ad actum et exercitium.' The terms in question are, of course, the common–coin of scholastic philosophy: see for instance the lengthy discussion of *habitus* in Aquinas, *S. T.*, 1a 2ae, 49, 1–4. See also Baldus ad D.1.3.9 (fol. 14r) for definitions of *habitus*. For earlier juristic use of these terms see Jacobus Butrigarius ad D.3.2.6, n. 8 (p. 190), 'Non sunt paria, esse in potentia et esse in actu.'

[75] Ad *Feud.*, 2.54 (fol. 79v), 'In magistratu [iurisdictio] est tanquam in subiecto animato sine quo per se iurisdictio nihil agit, ut [D.1.2.2, 13]...Iurisdictio quandoque est in habitu, quandoque in actu. Nam in habitu est per potentiam, in actu per exercitium, dixi [D.1.12.1] per Bartolum [D.2.1.1]...Sed prout inest ipsi magistratui est regentis officium magistratus, quod in habitu actuque consistit, iuxta no. per modernos in [D.2.1.1 & 3].' The distinction between *habitus* and *actus* does not appear in Bartolus ad D.2.1.1, but note the following there: 'officium est exercitium illius iurisdictionis'

subordinate to the people: he has only as much power as it concedes to him;[76] he is bound like any magistrate to observe its statutes in the exercise of his jurisdiction;[77] as a reflection of the general custom he is at the end of his term of office held to account by the people which is thus in the position of his superior, his *dominus*;[78] and, as we have seen, this accountability is likened to that of a tutor on behalf of his ward, but in such a way that the people is in no way seen as a minor in relation to its rector.[79]

In his commentary on X.1.2.8 Baldus clearly treats the *populus* as a corporate entity distinct from its human members, and considers it to be as such the internal sovereign within an independent city-republic: it is 'the lord and *princeps* of its citizens' and the source of jurisdictional authority. Although the citizen-body may as the corporeal members of the corporation be understood as being to that extent partakers in sovereignty, the citizens taken as individuals are in the position of subjects in relation to the *populus* as a corporate whole.[80]

Baldus' treatment of the relationship between the *podestà* and the priors or *antiani* reflects their relative position in republics in which the *popolo* had become dominant. He certainly respects the specific functions of the *podestà* and, indeed, terms both him and the priors or *antiani* as being the 'head' of the citizen-body,[81] but he nevertheless considers that the *antiani* or priors are superior to the *podestà*. Thus when a designated judge of appeal is lacking (such as the *iudex iustitiae* at Perugia),[82] appeal may be had from the court of the *podestà* to the council of priors or *antiani* as to a superior.[83] Baldus' thinking clearly

(n. 9, fol. 46v). See also Baldus ad C.7.62.6 (fol. 256r), 'Lex et magistratus auctoritate legis faciens sunt unum et idem sicut potentia in actu deducta efficitur unum et idem cum actu.'

76 Baldus ad X.1.36.3, n. 2 (fol. 163v).

77 Id. ad Auth., 'Sed novo iure' (ad C.6.1.3), fol. 3v; id. ad X.2.24.19, n. 2 (fol. 303v); id. ad Auth., 'Hodie' (ad C.3.1.14), fol. 149r; and id. ad D.1.1.9 (above, p. 111, n. 59).

78 Id. ad D.1.16.4, 2 (fol. 50v); and id., *Tractatus de syndicatu officialium*, n. 34, fol. 446r (ed. Lyon, 1549), for the identical view.

79 Above, p. 197.

80 Cp. id. ad C.7.46.2 (fol. 220r).

81 As 'caput civium' the *podestà* enjoys the privileges of a citizen (ad D.1.16.4, 2, fol. 50v); cp. id. ad D.46.8.9 (fol. 43v). See also id. ad X.2.28.Rubr., n.2 (fol. 346v), 'Vbi sunt anciani, sive decuriones, qui sunt caput civitatis, tota civitas esse videtur.'

82 See Blanshei, *Perugia*, pp. 54–5. In that he is a judge of appeal the *iudex iustitiae* is in this respect superior to the *podestà* (Baldus, *Cons.*, 2.486, n. 1, fol., 130v, ed. Venice, 1575).

83 Id. ad D.1.10.1 (fol. 42v), 'Quero civitas habet consules et antianos suos et vacat iudex appellationis, an a sententia potestatis potest appellari ad antianos, cum non sit alius superior. Dicit Bartolus quod sic in [D.26.5.19]…Sed Innocentius dicit quod deficientibus etiam rectoribus penes universitatem non est exercitium iurisdictionis, et

is that in cities which truly possess powers of jurisdiction the *antiani* act directly as the officers of the *populus* and articulate its will. This mirrors the arrangements in popular regimes in which the priors or *antiani* were the governmental embodiment of the *populus* and the *podestà* a judicial (and to some extent executive) officer appointed ultimately on the authority of the *populus*. Indeed, for Baldus the priors or *antiani* are the ultimate court of appeal and final institutional embodiment of the people's justice. In whatever circumstances there has to be some place where justice can be found. If all other judicial arrangements fail then the priors or *antiani* supply what is lacking. Baldus thus likens their role to that of the *pontifices* in an early period of Republican Rome.[84] They are, as it were, the personified norms of justice ('sunt sicut regule in sua civitate durante officio'). Indeed, in a sovereign city they are the heirs to the appellate jurisdiction of the *princeps* himself.[85] In terms of the administration of justice they are the final organ for the exercise of the people's sovereign jurisdiction.

Clearly the application of the name *praeses provinciae* to the *podestà* and of that of *decuriones* to the priors or *antiani* is in Baldus' works no longer truly apposite. According to the strict interpretation of Roman law the *praeses provinciae* possesses *merum imperium* and is superior to the *decuriones* who do not, being mere municipal officials.[86] Such an interpretation obviously does not tally with Baldus' treatment of the city's officers. In employing these terms he is clearly working within the juristic tradition, but he recognises that the use of the term *decuriones* is in this context to some degree misleading. He cites the case of the priors of the independent cities of Tuscany (amongst which Perugia was, as we have seen, deemed to be numbered):[87] 'Priors, who

---

si non est apud populum multominus est apud decuriones. Opinio Innocentii est vera in universitatibus iurisdictionem non habentibus, sed in habentibus iurisdictionem est vera opinio Bartoli. Huiusmodi sunt insignes civitates habentes hoc ex consuetudine, vel privilegio, ut ex pacto vel ex pace Constantie, vel alia ex pace, que fieret hodie. Nam a talibus antianis seu prioribus, tanquam a pontificibus civitatis iura possunt impetrari, arg. supra [D.1.2.2, 6]; nam sunt sicut regule in sua civitate durante officio, unde eorum cura precipua est curare ne aliquis quid patiatur iniustum.' Cp. Bartolus ad D.26.5.19, n. 1 (fol. 52v) where it is unclear whether, in this case, he treats *priores* as *decuriones*, although Baldus, ibid. (fol. 28r) appears to consider that he does. For the superior position of the priors or *antiani* see also Baldus ad D.1.18.14 (fol. 58v).

[84] See D.1.2.2, 6 to which Baldus refers here. See also Baldus, *Cons.*, 2.486, n. 1, fol. 130v (ed. Venice, 1575), for such appeal to the Perugian *priores artium* from the sentence of the *capitano del popolo*, when there is no *podestà* or *iudex iustitiae*, 'semper enim in republica debet esse qui iura dederat.' For the *capitano* see Blanshei, *Perugia*, p. 54.

[85] Baldus, *Cons.*, 2.486, n. 1, fol. 130v (ed. Venice, 1575), 'Ad principem propter novum casum recurrendum est...Princeps autem nunc est collegium priorum artium.'

[86] See above, p. 126 (the *decuriones* would elect the *defensores civitatis*).

[87] See above, p. 127, n. 120.

according to Roman law are called *decuriones*, can be tried for fraud and any crime. I think the position is otherwise with the priors of a Tuscan city who acquire power for themselves and can thus be called magistrates.'[88] This means that the strict interpretation of the Roman law places the priors in the position of *decuriones* subordinate to a magistrate (such as the *podestà*) who would cite them for their offences, whereas in practice they have obtained in Tuscany the power of magistrates rather than that of mere municipal officials, and thus as a group, and in their official capacity, cannot be cited by another magistrate.[89]

Although the priors or *antiani* normally constitute the governing body of the city, the *populus* is at liberty to grant the exercise of its authority to whom it pleases: thus quite apart from being able to give unrestricted power to its priors or *antiani* if it so wished,[90] it could also, for example, grant all its authority to *sapientes* (wise men), the *ad hoc* committees of *savi* which were such a common feature of the government of Italian cities.[91] Ultimate authority lies with the *populus* which has a free hand in determining the structure of offices through which that authority is exercised. Similarly it establishes *statutarii* to draft its legislation but does not thereby alienate any of its authority to these officers but rather acts through them. Thus since it is essentially the *populus* which makes the statute, the *populus*, not the *statutarii*, must interpret it,[92] a view which coincides with the *communis opinio* of other jurists,[93] and which although applicable to non-sovereign cities reflects in the theories of Bartolus and Baldus their contention that the sovereign *populus* retains that sovereignty throughout its legislative process.

BALDUS AND THE IDEA OF THE STATE

The major significance of Baldus' conception of the sovereign city-*populus* as a corporation composed of political men lies in its implications for the development of the idea of the state. It is here that Baldus' unique contribution to political thought truly appears. His

---

[88] Ad C.9.22.21 (fol. 376r).
[89] This explains Baldus' meaning ad C.10.32.2 (fol. 30r), 'Nota primo quod magistratus possunt citare priores sive ancianos; alias compellantur consiliarii, quos Perusini appellant priores.'
[90] Id., *Cons.*, 5.32, fol. 10v (ed. Brescia, 1491).
[91] Id. ad D.1.3.1 (fol. 13r).
[92] Id. ad X.2.22.8, n. 1–2 (fol. 289r). Cp. id. ad D.1.4.1 (fol. 21r).
[93] See, for instance, Bartolus ad D.1.1.9, n. 56 (fol. 13r): for this part of Bartolus' theory see Ullmann, 'Concilium repraesentat mentem populi', pp. 720–1. For the same argument see Raynerius de Forlì, *Rep.*, ibid., n. 88 (fol. 23v).

conception of such a city-*populus* may be summarised thus: it is a corporation which is in its abstract aspect an entity distinct from its members and government but which is in its parallel corporeal form a body composed of natural, political men (citizens); as such it exists within a thoroughly this-worldly dimension; it is furthermore perpetual and territorially sovereign within the overall structure of the hierarchy of sovereignty and within the limitations imposed on secular internal sovereignty by ecclesiastical jurisdiction and higher norms. This view is clearly an idea of the state which is late medieval insofar as it accepts such a hierarchy and such limitations; but it also exhibits a requirement generally accepted as part of any modern conception of the state: that the state is envisaged as an abstract entity distinct from its members and government. Quentin Skinner considers that the acquisition of this latter concept can be dated to the second half of the sixteenth century.[94] It was however Bartolus and Baldus who developed this part of the modern state concept by applying juristic corporation theory to the territorially sovereign city. In this respect Baldus is clearly walking the same path as Bartolus. Both jurists through the use of corporation theory are making a distinctive contribution to political thought, one which is couched in a specific juristic language. Its very distinctiveness is made even clearer when this juristic view is compared with contemporary ideas of the state. The Aristotelian tradition tended to identify the state with its members. Thus Walter Ullmann, for instance, considered that the major effect of the rediscovery of Aristotelian political ideas in the thirteenth century was the acquisition of the concept of the state in the sense of a congregation of natural political men, of citizens.[95] Aquinas for example certainly identified the state with its members;[96] even when he stressed the unitary aspect of a political community by saying, 'In civil matters all those who belong to one community are considered, as it were, one body, and the whole community, as it were, one man,'[97] he was not thereby considering it as an entity distinct from its members. If one turns furthermore to a nominalist approach, there is no doubt that it was completely opposed to Bartolus' and Baldus' view. Thus, as we have seen, Ockham through identifying any group only with the individuals who composed it expressly rejected the basis of the corporation theory of Bartolus and Baldus.[98] The position of Marsilius however is more open to debate:

[94] *Foundations*, II, 352–8.
[95] See, for instance, *Medieval Foundations*, pp. 94–5.
[96] See, for instance, Gilby, *Principality and Polity*, pp. 253–60; and Lewis, *Medieval Political Ideas*, I, 206–7.
[97] *S.T.*, 1a 2ae, 81, 1 ('Leonine' ed., p. 88).   [98] Above, p. 191, n. 22.

although his concept of the state owed much to Aristotle, Michael Wilks has argued that Marsilius did possess a conception of the *universitas civium* as a corporate entity distinct from individual citizens, but that this was derived from juristic sources, an argument which Helmut Walther rejects.[99]

Baldus' unique contribution to political thought is to combine a fully articulated juristic corporational view with an ultimately Aristotelian conception of the state as a congregation of natural political men. In doing so he goes beyond Bartolus' approach by placing the *de facto* state within the philosophical context of a natural, this-worldly, and thus avowedly political dimension. In identifying the territorial state's physical aspect with the congregation of political men Baldus draws this Aristotelian idea into his juristic corporational view and thus succeeds in grafting an abstract dimension onto an Aristotelian idea of the state. The concept of the territorial state that results is thus both more complex and fuller than had previously existed either in jurisprudence or Aristotelian-based *scientia politica*; and Baldus has therefore made an innovative contribution to the development of the idea of the state. His theory has its special character because he adopts an Aristotelian stand-point but argues from the very centre of juristic thought whereas Marsilius, insofar as he did use jurisprudence, certainly applied only a piecemeal and very limited juristic knowledge. It has been maintained that to identify the *populus* with a corporation was to prevent the emergence of the idea of the state through obscuring the crucial differences between the state and lesser corporations.[100] Yet in the cases of both Bartolus and Baldus the application of corporational concepts does not detract from the idea of the territorial state: rather the state is a special kind of corporation. For both jurists corporation theory is central to their ideas of the state. Although it is true that Baldus only uses the term 'political' in the context of city-states and that thus his elaboration of the concept of the territorial state is fullest in his treatment of city-*populi*, he does not restrict his idea of the territorial state to cities but also makes a major contribution to the theory of kingdoms as states.

[99] See Wilks, 'Corporation and representation', esp. pp. 254–6, and Walther, *Imperiales Königtum*, p. 162, n. 179.
[100] See, for instance, Ullmann, 'Juristic obstacles', pp. 51–2.

Chapter 6

KINGSHIP AND *SIGNORIE*

The remaining area of Baldus' political thought concerns his theory of the territorial rule by one man. He devotes attention both to kingship and *signorie*. Indeed, in his treatment of the nature of kingship and the relation of the king to the crown and the community of the realm he produces a major contribution to late medieval jurisprudence. The comparison with Bartolus in this respect is instructive: although Bartolus produces an important discussion of certain aspects of kingship in his tract, *De regimine civitatis*, he neglects the subject in his commentaries.[1] Baldus, in contrast, in his commentaries and in his *consilia* gives a far more profound and extensive treatment to kingship. Whereas the substantive point which Bartolus makes in that tract is to relate the suitability of the form of regime to the size of state, and thus to consider that monarchy is suited to a state of the largest magnitude, the most significant part of Baldus' discussion exists on a deeper level – through the application of corporation theory he provides a structure for the sovereign monarchical state itself. The comparison with Bartolus is even more striking as regards the treatment of *signorie*. Bartolus is unsympathetic to *signori* and tends to condemn them as tyrants.[2] Baldus, however, accepts their existence as a political fact and in his *consilia* accommodates them into his political theory in a constructive manner.

As we have seen, Baldus treats kingship within his overall *de iure–de facto* structure and accords to kings an essentially *de facto* sovereignty.[3]

[1] See Woolf, *Bartolus*, pp. 107–12. For Bartolus, *De regimine civitatis*, see especially Quaglioni, 'Regimen ad populum', and above, p. 7, n. 31; and Skinner, *Foundations*, I, 53–6.

[2] See Woolf, *Bartolus*, pp. 162–73; Quaglioni, 'Il "Tractatus de tyrannia" di Bartolo'; id., 'Un "Tractatus de tyranno"', pp. 65 and 66; id., *Politica e diritto*, pp. 57–71; and Skinner, *Foundations*, I, 55–6.

[3] Above, pp. 64–8. For aspects of Baldus' theory of monarchy and kingship see Wahl, 'Immortality and inalienability', and 'Baldus and foundations'. My approach to Baldus' thought is different from that of Wahl who does not treat Baldus' fundamental

In doing so he is going beyond Bartolus by applying a developed *de facto* argument for the sovereignty of kings as well as of city-*pópuli*. According to Baldus, in the case of kings as of city-*populi* the source of power within the *de facto* dimension lies with the people, which on the basis of the *ius gentium* itself through the exercise of its natural reason elects its monarch, as in the case of Castile:

The question is whether these days a province can elect a king for itself. And it seems that it cannot, for provinces are under the natural dominion of the emperor, and therefore they cannot confer *merum imperium* on anyone, as in Auth., 'De defensoribus civitatum' [Coll., 3.2, 1 = Nov., 15, 1]. But you are to say that it can, if it is such a province as is not subject to the emperor, like Spain. For if the lords of Castile were to become totally extinct, the inhabitants of the kingdom could elect themselves a king through the *ius gentium*, as here. Were jurisdictions therefore introduced through the *ius gentium*? You are to say that they were, because being a king means that one possesses jurisdiction. Since, therefore, there were kings through the *ius gentium*, there were also jurisdictions.[4]

Baldus is commenting here on the passage in the *Digest* which derives the foundation of kingdoms from the *ius gentium*.[5] Indeed, in terms of the *Corpus Iuris Civilis* this is the only source of the authority of kings as such. The question is whether this original right under the *ius gentium* had been superseded by the establishment of the Roman empire. Like all jurists Baldus holds that before the creation of legal systems all peoples could elect their kings on the basis of the *ius gentium*: 'By the *ius gentium* kings originated without any formality solely from the consent of those who elected them, since there were kings before there were laws, when they reigned in their first purity and only nature made law for man [D.1.1.5; D.1.2.2, 1] and Auth. "Quibus modis naturales efficiuntur sui" [Coll., 7.1, 1 = Nov., 89, 1].'[6] The crucial point is that Baldus maintains that a kingdom's inhabitants by virtue of the *ius gentium* still continue to possess this right to elect their kings in his own

de iure–de facto structure, and who tends to mix in together texts relating to the emperor, kings, the *populus* and the *respublica*. In contrast, it is essential to distinguish in Baldus' thought the specific forms of government and political entities which he considers. Thus, for instance, to discuss 'the ruler', as does Wahl, is misleading: it is necessary to know which ruler Baldus has in mind. Furthermore neither in these articles nor in his thesis (above, p. 1, n. 2) does Wahl treat Baldus' theory of the sovereignty of city-*populi* and the republican form of government. Likewise Curcio in 'La politica di Baldo' (above, ibid.), although he perceives that Baldus attributes sovereignty to the city-*populus* (p. 128), nevertheless neglects the whole republican aspect of his thought and considers that he only advocates a monarchical government for such cities.

4 Ad D.1.1.5 (fol. 7r).   5 See above, p. 26, n. 32.
6 *Consilium* on the Great Schism (ad C.6.34), fol. 99r. Cf. D.1.2.2, 1.

day.[7] The full significance of this view emerges when it is seen in the context of Baldus' use of the *ius gentium* as the juristic expression of the this-worldly dimension of human government and society.[8] Peoples, deriving their origin from the *ius gentium*, can on this basis through natural reason establish their form of government, whether this is republican in the case of city-*populi* or monarchical in that of kingdoms. Free kingdoms which elect their own kings possess *maiestas* on a par with that of the Roman people,[9] and through the exercise of *de facto* consent in the form of custom are not subject to the emperor, with the result that their kings, as in the case of France or Castile, are themselves not subject to him either. As has been noted, however, there is a difference between the relationship of a sovereign king to the emperor and that of a sovereign city. Although both are subject to the universal sovereignty of the emperor *de iure*, within the context of *de facto* sovereignty the king's is of a higher form: whereas his kingdom is fully independent from the emperor (thus according to Baldus the kingdom of France is not part of the empire),[10] a city of the *terrae imperii*, while in normal circumstances it enjoys practical sovereignty, is slightly more directly under the ultimate sovereignty of the emperor who might conceivably appear in the city to take up his authority.[11] Thus there is a hierarchy of sovereignty both in terms of the *de iure–de facto* distinction and within *de facto* sovereignty itself. Baldus' view is clearly different from that of the Neapolitan school of jurists. Unlike them he does not use the *ius gentium* to deny the *de iure* authority of the emperor over kings and thus to maintain with Andreas de Isernia that the world has thereby returned to its pristine condition before the conquests of Rome.[12] According to Baldus the universal empire

[7] See also Baldus ad C. Const., 'De novo codice componendo', Rubr. (fol. 1v); and id. ad X.1.3.36, n. 2 (fol. 61r). Once a king has been elected the kingship can then pass by succession: Baldus, *Cons.*, 1.359, fol. 109v, ed. Brescia, 1490 (= *Cons.*, 3.159, ed. Venice, 1575).

[8] See above, pp. 104–13, and p. 158.

[9] See Baldus, *Cons.*, 1.359, fol. 109v, ed. Brescia, 1490 (= *Cons.*, 3.159, ed. Venice, 1575), 'Incidit in crimen perduellionis veniendo contra maiestatem regni seu reipublice; nam ipsa respublica maiestatem habet ad instar populi romani, cum libera sit, et ius habeat creandi regem, ut [Inst., 3.1].'

[10] See above, p. 66; and Baldus, *Cons.*, 1.417, fol. 129r, ed. Brescia, 1490 (= *Cons.*, 3.217, ed. Venice, 1575), where he refers to the king of France 'qui francus est a iure romano, et dedignatur legibus subiici.' Sicily is of course the great exception being subject to the papacy: Baldus says of Henry VII's process against Robert of Naples, 'ibi processit imperator contra non subditum sibi principaliter sed ecclesie romane' (ad C.7.62.15, fol. 260v).   [11] See above, p. 116.

[12] See above, p. 70, n. 176. Andreas de Isernia considers that the Roman people and other free peoples are on a par in their capacity to create their rulers on the basis of the *ius gentium* (ad *Feud.*, 2.56, n. 18, fol. 291v).

coexists with the people's persisting right under the *ius gentium*, which indeed originated in mankind's primitive condition.[13] The crucial point for Baldus however is that times have changed since then: the sempiternal and divinely sanctioned empire has in the meantime been established and it is not possible to put the clock back. As we have seen, he has a developed historical sense and considers that any apparent difficulty in understanding old laws and legal claims can be resolved by realising that they had a different meaning and application at the time at which they were made, but that they must now be applied in a way which suits contemporary conditions: thus, for instance, on this basis he is able to reject any argument which is founded on the French king's supposed position in the distant past and which thereby denies his *de facto* non-subjection to the emperor.[14]

To describe the sovereign power of the king Baldus uses the language developed by canonists and civilians from the last decade of the twelfth century onwards. The emperor provides the model for the king's sovereignty. Thus Baldus applies the classic formula, *rex in regno suo est imperator regni sui*, to a king who does not recognise a superior in his kingdom.[15] He expresses with admirable clarity the true meaning behind this idea: that the king possesses within the ambit of his kingdom those sovereign powers which the emperor enjoys in the empire as a whole.[16] It is indeed of the essence of royal power that it is territorially confined.[17] Furthermore, as has been noted in the case of sovereign cities, the non-recognition of a superior contains that

[13] See also Baldus, *Cons.*, 2.389, n. 1, fol. 104r (ed. Venice, 1575), 'Et questio feratur in regno libero, et non solum ubi vigent iura civilia in observantia sed etiam cum sumus in regnis que hodie reguntur quomodo regebantur cum sola natura et dictamen rationis naturalis hominibus sanciebat.' This *consilium* is divided into two distinct parts. The second purports to be a report of Baldus' conclusions (n. 10, fol. 105r). There is no good reason to doubt the genuineness of the section quoted.

[14] 'Et no. glo. hic positam que dicit quod rex francorum est sub [super *ed. Pavia, 1495*] imperio romanorum et arguit quod semel fuit ergo est, quia semel verum semper verum. Sed ista ratio non concludit quia *distingue tempora et concordabis scripturas*, ut [C.6.2.21]', ad *Feud.*, 2.53, fol. 74v (see above, p. 66). Cp. Accursius, gl., ibid., ad v. 'Hoc edictali' (fol. 187r), 'Nunquid tenet [i.e. lex ista] francigenas et alios ultra-montanos qui ei non sunt subditi?...Dicas quod eos similiter tenet quoniam licet ei non sint sacramento subditi, subditi tamen sunt ei ratione populi romani sub quo esse debent cum ipsi fuerint de imperio iustiniani.' For Baldus' historical sense see above, p. 6.

[15] Ad X.2.27.33, n. 5, fol. 344r; ad C.4.19.7 (fol. 241r); ad X. Proem, 'Rex pacificus', n. 15, fol. 5r; and ad X.1.33.6, n. 1 (fol. 158r).

[16] 'Quod potest princeps universaliter possunt isti [i.e. reges et principes] in terris sibi subiectis, cum in eisdem iure principis illi fungantur' (ad Inst., 1.2, 1, n. 8–9, fol. 3r, ed. Venice, 1615).

[17] See Baldus, *Rep.* ad C.1.1.1, n. 51, p. 19 (ed. Meijers); and id., *Cons.*, 2.395, n. 4, fol. 106v (ed. Venice, 1575). Cf. Johannes de Imola ad *Clem.*, 2.11.2, n. 41 (fol. 69v).

crucial element of will required in the creation of *de facto* territorial sovereignty, whereas under the *de iure* structure, in which the emperor's direct sovereignty is not thus rejected, true sovereignty is not possible for his subject.[18]

Since the king as the emperor of his kingdom recognises no superior, and is thus the possessor of *principatus* in his realm, Baldus accords to such a monarch powers which he otherwise applies only to the emperor or the pope: plenitude of power and supreme power.[19] Indeed, as he trenchantly says, 'a king in his kingdom can freely do anything';[20] and from the judgment of such a king there can be no appeal.[21] As we have seen, the reservation of plenitude of power and supreme power to emperors, popes and kings reinforces the interpretation that Baldus places kings above city-*populi* in the hierarchy of sovereignty.[22] This may be another reason why he is content to apply the formula, *rex in regno suo est imperator regni sui* (apart from juristic tradition and the personal form of sovereignty common to kings and the emperor), whereas he draws back from employing the formula, *civitas sibi princeps*, in the case of *de facto* sovereign Italian cities all of whose ultimate superior just might appear in the city to exercise his jurisdiction.

There is, however, an apparent problem in that Baldus, although he considers kingship to have an essentially this-worldly origin, nevertheless also applies theocratic language to describe the sovereignty of kings. The king is *vicarius dei*.[23] Furthermore the king as the emperor in his kingdom has the theocratic powers of the emperor, being 'like a corporeal god' ('tanquam quidam corporalis deus') to his subjects, although this does not make him literally a second emperor.[24] The emperor as 'a corporeal god to the world' ('corporalis mundo deus') is the avowed model for the king here,[25] although there is also a

---

[18] See above, p. 115.

[19] *Cons.*, 1.359, fol. 109v, ed. Brescia, 1490 (= *Cons.*, 3.159, ed. Venice, 1575); and id. ad D.1.2.2 (fol. 12v). Not all jurists agree that a king has plenitude of power: see Johannes Andreae ad X.3.49.2 (fol. 160r).

[20] Ad X. Proem, ad v. 'Rex pacificus', n. 11 (fol. 5r).

[21] Ad D. V. Proem, ad v. 'Quoniam omnia' (fol. 1r).

[22] Above, p. 65.

[23] See Baldus ad X.1.29.38, n. 5 (fol. 141r).

[24] Ad *Feud.*, 2.55 (fol. 86r). Baldus is here specifically concerned with the king of France, and is arguing that a feudal oath must not harm a man's king just as it must not the emperor. But see Baldus ad C.2.4.41 (fol. 105v), 'Vltimo no. quod princeps indignatur quando nomen suum apponitur in iuramento et non servatur iuramento; quod ipse equiparat se deo, quia est deus in terris. Nec habet locum hoc nisi in monarcha, scilicet imperatore et papa, non in regibus.'

[25] Id. ad *Feud.*, 2.55, fol. 86r (above, p. 25): the protection accorded there to the emperor's rights reflects the reality of feudal authority in Italy.

well-known Thomist source for this idea.[26] In addition Baldus gives a theocratic definition of the king's law-creating function. He thus explains why law is defined in D.1.3.2 as 'an invention and gift of God' ('inventio et donum dei') in this way: 'because the king is the living law, and as long as he concedes his own majesty [i.e. in law-giving], this is a grace freely given, and his subjects can then say, "I sleep, and my heart, that is my king, keeps watch".'[27] This passage intimates that the king here is as God's representative the embodiment of the law and concedes it by his *grace* to his subjects.

Bartolus in *De regimine civitatis* had combined the human and the divine sources of kingship with the emphasis on the human in the case of kings other than the *Rex Romanorum*:

> Every king is either immediately chosen by God or by electors under the eye of God…And note from this that rulership through election is more divine than that through succession…And thus the choice of the emperor who is the universal king is made through the election of prelates and princes, and does not go by succession…For 'God constituted this empire from heaven'…*Individual kings however are more from human constitution*, as in [D.1.1.5].[28]

For the interpretation of Baldus' theory of kingship, however, with its articulated *de facto* thesis based on the *ius gentium*, the acceptance of theocratic language does pose distinct problems. On the face of it the *de facto*, and the theocratic theses appear to set forth totally different sources for royal power: the one purely human and the other divine. There were of course ways round the problem, such as the resolution, we have seen, of the divine and human sources of imperial power, and the idea that royal power derives ultimately from God but is mediated by the people.[29] It could be that election by the people is essentially declaratory of the divine will, and that after his election the king is a purely theocratic monarch. The trouble is that Baldus produces no explanation of his use of both *de facto* and theocratic sources for the

---

[26] Aquinas, *De regimine principum*, 1.9 & 12: see Quaglioni, 'Regimen ad populum', p. 213, n. 46; and Wilks, *Problem of Sovereignty*, pp. 213–14.

[27] Ad D.1.3.2 (fol. 13v). Cp. Baldus, *Cons.*, 2.395, n. 2, fol. 106v (ed. Venice, 1575). For the emperor as *lex animata* see Nov., 105, 2, 4. The concept is of Greek origin: see Steinwenter, 'Νόμος ἔμψυχος'. For the connection between *lex* as the *anima* of the *corpus* of the community and the role of the theocratic monarch as *lex animata* embodying the law, see Ullmann, *Individual and Society*, pp. 46–9. See also Wilks, *Problem of Sovereignty*, pp. 152 and 162.

[28] Ed. Quaglioni, *Politica e diritto*, p. 166. Baldus in *Cons.*, 1.359, fol. 109v, ed. Brescia, 1490 (= *Cons.*, 3.159, ed. Venice, 1575), thus exemplifies elective kingship: 'ut est regnum romanorum; et tale regnum a deo hominibus mittitur.'

[29] See above, p. 26; and Wilks, *Problem of Sovereignty*, p. 187.

origin of kingship. It may be that there is an inconsistency here in the context of his basic *de iure–de facto* structure. In any case it is impossible to determine what Baldus' answer to this question would be. What, however, is certain is that he does not apply to kings his solution of the divine and human origins of imperial power, which includes that of the *Rex Romanorum* whose authority is different in nature from that of other kings.[30]

The most notable aspect, however, of Baldus' theory of kingship is his use of corporation theory. This is revealed primarily in *Cons.*, 1. 359, ed. Brescia, 1490 (= *Cons.*, 3.159, ed. Venice, 1575), in the course of his argument to demonstrate that a king's contracts made in the name of his kingdom are binding on his successors, for 'Some things, however, derive from office, and these are always perennial and eternal... Of this kind are the contracts of kings who make contracts in their own name and that of their kingdom or people.'[31] The kingdom itself, he continues, apart from being a territorial entity, is in its corporeal aspect identified with its human members: 'For the kingdom contains within itself not only its material territory: the races and peoples of the kingdom themselves are also collectively the kingdom.'[32] Yet the kingdom as a corporation also possesses an abstract aspect distinct from its human components – it is an immortal legal person as is furthermore the royal office, or *dignitas*, which is thus also distinct from its mortal incumbents:

In a kingdom the office which does not die should be considered, and also the corporation or *respublica* of the kingdom which lives on even when kings have come to an end, for the *respublica* cannot die; and for this reason it is said that the *respublica* does not have an heir because it lives forever in itself.[33]

The undying corporation of the kingdom concedes authority to its mortal king by conferring on him this immortal *dignitas* which he puts into operation and acts thereby for the kingdom which does not act for itself:

The person who concedes is not dead here, namely the *respublica* itself of the kingdom, for it is true to say that the *respublica* does nothing for itself; the ruler of the *respublica*, however, acts in virtue of the *respublica* and the office conferred on him by the same *respublica*.[34]

[30] See above, pp. 26–41.
[31] Fol. 109v.   [32] Ibid., (fol. 109v).
[33] Ibid. Cf. id. ad X.1.2.7, n. 38 (fol. 19v). For Baldus' conception of the relationship between the king, his *dignitas* and the kingdom see Kantorowicz, *King's Two Bodies*, pp. 397–401 and 437–9.
[34] Id., *Cons.*, 1.359, fol. 109v (ed. Brescia, 1490).

In a classic formulation of the theory of 'the king's two bodies' Baldus considers that there are thus two completely different kinds of person in the king – his human and mortal person and an abstract and perpetual legal person (his *dignitas*):

Moreover, two things coincide in the king: his human person and what he signifies [i.e. his *dignitas*]. And that signification itself which is something relating to the intellect perseveres forever in a mysterious manner, although not in a corporeal one. For although the king may expire, what does that matter? The king certainly fills the place of two persons, as in [D.34.9.22].[35]

The human king is thus no more than the instrument or organ of his *dignitas* which therefore appears as the principal source of royal actions:

And the person of the king is the organ and instrument of that intellectual and public person; and that intellectual and public person is the principal source of action, because more attention is paid to the capacity of the principal than of the instrument.[36]

Thus when the individual ruler acts in the role of king, he acts not as himself but as the personification of his *dignitas*. Royal contracts, therefore, made through the exercise of the royal *dignitas* bind the king's successors because they are made ultimately on the authority of the immortal *respublica regni* which the king represents: 'The clear conclusion is that the said contract passes on because of its form, and also on account of the *dignitas* and authority of the person agreeing to it, as well as of the represented *respublica* itself which, as I have said, does not die.'[37]

The same considerations apply in determining whether the king can make contracts binding the fisc. The fisc is not the private possession of the king but is part of the *respublica regni* itself.[38] As such the fisc, like the *respublica regni*, is also an undying legal person; in consequence any contracts which the king makes binding the fisc or the *respublica regni* are perpetual:

[35] Ibid. Cf. id., *Cons.*, 1.417, fol. 129r, ed. Brescia, 1490 (= *Cons.*, 3.217, ed. Venice, 1575); id. ad C.6.51.1, 6 (fol. 152v); and id. ad C.7.55.1 (fol. 247v).

[36] Id., *Cons.*, 1.359, fol. 109v (ed. Brescia, 1490). Cp. id., *Cons.*, 1.322, fol. 98r, ed. Brescia, 1490 (= *Cons.*, 3.121, ed. Venice, 1575); id. ad C.7.61.3 (fol. 252v); and id. ad C.6.43.3 (fol. 134r).

[37] Id., *Cons.*, 1.359, fol. 109v (ed. Brescia, 1490).

[38] See Baldus, *Cons.*, 3.241, fol. 72r, ed. Brescia, 1491 (= *Cons.*, 1.271, ed. Venice, 1575). Baldus does, however, sometimes speak more loosely treating the fisc as the king's possession: 'Reges habent regalia fisci circumscripta tamen secundum regnum suum' (ad C.6.49.3, fol. 142v); and 'Fiscus idem est quod saccus cesaris vel regis vel reipublice' (ad C.7.73. Rubr., fol. 283r). For Baldus on the *rex*, the *regnum* and the *fiscus* see Kantorowicz, *King's Two Bodies*, pp. 170–90; and Wahl, 'Immortality and inalienability', pp. 320–2.

It has become customary concerning contracts to ask whether a king's or the emperor's contract can bind the *respublica* or the fisc. For if it can bind them, since the *respublica* and the fisc are essentially eternal and perpetual entities (although their dispositions often change), for the fisc never dies, as is noted in [D.2.3.1, 4], it at once follows that the *respublica* of the kingdom and the fisc would be bound once and for all by a royal contract, especially because personal obligations of their nature are perpetual, as in [Inst., 4.12; D.44.7.44]...And on this point it is to be said that the king can bind the fisc of his kingdom.[39]

Baldus' achievement is thus to produce a theory of the relationship of king to kingdom in the context of a territorially sovereign state viewed in corporational terms. In doing so he breaks new juristic ground through the way in which he applies corporation theory to kingdoms and kings understood as sovereign within the *de facto* structure. His approach bears comparison with his theory concerning city-republics. The free kingdom exists within a this-worldly *de facto* dimension and possesses both a corporeal and an abstract aspect distinct from its human members and government. It is however different from the city-republic because it elects one man to rule it. This ruler is sovereign being given this authority by the people of the kingdom itself. Just as the city-republic in its abstract aspect requires its members or their representatives to act for it since it cannot directly act of itself, so also the kingdom in its abstract form needs the human king to act on its behalf. The main difference, however, between Baldus' treatment of the kingdom and the city-republic as corporations is that the government of the kingdom exhibits an extra stage of complication. Between the individual king and the kingdom Baldus has inserted the medium of the abstract royal *dignitas* which, since it is abstract and immortal, he perceives as being generated by an entity of the same juristic kind, the undying legal person of the *respublica regni*. Through thinking in these terms Baldus indicates the perpetual nature both of the kingdom as a state and of its government. There is thus a form of continuous creation of the royal office by the *respublica regni* with the result that the derivation of royal power from the people is a permanent and ongoing phenomenon and is not just limited to the particular election of an individual king or dynasty.

[39] Id., *Cons.*, 3.241, fol. 72r (ed. Brescia, 1491). See also id. ad X.2.14.9, n. 38 (fol. 227v–28r), 'Fiscus est persona incorporalis, et ideo ubique, ut no. in [C.7.37.1]. Quandoque est [i.e. possessio] de non corpore in non corpus, ut fiscus vel ecclesia in abstracto, id est prout est quoddam mere intellectuale, quod intellectu concipitur per regulas sumptas a rationabilitate intellectus, quasi possidet patrimonium suum in genere complexum corporalium et incorporalium, ideo possidetur mistice, ut [D.5.3.9]'; and id., *Cons.*, 3.12, fol. 4v (ed. Brescia, 1491).

The setting up of a king involves a true transfer of sovereignty by the people in the sense that the royal dignity once created cannot be removed. A hierarchy of authority is established in which the physical members of the *respublica regni* become the subjects of their ruler. Thus Baldus considers that subjects, although they may *de facto* expel a tyrannical king, nevertheless cannot deprive him of his royal dignity, because he remains in legal right their superior:

The second question is whether subjects can expel their king on account of his intolerable injustices and tyrannical actions. And it seems that they can, as below [D.1.2.2], for a bad king becomes a tyrant...The contrary is true because subjects cannot derogate from the right of their superior. Therefore, although they may expel him in fact, their superior does not however lose his dignity [C.4.55.4].[40]

There is no problem involved in understanding this transfer of sovereignty within the context of Baldus' fundamental *de facto* view of kingship: it can be seen to underlie his conception of royal sovereignty. This transfer can be understood both as taking place at the election of a king or the establishment of a royal dynasty, and in a corporational sense as a continuous interaction between the *respublica regni* and the royal *dignitas*. The people is perfectly free to establish such a monarch. Yet Baldus here confronts the problem of what happens when such a people removes its obedience from its king. Since the essence of the *de facto* argument is the acceptance of political reality, he admits that there is no substance to the rule of a king who is not obeyed: 'A king could not be said to reign if his peoples were to withdraw their obedience, as in [D.1.2.2, 3].'[41] He retains, however, the hierarchical principle that a subject even when he removes his obedience cannot thereby derogate from his superior's jurisdiction.[42] Thus in the case of kings Baldus' solution reconciles both the permanent establishment of the royal dignity and the *de facto* capacity of subjects to exercise their fundamental right to withdraw consent when faced with tyranny. It is crucial that he does not condemn the ejection of a tyrant. Clearly the transfer of sovereignty differentiates a royal from a city-republican regime; but the *de facto* popular source of authority is common to both, being shown in the case of the kingdom not only by popular election of the monarchy, but also by the view that rulership in the state derives its authority continuously from the corporation of

---

[40] Ad D.1.1.5 (fol. 7r).
[41] *Cons.*, 1.359, fol. 109v, ed. Brescia, 1490 (= *Cons.*, 3.159, ed. Venice, 1575).
[42] Cp. id., *Cons.*, 5.135, n. 2, fol. 35r (ed. Venice, 1575).

the people, and the recognition of a surviving right of popular resistance against a tyrannical king.

Are there any limitations on the sovereignty of a king apart from this final sanction of a withdrawal of obedience by his subjects? Like the emperor, the king rules within the context of higher norms[43] as well as the restraints of both feudal law[44] and the requirements of his office. It is, however, in this latter area of the limitations imposed by the royal *dignitas* that Baldus makes another important contribution to the theory of kingship. Precisely because the royal office is set up by the kingdom as a corporation, kingship is seen by him as a function limited by the purpose for which it is instituted. That purpose is to protect and therefore not alienate the rights which the kingdom possesses because it is a separate entity and the source of the monarch's authority. Thus all medieval kings according to Baldus should swear a coronation oath to conserve the rights of their kingdoms symbolised in the imagery of the crown: 'Note that all the kings in the world should swear at their coronation to conserve the rights of their kingdom and the honour of their crown. Also bear in mind that those two are equal: the rights of the kingdom and the honour of the crown.'[45] The king should thus act as a tutor for his kingdom which, as we have seen, does not act for itself. This tutorial function derives fundamentally from the nature of the royal office itself, the duties of which are only formalised by the coronation oath: 'The king ought to be the tutor of his kingdom, not its pillager or destroyer... Note that perjury is not the final cause why alienations should be revoked, because alienation is not valid, even if it is supported by [another] oath, on account of the nature of his office, for the king ought to protect the welfare of the *respublica* [D.1.15.1].'[46] The point is that the kingdom in appointing a king has not thereby abdicated its freedom with the result that its

---

[43] See, for instance, id., *Cons.*, 1.359, fol. 110r, ed. Brescia, 1490 (= *Cons.*, 3.159, ed. Venice, 1575); and id., *Cons.*, 1.417, fol. 129r, ed. Brescia, 1490 (= *Cons.*, 3.217, ed. Venice, 1575). For the king's duty to observe the *utilitas publica* see above, p. 90.

[44] See id., *Cons.*, 2.308, fol. 82r, ed. Brescia, 1490 (= *Cons.*, 5.182, ed. Venice, 1575); and above, p. 82.

[45] Ad X.2.24.33, n. 3 (fol. 315r). For the concept of the visible and the invisible crown (as applied to the emperor) see id., *Cons.*, 1.359, fol. 109v, ed. Brescia, 1490 (= *Cons.*, 3.159, ed. Venice, 1575). On the crown as abstraction see Kantorowicz, *King's Two Bodies*, pp. 336–83. For Baldus on the *corona* see Wahl, 'Immortality and inalienability', pp. 326–8.

[46] Baldus ad X.2.24.33 (fol. 314v) – for this decretal see above, p. 49, n. 104. Cf. Baldus, ibid., n. 3 (fol. 315r), 'Nota quod omnes reges mundi in sua coronatione debent iurare iura regni sui conservare et honorem corone.' For the promise of non-alienation at royal coronations (especially in England) see Richardson, 'English coronation oath'; Kantorowicz, 'Inalienability'; and id., *King's Two Bodies*, pp. 347–58.

rights remain inalienable: 'A king cannot alienate his people nor give it another king, because the people is free, although it is under a king.'[47] The minority-thesis, which we discussed above, does not apply to Baldus' concept of kingship, because the kingdom is the source of the king's authority, with the result that the king's tutorial role as protector and preserver is similar to that of the *rectores terrarum* in city-republics.[48] The king, however, with his plenitude of power has greater independence in that he cannot be brought to account for his actions: 'Nor, again, is a thorough investigation to be made of kings, since they have the fullest power and are not subject to account, as in [D.1.12.1, 4].'[49] Again, this shows that Baldus in using a tutorial concept is not intending to apply the full implications of a tutor's role, but wishes simply to stress the preserving role of the ruler. Infeudation, however, does not alienate the rights of the kingdom, and indeed increases the honour of the king through augmenting the dignity of his subjects.[50] The king as sovereign is clearly more than just the legitimate administrator or the governor of his kingdom, and especially so in the case of an hereditary monarch who has an element of dominion in his rule in that he can pass his kingdom onto his heirs, although even so his sovereignty is limited by his duty not to diminish the monarchy and his crown.[51]

There is, however, as we have seen in the cases of both the emperor and sovereign cities, a crucial distinction between limited and controlled government or rulership.[52] Baldus does not explore constitutional controls over the king: the remedies of feudal law apart, normative limitations or those deriving from the royal office cannot be enforced. As we know, this would not make such limitations any less important in his eyes since they provide the formative context within which kingship should operate. The lack of institutional controls is, however, clearly an aspect of royal sovereignty. The king is simply not limited by the consent of his subjects: thus although he should for instance take counsel from his people he is not obliged to follow this.[53] The *respublica regni* has transferred sovereignty to a monarch it cannot control, but

---

[47] Baldus ad D.V. Proem, ad v. 'Quoniam' (fol. 1v). For the inalienability of the rights of the kingdom see especially Hoffmann, 'Unveräusserlichkeit'.

[48] See above, p. 197. For the interpretation of the development of medieval kingship in terms of the king's tutorial role and the corresponding minority status of the community, whose rights it would be the royal duty to preserve and not to alienate, see Ullmann, *Carolingian Renaissance*, pp. 177–87; id., 'Schranken der Königsgewalt', pp. 12–18; id., 'A note on inalienability'; and id., *Medieval Foundations*, pp. 22, 36 and 109.

[49] Baldus ad X.2.24.33, n. 5 (fol. 315r).   [50] Id., ibid..

[51] Id., *Cons.*, 3.241, fol. 72r, ed. Brescia, 1491 (= *Cons.*, 1.271, ed. Venice, 1575).

[52] Above, pp. 91–2 and p. 157.

[53] Baldus ad X.2.24.18, n. 1 (fol. 302v); and ad D.1.13.1 (fol. 44r).

can only in extreme circumstances eject through taking the law into its own hands.

Baldus' treatment of *signori* is to be found almost entirely in *consilia* which he wrote towards the end of his life and which concern Bernabò and Giangaleazzo Visconti. Through accepting Giangaleazzo's invitation to lecture at Pavia in 1390 Baldus for the rest of his days threw in his lot with the Visconti and, as these *consilia* attest, fully supported the signorial regime of the state of Milan. These were, of course, the years which saw the expansion of the Milanese state and its growing threat to the remaining city-republics. Yet Baldus himself was not the apologist for any one form of government: he accepted the validity of both republican and signorial regimes – for him they existed in parallel. Thus he continued to adhere to his theory of sovereign city-republics as crucial passages in his commentary on the *Decretales* show.[54]

Baldus locates the Visconti's power within his overall *de iure–de facto* structure. That power exists on a *de iure* basis: it is derived firstly from an imperial feudal vicariate and then, as we have seen, from the feudal grant of an imperial dukedom in 1395.[55] In either case Giangaleazzo derives his power from the emperor in whose place he rules;[56] but unlike sovereign cities which take the emperor's place by the latter's default, Giangaleazzo does so by imperial grant. The emperor has thereby transferred a territorially limited plenitude of power to the prince of Milan, with the result that, while the primacy of the emperor himself is retained, Giangaleazzo possesses full imperial power in these lands, so much so that his privileges have the same force as if the emperor had made them himself.[57] It is, however, the dukedom which

---

[54] See above, p. 116, nn. 70 and 73.

[55] Above, p. 19. Wenceslas as king of the Romans had the power to grant imperial rights: see above, p. 37, n. 63. Wenceslas in 1380 gave back to Giangaleazzo the vicariate which the Visconti had forfeited in 1372 (see Bueno de Mesquita, *Giangaleazzo Visconti*, p. 26).

[56] See Baldus, *Cons.*, 1.51, fol. 20r (ed. Brescia, 1490), 'Magnificus [dominus] noster habet regalia ab imperatore et vicem eius per omnia gerit'; id., *Cons.*, 3.283, fol. 88v, ed. Brescia, 1491 (= *Cons.*, 1.333, ed. Venice, 1575); id., *Cons.*, 1.303, fol. 91r, ed. Brescia, 1490 (= *Cons.*, 3.105, ed. Venice, 1575); and id., *Cons.*, 1.110, fol. 39v (ed. Brescia, 1490). For a similar vicariate see id., *Cons.*, 1.196, fol. 65r (ed. Brescia, 1490).

[57] Baldus, *Cons.*, 3.359, n. 1–2, fol. 101v (ed. Venice, 1575). The *casus* for this *consilium* is printed at the end of *Cons.*, 3.358 (fols. 101r–v), and shows that it concerns Giangaleazzo. This *casus* refers in detail to the 1380 grant of the imperial vicariate

is truly crucial in Baldus' eyes. It further reinforces Giangaleazzo's possession of the powers of the emperor:[58] indeed he can demand the obedience due to the emperor whose place he physically takes – 'Our magnificent prince should be formally and totally obeyed in those things in which obedience would be due to the emperor himself, if he were to be present in Italy in his imperial person.'[59] Indeed, Baldus goes so far as to say that through the grant of this dukedom the Roman empire has risen from the dead.[60] As we have seen, Baldus believed that the empire had been eclipsed in Italy because the bond of faith that should exist between the emperor and cities and lords had been broken, a fact he accepted with some regret.[61] That precious bond is now re-established between Giangaleazzo and the emperor.[62] Thus right at the end of his life Baldus perceives a great change in the status of imperial authority in Italy and one which as a civilian he welcomes. In the state of Milan the emperor's authority embodied in the rule of Giangaleazzo Visconti has been given reality again: there the gap in the spread of imperial jurisdiction has been filled. The grant of such a feudal dukedom, as indeed of any vicariate, does not diminish the power of the emperor who remains the ultimate possessor of such power, and who thus, as we have seen, avoids disobeying his duty not to alienate the empire;[63] nor does such a grant diminish existing feudal rights – in the case of a dukedom the emperor is simply inserting another level in the feudal hierarchy.[64]

In Baldus' eyes Giangaleazzo is clearly not a sovereign ruler – he is

to Giangaleazzo. Although the *consilium* was written after the grant of the dukedom (Giangaleazzo is referred to as *dux* in the *casus*) it concerns Giangaleazzo's rights under the vicariate to grant confiscated property to someone else.

[58] Id., *Cons.*, 3.277, fol. 84r, ed. Brescia, 1491 (= *Cons.*, 1.327, ed. Venice, 1575).

[59] Id., *Cons.*, 3.276, fol. 83r, ed. Brescia, 1491 (= *Cons.*, 1.326, ed. Venice, 1575).

[60] See *Cons.*, 3.283, fol. 88r, ed. Brescia, 1491 (= *Cons.*, 1.333, ed. Venice, 1575), 'Nam tunc Romanum imperium surrexit a mortuis, si bene consideretur, quando dictam magnificam, illustrem et gloriosam gratiam fecit [i.e. imperator] domino nostro duci Mediolani comiti Papie et virtutum etc.' See above, p. 37, n. 63.

[61] See above, pp. 114–15.

[62] See Baldus, *Cons.*, 3.313, fol. 102r, ed. Brescia, 1491 (= *Cons.*, 1.363, ed. Venice, 1575).

[63] Above, p. 86. See id., *Cons.*, 3.359, fol. 101v (ed. Venice, 1575), where he says of the vicariate, 'Ista translatio facta per imperatorem plenissima est, licet radices imperii non evellat'; and id., *Cons.*, 3.283, fol. 88v, ed. Brescia, 1491 (= *Cons.*, 1.333, ed. Venice, 1575).

[64] This is what Baldus sets out to demonstrate in *Cons.*, 3.283, ed. Brescia, 1491 (= *Cons.*, 1.333, ed. Venice, 1575): he concludes, 'Ex quibus sequitur evidenter quod dominus noster vice regis romanorum, et ex dignitate sua, que est quedam monarchia creata iuxta contentum suum, potest requirere et mandare quod sibi iuramenta noviter instituta prestentur sine derogatione substantie dignitatum comitum et baronum, et absque subversione bonarum consuetudinum, que omnino servande sunt' (fol. 88v). See Magni, *Il tramonto del feudo lombardo*, pp. 75–9, for Baldus' support of Giangaleazzo

the emperor's subject: 'The emperor through granting a fief ennobles rulership, and it is to the advantage of the *respublica* to have just subjects rather than bad ones; and thus it is advantageous to have a subject duke rather than a tyrant.'[65] But Giangaleazzo is sovereign as far as his own subjects are concerned, because he exercises sovereign powers. As we have seen, he possesses *plenitudo potestatis*,[66] and is *lex animata* in his lands.[67] Furthermore, since Giangaleazzo is in the emperor's place, Baldus consistently refers to him as *princeps*, applying to him *leges* relevant to imperial powers.[68] Furthermore he possesses imperial fiscal powers,[69] can have treason committed against him,[70] and can legitimise.[71] His monarchy is a kingdom in all but name: according to Baldus it is the reality of power which matters, not whether Giangaleazzo is entitled *rex* or *dux*.[72] His rule is subject to the usual normative limitations; but whereas the emperor can transcend the requirements of the *ius gentium* through not requiring a cause to remove his subjects' private property, Giangaleazzo needs a just cause to do so, and thus lacks that most extreme attribute which Baldus accords to the sovereignty of the emperor.[73]

The *de iure* basis of Giangaleazzo's power raises in a fundamental sense the relationship between the *de iure* and *de facto* sources of jurisdiction. In *consilia* concerning Bernabò Visconti Baldus makes general statements accepting both *de iure* and *de facto* sources for the sovereign power exercised by *signori*. Thus he recognises both vicariates and custom as sources for the plenitude of power of *signori*,[74] and indeed maintains that it is an observable fact that their will has the force of

against existing holders of imperial fiefs who were complaining against the institution of the duchy over them: an oath of fealty to Giangaleazzo, which Baldus mentions here, was imposed on them by Wenceslas.

[65] Ibid. (fol. 88r).

[66] Above, p. 221, n. 57. See also id., *Cons.*, 3.312, n. 3, fol. 87v (ed. Venice, 1575). As these passages and those in the following notes make clear Giangaleazzo's vicariate as well as his dukedom was a source of sovereign powers.

[67] See id., *Cons.*, 3.359, n. 9, fol. 101v (ed. Venice, 1575).

[68] Id., *Cons.*, 3.359 (ed. Venice, 1575) is a major example of this; but see, for instance, also id., *Cons.*, 3.37, fols. 10v–11r (ed. Venice, 1575); and id., *Cons.*, 1.253, fols. 74r–74v (ead. ed.).

[69] Id., *Cons.*, 3.313, fol. 102r, ed. Brescia, 1491 (= *Cons.*, 1.363, ed. Venice, 1575) concerns the fiscal rights granted to Giangaleazzo through the dukedom: and see also id., *Cons.*, 3.359, nn. 2, 8 & 9, fol. 101v (ed. Venice, 1575).

[70] Id., *Cons.*, 3.213, fol. 60v, ed. Brescia, 1491 (= *Cons.*, 1.243, ed. Venice, 1575).

[71] Id., *Cons.*, 1.146, n. 1, fol. 44r (ed. Venice, 1575).

[72] *Cons.*, 3.278, fol. 85v, ed. Brescia, 1491 (= *Cons.*, 1.328, ed. Venice, 1575).

[73] Id., *Cons.*, 3.313, fol. 102r, ed. Brescia, 1491 (= *Cons.*, 1.363, ed. Venice, 1575).

[74] *Cons.*, 3.237, fol. 70r, ed. Brescia, 1491 (= *Cons.*, 1.267, ed. Venice, 1575).

law.[75] Above all, Baldus accepts the reality of power as regards *signori*:

But nevertheless because all the Lombard *signori* through customary usage, and, as it were, in theory and practice, employ here the words, 'by plenitude of power', and are in possession of that power, as it were, in word and deed, I think that, without substantially violating the truth, we must believe them when they use such language, because it does not appear true that they would use a deceitful mode of expression, see the argument in [C.9.27.6]. Otherwise...the decrees of such great *signori* would become illusory, as at the beginning of [D.5.1.75].[76]

Certainly Baldus is not going to speak out against the power of the *signori*: 'Neither do I nor would I dare to turn my face to heaven to give my opinion against the might of princes, because there could follow from this opinion many exceedingly bad and dangerous things to be avoided, because they would produce a very great scandal.'[77]

It remains true that for Baldus territorial sovereignty which does not recognise a direct superior can only be obtained in a *de facto* manner, and that cities or *signori* deriving their jurisdiction from *de iure* concession are thereby subordinate to their superior.[78] There are, however, grades of *de iure* power. *De iure* autonomy would certainly be inferior to *de facto* sovereignty.[79] The crucial point is, however, that Baldus considers *de iure* and *de facto* power to exist within two parallel structures of validity. Thus because of his respect for imperial and papal authority, Baldus in his treatment of *signori* does not seem to consider that the possession of sovereign powers *de iure* (that is without actually being sovereign) makes the holder inferior to a *signore* with *de facto* sovereign power: either justification is acceptable. The case of Giangaleazzo Visconti, however, is unique in that he embodies in his dukedom the highest level of sovereignty, that of the emperor. It is nevertheless difficult to know how far to take this argument: Baldus does not, for instance, draw the conclusion that Giangaleazzo's jurisdiction is thereby superior to that of cities or *signori* with *de facto* sovereignty, although, as we have seen, any such sovereignty must exist

---

[75] *Cons.*, 3.218, fol. 61v, ed. Brescia, 1491 (= *Cons.*, 1.248, ed. Venice, 1575). Cp. id., *Cons.*, 3.232, fol. 68r, ed. Brescia, 1491 (= *Cons.*, 1.262, ed. Venice, 1575), 'Sed dominus Bernabos...[erat] supra legem, quia poterat derogare legibus, sicut et quotidie faciunt gloriosi principes de domo Vicecomitum'; and id. ad C.5.16.26 (fol. 385v), 'In contrahendo non versatur publica utilitas, nisi imperatore vel rege vel alio, qui non ligatur legibus in suo territorio sicut sunt multi duces et marchiones.'

[76] *Cons.*, 3.237, fol. 70r, ed. Brescia, 1491 (= *Cons.*, 1.267, ed. Venice, 1575).

[77] *Cons.*, 3.218, fol. 61v, ed. Brescia, 1491 (= *Cons.*, 1.248, ed. Venice, 1575).

[78] See above, p. 115.   [79] See above, pp. 65–6.

on a level below that enjoyed by the emperor.[80] The case is rather that although the emperor's authority has been re-established in the state of Milan, *de facto* sovereignty still legitimately fills the gaps left elsewhere in the *terrae imperii* through the continuing absence of effective imperial jurisdiction.

Baldus is clearly happy to accept the *signoria* as a form of government in a way that Bartolus is not. Thus whereas Baldus simply accepts vicariates as a *de iure* validation, Bartolus admits their existence with considerable reservation, and indeed considers the tyrannical rule by *signori* with just title to be typical of Italy in his day.[81] It is, of course, pure speculation to try and guess what Bartolus' attitude to Giangaleazzo would have been. It is nevertheless possible that the grant of the imperial dukedom would have made all the difference in Bartolus' eyes as well. After all Bartolus treats dukedoms as a valid form of rule by one man – dukes only become tyrants when they act as such:

In the case of a particular lord he is sometimes said to rule over a kingdom, and sometimes over a dukedom, a march or a county, as in [*Feud.*, 2.55], § 'Preterea ducatus'. The common name however which we give to rulership [by one man] is natural lordship, and this is so, if the said lord strives towards a common and good end. But if he strives towards a bad end and his own advantage, his rule according to Aristotle is called tyranny, as it is also according to Roman law and custom.[82]

Baldus sometimes uses the term *tyrannus* in a non-pejorative sense to indicate a *signore*,[83] but he also, of course, uses it as a term of opprobrium to describe the unjust or illegitimate rule by one man. He condemns tyranny on moral grounds notably the traditional one of infringement of the common good: 'Broadly speaking, every city is under a tyrant when its subjects cannot freely speak up to defend the common good.'[84] Although he does not overtly adopt Bartolus' distinction between tyranny *ex defectu tituli* (by defect of title) and that *ex parte exercitii* (by acting as a tyrant) Baldus also condemns usurpatory rule as tyrannical:

And I say first of all that provinces which have been accustomed to be ruled by kings and princes are said to be beneath their natural lordship, that is by the law of peoples, as in [D.1.1.5]. And if someone else accepts lordship there

---

[80] See above, pp. 65–6.
[81] See *De tyranno*, pp. 196 and 204–5 (ed. Quaglioni, *Politica e diritto*).
[82] *De regimine civitatis*, p. 151 (ed. Quaglioni, *Politica e diritto*).
[83] Ad X.1.29.42, n. 10 (fol. 144r); and ad D.1.16.6, 3 (fol. 53v). See also above, p. 114.
[84] Ad C.1.2.16 (p. 80): I have used the critical text in Quaglioni, 'Un "Tractatus de tyranno"'.

against the will of the king or prince, he is a tyrant. The text for this is here. That lordship by usurpation is called tyranny.[85]

Indeed, a tyrant commits *laesa maiestas* against the emperor: 'If however the emperor allows someone to rule, not because that person rules well, but because he cannot expel him by force, that person is properly speaking a tyrant and a rebel against the empire, and is liable to the charge of treason, as in [D.48.4.1 & 2].'[86] The rule of a tyrant is simply invalid because he has no jurisdiction: 'And I say in the case where the tyrant himself has made a statute that the statute is not valid for this reason: since making statutes is an aspect of jurisdiction and he has no jurisdiction, he cannot therefore make statutes.'[87] A people, however, which is ruled by a tyrant still retains its jurisdiction: thus a people's statutes made under a tyrannical regime are invalid if the people acts out of fear of the tyrant, but valid if they act freely:

Either they [i.e. the people's statutes] were made with the tyrant's role in them disguised and are not valid, because they are presumed to have been made out of fear and pressure or an excess of deference, as in [D.27.6.7, 1 and D.44.5.1, 5]; or they were not made with the tyrant's role disguised, but for another and a just reason...and such statutes are valid because of both those who make them and the statute itself, as in [D.1.1.9]. For the people, through coming under a tyrant, does not thus lose the power to make statutes *de iure*, because the tyrant's crime does not prejudice the rights of the people.[88]

Thus Baldus, although he accepts the validity of *signorie*, is well aware of the possible corruptions of that form of regime.

As regards the source of the emergence of *signorie* Baldus singles out faction-fighting within cities:

Note that civil war is that which a people begins against itself...and where there is this division [i.e. in the city]...the sinews of the city, that is the important citizens, are torn apart. As a result a convulsion comes upon the city and commonly leads to a tyranny being necessary, as experience teaches, because the inexperienced and ignorant mob does not stand up to pressures for long. And some wise Genoese used to say that division in the city is the entry of the worm into the cheese.[89]

---

[85] Ibid., p. 79.
[86] Ibid., p. 80; see also id. ad C.9.5.1 (fol. 361v).
[87] Id. ad C.1.2.16, p. 81 (ed. Quaglioni). The same considerations apply to the tyrant's judicial activities (ibid., p. 82). Cf. id. ad D.5.1.2 (fol. 215r).
[88] Id. ad C.1.2.16, p. 81 (ed. Quaglioni). For the same view see id., *Margarita*, ad v. 'Fugiens propter metum' (fol. 14r); and id., *lectura antiqua* ad C.5.2.1 (fol. 376r). See also id. ad D.8.6.12 (fol. 249r).
[89] Ad C.6.51.1 (fol. 150r).

Clearly Baldus is not using tyranny in a pejorative sense here – after all he describes recourse to such a regime as a necessity in these circumstances. The hierarchical and oligarchical assumptions, however, underlying his conception of city-republics with their grades of citizens, are again revealed.

The treatment of kingship and *signorie* thus completes Baldus' political thought. Within his fundamental *de iure–de facto* structure, incorporating both universal and territorial sovereignty, he has been able to accommodate all the forms of government known to him: imperial, papal, royal, city-republican and signorial.

CONCLUSION

Baldus' fame and influence long outlived him: indeed, his works occupied a central position in European thought until at least the early seventeenth century. The large number of early printed editions of his writings still in existence bear physical witness to this. The reason for his lasting importance is to be found in the longevity of the medieval juristic tradition. Far from being superseded by humanist jurisprudence in the sixteenth century, scholastic legal science continued to flourish as the education for the practice of law. Thus humanist critics of the medieval approach nevertheless tended to accept its practical application. Andrea Alciato, for instance, held both Bartolus and Baldus in high regard: indeed, references to Baldus and discussions of his arguments are integral to Alciato's treatment of legal problems, notably in his *De verborum significatione*. Furthermore, François Hotman, notable for his adoption of the humanist *mos gallicus* and notorious for his later criticism of it and indeed all Roman law studies in his *Antitribonian*, nevertheless in his practical application of law in his *consilia* made frequent use of Baldus, thus drawing on his conservative juristic formation at Orléans. Within the surviving medieval tradition the dominant position of Bartolus and Baldus became increasingly consolidated. Thus in the sixteenth century, quite apart from Italian jurisprudence which continued almost universally to revere the medieval civilians and canonists, the works of those French jurists, who remained heavily influenced by the scholastic tradition, are full of references to Baldus: one need only consult the works of Claude de Seyssel, Nicholas Bohier, Charles Du Moulin, Bartholomé Chasseneuz and André Tiraqueau. In Germany too the reception of Roman law meant that Baldus' works became a pillar of legal education and practice, as for instance Ulrich Zasius' respect for his work reveals. Indeed, in all the countries where the medieval civilian and canonist tradition was studied or applied Baldus held a place of the highest honour within jurisprudence. Because law occupied such a central position in higher education this meant that study of the works of Baldus formed an important part of the formation of large numbers of men who followed not merely legal careers but governmental ones as well.

As far as political thought is concerned, scholastic jurisprudence also continued to exert a major influence into the seventeenth century, largely because of its role in education. Thus reference to Baldus is frequently to be found in political writers. Bodin, for instance, made a very large number of references to Baldus' works, although his use of Baldus has not yet been systematically studied.[1] Indeed, the treatment of so many topics raised in political debate during the sixteenth-century French wars of religion drew on late medieval jurisprudence: the *lex regia*, the *ius gentium*, ideas of the nature and limitations of kingship and feudal conceptions for instance. If the political thought of this period is fully to be understood, its relationship to its medieval background, including the works of Bartolus and Baldus, needs to be studied more deeply. Also, wherever an avowedly scholastic tradition in political thought flourished, medieval jurisprudence maintained its influence. Thus Francisco Suárez, for instance, in his *Tractatus de legibus ac deo legislatore* makes a multitude of direct references to Baldus. As regards the beginnings of the science of international law Bartolus and Baldus were also of prime importance: a reflection of this is to be found in the marginal references to Baldus in Hugo Grotius' *De iure belli ac pacis*.

It remains for future research to investigate Baldus' influence on political thought in these later centuries. The picture which will emerge will assuredly be a complex one involving acceptance, development, modification and often rejection of Baldus' ideas; yet whatever the reaction, Baldus' work, because of its central importance in late medieval and early modern thought, cannot be ignored, if a balanced picture of this period is to be achieved. This study has been an attempt to put Baldus in his rightful place as a seminal contributor to the juristic mainstream in the development of European political ideas.

---

[1] This is immediately evident from the briefest consultation of *Les six livres de la république*. Giesey in 'Medieval jurisprudence' has also noticed Bodin's debt, and refers to Baldus as 'Bodin's seemingly favorite commentator' (p. 175). Bodin's *marginalia* are replete with references to Baldus. See also Franklin, *Jean Bodin* for reference to Baldus in the elucidation of Bodin's thought.

APPENDIX I

*Latin text of passages translated into English and of the three sections
of Baldus ad D.1.1.9 referred to on pp. 104–13*

p. 6   Baldus ad D.1.1. Rubr.:
Omnis ars assumit sibi naturam pro materia...sed legista pro materia
assumit sibi facta hominum...Item ipsa interpretatur et sic ius nostrum
est fundatum super accidentibus, id est super casibus emergentibus...
nam iura ex factis nata sunt...Communis vero materia non versatur
in factis nature sed in factis hominum.

p. 24   Baldus, *Cons.*, 4.436:
Idque verissimum est quod imperator est dominus mundi quoad
omnimodam iurisdictionem et potestatem supremam, ut [D.14.2.9;
C.7.37.3; C.1.14.12; & X.1.33.6].

p. 25   Baldus, *De pace Constantie*, ad v. 'Imperialis clementie':
Nota quod omnes tenemur principi, quia ut deus princeps in celis, sic
imperatorem [imperator *ed. cit.*] vicarium suum et dominatorem
in fide ac veritate et iusticia constituit in terris...Preterea divina pagina
dicit, 'omnis anima subdita sit principi.'

p. 25   Baldus ad *Feud.*, 2.55:
Nota quod omnis qui iurat, sicut non iurat contra deum, ita nec iurat
contra imperium. Itaque ab omni iuramento fidelitatis excipitur
imperator quia princeps mundi est, et, ut ita dixerim, corporalis mundo
deus.

p. 26   Baldus ad C.1.14.4:
Nota quod auctoritas imperatoris pendet ex lege regia que fuit nutu
divino promulgata et ideo imperium dicitur esse immediate a deo.

p. 27   Baldus ad C.7.37.3:
In textu ibi, 'nutu divino', nota imperatorem constitui divinitus sicut
apostolatus et processit a deo imperium. Et ideo imperium et ecclesia
fraternizant ut in constitutione, 'Quomodo oporteat episcopos' [Coll.,
1.6 = Nov., 6], in principio. Innocentius tamen dixit quod nescit unde

imperium habuit originem. Potes dicere quod habuit initium ab ense permisso divino; voluit enim populo Romano totum orbeṁ subiugari. Deinde populus Romanus constituit imperatorem in quem transtulit potestatem omnem et postea confirmatum fuit expresso verbo divino dum dixit, 'Imago dei reddatur deo et imago Cesaris reddatur Cesari'; est etiam approbatum postea ab ecclesia.

p. 27   Baldus ad D.V., Proem, ad v. 'Quoniam omnia':
Et item illa dignitas suprema est a deo instituta, unde per hominem supprimi non potest. Hinc est quod imperium semper est in Auth., 'Quomodo oporteat episcopos' [Coll., 1.6 = Nov., 6] in fine.

p. 30   Bartolus ad D.49.15.24:
sed modicum ad nos de illis qui foris sunt.

p. 31   Baldus ad X. Proem, ad v. 'Gregorius':
[Papa] non solum est episcopus, sed culmen episcoporum et ceterorum, quos intellectus potest imaginari, cui data est clavium plenitudo, et summa et libera potestas, que appellatur potestas absoluta ab omnibus vinculis canonum et ab omni regula arctativa, preterquam ab evangelica et apostolica.

p. 31   Baldus ad X.2.24.18:
Nam quod dicitur quod papa omnia potest debet intelligi clave discretionis non exorbitante a divinis regulis et naturalibus preceptis.

p. 31   Baldus ad C.6.30.19:
De regno, cui rex puer erit, et intentionem suam et predecessorum potest apostolicus declarare, cum non sit sicut alii homines terreni, nec imperatorem excipio, cum apostolicus sit principalis vicarius Iesu Christi, et ultra humanam naturam habeat potestatem, que ex ore altissimi prodit [Eccl:23], unde ipse est princeps regum terre [Apoc:1].

p. 34   Baldus, *De pace Constantie*, ad v. 'Hoc quod nos':
Et remotis omnibus iuris ambagibus ego puto imperium electione deferri et non successione [X.1.6.34; X.1.35.5]...Sed illi qui ita eligunt auctoritatem eligendi ab apostolica sede acceperunt.

p. 34   Baldus ad X.1.6.34:
Ibi, 'ab apostolica sede', id est a catholica ecclesia, et a populo simul [D.1.2.2, 13].

p. 34   Baldus ad C.1.1.1:
Sed nunquid ecclesia sit mater [mater *ed. Venice, 1615*; iuris *ed. cit.*]

imperii? Dic quod sic...Vnde ecclesia est mater conservans non generans; nam imperium immediate a populo processit, ut in Auth., 'De instrumentorum cautela et fide' [Coll., 6.3 = Nov., 73], Auth., 'Quomodo oporteat episcopos' [Coll., 1.6 = Nov., 6]. Ecclesia ergo mater est protectione, ut in Auth., 'Vt determinatus sit numerus' [Coll., 1.3 = Nov., 3], et approbatione infule imperialis seu corone.

p. 35   Baldus ad X. Proem, ad v. 'Rex pacificus':
Rex etiam Romanorum statim cum electus est habet imperium plene formatum auctoritate potestatis, licet coronam expectet.

p. 35   Baldus ad X.2.24.33:
Coronatio in imperatore non addit nisi corruscationem et honoris augmentum; sed veram essentiam habet ex sola electione concordi... Ex hoc sequitur quod administratio potest precedere coronationem et etiam sequi.

p. 36   Baldus ad X.1.6.34:
Ibi, 'coronamus', tribus coronis coronatur imperator, ut notatur in d. [*Clem.*, 1.3.2]. Tamen corona aurea non est necessaria quantum ad administrationem ei conferendam, quam habet statim quod est electus legitime in concordia vel a maiori parte, ut notat Cynus in [C.7.37.3]. Quid ergo operatur corona? Respondeo quia est postrema confirmatio...Dic quod ultima corona de auro que fit Rome dat postremam perfectionem et est culmen omnium coronarum, que sub celo sunt.

p. 36   Baldus ad C.1.1.1:
Sed nunquid ecclesia sit mater imperii? Dic quod sic, quia imperator debet ab ea recipere insignia imperialia, quamvis et ante est imperator.

p. 38   Baldus, *Cons.*, 3.283:
[Princeps Romanus] non habet aliquem supra caput nisi deum, a quo tamen punitionem expectet si facit iniustitiam, et interdum propter enorme regimen papa privavit eum, ut in [*Sext.*, 2.14.2], quia magis est vicarius dei papa quam imperator, quia papa equiparatur soli qui maior est quam luna quantitate, dignitate, officio et sublimitate.

p. 38   Guilelmus de Cuneo ad C.1.1.1:
Duo sunt luminaria: luminare maius, scilicet ecclesia vel papa, et luminare minus, scilicet imperator, ut in Auth., 'Quomodo oporteat episcopos', § 'quia vero' [Coll., 1.6 = Nov., 6].

p. 38   Albericus de Rosciate ad C.7.37.3:
Ad illud quod dicitur de sole et luna per c. 'Solite' [X.1.33.6], licet

hoc communiter teneatur, tamen ipse Dantes negat verum esse quod in hoc figurentur sacerdotium et imperium; et hoc probat in dicta questione per subtiles et probabiles rationes.

pp. 38–9   Baldus, *De pace Constantie*, ad v. 'Hoc quod nos':
Examinatio tamen, promotio, unctio, consecratio, coronatio, manus impositio ad dominum papam spectant, ut d. [X.1.6.34]...Vnde dominus papa ex causa poterit principem deponere, ut in [*Decr. Grat.*, C.15, q.6, c.3].

p. 39   Baldus ad C.1.14.12:
Vlterius nota...quod nihil est maius et sanctius imperio. Intellige nisi apostolatus beati Petri. Cum enim apostolicus confirmet principem, istud est manifestum signum superioritatis, ut in Auth., 'De defensoribus civitatum', § 'interim' [Coll., 3.2 = Nov., 15], et ideo imperator iurat domino pape fidelitatem [X.1.6.34; *Clem.*, 2.9.1].

p. 39   Baldus ad D.1.14.3:
Sed hic quero nunquid imperator possit renunciare imperium in manibus electorum; et dico quod non, quia non sunt eius superiores... sed electores postquam imperator est confirmatus et coronatus vel confirmatus tantum non habent potestatem destituendi, ergo in eorum manibus non potest renunciari.

p. 40   Baldus, *De pace Constantie*, ad v. 'In nomine Christi membrum':
Potest ergo princeps deponi...sed si papa deponit imperatorem dolo vel ambitione sine legitima et ardua causa depositio ipso iure est nulla.

p. 40   Baldus, ibid.:
Et est alia ratio quia ecclesia debet vasallo vicem, et de suo imperio non potest eum [i.e. imperatorem] ledere. Immo papa se facit alienum a potestate si talem iusticiam non reddit imperatori qui iuravit fidelitatem...Et imperator potest se defendere cum exercitu suo.

p. 43   Baldus ad X.1.6.34:
Nota quod officium imperatoris est defendere ecclesiam, ut hic, et papam exaltare...hac ratione ne catholicus populus [populus ed. *Venice, 1595; om. ed. cit.*] propter schisma veniat in ruinam, imperator potest apponere remedia extrinseca, non dico intrinseca, quod disponat de papatu...Nota quod omnis persecutor catholice ecclesie est exterminandus, quod est contra papas, qui gubernant schisma.

p. 43   Baldus ad X.1.6.42:
Concilium est necessarium in hac causa ut clerus Romanus, in quo

continentur omnes veri et indubitabiles cardinales mundi, habeat ipsum congregare, requisito ad hoc rege Romanorum, et aliis regibus, et principibus, quorum interest.

p. 44   Baldus ad D.1.14.3:
Imperator vero superiorem habet, scilicet papam...papa iustus est supremus vicarius dei. Qui dicit contrarium mentitur. Imperator quantum ad mundum est maior quam papa, et papa maior quantum ad deum, si est iustus, non est maior ipso in hoc mundo.

p. 46   Baldus ad *Specul.*, 2.2.7:
Illud certum est...quod temporalis iurisdictio est in imperatore tanquam in radice.

p. 46   Baldus, *Cons.*, 2.37:
Imperator habet imperatoriam maiestatem ubique quia maiestas non dividit se, sicut nec character, nec fama; sed non habet ubique imperatoriam administrationem, nam divisum habet imperium cum apostolico, ita quod terre ecclesie Romane non subsunt imperatori immediate nec mediate...Item sicut papa non legitimat in terris imperii, sic nec econtra, d. [X.4.17.13], nam in terris pape imperator redactus est ad instar privati, et si non potest ius dicere ergo nec privilegiare.

p. 47   Bartolus ad D.49.15.24:
Ecclesia Romana exercet illis [illas *ed. cit.* & *ed. Basel, 1589*] in terris iurisdictionem, que erat imperii [imperii *ed. Milan, 1491*; imperio *ed. cit.* & *ed. Basel, 1589*] Romani et istud fatentur; non ergo desinunt esse de populo Romano, sed administratio istarum provinciarum est alteri concessa.

p. 49   Baldus ad X.2.24.33:
Nota quod iuramentum regis etiam eo vivo non officit iuribus regni. In contrarium facit donatio Constantini. Sed ibi Constantinus non iuraverat non alienare, vel illud fuit miraculum propter defensionem fidei catholice. Imperatores autem moderni primo confirmant dona authoritate pape, postea prestant iuramentum, et hoc salvo iurant, ut hic continetur. Alii dicunt quod ecclesia usurpat, sed ista opinio non est bene catholica, quia suprema authoritas pape et catholice ecclesie ab omni lege et constitutione videtur excepta, nec papa intelligitur recipere iuramentum contra seipsum, supra [X.2.24.19; D.33.8.6, 4]. Questio ista nunquam fuit ita determinata quod partiales imperii non revocaverunt eam in dubium, quia imperium minui non potest, nam eadem ratione

per particulas posset totum dissolvi. Ista ratio est nervus valde difficilis ad dissolvendum super quo fundat se Accursius in Auth., 'Quomodo oporteat episcopos' [Coll., 1.6 = Nov., 6] in principio; et nemo unquam dicit quod Accursius ex hoc fuerit hereticus. Etiam videmus quod hodie est valde diminutum imperium; sed somnia sunt quicquid dicitur contra statum universalis ecclesie, a quo dependet imperium et totus universalis orbis.

p. 51   Baldus ad *Feud.*, Proem, ad v. 'Expedita':
Istam questionem determinaverunt antiqui tangendo illam questionem de donatione facta ecclesie que potius fuit divinitatis quam humanitatis, et dixerunt quoad expropriationem territorii, dignitatis vel iurisdictionis non valere nec possibile esse; commoda tamen et utile dominium concedi posse salva semper ab imperio recognitione ac fide. Quod enim imperator seipsum mutilet, id est membra imperii a se amputet, dicere esset species fatuitatis...et ideo si donatio Constantini non processisset a fide catholica sicut processit sed a mero iure imperialis officii non potuisset caput imperii, id est Romam, a ceteris membris mutilari, quia capitis truncatio non est pars quota sed tota.

p. 52   Baldus ad *Specul.*, 2.2.3:
Solutio. Contra imperatorem, qui pretendit ex institutione divina iurisdictionem temporalem, non potest prescribi ab ecclesia: bene habet decimas ex institutione divina, sed temporalem iurisdictionem ex institutione et providentia humana. Sed quia ecclesia dubitat de veteri donatione, fecit sibi de novo donari per imperatorem Carolum, contra quam novam donationem non potest opponi prescriptio temporis, quia recens donatio est.

p. 53   Baldus ad D.V. Proem, ad v. 'Quoniam':
Prescriptio pape enervat perpetuo ius imperatoris...Et licet inferior non possit prescribere regalia contra superiorem, ut [C.7.39.6], tamen papa potest prescribere regalia contra imperatorem et subditos quia est capax supreme potestatis, sicut unus rex potest prescribere contra alium regalia regis.

p. 54   Baldus ad C. Const., 'De novo Codice componendo':
Constat enim quod secundum naturalem rationem et secundum ius gentium provincie eligunt sibi regem, ut [D.1.1.5]. Et ideo quod est a principio approbatum istud censetur de iure gentium. Sed per provincias et per civitates istud fuit semper approbatum et prestitum iuramentum fidelitatis ipsi pape; ergo tales provincie et civitates subsunt domino pape de iure gentium secundum naturalem rationem. Et istam

partem teneo et confirmo, quia posito quod donatio non tenuisset ecclesia tamen prescripsisset non obstante [C.4.21.20], quia subditus non prescribit ut ibi, sed ecclesia est par imperio.

pp. 54–5   Baldus, ibid.:
Si imperator debet habere propositum augendi et facit contrarium, tunc facit quod non debet facere, et ideo non preiudicat successori, et quia est officialis et non dominus...et hanc opinionem tenebat hic Iacobus Butrigarius in lectura dicens quod non tenet alienatio nec quo ad se nec quo ad successorem, licet de successore sit minus dubium secundum ipsum. Postea mutavit opinionem et bene, quia cum papa sit superior, ex hoc acquisitum est ius superiori, unde inferior non potest revocare.

p. 57   Cynus ad C.1.14.12:
De his opinionibus tene que magis tibi placet, quia ego non curo. Nam si populus Romanus faceret legem vel consuetudinem de facto, scio quod non servaretur extra urbem.

p. 58   Baldus ad D.1.2.2, 11:
Causa vero efficiens fuit populus Romanus qui dedit ei [i.e. imperatori] imperium. Et nota verbum, 'dedit'; ergo populus perdidit.

p. 58   Baldus ad C.8.47.2:
Item nota quod auctoritas populi fuit redacta in principem. Ideo dicit littera, 'olim', continens quod apud populum non resideat illa iurisdictio; unde aliud est quando populus committit iurisdictionem, aliud quando transfert, et a se abdicat. Vnde si quis possit ponit sibi superiorem, ipse remanet inferior et subiectus, et perdit auctoritatem superioritatis. Vnde ista littera innuit quod apud populum Romanum non sit hodie imperium.

p. 59   Baldus ad C.1.14.12:
Queritur utrum hodie populus Romanus possit legem facere. Dicendum est quod non, quia denudatus est generali potestate, cum illa translata fuerit in principem, facit supra [C.1.14.8], et per principem postea translata fuerit in apostolicum.

pp. 59–60   Baldus ad D.V., Proem, ad v. 'Quoniam omnia':
In contrarium quod donatio valuerit, facit quia fuit facta a Constantino cum senatu et toto populo. Valet ergo ex nova lege regia que de imperio lata est, quia non processit a minori potentia cause quam prima lex regia, sed ab eadem vi ac potestate, vel maiori [D.1.14.3] fi., argu. infra [D.20.6.8, 11]; sic valet auctoritate populi quod per se non valeret; et quia populus numquam moritur [D.5.1.76], ideo non curatur mors

Constantini, ita probatur in simili, infra [D.2.2.1, 1]; et ideo urbs Romana est ecclesie, non Cesaris, ut no. in [D.1.12.1].

p. 61   Baldus ad D.1.3.9:
Solutio. Populus Romanus potest eum [i.e. imperatorem] privare...
Contrarium videtur quia populus Romanus est sub papa, et ideo in papa residet hec potestas, quia in eo residet cerebrum et vertex totius populi, et quia populus non potest confirmare imperatorem, nec ergo privare, sed quia imperator non iurat fidelitatem populo sed domino pape, et hec est veritas, licet Cynus et Raynerius de Forlivio isti dicant quod populus possit privare, tamen non est verum, cum non possit eligere nec confirmare, in Auth., 'De defensoribus civitatum' [Coll., 3.2 = Nov., 15].

p. 61   Baldus ad *Feud.*, 1.26:
Olim ergo poterat; hodie non potest... et ideo caveat populus Romanus a vanis opinionibus et cogitationibus.

p. 63   Baldus ad X.2.1.12:
In summa quicquid potest rex in suo regno, potest papa in ecclesiastica monarchia, et sicut olim omnia a manu regis gubernabantur, ut [D.1.2.2, 1], ita et quicquid regi placet legis habet vigorem.

p. 63   Baldus, *Cons.*, 3.274:
Papa enim debet esse conservator papalis regni et corone, quia tenetur honorem corone illesum servare et etiam si iuraret contrarium non valet iuramentum. Idem in seculari, quia honor corone non est alienabilis nec alteri concessibilis nec alteri transmutabilis, licet sit communicabilis.

p. 64   Baldus ad D.V., Proem, ad v. 'Quoniam omnia':
Subditi ergo habent parere donatario nisi quatenus seve et tyrannice uteretur iurisdictione, ut infra [D.1.1.3; D.1.2.2, 3], et quod notatur [D.49.15.24] per Bartolum, nam si dominus non impendit subditis officii debitum subditi non tenentur ei ad servitutem, infra [D.1.4.1] in verbo 'ei et in eum', et nota [D.1.6.2], § 'dominorum', scilicet quamdiu non servatur quod debetur.

p. 64   Baldus ad C.1.1.1:
Merito non ponitur restrictive habita relatione ad ius, sed habita relatione ad factum posset poni restrictive secundum Bartolum, quod est novum et notandum dictum et bene.

p. 66   Baldus ad *Feud.*, 2.53:
Respondeo omnes sunt subiecti [i.e. imperatori] de iure, et merito; sed

non omnes sunt subiecti de consuetudine; et peccant sicut Francigene et multi alii reges...et licet regnum Francorum non sit de Romano imperio, tamen non sequitur, ergo imperium non est universale, nam aliud est dicere universale, aliud integrum, ut no. [D.50.16.25].

p. 67   Jacobus de Ravannis ad D. V. Proem:
Quidam dicunt quod Francia exempta est ab imperio; hoc est impossibile de iure. Et quod Francia sit subdita imperio habes... [C.1.27.2, 3]. Si hoc non recognoscit rex Francie, de hoc non curo.

p. 72   Baldus ad X.1.2.1:
Plenitudini potestatis nihil resistit, nam omnem legem positivam superat, et sufficit in principe pro ratione voluntas [D.1.4.1].

p. 72   Baldus ad C.3.34.2:
Est autem plenitudo potestatis arbitrii plenitudo nulli necessitati subiecta nullisque iuris publici regulis limitata.

p. 72   Accursius, gl. ad D.48.19.4 ad v. 'Ex aliqua causa':
Ex aliqua causa. Magna et iusta causa est eius voluntas.

p. 72   Baldus ad D.1.3.31 (Additio Baldi):
Ibi, 'legibus', id est iure civili, non naturali, vel divino.

p. 73   Baldus, *Cons.*, 3.283:
Nos iuriste debemus dicere quod imperator est dominus mundi etiam si male administret, quia non potest inferior corrigere superiorem, licet papa posset ex maxima causa eum deponere.

p. 73   Baldus, *Cons.*, 3.278:
Quicquid tamen agitur supra legem absoluta potestas est nec est subditorum corripere, quia ut ait Aristoteles, nullum inferius participat id quod superius est, sed obedire oportet.

p. 75   Baldus ad C.1.14.4:
Princeps debet vivere secundum leges quia ex lege eiusdem pendet auctoritas h.d. Intellige quod istud verbum, 'debet', intelligi de debito honestatis que summa debet esse in principe. Sed non intelligitur precise, quia suprema et absoluta potestas principis non est sub lege, unde lex ista habet respectum ad potestatem ordinariam non ad potestatem absolutam...Nota quod imperator dicit se esse legibus alligatum et hoc ex benignitate non ex necessitate.

pp. 75–6   Baldus, ibid.:
Vltimo nota quod nemo potest imponere legem successori dignitatis vel officii vel imperii. Ratio quia par in parem non habet imperium.

p. 76   Baldus ad D.1.4.1:

Nota tamen quod hec auctoritas, 'quicquid principi placet', debet intelligi scilicet 'possibile' et 'honestum', nam impossibilia princeps non potest. Illud autem est impossibile, cuius contrarium est necessarium. Est autem necessarium ius divinum, item ius naturale...sic non potest tolli ius gentium, supra [D.1.1.11; Inst., 1.2, 1]. Et ideo si principi placet quod deo non placet, non habet legis vigorem.

p. 77   Baldus ad X.2.1.12:

Illud tamen scias quod de potentia principis non est disputandum quia suprema potestas eius nulli subiacet regule, nisi soli legi divine vel naturali, ut plene no. [C.1.22.6].

p. 77   Baldus ad C.3.34.2:

Lege positiva princeps obligatur a dictamine rationis, quia est animal rationale, ideo ea non est princeps solutus. Nulla enim auctoritas, neque principis neque senatus potest facere quod princeps non sit animal rationale mortale nec eum absolvere a lege nature vel a dictamine recte rationis vel legis eterne [D.7.5.2].

p. 78   Baldus, *Cons.*, 3.277:

Princeps est creatura rationabilis [creatura rationabilis *ed. Venice, 1575*; natura rationalis *ed. cit.*] habens potestatem supremam, sed inquantum est rationalis debet obedire rationi, ut notatur in Auth. 'De monachis' [Coll., 1.5 = Nov., 5] in principio.

p. 78   Baldus, *Cons.*, 3.295:

Non posset imperator dare licentiam quod quis posset propria auctoritate expellere iustum et legitimum possessorem, quia talis licentia contineret flagitium [C.8.4.6]...Nec obstat clausula de plenitudine potestatis quia illa clausula intelligitur de plenitudine potestatis bone et laudabilis non vituperabilis vel tirannice, nam non dicitur imperator posse nisi quod de iure potest...Item quia plus potest naturalis et civilis ratio quam imperator. Item quia et imperator est animal rationale mortale.

p. 79   Baldus ad D.1.4.1:

Item nota quod non presumitur aliquid placere principi nisi iustum et verum...Et princeps vult omnes actus suos regulari a iustitia poli et fori.

p. 80   Baldus, ibid.:

Item nota quod sicut princeps non *debet* alicui auferre dominium sine causa, ita nec propriam iurisdictionem, ut [D.1.5.20], sed iurisdictionem commissam vel precariam auferre potest libere, ut infra [D.5.1.58].

pp. 80–1   Baldus ad X.2.26.13:

Nota quod omnia iura fiscalia sunt principis et ea concedere potest cuilibet persone, sed iura singularium personarum non sunt principis, nec veniunt in eius possessionem...nisi princeps ex potestate absoluta et rationabili causa aliter et specialiter provideret [D.31.1.78, 3; D.40.11.3]. Nam propter publicam utilitatem ecclesie vel populi posset uni concedi et alio auferri, item propter libertatem ecclesie.

p. 81   Baldus ad C.1.19.7:

Tertio querunt doctores nunquid imperator possit [potest *ed. cit.*] rescribere contra ius gentium. Glossa videtur dicere quod non; unde per rescriptum principis non potest alicui sine causa auferri dominium, sed cum aliquali bene potest [D.40.11.3; D.21.2.11; D.31.1.78, 1; D.6.1.15]; et *habetur pro causa quelibet ratio motiva ipsius principis.*

p. 81   Baldus ad C.3.34.2:

Solius enim principis privilegium est iura unius auferre et alteri dare ex plenitudine potestatis.

p. 82   Baldus ad *Feud.*, 2.7:

Nam princeps est subiectus consuetudinibus feudorum tanquam sit ius naturale istius posterioris inventionis, quia ius naturale quotidie nascitur.

p. 83   Baldus, *Cons.*, 3.277:

Bene tamen concedo quod imperator vel papa possunt creare et supprimere dignitates, ut no. [X.1.2.8]. Tamen illud est verum dignitate vacante, et dum dignitas est in abstracto, sed si est in substantia non potest supprimere sine causa, quia ius quesitum alteri non potest supprimere, sed de iure sibi aperto bene potest disponere pro libito voluntatis...Item princeps de perpetuo potest facere corruptibile, non tamen in preiudicium alterius, licet mundi dominus sit, quia illud intelligitur quoad bonum et naturale regimen, ne iniuriarum nascatur occasio, unde iura nascuntur, ut [C.8.4.6].

p. 84   Baldus ad *Feud.*, 1.7:

Pone quod imperator vel rex Francorum creat aliquem ducem et investit eum de ducatu; vel marchionem, et investit eum de marchionatu; vel comitem, et investit eum de comitatu; vel baronem, et investit eum de baronia. Nunquid potest pro libito divestire eum? Respondetur quod non, sed demum propter convictam [coniuncta *ed. cit.*] culpam vel felloniam. Adde quod nec successores in imperio vel regno possent, ut no. [X.2.1.13]. Nec obstat quod imperator habeat plenitudinem potestatis, quia verum est quod *deus subiecit ei leges, sed non subiecit ei contractus* ex quibus obligatus est, ut notatur et traditur in [C.1.14.4].

p. 85   Baldus ad D.1.4.1:
Licet princeps non ligetur lege legis, ligatur lege conventionis [C.1.14.4] per Cynum et infra [D.2.1.14]; ipse dico non successor, quia contractus principis non transit in successorem...quia ius non transit ad successorem, sed de novo creatur per electionem [X.3.5.25]...Et hoc verum nisi faciat ea que sunt de natura vel consuetudine sui officii, sicut est infeudare, ar. in Auth., 'Vt nulli iudicum liceat habere loci servatorem', § 'et hoc vere iubemus' [Coll., 9.9, 6 = Nov., 134, 6], et in Auth., 'Constitutio que dignitatibus', § 'illud' [Coll., 6.9, 2 = Nov., 81, 2].

p. 85   Baldus, *Cons.*, 3.277:
Quidam vero sunt sub imperatore ratione solius feudi; et isti ad nihil aliud tenerentur alicui salvo quod ipsi imperatori tenentur facere fidelitatem; et vice versa imperator tenetur omnibus servare fidem et non violare.

p. 86   Baldus ad C. Const., 'De novo Codice componendo':
Imperator 'augustus' nominatur. Quero, quare sic nominatur? Respondet glossa quia debet esse eius propositum ut augeat...Est considerandum ius alienationis an de iure teneat...Quando imperator concedit in feudum, et tunc sine dubio potest, eo quia tunc ius superioritatis remanet sibi.

p. 86   Baldus ad Auth., 'Omnes peregrini' (ad C.6.59.10):
Consuetudo feudorum dicit quod princeps non possit privare duces nisi prius per pares iudicentur indigni. An imperator possit statuere contrarium et abusivas facere dignitates? Respondeo non, ut in [*Feud.*, 1.7], nam consuetudo que disponit in ipsum principem maior est ipso principe nisi consuetudo tendat ad eversionem vel quasi status imperii.

pp. 86–7   Baldus, *Cons.*, 3.277:
Sed imperator non potest proprietatem a se eradicare vel vendere, quia non habet eam iure suo sed iure legis regie, et non transmittitur ergo nec alienatur. Et quidem imperator est procurator maximus tamen non est proprietatis imperii dominus, sed potius officialis.

p. 87   Baldus ad *Specul.*, 2.2.7:
Non tamen potest imperator tantum donare quod vilescat sua auctoritas, in Auth., 'Quomodo oporteat episcopos' [Coll., 1.6 = Nov., 6], in

princ. glo., et arg. not. [D.32.1.34, 1], quia minorem se facere non potest in fraudem imperii, arg. [D.37.14.16].

p. 87   Baldus ad X.2.19.9:
Non tamen posset imperator donare claves imperii, sicut ille qui tenet claves portarum tenetur eas resignare successori, alias potest dici proditor, ut not. [C.7.32.12; D.31.1.77, 21]. Item non potest viscera imperii eviscerare, quia esset homicida sue dignitatis...Item nec unam baroniam concedere, que posset subvertere maiestatem imperii, quia esset periurus.

pp. 87–8   Baldus ad *Feud.*, Proem, ad v. 'Aliqua':
Princeps Romanus ex certa scientia omnia potest, scilicet imperator in temporalibus, salva semper maiestate imperii sui.

p. 88   Baldus, *Cons.*, 1.177:
Nihil potest crescere vel decrescere contra ipsius rei naturam seu diffinitionem, ut d. [D.23.8.6, 1]. Ideo Romanum imperium non potest crescere vel decrescere quoad iuris dispositionem.

pp. 88–9   Baldus, *Rep.* ad C.1.1.1:
Imperator posset hodie corrigere Auth., 'Quas actiones' [ad C.1.2.23], sicut correxit [C.1.2.23], nam non minus potest hodie imperator quam tunc, quia imperium nunquam moritur, ut in Auth., 'Quomodo oporteat episcopos' [Coll., 1.6 = Nov., 6],

p. 90   Baldus ad C. Const., 'De novo Codice componendo', ad v. 'Hec que necessario':
Deinde videtur hic quod imperator utatur verbo, 'oportet'; contra quia sibi nihil est necessarium, nam imperator libere agit ad similitudinem dei qui est agens omnino liberum, ut [D.1.4.1]. Solutio: verbum, 'oportet', exponitur, id est 'oportunum', vel 'utile' est, scilicet subditis, sic [D.1.11.1].

pp. 90–1   Baldus ad *Feud.*, 1.14:
Et dicit Innocentius, 'cuius est civitas ecclesie?' Respondetur quod ecclesie, immo magis civium cuius est civitas. Bononia ecclesie, immo magis Bononiensium, quia ecclesia nihil habet ibi auctoritatis nisi tanquam respublica, cuius reipublice imaginem et nomen gerit. Item queritur, 'cuius est civitas Senarum?' Respondeo Cesaris, immo magis Senensium, nam respublica, fiscus et princeps presupponuntur quasi pro eodem, ut no. [C.6.1.7]. Respublica est sicut vivacitas sensuum. Fiscus est reipublice stomacus, saccus et firmitudo. Vnde imperator quasi tyrannus esset si non tanquam respublica gereret se, et multi alii reges

qui private sue utilitati negociantur, quia predo est qui non utilitati domini sed proprie studet.

p. 91   Baldus, *Cons.*, 3.283:

Notandum est ergo quod originalis intentio creationis imperii fuit bonum et utilitas rei publice non private, puta Caroli imperatoris. Ergo si imperator in respublicas seviret, excutere ab eo iugum tante servitutis non esset contrarium rationi naturali.

p. 91   Baldus ad D.1.8. Rubr.:

Princeps relative dicitur sicut pater et sicut subditi sunt obligati bene obedire, ita ipse est obligatus bene imperare.

p. 95   Hostiensis, *Lectura* ad X.1.31.3:

Vnde et hec iura collegiorum sive corporum vigent in civitatibus potissime Lombardie, que etsi dominum habeant, ipsum tamen non, ut expediret reipublice, recognoscunt, sicut nec rex Francie.

pp. 98–9   Baldus ad Inst., 1.2, 1:

Et primo queritur nunquid omni populo liceat statuta condere absque licentia superioris. Videtur quod non, arg. [C.10.65.5], ad hoc facit in Auth., 'De defensoribus civitatum' [Coll., 3.2 = Nov., 15]. Solutio. Dic, aut populus qui vult facere statutum nullam [nullam *ed. cit. & ed. Venice, 1615*; multam *ed. Lyon, 1585*] habet iurisdictionem, sed subest alicui civitati, sicut sunt ville et castra comitatus. Aut habet iurisdictionem plenam in temporalibus civilibusve et in criminalibus concessam [*add.* eis *ed. cit.*; *om.* eis *eds Lyon, 1585, & Venice, 1615*] a principe vel prescriptam [prescriptam *ed. Venice, 1615*; prescripta *ed. cit. & ed. Lyon, 1585*] consuetudine, quod esse potest ut in Auth., 'De defensoribus civitatum', § 'iusiurandum' [Coll., 3.2, 1 = Nov., 15, 1] in fine magne gl. Aut habet iurisdictionem limitatam, puta in civilibus tantum. Si nullam iurisdictionem habet, et tunc aut vult facere statuta circa distributionem pecunie vel alterius rei, que iurisdictionem non attingat, et tunc facere potest dummodo tale statutum non sit ambitiosum, quia tunc non valeret, ut in [D.50.9.4]. Aut vult facere statuta circa diffinitionem et cognitionem causarum, et tunc non potest sine licentia superioris per predicta iura, pro hoc facit [X.1.2.8 & 9]. Et est ratio quia condere talia statuta est iurisdictionis ut patet ex diffinitione iurisdictionis posita in gl. [D.2.1.1], unde cum iurisdictionem non habeat, non potest habere ea que a iurisdictione proveniunt, arg. [D.23.1.16]. Si querimus de populo habente iurisdictionem, et tunc potest absque superioris auctoritate...ut patet in hoc § et in [D.1.1.9], verb. 'populus', ubi indistincte datur licentia condendi statuta. Hoc probatur a similibus; nam consuetudo et statutum ambulant pari passu, ut dicam in [Inst., 1.2, 3], et consuetudo ex tacito consensu inducitur absque [ab *ed. cit. & eds Lyon, 1585, & Venice, 1615*] auctoritate superioris, ut [D.1.3.32], ergo et statutum. Et quod iste § debeat intelligi de populo habente iurisdictionem, patet quia lex exemplificat de populo Romano et Atheniensium, quos non est dubium iurisdictionem habere. Aut loquimur de populis iurisdictionem limitatam habentibus, et illi possunt statuta quantum ad illam iurisdictionem eis competentem condere sine auctoritate superioris, alia vero non.

p. 100   Baldus, *Secunda lectura* ad D.1.3.32:
Item nota quod de substantia consuetudinis est tacitus consensus populi scilicet tempore roboratus [roborationis *ed. cit. & ed. Venice, 1616*]...Ego dico...quod robur temporis requiritur non ad inducendum sed ad solennisandum consensum.

pp. 100–1   Baldus ad C.8.52. Rubr.:
Secundo querit glossa nunquid ad inducendam [inducendum *ed. cit.*] consuetudinem, ita quod ex ea ius fiat, sufficiat unus actus in quo consistit populus...Veritas est quod requiritur actuum pluralitas vel frequentia quia per pluralitatem et frequentiam actus apparet evidentius de consensu populi.

p. 101   Baldus, *Secunda lectura* ad D.1.3.32:
In lege scripta requiritur scriptura ad solennitatem non ad consensum.

p. 101   Baldus ad C.4.30.3:
Licet enim statutum sit consensus civium; tamen est consensus non simplex, sed lege munitus.

p. 101   Baldus ad C.8.52.2:
Consuetudo et statutum non differunt penes causam efficientem et eius potestatem, sed differunt penes modum et formam.

p. 101   Baldus ad D.1.3.32:
Nota...in versiculo, 'Nam cum ipse', statim addit tertium substantiale, scilicet tacitum consensum populi. Item ex comparatione quam facit de statuto ad consuetudinem patet quartum substantiale, scilicet quod est populus talis qui possit statuere. Nam si non potest in expresso nec in tacito cum utrobique requiratur par potentia cause efficientis.

p. 102   Baldus ad Auth., 'Omnes peregrini' (ad C.6.59.10):
De substantia consuetudinis est quod inducentes consuetudinem habeant statuendi potestatem.

p. 102   Baldus ad Auth., 'Et qui iurat' (ad C.7.72.9):
Est enim consuetudo tacitum statutum.

p. 104   Baldus ad D.1.1.9 (fol. 9r–9v):

a) First section

Nota ergo quod populi possunt sibi facere statuta…Modo restat videre
nunquid in tali statuto requiratur auctoritas superioris et videtur quod
non, quia populi sunt de iure gentium ergo regimen populi est de iure
gentium, ut supra [D.1.1.5]. Sed regimen non potest esse sine legibus
et statutis, ergo eoipso quod populus habet esse habet per consequens
regimen in suo esse, sicut omne animal regitur a suo spiritu proprio
et anima, et si bene se regit non potest superior se impedire, quia propter
bene viventes non sunt facte leges prohibitorie sed propter errantes, nam
si naturaliter ea que legis sunt faciunt, ipsi sibi sunt lex, et sanis non
est opus extranea medicina. Si ergo statuta sunt bona secundum
exigentiam et conservationem publicam illius loci non indigent alio
directore, quia confirmata sunt ex propria naturali iusticia. Preterea
quantum unumquodque habet de forma essentiali tantum habet de
virtute activa; sed populus habet formam ex se, ergo et exercitium
conservandi se in esse suo, et in forma propria; nam hoc est naturale
et permissum quod unumquodque studeat conservationi sui esse, supra
[D.1.1.3]. Preterea populi prohibentur statuere illicita, ergo licita sunt
permissa, patet primum [C.4.59.1]. Preterea non debemus requirere
plusquam lex requirat, ut infra [D.2.2.2], quia termini qui placent legi
debent placere nobis sine alia subauditione vel interpretatione…quia
contenti esse debemus de eo in quo lex figit pedes. Sed lex contenta
est consensu populi, ergo et nos, infra [D.1.3.32], nec potest dici quod
ibi loquatur solum de populo Romano, nam ibi ponitur ratio ad
principium legis, et in principio loquitur solum de alio populo. Preterea
populus potest inducere ius tacitum sine consensu et conscientia
superioris, nam inducit consuetudinem nesciente superiore, ut in
[*Sextus*, 1.2.1], ergo potest inducere ius expressum, id est statutum, quia
ius expressum et tacitum ubi non attenditur forma verborum sed
consensus idem operantur, quia convenerunt in causa et radice et
potentia, ergo in effectu. Sic enim arguit iurisconsultus in d.
[D.1.3.32]…

b) Second section

In contrarium facit nam populus non potest disponere super magistratu
nisi confirmetur a superiore, ut in auth. 'De defensoribus civitatum'
[Coll., 3.2 = Nov., 15], ergo non potest disponere super iure reddendo

a magistratu, quia cum magistratus sit superior populo ratione con-
firmationis superioris, ergo populus non potest imponere legem
magistratui, quia non potest inferior imponere legem superiori, ut no.
infra [D.1.4.1]. Preterea ego video quod populus non potest unum
minimum actum iurisdictionis exercere nisi interveniat magistratus,
unde non potest apud populum aliquis emancipari, ut [C.7.9.1]. Sed
statuta condere est iurisdictionis, quia qui statuit ius dicit; immo facit
quod plus est quam dicere ius vel reddere, infra [D.2.2.1]. Preterea est
de forma legis quod magistratus faciat propositam et interrogationem
in consilio vel in parlamento populi, ut infra [D.1.3.1] in glo. Nam
consul ibi vices magistratus gerit. Preterea omne quod est necessarium
ad ordinem rei est necessarium ad esse rei. Sed populus non debet vocari
nisi per magistratum, ut [C.10.32.2]. Preterea videtur lex expressa
[C.10.65.5]. Preterea clerus sine episcopo non potest facere statuta quia
essent membra capite mutilata, ergo idem in populo; populus enim
debet subesse non preesse, cum magistratus sit eius princeps [D.27.1.15].
Preterea nullus populus videtur sani capitis, quia quanto maior numerus
tanto minor intellectus [D.49.1.12; D.40.9.17; D.50.12.6]. Preterea
populus Romanus in quo erat omnium populorum vis ac potestas
abdicavit a se imperium, ergo non remansit in membris, quia cum capite
fortunas suas transtulit [C.1.14.12]...Preterea a quo removetur genus
removetur et quelibet eius species [C.2.4.32]. Sed a populo removetur
omnis iurisdictio ergo removetur iurisdictio statuendi, unde dicit
Innocentius quod penes populum iurisdictio nulla residet hodie
[X.1.2.8]. Item ibi notat Compostellanus quod nulla universitas potest
facere constitutionem absque magistratu. Et hec opinio severa est et [et
est *ed. cit.*] tenaciter servatur in terris ecclesie, adeo ut si tota provincia
Marchie vel Ducatus faceret statutum non admitteretur per ecclesiam
nisi esset approbatum sicut si castrum faceret statutum non admitteretur
nisi per commune civitatis approbaretur, ut d. [C.10.65.5], et ibi per
Bartolum. Sed Innocentius dicit quod in constitutione non requiritur
consensus nec scientia superioris, secus in consuetudine [X.2.22.15] per
Innocentium; sed nihil allegat. Idem tenet Iacobus Butrigarius, infra
[D.2.2.1]. Sed puto verum in his que non tangunt aliquo modo ius vel
interesse superioris. Vnde civitates habentes suum fiscum possunt facere
penalia statuta, quia de iure suo licitum est eis statuere, sed non in
alienum falcem mittere [C.3.39.4]. Et ideo de iure communi sic
distinguendum est. Aut princeps vetat statutum suo magistratu incon-
sulto, et tunc non valet statutum, quia princeps potest cassare statuta
facta et fienda; tamen hoc statutum sapit tyranniam nisi fiat ex iusta
causa, auth. 'Navigia' [ad C.6.2.18]; que tamen iusta causa presumitur

esse contra omnes qui non obediunt, vel consueverunt facere mala statuta, arg. infra [D.48.2.7]. Aut princeps non vetat, et tunc refert, aut statutum venit in derogationem iurisdictionis principis, puta quod non appelletur in casibus in quibus appellatio est permissa, et tunc non valet statutum factum super hoc directe vel indirecte [X.2.24.19], et no. [C.7.62.31] per Cynum [D.28.7.8] per Bartolum. Et illud est verum nisi natura facti non recipiat appellationem, quia illa est tunc potius observantia iuris communis quam sit statutorum [C.7.65.2]. Aut non veniunt in derogationem iurisdictionis superioris, et tunc refert, aut ʾquis statuit super reservatis superiori, ut super legitimatione spuriorum, et non valet. Et intelliguntur reservata omnia que concernunt supremam potestatem, ut in auth. ʿQuibus modis naturales efficiuntur suiʾ [Coll., 7.1 = Nov., 89] et in [*Feud.*, 2.56]. Aut quis statuit super aliis non reservatis, et tunc valet statutum, quia est concessum fieri per hanc legem et similes; et hoc verum ad ordinationem negociorum vel iudiciorum. Item ad causarum decisionem civilem non criminalem, quia criminalia respiciunt ius fiscale et sic superioris. Vel dic quod in favorem fisci possunt facere populi statuta sed non in lesionem fisci...Sed Innocentius dicit quod populus non potest facere statuta penalia, et hoc verum est quod iudici non potest imponere penam, quia imponeret superiori, sed inter se possunt, ut no. [C.10.47. Rubr.].

c) Third section (fol. 9v)

Et hec vera de iure communi quia magistratus confirmatur per superiorem. Sed si talis est civitas, cuius magistratus de consuetudine vel de iure non confirmatur per superiorem, tunc apud talem civitatem est plena iurisdictio, ut no. in auth. ʿDe defensoribus civitatumʾ [Coll., 3.2, 2 = Nov., 15, 2] in fine magne glo. Et iurisdictio est dominium, ut infra [D.1.5.20]. Et sicut dominus est moderator et arbiter, ita talis civitas, ut no. infra [D.2.2.1, 1] in glo. ordi., et potest in subditos omnia statuere, et in summa quantum habet iurisdictionis tantum habet auctoritatis condendi statuta, quia statuta condere est iurisdictionis, et uno posito ponitur reliquum, et remoto uno removetur reliquum secundum Bartolum. Et quandoque est meri imperii vel mixti secundum causas quas decidit...per Bartolum; tamen sicut ius dicens non potest tollere naturalem obligationem sic nec statutum, unde penalia statuta non absorbent obligationem naturalem, infra [D.2.2.4]. Item contra leges derogatorias clausula ʿnon obstanteʾ apposita in statuto nihil operatur [D.2.2.4] per Iacobum Butrigarium. Tamen illa ratio est indiscreta, nam si statuta ex iurisdictione vim capiunt, ergo non teneret statutum quod potestas teneatur exequi instrumenta, quia populus in magistratum non habet iurisdictionem. Item si illa sunt connexa, ergo quilibet magistratus posset facere statuta, quod est falsum [C.7.45.10]. Et si princeps expresse non permitteret, statutum non valeret [X.2.22.15] per Innocentium ... Item si imponitur pena centum venienti contra statuta loci, ista pena non habet locum hic quia non potest dici statutum nisi ex commissione populi magistratus fecerit... Alii multa dicunt de quibus non curo. Dico ergo quod statuta condere est potius de quadam iuris permissione quam sit annexum iurisdictioni. Idem dico quod magistratus tenetur sequi statutum sicut pactum, ar. infra [D.1.3.35]; et si non servat facit litem suam; nec ligatur auctoritate statuentium sed auctoritate iuris communis approbantis statutum [C.1.17.1].

p. 105   Baldus ad D.1.1.1, 4:
Ius gentium est quod procedit a ratione et intellectu gentium, quo omnes gentes quasi pereque utuntur, quod semper est bonum et equum, et sine quo homines non possent vivere ut hic, et infra [D.1.1.9; D.1.1.11; Inst., 1.2, 1], et distat a naturali sicut distat cerebrum hominis a cerebro animalium.

p. 105   Baldus ad D.1.1.5:
[Loquitur] hic in populis et urbibus vel villis: nam illa sunt de iure gentium et possunt fieri absque auctoritate superioris.

p. 111   Baldus ad D.2.1.1:
Dicit Bartolus quod facere statuta est iurisdictionis. Dominus Raynerius de Forlivio dicit contrarium, quia populus facit statutum et tamen penes ipsum non residet iurisdictio, in Auth., 'De defensoribus civitatum', § 'interim' [Coll., 3.2, 1 = Nov., 15, 1], et no. per Innocentium [X.1.2.6]. Vnde dicit dominus Raynerius quod populus non facit statutum iurisdictionis, sed vi permissionis [D.1.1.9], quod est ipsa veritas.

p. 112   Baldus ad X.1.2.6:
Dicit hic Hostiensis quod hodie populi tanquam principales et clarissimi non possunt statutum aliquod condere nisi princeps eis hoc expresse concedat vel confirmet; et probat ex eo quia populus Romanus in quo omnis populus includitur omne suum imperium transtulit in principem. Sed tu dic quod potestas statuendi et iurisdictio sunt annexa, et qui habet unum habet et reliquum eiusdem qualitatis. Nec aliquid valet ratio Hostiensis quia [D.1.1.9] est approbata per Iustinianum et per Cesarem, et ideo debet haberi pro imperiali constitutione, presertim quia Iustinianus fuit post Cesarem Augustum, ut no. [D.4.4.38] in fine. Et

ideo dicas statuta populorum valere, nisi eis sit expresse inhibitum per
principem eorum... Item sitiunt iurisdictionem quemadmodum cervus
desiderat ad fontes acquarum secundum quosdam.

p. 113   Baldus ad C.7.46.2:
In civitate tamen non puto quod possint facere sine auctoritate
superioris qui sit superior actu et potestate. Civitates vero que vivunt
in propria libertate et absolute proprio regimine non indigent alieno
adminiculo quia suis iuribus utuntur. Idem si faciunt auctoritate
privilegii vel consuetudinis prescripte.

p. 114   Baldus ad C.9.12.7:
Hodie de facto non est superioris copia cum civitates non obediant
Cesari.

p. 114   Baldus ad Auth., 'Sed omnino' (ad C.4.12.4):
Satis dicitur deficere [superior] cum non possit efficaciter consulere sicut
imperator et papa contra tyrannos Lombardie et etiam contra populos
qui vivunt sicut sui iuris in libertate facti.

p. 114   Baldus ad D.1.8. Rubr.:
Sed ut dixi civitates que realiter superiores non recognoscunt et infiscant
sibi regalia hoc habent de consuetudine et minime mutanda videntur
que consuetudinem certam semper habuerunt, supra [D.1.3.23]. Equa-
nimiter tolleremus, quia non ipsi facimus. Sed de iure constat potestatem
soli principi reservatam a civitatibus esse exemptam [C.10.32.19 &
C.4.62.2]... Sed olim erat princeps auctoritatem et utilitatem publice
rei prospiciens; nunc vero non eadem fides est in principe nec in
subditis, perempto enim seu mortificato nimis uno extremorum aliud
extremum pati necesse est.

p. 116   Baldus ad X.1.29.41:
Respondeo cum eligatur ab imperatore, sufficit quelibet etas... Idem si
eligatur a populo *vice* imperatoris, quia in territorio suo princeps est.

p. 116   Baldus, *Cons.*, 2.49:
vicem ergo et *imaginem* principis habent.

p. 116   Baldus, *Cons.*, 5.406:
civitas enim francha a superis concedere potest franchisiam inferis, quia
vicem principis in suo gerit solio.

p. 116   Baldus ad X.1.2.13:
in suo territorio *vice* principis funguntur.

pp. 116–17   Baldus ad X.1.2.1:

Imperator non solet legitimare nisi reservata forma, id est clausula non obstantium adiecta. Sed populus, qui est minoris auctoritatis, non potest istam clausulam derogatoriam apponere, quia ista clausula est de suprema iurisdictione, que vocatur plenitudo potestatis, que non est apud populos.

p. 118   Baldus ad C.7.38.1:

Dico quod licet contra imperium et Romanam ecclesiam non prescribitur super his que reservata sunt in signum specialis prelationis et preeminentie, ut notat Ioannes Andree in [*Sext.*, 1.6.1], tamen forsan tanto spacio centum annorum prescribitur. Vnde prescripsit populus Romanus libertatem, facit [D.49.15.24], ubi loquitur de populis liberis, et quia non est dubium quin imperator possit [quia imperator potest *ed. cit.*] libertatem concedere populo Romano per suum privilegium et rescriptum et concedere ei omnia iura regalia et merum imperium, ut in decima collatione, 'Que sint regalia' [*Feud.*, 2.56], et ita Fedricus in decima collatione concessit Lombardis in pace Constantie, et habes in Auth., 'De defensoribus civitatum', § 'et iudicare' [Coll., 3.2, 3 = Nov., 15, 3], ergo et eodem modo per patientiam tribuere, quia non minus operatur animi patientia firmata longi temporis causa quam concessio.

p. 120   Bartolus ad D.5.3.30, 7:

Nota glossam que dicit quod bona vacantia non applicantur alteri civitati sed fisco. Et verum dicit in civitatibus que recognoscunt superiorem; sed in his que non recognoscunt superiorem de iure vel de facto ut civitates Tuscie est ipsamet civitas fiscus. Vocatur enim populus liber de quo fit mentio in [D.49.15.24]...In illis vero civitatibus que non recognoscunt aliquem in dominum que dicuntur de fisco intelliguntur de suo communi.

p. 120   Baldus ad D.1.8. Rubr.:

Et an civitates habeant proprium fiscum suum? Dico quod non, nisi quedam que superiorem non recognoscunt, que per sua statuta et consuetudines habent iura fisci.

p. 121   Baldus ad C.4.39.1:

Nulla bursa dicitur fiscalis proprie loquendo nisi bursa principis vel reipublice Romane, ut [D.39.4.6 & D.50.16.16], salvis civitatibus que prescripserunt iura fiscalia.

p. 121   Baldus, *Rep.* ad C.1.1.1:

quelibet civitas in suo territorio succedit in locum fisci.

p. 122   Baldus ad X.1.32. Rubr.:
Officium potestatis debet vigilare contra eos qui populum in turbas
[turba *ed. cit. & ed. Venice, 1595*] sollicite tentant, ut in Auth., 'De
mandatis principum' [Coll., 3.4, 17 = Nov., 17, 17], et inquirere et
requirere et punire. Et sic punitur pena mortis qui intentat mutare
statum populi cum armis [C.9.42.2], quia est crimen lese maiestatis.

p. 122   Baldus ad C.9.24.2:
Dicerem in civitate ista quod esset crimen simile lese maiestati, si quis
subditus istius civitatis falsaret istam monetam. Ideo dico subditus
[subditis *ed. cit.*] quia non subditus non incidit in crimen lese maiestatis,
ut notat Paulus in [*Clem.*, 2.11.2]. Vnde qui vult prodere populum
incidit in crimen lese maiestatis. Istud est verum de subdito, secus de
non subdito.

pp. 123–4   Baldus ad D.V. Const., 'Omnem':
Nota quod respublica dicitur tribus modis: primo modo pro tota
congregatione fidelium imperii, seu pro toto imperio; secundo modo
pro republica urbis Rome; tertio modo pro qualibet civitate. Et sic
respublica quandoque stat pro capite et membris simul, quandoque pro
capite tantum scilicet pro urbe Romana, quandoque pro aliis membris.

p. 124   Baldus ad C.7.73. Rubr.:
Fiscus idem est quod saccus Cesaris vel regis vel reipublice, ut no.
[C.12.49.4]; municipia enim proprie fiscum non habent, ut [C.10.10.1],
licet habeant bursam communem, ut [D.3.4.1, 1].

p. 124   Baldus ad C.7.49.1:
Dic quod respublica universitatem significat; fiscus autem significat
rem ipsius universitatis.

pp. 124–5   Baldus, *Cons.*, 2.369:
Ista enim iura pedagiorum sunt specialiter reservata superiori in signum
superioritatis, ut [C.7.39.6], superior autem secundum consuetudinem
Italie sunt ipse civitates que per se reguntur, ut [D.49.15.7 & 24], nam
ipse dicuntur respublice non castra vel ville.

p. 126   Accursius, gl. ad C.7.33.12 ad v. 'Id est in una provincia':
Et nota unum locum appellari unam provinciam: sed hodie non videtur
habere locum sed in eadem civitate esse debent, cum singule civitates
habeant sua regimina ut olim singule provincie.

p. 126   Baldus ad C.7.33.12:
In glossa que incipit ibi 'in una provincia', § 'cum singule civitates',

ista glossa est singularis in iure et non habet sociam secundum Accursium, quod unaqueque civitas que habet suum regimen proprium et distinctum non supponitur de facto iurisdictioni superioris dicitur provincia. Exemplum pone in Florentia, Perusio, et in civitate Senarum: habentur loco unius provincie. Vnde exercentes in eis imperium tenent locum presidis. Vltimo esset hic videndum quis locus debeat appellari provincia; dic ut hic per Cynum qui clare dicit.

p. 128   Baldus ad C.6.24.1:
Bannum non afficit personam nisi in territorio unde est bannitus. Hec ergo est pena persone in loco et non persone simpliciter, nam iurisdictio coartata quoad locum extra ipsum locum se non extendit, ut [D.1.16.1 & 2; D.1.12.1, 4; D.2.1.20], nam iurisdictio coheret territorio, ut [C.2.26.3], sed territorium habet suos fines limitatos...et sic, ut ita dixerim, tales banniti sunt a certa parte banniti, scilicet de territorio bannientis, et pro alia parte non banniti, scilicet in aliis locis, in quibus liberas edes habent.

p. 128   Baldus, ibid.:
In universo orbe manere licet [bannito] excepta terra unde exulat...licet [banniti] amittant iura et bona proprie civitatis, tamen non amittuntur iura communia civium Romanorum.

p. 129   Baldus ad D.1.18.3:
Querit hic Guilelmus, iudex domicilii procedit, iudex loci delicti petit remissionem, utrum debeat fieri, et determinat quod sic, quod est notandum, quod debet remittere etiam ille, qui per se potest punire... Hodie tamen non utimur istis remissionibus nisi in terris que sunt sub uno principe generali, non autem in terris que non subalternantur regimini alicuius; et ita se habet consuetudo que est servanda quia generalis et prescripta. Vnde videmus quod banniti de civitate Pisarum possunt hic secure morari, non tamen timent remissionem quia non est in usu quod fiat de pari ad parem.

p. 130   Baldus ad D.1.1.9:
Queritur ulterius nunquid intrinseci possint [possunt *ed. cit.*] facere statuta contra expulsos. Et videtur quod sic, quia intrinseci faciunt populum, non dispersi et vagi per mundum [X.5.32.2] per Innocentium...In contrarium...ex quo sunt expulsi desierunt esse de illa universitate et de illo corpore [D.4.5.5, 1], ergo tanquam extranei non sunt sub statuto. Dic quod siquidem sunt expulsi ex iusta causa valet statutum, quia delictum non debet eis prestare exemptionem d. [D.4.5.5, 1; D.50.12.8; D.42.4.13]. Et concedo quod iurisdictio remanet

penes intrinsecos, quia coheret territorio, et intrinseci possident territorium. Item intrinseci sunt universi et expulsi sunt singuli.

pp. 132–3 Baldus ad C.1.2.12:
Tertio nota quod ubi lex est contraria canoni debet servari canon et non ius civile. Circa quod dic, aut loquimur in spiritualibus et pertinentibus ad fidem et stamus canoni, ut hic in glossa, idem in rebus ecclesiasticis vel aliis iuribus ecclesiarum, ut [X.1.2.10]; aut loquimur in meris temporalibus et tunc aut in terris ecclesie, et in utroque foro servamus canones, aut in terris imperii, et tunc in foro civili servamus leges nisi talis observantia induceret peccatum, ut [X.4.17.13], sed in foro episcopi stamus potius canonibus.

p. 133 Baldus ad X.2.28.7:
Et per textum capituli nostri dico quod in civitatibus Romani imperii statuta civitatum prevalent sacris canonibus summorum pontificum, per istud capitulum, quia si ad papam non potest appellari, ergo iurisdictionem superiorem non habent; unde in feudis constitutiones principum et dominorum magis debent servari quam constitutiones episcoporum nisi feudum esset ecclesiasticum, ut in [*Sext.*, 2.15.3].

p. 133 Baldus ad X.2.18.7:
nota quod iurisdictio temporalis est omnino divisa a iurisdictione ecclesie, nisi in terris ecclesie.

p. 134 Baldus ad Auth., 'Statuimus' [ad C.1.3.32], fol. 37v:
Nota hic quod nulla persona ecclesiastica potest trahi ad iudicium iudicis secularis, et omnia iura vetera que contrarium permittebant sunt correcta. Dicunt canoniste quod hoc non est ius novum sed est recedere ab errore veterum legum quia clerici nunquam fuerunt de iurisdictione temporali iudicum laicorum. Et ista est ipsa veritas, quia deus a principio istas iurisdictiones distinxit ut in [*Decr. Grat.*, D.96, c.6] et Auth., 'Quomodo oporteat episcopos' [Coll., 1.6 = Nov., 6].

pp. 134–5 Baldus, ibid. (fol. 38r):
Que autem statuta dicantur contra libertatem ecclesie? Dicit Innocentius quod omnia illa que sunt contra privilegia concessa universali ecclesie, sive a deo, sive a dei vicario, sive ab imperatoribus, ut notatur per eum [X.5.39.49], Cynus refert in Auth., 'Cassa et irrita' [ad C.1.2.12].

p. 136 Baldus ad Auth., 'Item nulla' (ad C.1.3.2):
Communitates nullam habent potestatem in ecclesiam vel ecclesiasticas personas nec possunt eis imponere collectas.

pp. 136–7   Baldus, *Cons.*, 1.148:

Et opinio Bartoli propter publicam utilitatem et publicas necessitates
est in usu; et alias esset damnare totum mundum. Sed Iacobus
Butrigarius in dicta Auth., 'Item nulla communitas', in lectura [ad
C.1.3.2] non confirmat [se firmat *ed. cit. & ed. Venice, 1575*], tamen satis
dat intelligere quod antequam collecta sit imposita bona non sint
hipothecata, quasi hoc sit impossibile, et sic principium acquisitionis
dominii erit liberum et non affectum. Et ex hoc sequitur statim quod
clerici non tenentur ad novas collectas, quia eorum predia quantum ad
hoc non videntur esse de territorio sive de districtu laicorum. Et ista
est tutior opinio quia periculosum est in istis loqui contra ecclesias et
clericos. Tamen opinio Bartoli de facto servatur, nisi sit alius modus
ubi per obligationes antecessorum quod clerici pingues teneantur pro
bonis patrimonialibus una cum suis concivibus conferre ad ea que
reipublice expediunt, in quibus universorum salus et incolumitas
procuratur.

p. 137   Baldus, ibid.:

Et certe in casibus necessitatis ipsi [i.e. clerici] deberent seipsos offerre
ut quod omnes tangit ab omnibus sentiatur. Per hoc tamen non dico
quod laici faciant statuta alias non facturi nisi odio clericorum; nam
tunc factum in fraudem ecclesiastice libertatis crederem non valere.

p. 138   Cynus ad C.8.52.2:

Queritur nunquid consuetudo populi liget clericos. Et dicimus quod
non duabus rationibus. Vna quia duo sunt populi, quod patet quia duo
sunt iudices, ergo etc., ut [D.1.22.3]. Vnde nihil habet commune cum
actibus plebeis, ut [C.1.3.17]. Alia quia clerici sunt maiores respectu
laicorum... Sed statuta minorum non ligant maiores... ergo etc., nisi
clerici voluerint.

p. 139   Baldus ad *Feud.*, 2.21:

An sacerdos possit vel debeat reputari de universitate civium? Dic quod
sic [D.35.1.33, 1; X.2.2.17], sicut et ecclesie sunt de corpore civitatis
secundum Oldradum.

p. 139   Baldus ad X.1.2.7:

Clerici sunt de populo quoad favorem eorum, sed non quoad damnum
ecclesie.

p. 139   Baldus, *Cons.*, 1.243:

Ea que a iure communi statuta sunt in favorem clerici ad clericos
extenduntur... et idcirco clerici civium [cives *ed. cit. & ed. Venice, 1575*]
privilegiis et favoribus gaudent, et ad hoc [*Decr. Grat.*, C.12, q.1, c.7].

p. 140   Paulus de Castro ad D.1.1.9:
Item an clerici gaudeant beneficio laicorum? Dic quod sic, quia sunt
de populo, et insimul cum laicis faciunt unam rempublicam...et ita
tenuit Oldradus consulendo, et allegat [*Decr. Grat.*, D.10.7], licet sint
exempti ab oneribus laicorum; sed hoc non minus facit eos esse de
populo, et gaudere statutis, quia plures alii laici sunt exempti et
privilegiati, tamen gaudent, quia privilegium non debet eis [ei *ed. cit.*]
esse nocivum.

p. 140   Baldus ad D.1.1.1, 2:
Deinde nota quod ius publicum consistit in rebus, id est in sacris rebus,
consistit etiam in actibus hominum, id est in sacrificiis, infra [D.1.1.2];
consistit etiam immediate in personis, id est sacerdotibus propter
sacerdotium, quod est publicum ministerium, et in magistratibus
propter publicum officium...Sacerdos qui est preses animarum, et
magistratus qui est preses iudiciorum, non sunt instituti propter Titium
et Seium, sed propter incertum de incertis, unde quicunque sit ille qui
agit sacerdotium vel magistratum non curatur sed respublica attendit
ut recte regatur. Et nota hic de iure publico. Sed quero econtra de
iniuria, id est que dicatur publica? Respondeo, que omnibus fit sub
ratione pari...Item quia ius censuerit esse publicam...propter persone
publice dignitatem, ut quia infertur magistratui vel sacerdoti qui
representat rempublicam.

p. 141   Baldus, ibid.:
Extra nota argumentum quod sacerdotes sunt partes reipublice, et sunt
de districtu civitatis, ut notat Ioannes Andree in [X.1.3.43] in novella,
et facit ad statutum quod nemo trahat aliquem extra curiam Perusinam,
ut non includat trahentes ad curiam episcopalem; nam et illa dicitur
Perusina, sicut dicitur ecclesia Perusina [X.2.12.3].

p. 143   Baldus, *Cons.*, 1.442:
Modo queritur utrum istud capitulum quod non facit mentionem de
clericis restringere habeat primum capitulum quod facit de clericis
mentionem. Et breviter est dicendum quod quicquid princeps in
favorem clericorum vel ecclesiarum ordinat nunquam intelligitur esse
revocatum per aliquod aliud decretum eorum nisi nominatim fiat
mentio de clericis, textus est [C.1.2.12]. Et ideo primum capitulum circa
clericos formatum servandum est. Ad hec etiam facit quod [verba] dicti
serenissimi principis etiam clericos vocant subditos in materia ista que
est circa protectionem [*Decr. Grat.*, D.10.7].

p. 143   Baldus, ibid.:
Item et clerici pars civitatis sunt, et quidem honorabilissimum membrum, nec si omnino ab universali corpore alieni, quia auctus sit honor eorum [D.35.1.33, 1].

p. 144   Baldus ad X.2.28.7:
Et nota quod potestas secularis et ecclesiastica debent sibi invicem auxilia mutuare, quia fraternizant, licet in ista fraternitate ecclesia sit maior et magis libera, ut in Auth., 'De non alienandis ecclesiasticis rebus' [Coll., 2.1 = Nov., 7].

p. 144   Baldus ad C.6.33.3:
In eadem civitate ille est principalior forus sub quo sunt alii, unde... forus episcopi est maior foro potestatis, quia potestas quandoque est sub episcopo, non econtra, ut no. [D.3.1.9].

p. 145   Baldus, *Cons.*, 4.496:
Sicut laici non possunt tollere libertatem clericorum, ita nec clerici libertatem et iurisdictionem laicorum in subditos laicos.

p. 145   Baldus ad C.3.1.3:
Secundum ius canonicum causa spiritualis incidens civili non cognoscitur apud civilem, scilicet secularem iudicem, sed econtra si causa fori civilis incideret cause spirituali pertinet ad iudicem spiritualem, id est ad episcopum, ut [X.4.20.3]. Sed istud dicunt canoniste quia student attribuere sibi iurisdictionem et totam suam facere ex ambitu iurisdictionis secundum Cinum. Sed male dicit. Nam considerandum est quod quedam sunt cause diversi fori principalis, ut civilis et secularis, et ecclesiastica et [*om. ed. cit.*] spiritualis; tunc secularis iudex non posset cognoscere etsi esset imperator, quia talis iurisdictio ab eo distincta est a lege divina, unde ipse non est capax huius iurisdictionis per aliquam legem vel rationem humanam, ut d. [X.2.10.3]. Non obstat quod econtra episcopus cognoscat de temporali incidenti spirituali vel ecclesiastice cause; nam illud est ideo quia ille cause sunt digniores, ideo trahunt ad se minus dignum secundum dictamen naturalis rationis.

pp. 145–0   Baldus, *Cons.*, 2.310:
Propter pretensam iniusticiam statuti ad curiam ecclesiasticam recursus habetur...Constat ergo quod ratione iniusticie et peccati quod nulla potest tergiversatione celari aditur ecclesiam [ecclesia *ed. cit. & ed. Venice, 1575*] in subsidium laicorum, secus si proprie non sit peccatum vel probari non liceat.

p. 146   Baldus, ibid.:
De foro episcopi et potestatis terre constat quod sunt distincta distinctione principali que est inter imperatorem et ecclesiam quorum isti sunt membra. Tamen sol nobilior est luna...Alter autem alterius officium tangere non debet nisi eatenus quatenus, nam oportet sacras regulas pro legibus valere, in Auth., 'Quomodo oporteat episcopos', § ii [Coll., 1.6, 2 = Nov., 6, 2]; immo non [non *ed. Venice, 1575; om. ed. cit.*] solum valere sed etiam prevalere, quia leges non dedignantur sacros canones imitari [imitari *ed. Venice, 1575; immutari ed. cit.*], in Auth., 'Vt clerici apud proprios episcopos' [Coll., 6.11 = Nov., 83].

p. 147   Baldus ad Auth., 'Clericus quoque' (ad C.1.3.32):
Quando tamen episcopus remittit hereticum ad iudicem secularem iudex secularis tenetur stare actis episcopi, quia ista remissio fit tanquam de superiori ad inferiorem; unde inferior solum habet exequi non cognoscere de crimine, de hoc per Bartolum...et hic per Iacobum Butrigarium.

p. 149   Baldus ad D.24.3.1:
Est enim ius commune sicut genus, municipale sicut species; et si municipale esset contra ius, derogatur iuri communi, tunc quia posterius, tunc [tum *ed. cit.*] quia species derogat generi, ut [D.1.3.32].

p. 150   Baldus ad D.1.3.32:
Dico quod consuetudo localis vincit ibi usum id est observantiam legis, non autem dico quod funditus eradicet de illo legem, nam illa sunt diversa. Si enim radicitus eradicaret [radicaret *ed. cit. & ed. Venice, 1616*] legem de illo loco, et ponamus quod fiat statutum quod consuetudo sit cassa, ille locus remaneret sine ulla lege [D.1.2.2, 1]. Sed quia non est abolita lex, sed effectus legis, tunc sublata consuetudine remanemus in iure communi, et hec res revertitur ad naturam suam, quia non erat omnino extincta, sed velata.

pp. 150–1   Baldus, ibid.:
Tertio opponitur et videtur quod consuetudo non tollat legem, sed tollatur per legem, quia imperiales constitutiones in omni loco prevalere oportet [D.47.12.3, 5]. Solutio: aut consuetudo est introducta post legem, et prevalet consuetudo, ut hic, aut econtra constitutio est facta post consuetudinem et tollitur consuetudo per constitutionem ut in contrario. Quarto contra hanc solutionem opponitur quod consuetudo specialis non tollatur per legem generalem sequentem, ut in [*Sext.*, 1.2.1]. Solutio: aut constat de mente legislatoris, scilicet quod vult tollere consuetudinem, et tunc statur legi tanquam superiori; aut

constat contrarium, et tunc statur consuetudini in loco suo; aut dubitatur, et tunc aut id quod consuetudo permittit nova constitutio censet esse delictum vel malum publicum, et penam imponit, et tunc lex prevalet, quia ubi lex credit inesse delictum, non posset de novo consuetudo fieri, ergo nec in futurum permanere, ut d. [D.47.12.3, 5], et adde quod notatur in [*Clem.*, 1.3.7]. Aut lex non iudicat illud esse delictum quod est preambula consuetudine introductum, et tunc non tollitur consuetudo certi loci per legem generalem, quia species a genere semper eximitur, et quia princeps non creditur velle quod nescit, voluntas enim est actio intellectus cognoscentis, unde nemo dicitur velle quod in mente non cogitavit, ut infra [D.33.10.7].

p. 152   Baldus ad C.8.52.2:

Alii dicunt... quod aut consuetudo est introducta contra legem ex certa scientia aut per errorem iuris... Ad id quod dicis de errore respondeo quod non est verum, quod hic cesset consensus, nam error in causa seu ratione non facit consensum abesse sive deesse... Ex hoc nota quod licet prorogationem iurisdictionis que fit per singularem personam impediat error, tamen secus quando talis prorogatio iurisdictionis fit per universitatem seu populum, nam per tales actus inducitur consuetudo que est apta et potens dare novam iurisdictionem.

p. 152   Baldus ad C.3.13.7:

Nota quod collegia approbata possunt habere proprios iudices et prepositos... Vlterius nota quod collegia artium et artifices licet habeant proprios iudices tamen nihilominus possunt conveniri sub potestate, et quod potestas dicitur superior non solum artium sed artificum et etiam prepositorum ipsorum.

pp. 152–3   Baldus ad D.1.1.9:

Hic queritur an collegia, puta mercatorum artis lane, possint facere inter se statuta specialia contra statuta generalia illius civitatis; et videtur quod sic, nam eo ipso quod collegium est approbatum potest facere statuta inter suos iuratos [C.4.18.2]... Solutio: inter ipsos possunt habere propria statuta a generali lege discrepantia facta super factis illius artis, vel professionis, non super aliis, puta super hereditatibus... Hec tamen statuta non nocent aliis quam ipsismet, et heredibus eorum, nam talia statuta dicuntur conventiones, ut infra [D.1.3.25], ergo aliis non nocent.

p. 153   Baldus ad C.9.21.1:

Guelphus et Gebellinus sunt passiones et partialitates animi sicut amor et odium et ideo secundum rei veritatem non sunt iste passiones innate que veniunt a principiis rationis loquendo secundum rationem.

p. 153   Baldus ad X.2.19.2:
Et nota quod prava statuta terrarum sunt per superiorem reprobanda, facit [D.50.9.4], et maxime quando sapiunt monopolium seu factum illicitum, ut contingit interdum in statutis Guelphorum contra Gebellinos et econtra; que enim procedunt de fonte irrationabilis odii, extirpanda sunt, quia dolus est.

p. 154   Baldus ad D.3.4.1:
Hec est ipsa veritas circa rem publicam nisi forte esset expulsa maior pars civitatis, quia tunc sub nomine maioris partis, non sub nomine secte, facerent collegium licitum.

p. 154   Baldus ad D.30.1.32, 2:
Dicit Bartolus quod si due sunt partes in una civitate, una intrinseca, alia extrinseca, ut quia expulsa, quod si iste partes submittunt civitatem separatim, quod non valet. Sed tu dic quod valet si fiat a maiori parte, ut in [X.5.32.2], scilicet quantum ad preiudicium facientium sed non superioris.

p. 156   Baldus ad C.9.1. Rubr.:
Nam ius divinum est ius naturale nature create.

p. 157   Baldus ad C.1.19.7:
Secus est in statuto populi, quia non debet inesse causa motiva, sed debet inesse causa probabilis et condigna, alias non valet, ut [D.40.9.17].

p. 157   Baldus ad X.2.26.20:
Secundo nota quod ratione peccati papa potest cassare leges imperatorum, regum et populorum, ergo non valent statuta permittentia homicidia, quia qui non habet gladii potestatem, et facit homicidia, peccat mortaliter. Ego dico quod non valet statutum tanquam statutum licentie, quia impossibile est quod peccare mortaliter sit licitum... Oppo. quod papa non possit se intromittere de rebus laicorum cum sit iudex incompetens in causis eorum... Solutio: hoc contingit hic ratione peccati.

p. 159   Baldus ad C.7.53.5:
Dic incidenter quod homo potest tripliciter considerari. Vno modo prout est per se quoddam individuum ex anima et corpore naturaliter constitutum, ut [D.21.2.56, 2]. Secundo modo potest considerari prout est quoddam corpus iconomicum, id est, princeps familie, ut [D.50.16.195, 1], sicut est paterfamilias et abbas monasterii. *Tertio modo potest considerari prout est quoddam corpus civile seu politicum* sicut est episcopus civitatis et potestas, et hoc si consideretur in preeminentia.

*Sed si consideratur in congregatione tunc homo naturalis efficeretur politicus,
et ex multis aggregatis fit populus*, ut [D.41.3.30]. Iste populus quandoque
muris cingitur, et incolit civitatem; et idem proprie dicitur politicus
a polis quod est civitas. Alius est populus rusticanus qui habitat in castris
vel villis, et ibi habet suum domicilium, ut supra [C.6.23.31].

p. 160   Baldus ad D.1.1. Rubr.:
Causa finalis [artis nostre] est triplex, scilicet in homine, ad hominem,
et ad rempublicam. In homine, ut bonus sit; et hoc pertinet ad ethicam.
Ad hominem, ut quis bene regat familiam; et hoc pertinet ad
economicam. Ad rempublicam, ut respublica salubriter regatur; et hoc
pertinet ad politicam, supra in [D. Const., 'Omnem', 11).

p. 161   Aquinas ad *Pol.*, Proem, 5:
Cum igitur hoc totum quod est civitas sit cuidam rationis iudicio
subiectum, necesse fuit ad complementum philosophiae de civitate
doctrinam tradere quae politica nominatur, idest civilis, scientia.

pp. 161–2   Guilelmus de Cuneo ad D.V., Proem (ed. Brandi):
Queritur quid sit subiectum in ista scientia...Dicit alibi quod immo
quod iusticia civilis est subiectum homo politicus, prout aptatur ad
regnum rei publice...Nunquid ergo homo politicus est subiectum? Hic
dico quod sic, quia ideo principaliter tractatur in iure ut homo; cum
gratia hominum omnia iura facta sunt, infra [D.1.5.2]. Dico tamen circa
hoc quod subiectum bene regatur, quia homo civiliter vivens potest
dici subiectum...Item operaciones [oposiciones *ed. cit.*] hec possunt dici
subiectum inspecto homine prout operatur civiliter: unde nihil videtur
interesse utrum dicamus hominem politicum idest vivens civiliter,
dicatur esse subiectum, vel an operaciones humane, ar. infra [D.34.5.19].

id., ibid. (Bodleian MS, Can. Misc. 472):
Set circa istam materiam queritur quid est subiectum in ista materia...
dicit allibi quod iusticia civilis est subiectum homo pollicitus prout
aptatur ad regimen rei publice...Nunquid ergo homo pollicitus est
subiectum? Hic dico quod sic, quia de eo principaliter tractatur in iure
ut homo bene regnatur. Quare homo civiliter vivens [?] potest dici
subiectum, cum gratia hominum...iura omnia facta sunt...Item
opiniones humane possunt dici subiectum inspecto homine prout operatur civiliter, unde nichil videtur interesse utrum dicamus hominem
pollicitum, id est vivens [veniens *MS*] civiliter dicatur esse subiectum
vel an opiniones humane.

Appendix I

p. 163   Azo, *Summa Codicis*, ad v. 'Incipit materia ad Codicem':
Supponitur ethice, quia tractat de moribus, sicut et omnes libri legalis
scientie.

p. 163   Bartolus, *De regimine civitatis*:
Istud regimen vocat Aristoteles politiam seu politicum. Nos autem
vocamus regimen ad populum.

p. 165   Baldus ad *Feud.*, 1.8 (Additio):
Vbi vero est tribunal, ibi aliquam politicam et regulam necesse est esse
[esse *ed. Lyon, 1585*; et *ed. Pavia, 1495*] que dici potest ius civile, id est
ius vivendi sub quadam specie civilitatis.

p. 166   Baldus ad D.1.1.1, 1 (Additio):
Quia homo est animal sociale, ut in primo Politicorum, competunt sibi
iura, que societatis sunt, et iura civitatis sue.

p. 166   Aquinas, *S.T.*, 1a 2ae, qu. 72, art. 4:
Homo est naturaliter animal politicum et sociale, ut probatur in I
Politicorum.

p. 166   Aristotle, *Pol.*, trans. William of Moerbeke, p. 7:
Ex hiis igitur manifestum, quod eorum quae natura civitas est, et quod
homo natura civile animal est.

p. 166   Aquinas ad *Pol.*, I, *lectio* 1:
Deinde cum dicit, 'ex iis igitur', ostendit, quod homo sit naturaliter
civile animal. Et primo concludit hoc ex naturalitate civitatis. Secundo
probat hoc per operationem propriam ipsius, ibi, 'Ex quo patet sociale
animal etc.'

p. 171   Bartolus, *Cons.*, 1.62:
Punctus talis est: Quidam est effectus civis alicuius civitatis per statutum
vel reformationem. Queritur, an dicatur vere civis, an improprie? In
questione predicta sciendum est quod aliquem esse civem non est actus
naturalis, sed iuris civilis, quod apparet. Primo, ex ipso nomine, quia
civis dicatur a civitate. Secundo, quia de iure naturali non erat civitas
et nascendo quis non efficiebatur civis. Est ergo constitutio iuris civilis
que facit aliquem civem propter originem vel propter dignitatem vel
propter adoptionem, ut [C.10.40.7]. Vnde non est dicendum quod
quidam sunt cives naturaliter, quidam civiliter. Immo est dicendum
quod omnes sunt cives civiliter: aliqui tamen propter naturalem
originem, aliqui propter aliam causam. Vnde si civitas facit statutum
quod quicunque habet ibi domum sit civis, vere erit civis, ut

[D.50.16.139] et ibi not. et [D.50.16.190 & D.1.5.17]; et vere et proprie civis est, quicunque recipitur, ut munera subeat. Sed iste est sic receptus, ergo vere et proprie civis est, ut [D.50.1.1] ibi 'proprie quidem' etc. Vnde debet tractari ut civis illius civitatis que eum civem facit.

p. 172   Baldus ad C.6.23.9:
Nomen civis est civile eque bene sicut naturale, et ideo potest vere introduci per statutum et privilegium.

p. 172   Baldus, *Cons.*, 5.409:
Verus civis non natura sed arte, quia civilitas est quid factibile et non solum nascitur sed creatur [creatur *ed. cit.*; causatur *ed. Kirshner, p. 326*].

p. 172   Baldus ad C.6.8.2:
Et facit ad statutum quod comitativi habeantur pro civitatensibus. Nam hoc nomen, 'civitatensibus', ponitur naturaliter; et ius originis non potest mutari nisi per fictionem, ut [D.50.1.6; & C.10.40.9]. Sed Bartolus dicit quod istud statutum in veritate disponit, non in fictione [D.41.3.15]. Sed tu dic quod duplex est civilitas, scilicet originaria, et quoad istam est fictio, et civilitas in genere, et quoad istam est veritas, quia predicatur de multis speciebus, et ideo species contenta sub genere ex propria [ex propria *ed. Lyon, 1585*; prior a *ed. cit.*] natura generis inest ei secundum veritatem, ergo etc., ut [C.10.40.7].

p. 172   Baldus ad X.2.26. Rubr.:
Dubitatur an quis possit prescribere civilitatem et privilegia civium alicuius terre. Videtur quod sic, excepta origine que prescribi non potest; sed commoda originis bene possunt prescribi, et erit simul iste civis verus et fictus originarius, id est in hac specie civilitatis, que naturalis sive in naturali est, et verus in vero iure civilitatis in genere [D.41.3.15] per Bartolum.

p. 173   Baldus ad D.12.1.14:
Et facit arg. ad forenses qui recipiuntur in cives originarios, quia hoc est per fictionem: pura enim civilitas potest induci per veritatem, sed originaria non, ut [D.50.1.6]; pares [pares *ed. Venice, 1616*; patris *ed. cit.*] ergo erunt per omnia iste civilitates.

p. 173   Baldus ad X.1.6.6:
Verbum, 'habeatur', positum super vero [vero *ed. Venice, 1595*; verbo *ed. cit.*] significat veritatem, quod si super ficto significat fictionem. Et facit ad questionem statuti dicentis quod mercatores forenses pro civibus habeantur, quia denotat similitudinem non unitatem, quia contra naturam sermo prolatus fictionem inducit...Si

262

igitur gentem consideres, id est patriam, fictio est; si meram civilitatem, potest esse veritas, ut hic et notatur per Bartolum [D.41.3.15].

pp. 174–5   Baldus ad D.V., Const., 'Omnem':
Sicut aliud est naturaliter et originaliter civem esse Padue aliud habere iura cum civibus, ut no. in [D.50.16.66], sicut aliud est esse naturaliter legitimum et aliud civiliter legitimatum, licet uterque legitimus habeat iura in succedendo. Quid autem si ista verba simul iungantur, videlicet 'et habeatur et sit'? Respondeo, significant veritatem si possunt, infra [D.2.2.1, 2] ubi textus eo casu loquitur ibi dum dicit, 'quoniam pro nullo habetur', nec est nisi quia iugimus iuris intellectum veritati. Et nota quod illud quod non simpliciter dicitur est magis simile quam idem, quia qualitas est una sed substantia sive natura est diversa. Non obstat quod notat Bartolus [D.41.3.15], ubi dicit quod illa verba, 'habeantur pro cive', faciant vere civem, quia civilitas in genere est vera quia una species eius est per accidens, sed civilitas in specie, id est relatione facta ad originalem civilitatem non est vera sed ficta, quia accidens non potest esse verum sed potest esse simile vel fingi idem. Nulla enim ars et nullum ingenium hominis poterit facere eum esse originalem verum in carentibus origine, sed bene poterit inducere similitudinem esse et fictionem esse, facit [C.6.8.2] et quod ibi plene no. et facit infra [D.1.7.1 & D.1.7.38] et infra [D.1.5.17] et infra [D.50.16.139 & D.41.3.2].

p. 178   Baldus ad C.6.23.9:
Quero, hic dicitur 'patrie tue', an patria tua dicatur in qua tu civis es adoptivus et non naturalis. Et videtur quod sic, si ibi sicut originarii publicos honores habes, nam cives muneribus et honoribus cognoscuntur, ut infra [C.10.40.7]. Qui autem non participant in publicis honoribus non dicuntur proprie cives, quia non tractantur ut cives in eo quod est supremum et maximum civilitatis argumentum.

p. 178   Baldus, *Cons.*, Lucca, 358:
Arguo civilitas est ultro citroque obligatoria... mutuum enim vinculum contrahitur hinc et inde; enim sicut ipsi sunt protegendi ex offitii debito, ita ipsi tenentur obedire et subesse civilitati nostre et vinculo... unde non potest acceptari emolumentum et respui detrimentum... Cum ergo consenserit est civis effectus vere et plene [D.41.3.15] per Bartolum, ergo suppositus est iurisdictioni; factus est enim civis allectione non secundum quid sed per omnia [C.10.40.7] ubi ista tria parificantur: origo, incolatus et allectio; et sic forum sortitur... Cum civis est effectus... ista est submissio, non simplex prorogatio... Iam prorogatio

enim proprie non facit quem subditum, sed civilitas sic, circa id de quo queritur.

p. 179 Baldus ad C.6.23.9:
Et in summa, si naturalis civilitas potest aliquid augere circa ipsius iura et statum, non dicitur simpliciter civis. Si autem ex naturali statu non posset augeri effectus, quia est effectus civis in omnibus et per omnia, tunc continetur appellatione civium, ar. [D.28.2.29, 5] et supra [C.1.3.54] et adde quod notatur per Bartolum [D.48.5.4 & D.41.3.15].

p. 180 Baldus ad D.1.1.9:
Sed pone quod statuto cavetur quod nullus possit esse de prioribus nisi sit originarius civis. Modo Titius receptus est in civem cum clausula quod habeatur pro originario quoad omnia, queritur an poterit esse de prioribus? Et videtur quod non, quia ille est idem casus fictus non verus... In contrarium facit infra [D.45.1.132 & D.27.1.44], nam ex quo sic habetur ac si esset oriundus, ista species temperat genus, id est derogat generi, nam ex quo esse talem [talis *ed. cit.*] et haberi pro tali est expressum et singulariter ordinatum, debet pari iure censeri.

p. 181 Baldus, *Cons.*, 3.299:
Satis obtinet licentiam civium etiam naturalium, qui propter suam nobilitatem efficitur civis per statutum, quia iam est de grege civium et numerarius vel supernumerarius eorum, et de eodem civili corpore et universitate active et passive, ut [D.29.1.20]; nam cum iura [iura *ed. Venice, 1575*; iure *ed. cit.*] civium sortiti sint pro extraneis haberi non possint.

pp. 182–3 Baldus, *Cons.*, 2.394:
Nam matrimonium est istius virtutis ac nature quod transfundit originem uxoris in originem viri... hoc etiam probatur ex virtute unionis in qua id quod potentius est trahit ad se id quod minus dignum... sed nulla est maior unio quam unio coniugalis per quam vir et uxor efficiuntur una caro: etiam est una substantia in duabus personis... Et ideo dicta domina Agnes tanquam naturalis et originaria civis dicte terre Castellioni debet reputari, cum iure divino sit una caro et ius divinum consistat in veritate et non in fictione. Sequitur proprie uxor est coeffecta concivis viri, et ita tenet glossa in [C.10.40.7] et Bartolus [D.50.1.38, 1].

p. 183 C.10.39.4:
Origine propria neminem posse voluntate sua eximi manifestum est.

p. 183   Accursius, gl. ibid.:
Origine, ut et [D.50.1.6] in princ., hoc autem fallit propter matrimonium, ut [C.10.64.1] et [D.50.1.38, 1].

p. 186   Accursius, gl. ad D.3.4.7:
Vniversitas nil aliud est nisi homines qui ibi sunt.

p. 187   Baldus ad C.7.53.5:
Nec obstat quod glossa dicit in [D.3.4.7] quod populus non est aliud quam homines, quia debet intelligi de hominibus collective assumptis, unde homines separati non faciunt populum, unde populus proprie non est homines, sed hominum collectio in unum corpus misticum et abstractive sumptum, cuius significatio est inventa per intellectum.

p. 188   Baldus ad X.1.31.3:
Omnis universitas dicitur corpus, quia compositum et aggregatum, ubi corpora sunt tanquam materia, dicitur autem forma, id est formalis status [D.8.2.11]. Est igitur collegium imago quedam, que magis intellectu quam sensu percipitur [D.41.3.30; & D.4.2.9, 1; & X.5.39.53].

p. 189   Baldus ad C.6.26.2:
Omnis numerus eorum, qui loco unius substituuntur, pro singulari persona habendus est, ut [D.35.1.56]. Est et quedam persona universalis que unius persone intellectum habet, tamen ex multis corporibus constat, ut populus, ut [D.46.1.22]; et hec persona similiter loco unius habetur et individuum corpus reputatur...facit [D.4.2.9, 1]. Patet ergo quod hoc nomen, 'persona', quandoque ponitur pro singulari quandoque pro universali quandoque pro capite sive prelato, ut [X.3.5.28].

p. 189   Baldus, *De pace Constantie*, ad v. 'Imperialis clementie':
Quero nunquid civitas durans in novis civibus non naturalibus sed adventiciis dicatur eadem civitas? Respondeo sic...quia quod universale est non potest morte perire sicut homo in genere non moritur.

p. 195   C.2.53.4:
Res publica minorum iure uti solet ideoque auxilium restitutionis implorare potest.

p. 195   Baldus, ibid.:
Sed Iacobus Butrigarius dicit contra quod magna castra et magne ville que reguntur per alios equiparantur minoribus et restituuntur in integrum, secus in parvis castris vel villis, et idem in parva civitate, ut est in Gallia, Iacobus Butrigarius in lectura, idem tenet Bartolus. Ego

credo opinionem Iacobi de Arena veriorem nam si restituitur legatus municipii ergo multo fortius municipium...et distinctio inter parvam civitatem et magnam universitatem non probatur lege nec ratione, quia sive parva, sive magna non est ibi reperire verum consensum, nec veram negligentiam sed fictam, cum multi sint in universitate qui non possunt [possint *ed. cit.*] vere consentire, et multi sint [sunt *ed. cit.*] ibi pupilli et minores, quorum favore universitas civitatis, castri vel ville meretur beneficium restitutionis, quia sunt in eodem corpore ipsius universitatis. Et ita teneo.

p. 196   Baldus ad D.4.6.8:

Nota argumentum, quelibet civitas, castrum vel villa potest in integrum restitui adversus prescriptionem, quia si hoc conceditur legato eius ergo multo fortius sibi...Communiter nos tenemus quod universitates fungantur [fungantur *ed. Venice, 1616*; fingantur *ed. cit.*] iure minoris et possint [possint *ed. Venice, 1616*; possunt *ed. cit.*] restitui...Et est ratio quia semper sunt sub protectione et gubernatione administratorum, et ideo equiparantur ecclesiis et minoribus.

p. 200   Baldus ad C.7.53.5:

Si est congregata [i.e. universitas], personaliter citabitur, quia ista congregatio est quasi quedam persona politica.

pp. 205–6   Baldus ad C.9.22.21:

Priores qui de iure communi vocantur decuriones possunt conveniri de falso et de quolibet crimine. Secus puto in prioribus civitatis Tuscie qui usurpant sibi potestatem et ideo possunt vocari magistratus.

p. 207   Aquinas, *S.T.*, 1a 2ae, 81, 1:

In civilibus omnes qui sunt unius communitatis reputantur quasi unum corpus, et tota communitas quasi unus homo.

p. 210   Baldus ad D.1.1.5:

Queritur an hodie provincia possit sibi eligere regem. Et videtur quod non, nam provincie sunt sub naturali dominio imperatoris, ergo non possunt conferre alicui merum imperium, in Auth., 'De defensoribus civitatum' [Coll., 3.2, 1 = Nov., 15, 1]. Sed tu dic quod sic, si est talis provincia que non subsit imperatori, ut Hispania. Nam si dominus Castelle deficeret in totum, regnicole possent sibi eligere regem de iure gentium, ut hic. Nunquid ergo iurisdictiones fuerunt introducte de iure gentium? Dic quod sic, quia rex significat se habere iurisdictionem; cum ergo de iure gentium fuerint reges, ergo et iurisdictiones.

p. 210   Baldus, *Consilium* on the Great Schism (ad C.6.34):
Ex iure gentium reges orti sunt ex solo consensu eligentium omni solennitate circumscripta, cum prius fuerint reges quam leges quando regebant in puritate prima et sola natura hominibus sanciebat [D.1.1.5; D.1.2.2, 1] et in Auth., 'Quibus modis naturales efficiuntur sui' [Coll., 7.1, 1 = Nov., 89, 1].

p. 213   Baldus ad X. Proem, ad v. 'Rex pacificus':
Rex in regno suo libere potest omnia.

p. 214   Baldus ad D.1.3.2:
Quia rex est lex animata et donec concedit propriam maiestatem est gratia gratis data, et subditi possunt tunc dicere, 'ego dormio et cor meum, id est rex meus, vigilat.'

p. 214   Bartolus, *De regimine civitatis*:
Omnis rex aut immediate a deo eligitur, aut ab electoribus inspiciente deo...Et ex hoc nota, quod regimen quod est per electionem est magis divinum, quam illud quod est per successionem...Et ideo electio principis qui est rex universalis fit per electionem prelatorum et principum; non autem vadit per successionem...'Hoc' enim 'imperium deus de celo constituit'...*Reges vero particulares sunt magis ex constitutione hominum*, ut [D.1.1.5].

p. 215   Baldus, *Cons.*, 1.359:
Quedam vero procedunt a sede, et ista semper sunt perennia et eterna...huiusmodi sunt contractus regum, qui contrahunt nomine suo et regni seu gentis sue.

p. 215   Baldus, ibid.:
Nam regnum continet in se non solum territorium materiale, sed etiam ipse gentes regni et ipsi populi collective regnum sunt.

p. 215   Baldus, ibid.:
In regno considerari debet dignitas, que non moritur, et etiam universitas seu respublica regni, que etiam exactis regibus perseverat, non enim potest respublica mori, et hac ratione dicitur quod respublica non habet heredem quia semper vivit in semetipsa.

p. 215   Baldus, ibid.:
Non est mortua hic persona concedens, scilicet ipsa respublica regni, nam verum est dicere quod respublica nihil per se agit, tamen qui regit rempublicam agit in virtute reipublice et dignitatis sibi collate ab ipsa republica.

p. 216 Baldus, ibid.:
Porro duo concurrunt in rege persona et significatio. Et ipsa significatio, que est quoddam intellectuale, semper est perseverans enigmatice, licet non corporaliter. Nam licet rex deficiat, quid ad rumbum? Nempe loco duarum personarum rex fungitur [D.34.9.22].

p. 216 Baldus, ibid.:
Et persona regis est organum et instrumentum illius persone intellectualis et publice; et illa persona intellectualis et publica est illa que principaliter fundat actus, quia magis attenditur virtus principalis quam virtus organica.

p. 216 Baldus, ibid.:
Manifeste concluditur quod dictus contractus est transitorius ex forma, ac etiam ex dignitate et authoritate concedentis, necnon ex ipsa republica representata [representata *ed. Venice, 1575*; representatione *ed. cit.*], que ut dixi non moritur.

p. 217 Baldus, *Cons.*, 3.241:
Queri consuevit de contractibus, an contractus regis vel principis possit obligare rempublicam vel fiscum, quia si obligare potest, cum respublica et fiscus sint quid eternum et perpetuum quantum ad essentiam, licet dispositiones sepe mutentur, fiscus enim nunquam moritur, ut no. in [D.2.3.1, 4], statim sequitur quod ex regio contractu respublica regni et fiscus semel obligetur pro semper presertim quia personales obligationes natura sua sunt perpetue, ut [Inst., 4.12; D.44.7.44]...super quo articulo dicendum est quod rex potest obligare fiscum regni sui.

p. 218 Baldus ad D.1.1.5:
Secundo queritur an regem propter iniusticias suas intollerabiles et facientes tyrannica subditi possint expellere. Et videtur quod sic, infra [D.1.2.2], nam malus rex tyrannus fit...Contrarium est verum, quia subditi non possunt derogare iuri superioris; unde licet de facto expellant, tamen superior non amittit dignitatem suam [C.4.55.4].

p. 218 Baldus, *Cons.*, 1.359:
Circumscripta obedientia populorum rex non posset dici regnare, ut [D.1.2.2, 3].

p. 219 Baldus ad X.2.24.33:
Nota quod omnes reges mundi in sua coronatione debent iurare iura regni sui conservare et honorem corone. Item quod ista duo sunt paria, iura regni et honor corone, tene menti.

p. 219 Baldus, ibid.:
Rex debet esse tutor regni, non depopulator nec dilapidator...Nota quod periurium non est causa finalis quare revocentur alienata, quia ex natura officii etiam in iuramento non valeret, nam rex debet salutem reipublice tueri [D.1.15.1].

p. 220 Baldus ad D.V. Proem, ad v. 'Quoniam':
Rex non potest alienare populum suum nec dare ei alium regem, quia populus est liber, licet sit sub rege.

p. 220 Baldus ad X.2.24.33:
Item nec scrupulosa inquisitio est regibus exigenda, cum ipsi habeant plenissimam potestatem et non sint suppositi calculis rationum, ut [D.1.12.1, 4].

p. 222 Baldus, *Cons.*, 3.276:
Magnifico principi nostro debet formaliter et totaliter obediri in his in quibus esset obediendum ipsi imperatori, si eius persona principaliter et personaliter interesset in Italia.

p. 223 Baldus, *Cons.*, 3.283:
Princeps dando feudum nobilitat regnum, expeditque reipublice potius habere iustos subditos quam perversos; et sic expedit habere subditum ducem quam tyrannum.

p. 224 Baldus, *Cons.*, 3.237:
Sed tamen quia omnes domini Lombardie de consuetudine usuali et quasi de quadam theorica et practica ponunt hic verba de plenitudine potestatis, et sunt in quasi possessione verbi et facti, puto salva substantia veritatis credendum [esse] eorum sermoni, quia non est verisimile quod falsa voce uterentur, arg. [C.9.27.6]. Alioquin...illusoria fierent decreta tantorum dominorum, ut [D.5.1.75] in prin.

p. 224 Baldus, *Cons.*, 3.218:
Nec audeo, nec auderem, ponere os in celum ad consulendum contra potentiam principum, quia multa ex hac opinione possent sequi valde mala et periculosa et cavenda, quia generarent valde magnum scandalum.

p. 225 Bartolus, *De regimine civitatis*:
Si vero [est dominus] particularis aliquando appellatur regnum, aliquando ducatus, marchia vel comitatus, ut [*Feud.*, 2.55], § 'Preterea ducatus'. Communi vero nomine appellamus regnum dominium naturale, et hoc si dictus dominus in communem et bonum finem tendit.

Si vero tendit in malum finem et in proprium commodum, secundum Aristotelem appellatur tyrannides, sic etiam secundum leges et mores appellatur.

p. 225   Baldus ad C.1.2.16:
Largo modo loquendo omnis civitas est sub tyrannide quando subditi non possunt libera voce defendere bonum publicum.

pp. 225–6   Baldus, ibid.:
Et dico in primis quod provincie que consueverunt regi per reges et principes dicuntur esse sub eorum dominio naturali, id est de iure gentium, ut [D.1.1.5]. Et si alius accipit ibi dominatum contra voluntatem regis vel principis, ille est tyrannus. Textus est hic. Ista igitur usurpatoria dominatio vocatur tyrannides.

p. 226   Baldus, ibid.:
Si autem imperator patitur aliquem regere, non quia regat bene, sed quia non potest ipsum expugnare, iste est tyrannus proprie et est rebellis imperii, et tenetur crimine lese maiestatis, ut [D.48.4.1 & 2].

p. 226   Baldus, ibid.:
Et dico quod aut statuit ipse tyrannus et non valet statutum quia, cum statuere sit iurisdictionis et ipse nullam habeat iurisdictionem, ergo non potest statuere.

p. 226   Baldus, ibid.:
Aut sunt facta [i.e. statuta populi] obtentu persone tyranni, et non valent, quia presumuntur quod sint facta metu et impressione vel nimia reverentia, ut [D.27.6.7, 1; & D.44.5.1, 5]. Aut non sunt facta obtentu persone tyranni, sed ob aliam iustam causam...et talia statuta valent ratione statuentium et ratione ipsius statuti, ut [D.1.1.9], nec enim ideo perdit populus potestatem statuendi de iure quia fit sub tyranno, quia delictum tyranni non preiudicat iuribus populi.

p. 226   Baldus ad C.6.51.1:
Nota quod bellum civile est quod in se populus movet...et ubi est ista divisio [i.e. civitatis]...abscinduntur nervi civitatis, id est magni cives. Vnde civitati advenit spasmus et plerunque inducitur ad necessitatem tyrannidis sicut experientia docet quia imperitum et ignorabile vulgus non diu sustinet pressuras. Et dicebat quidam sapiens Ianuensis quod divisio in civitate est vermis ingressus in caseo.

APPENDIX II

Notes on civilians and canonists mentioned in the text

ACCURSIUS, FRANCISCUS

b. 1181/5 into a family from the Florentine *contado*. Student of Azo at Bologna. Professor at Bologna. d. 1259/63.

WORKS: Produced the *Glossa ordinaria* on all parts of the *Corpus Iuris Civilis*. He transcribed, condensed and conflated all he thought worthwhile from his predecessors' work: main sources, Azo and Hugolinus. Accursius' Gloss was the culmination of the work of the school of Glossators, and remained the fundamental text for the scholastic theory and practice of law until the early seventeenth century.

ALBERICUS DE ROSCIATE

b. ca. 1290 near Bergamo. Studied at Padua under Oldradus de Ponte and Ricardus Malumbra. Lived at Bergamo, where he was a practising lawyer and took part in public life. There is no mention of any academic post held by him. Reformed the statutes of Bergamo in a sense favourable to the signorial regime. In his legal commentaries influenced by the scholastic methods of the early French Commentators. d. 1360.

WORKS: *Commentarium de statutis*: a most important and informed contribution to the early development of the study of private international law. *Commentaria* on the Digest and the Code. *Dictionarium iuris*: first great lexicographical undertaking in jurisprudence.

ANDREAS DE ISERNIA

d. ca. 1316. Judge at the *Magna regia curia* at Naples from 1288. Professor of civil law, University of Naples from 1289. Magistrate. Juridical adviser to the Neapolitan monarchy. 1309: accompanied King Robert of Naples on embassy to Avignon.

WORKS: *In usus feudorum commentaria* (composed ca. 1300); *Lectura* on the *Liber constitutionum* of Frederick II (composed after 1305); *Riti* of the *Magna curia* of the *maestri razionali* (treasurers) of the Kingdom of Naples.

ANGELUS DE UBALDIS

Younger brother of Baldus. Chair at Perugia, 1351. Served on embassies. Exile from Perugia, 1384–94, during which taught at Padua, Florence and Bologna. d. Florence ca. 1400.

WORKS: Commentaries on all parts of the *Corpus Iuris Civilis* except the Institutes. *Consilia*.

AZO PORTIUS

Born at Bologna where he taught from at least 1191. Brought the school of the Glossators to its highest development and was thus a major source for Accursius. d. 1220.

WORKS: *Summa Codicis* (1208–10) and *Summa Institutionum* (there had been an earlier draft of both works: 1185–90) – immense influence. *Lectura ad Codicem* (last work) – written down by a scholar. Fragments survive of glosses on various parts of the *Corpus Iuris Civilis*. *Brocarda* (brief rules of law); *Quaestiones*; *Distinctiones*.

BARTHOLOMAEUS DE SALICETO

Born into an illustrious Bolognese legal family. Teaching at Bologna by 1365. 1370–4: lectured at Padua. Returned to Bologna: 1375. 1376–89: most constructive period of his teaching at Bologna. 1399–1403: in exile. Returned to Bologna and retired in 1408. d. 1411.

WORKS: Commentary on the Code (begun, 1365–70; finished, 1400), and on the second part of the *Digestum vetus*.

BARTOLUS DE SASSOFERRATO (Bartolo da Sassoferrato)

b. 1313/14; d. 1357. Studied under Cynus de Pistoia at Perugia; completed his studies at Bologna: *baccalaureus*, 1333, doctor, 1334 (promotor, Jacobus Butrigarius; Raynerius de Forlì one of his examiners). Assessor at Todi, 1336; magistrate at Pisa, 1339. 1339 professor of law at Pisa. From 1343 to his death, professor of law at Perugia.

WORKS: Commentaries on all parts of the *Corpus Iuris Civilis*, although that on the Institutes attributed to him in sixteenth- and seventeenth-century editions is not by him but is considered to be by Jacobus de Ravannis; *Consilia*; *Quaestiones*; *Tractatus*.

CYNUS DE PISTOIA (Cino da Pistoia)

b. 1270; d. 1336/7. Studied at Bologna where taught by Dynus de Mugello, Lambertus de Ramponibus and Franciscus Accursius (junior). Also studied in France where heavily influenced by Jacobus de Ravannis and, above all, Petrus de Bellapertica. Finished his career lecturing at

Perugia. Bartolus of Sassoferrato his pupil. Highly important in introducing from France into Italy the scholastic techniques of the school of the early Commentators on Roman law. Jurist of the first rank exerting great influence on Bartolus and Baldus. Major vernacular Italian poet and friend of Dante. His juristic works give no clue that he was also a poet. Originally a Ghibelline and supporter of Henry VII's claims in Italy, but came at the end of his life to adopt pro-papal position.

WORKS: *Lectura super aureo volumine Codicis* (his major work, 1312/14); *Lectura super Digesto veteri*, ed. Frankfurt, 1578; *Lectura super Digesto veteri* (his major and final version composed ca. 1330–6, which is partially preserved in MS, Bibl. Savigny 22, Preußische Staatsbibliothek, Berlin, and MS, Urb. Lat. 172, Biblioteca Apostolica Vaticana, and which is different from that in the printed editions); some surviving *consilia* and *quaestiones*.

DIPLOVATACCIUS, THOMAS
b. Corfu, 1468. Studied civil and canon law at Bologna. Studied at Padua, 1485–8, under Jason de Maino. Lived at Pesaro. d. 1541.
WORKS: *De claris iuris consultis* – lives of jurists. Editions of Bartolus' commentary on the *Digestum vetus* and of his *Consilia, Quaestiones* and *Tractatus*.

FRANCISCUS ZABARELLA
b. ca. 1335 at Padua. Studied at Bologna under Johannes de Lignano, and also at Florence. Lectured at Bologna and Florence and then at Padua. John XXIII made him bishop of Florence in 1410 and cardinal in 1411. Papal legate at Council of Constance where he died in 1417.
WORKS: Commentaries on the *Decretales* and *Clementinae*; *Consilia* and *Repetitiones*.

GUIDO DE SUZARIA
d. ca. 1290. Law professor at Padua and Bologna; taught Jacobus de Arena and Guido de Baisio. Served Charles of Anjou, but opposed execution of Conradin.
WORKS: Famous for *quaestio* now lost but referred to by Cynus (ad C.1.14.4) concerning obligation of *princeps* to adhere to his contracts and privileges (see Cortese, *Norma giuridica*, I, 155–9, for attempted reconstruction). No editions of his commentaries on the Digest and Code but some fragmentary MSS. Tracts: *De ordine causarum, De testibus, De instrumento guarentigiato, Super causarum ordinatione*.

GUILELMUS DE CUNEO (Guillaume de Cunh)
d. 1335. Major luminary of the law school at Toulouse. His works had a considerable influence on those of Baldus.
WORKS: *Lectura super Digesto veteri*; *Lectura super Codice*.

HOSTIENSIS (Henricus de Segusio)
b. at Segusia in the diocese of Turin shortly before 1200. Studied at Bologna at the same time as Innocent IV. Lectured at Paris. 1236–44 in England in household of Eleanor of Provence, wife of Henry III. Served Henry III. Chaplain to Innocent IV (by 1241). Bishop of Sisteron (1244–50); archbishop of Embrun (1250–61); 1262, made Cardinal-Bishop of Ostia. A most important canonist. d. at Lyon, 1271.
WORKS: *Summa Decretalium* (1250–3); *Lectura super novellis Innocentii IV* (written before September, 1253); *Lectura in V Decretalium libros* (completed in the last year of his life).

INNOCENT IV (Sinibaldus Fliscus)
b. at Genoa at the end of the twelfth century. Taught canon law by Laurentius Hispanus, Vincentius Hispanus, Johannes Teutonicus and Jacobus d'Albenga; and Roman law by Azo, Accursius and Jacobus Balduinus. Lectured at Bologna. Canon of Parma. Held curial posts. Pontifical legate in the March. Made bishop of Albenga in 1235; vice-chancellor of the Roman Church; assistant to Hugolinus, cardinal of Ostia, future pope Gregory IX; elected pope, 1243. d. at Naples, 1254. A renowned canonist.
WORKS: *Commentaria super Decretalibus* (written ca. 1251). As pope promulgated three official collections of decretals.

JACOBUS DE ARENA
Taught at Padua from 1261, and then at Siena, Bologna, Reggio and then Padua from ca. 1286. 1296 recorded as teaching at Naples. d. ca. 1296.
WORKS: *Commentarii in universum ius civile.*

JACOBUS DE BELVISIO
b. 1270. Studied law at Bologna under Franciscus Accursius (junior) and Dynus. Taught at Naples, Bologna and Perugia. Judge at Naples and counsellor of Charles of Anjou. d. 1335.
WORKS: Commentaries on the *Libri feudorum* and the *Authenticum.*

JACOBUS BUTRIGARIUS

b. ca. 1274; d. 1348. Major teacher of law at Bologna: Bartolus his pupil. Considerable influence on the jurisprudence of Bartolus and Baldus.

WORKS: *Lectura super Codice*; *Lectura in Digestum vetus.*

JACOBUS DE RAVANNIS (Jacques de Révigny)

d. 1296. Major luminary of the juristic school of Orléans. Instrumental in introducing developed scholastic method into jurisprudence. Taught at Toulouse. Later auditor of the Rota.

WORKS: Commentaries on all parts of the *Corpus Iuris Civilis*: his *Lectura super prima et secunda parte Codicis*, ed. Paris, 1519, falsely attributed by the editor to Petrus de Bellapertica; considered to have been the author of the commentary on the Institutes attributed to Bartolus in sixteenth- and seventeenth-century editions. Some *quaestiones* also survive, and a *Tractatus de consuetudine.*

JASON DE MAINO

b. 1435. One of the last of the Commentators. Pupil of Alexander Tartagnus de Imola. Taught at Pavia from 1467 until his death in 1519 (with the exception of his teaching at Padua, 1485–8). His pupils included Andrea Alciato.

WORKS: His most important are his commentaries on the Digest and the Code, and his *consilia.*

JOHANNES ANDREAE

b. ca. 1270. Studied canon law at Bologna under Guido de Baisio. Taught at Padua and Bologna. One of the professors of canon law who were laymen. d. 1348.

WORKS: *Glossa ordinaria* on the *Liber Sextus* and the *Clementinae*; *Novella super Decretalibus*; *Novella in Sextum*; *additiones* to the *Speculum iudiciale* of Guilielmus Durantis.

JOHANNES DE IMOLA

b. 1367/72. Studied at Bologna (doctorate 1397). Taught at Bologna, Ferrara and Padua. Taught both Roman and canon law. d. 1436.

WORKS: *Commentaria in tres libros Decretalium*; *Commentaria super Clementinis*; *In primam et secundam Infortiati Digestique novi partes*; *Tractatus super Schismate*; and *Consilia.*

JOHANNES MONACHUS (Le Moyne)

b. ca. 1250 at Crécy. Studied at Paris. Canon of Amiens and Paris. Auditor of Roman Rota (1288–92). Dean of Bayeux; bishop of Meaux.

Adviser of Philip IV. 1294, made cardinal by Celestine V. Boniface VIII made him vice-chancellor of the Roman church and in 1302 sent him on embassy to Philip IV. d. 1313 at Avignon.

WORKS: *Glossa aurea super Sexto Decretalium*; and a commentary on the *Extravagantes communes* of Boniface VIII.

LUCAS DE PENNA

b. ca. 1320 at Penna near Pescara in the Abruzzi. Studied law at Naples. Graduated 1345. Probably never taught. An advocate and judge. d. 1390.

WORK: Commentary on the *Tres Libri Codicis* (not written for publication).

MARINUS DE CARAMANICO

d. 1288. Major jurist of the school of Naples.

WORK: *Glossa ordinaria* to the *Constitutiones regni Siciliae* of Frederick II (composed by 1282).

ODOFREDUS DE DENARIIS

An important post-Accursian jurist. From 1244 taught at Bologna. d. 1265.

WORKS: *Lecturae* on the Code and Digest; works on the *Libri feudorum* and the Peace of Constance; *consilia*; *disputationes*; and *repetitiones*.

OLDRADUS DE PONTE

d. 1335. Professor of law at Padua (perhaps also at Siena and Bologna). A canonist as well as a civilian – entered papal service at Avignon.

WORKS: *Consilia*.

PANORMITANUS (Nicholas de Tudeschis)

b. at Catania 1386; d. 1445. Most important canonist of his era. Studied at Bologna and Padua (under Franciscus Zabarella). Taught at Bologna, Parma, Siena and Florence. Took part in papal delegation to Council of Basel in 1431. Made archbishop of Palermo (hence called Panormitanus), 1435. Ambassador of Alphonso V of Aragon to Basel. Became conciliarist.

WORKS: Voluminous. Commentaries on *Liber Extra*, *Liber Sextus*, *Clementinae*; unfinished commentary on *Decretum*; 118 *consilia*; tract *De Concilio Basiliensi*.

PAULUS DE CASTRO

b. at Castro (west of Lake Bolsena). Pupil of Baldus. Also studied at Siena. Taught law at Avignon, Florence, Siena, Bologna and Padua.

1415: participated in the revision of the *Statuta populi et communis Florentie*. d. 1441.

WORKS: Commentaries on the Digest, Code and *Authenticum*; *consilia*.

PETRUS DE BELLAPERTICA (Pierre de Belleperche)
d. 1308. He and Jacobus de Ravannis were the major luminaries of the school of the early Commentators at Orléans: they pioneered the application of developed scholastic method to jurisprudence. Petrus had a great influence on Cynus and thus on Italian jurisprudence. Taught at Toulouse and Orléans. Died as royal chancellor.

WORKS: *Lectura Institutionum*; *Lectura super Digesto novo*; *Repetitiones in aliquot divi Iustiniani imperatoris Codicis leges* (MS, Peterhouse, Cambridge, no. 34; ed. 1571); *Quaestiones et distinctiones*; *Tractatus de feudis*.

PHILIPPUS DECIUS
b. Milan, 1454. Taught law at Paris and Siena. 1490, auditor of the Roman Rota. 1502, professor of canon law at Padua. Taught at Pavia, 1505. Professor at Valence; also taught at Rome and Pisa. d. 1536/7.

WORKS: Commentaries on the *Digestum vetus*, *Codex* and *Decretales*; *De regulis iuris*; *consilia*; and *repetitiones*.

RAYNERIUS DE FORLÌ (Ranieri Arsendi da Forlì)
Studied at Bologna. Taught at Bologna from 1319/20 to 1338 (students included Bartolus); at Pisa from 1338 (Bartolus his colleague); and at Padua from 1344 till his death in 1358. Applied scholastic techniques of early French Commentators, notably Guilelmus de Cuneo.

WORKS: These only survive in part. Printed editions include: *Lectura super Ia et IIa parte Digesti Novi*; *Repetitiones* (his notable one on D.1.1.9 is printed in Albericus de Rosciate, *Commentariorum pars prima super Digesto veteri*); *Additiones* to Guilelmus de Cuneo, *Lectura super Codice*; and a few *consilia*. MSS include *Annotationes* on the *Digestum vetus*, *Infortiatum*, *Digestum novum* and *Codex*; *Additiones* to Cynus, *In Codicem commentaria*; *Additiones* to Guilelmus de Cuneo, *Lectura super Digesto veteri* (including one supporting the validity of the Donation of Constantine); some *quaestiones* and *repetitiones* (that on D.1.1.9 is dated 19 October, 1355 in Cod. Vat. Lat. 2683); and a few *consilia*. His *Lectura super Digesto veteri* is lost.

BIBLIOGRAPHY

1. PRIMARY SOURCES

a) *Manuscripts*

Baldus de Ubaldis *Additiones super Innocentio*. MS, Cod. 187, Biblioteca Feliniana Capitolare, Lucca.

Consilia. MS, Cod. 351, Biblioteca Feliniana Capitolare, Lucca.

Consilia. MS 6, Joseph Regenstein Library, University of Chicago.

Super Sexto Decretalium. Cod. Vat. Lat. 5925, Biblioteca Apostolica Vaticana.

Cynus de Pistoia *Lectura super Digesto veteri*. MS, Bibl. Savigny 22, Preußische Staatsbibliothek, Berlin.

Lectura super Digesto veteri, MS Urb. Lat. 172, Biblioteca Apostolica Vaticana.

Guilelmus de Cuneo *Lectura super Digesto veteri*. MS, Can. Misc., 472, Bodleian Library, Oxford.

b) *Printed*

Accursius *Glossa ordinaria*. Venice, 1497–8.

Albericus de Rosciate *Commentariorum pars prima super Digesto veteri*. Lyon, 1545.

Commentariorum pars secunda super Digesto novo. Lyon, 1545.

Commentariorum pars prima super Codice. Lyon, 1545.

Commentariorum pars secunda super Codice. Lyon, 1548.

Commentarium de statutis. Lyon, 1552.

Albertus Magnus *Quaestiones de animalibus*, ed. Filthaut, E. Münster, 1955.

Andreas de Isernia *In usus feudorum commentaria*. Lyon, 1579.

Angelus de Ubaldis *Lectura super Codice*. Lyon, 1545.

Super tribus libris Codicis. Lyon, 1518.

Consilia. Lyon, 1539.

Aristotle *Ethica Nicomachea*, ed. Bywater, I. Repr. Oxford, 1962.

Politica, ed. Ross, W. D. Repr. Oxford, 1964.

Aristotelis politicorum libri octo cum vetusta translatione Guilelmi de Moerbeka, ed. Susemihl, F. Leipzig, 1872.

Augustine of Hippo, Saint *De civitate dei*, ed. McCracken, G. E. London, 1957.

Azo *Summa Institutionum*. Speyer, 1482.

Summa Codicis. Speyer, 1482.

Summa Codicis. Pavia, 1484.

Summa Codicis. Lyon, 1557.

Lectura ad Codicem. Paris, 1577 (anastatic reproduction, 1966).

Quaestiones, ed. Landsberg, E. Freiburg in Breisgau, 1888.

Bibliography

Baldus de Ubaldis *Lectura super primo secundo et tertio Codicis*. Venice, 1474.
Commentaria ad IV Institutionum libros. Pavia, 1489.
Lectura super tribus libris Codicis. Pavia, 1490.
Partes I–V Consiliorum. Brescia, 1490–1 (Parts 1, 2 and 4: 1490; parts 3 and 5: 1491).
Lectura super prima et secunda parte Infortiati. Venice, 1494.
Super usibus feudorum interpretatio. Pavia, 1495.
Commentarium super Pace Constantie. Pavia, 1495.
Lectura super prima et secunda parte Digesti veteris. [Lyon], 1498.
Lectura super prima et secunda parte Infortiati. [Lyon], 1498.
Lectura super Digesto novo. [Lyon], 1498.
Commentaria super I–V libris Codicis. [Lyon, 1498].
Lectura in VI–IX libros Codicis. [Lyon, 1498].
This edition of Baldus' commentaries is found in the Old Library, Queens' College, Cambridge, and is bound in four volumes: 1. *Dig. vet.*, *Pars prima*, n.p., 1498 (= Pellechet (*Catalogue générale des incunabules des bibliothèques publiques de France*, 1. Paris, 1897), 1730, *ubi* '[Lugduni], 1498'); *Dig. nov.*, n.p., 1498 (= Pellechet, 1735, *ubi* '[Lugduni], 1498'; Copinger (Supplement to Hain), 815). 2. *Dig. vet.*, *Pars secunda*, n.p., 1498 (= Pellechet, 1730, *ubi* '[Lugduni], 1498'; Copinger, 812); *Infort.*, *Pars prima et secunda*, n.p., n.d. (= Pellechet, 1734, *ubi* '[Lugduni], 1498'; Copinger, 813, *ubi* '1498'). 3 & 4. *Codex*, I–IX, n.p., n.d. (= Hain, *2279; Pellechet, 1722, *ubi* '[Lugduni, 1498?]').
Margarita ad Innocentiana commentaria. Lyon, 1525.
Partes I–V Consiliorum. [Lyon], 1543.
Super Decretalibus. Lyon, 1551.
Partes I–V Consiliorum. Lyon, 1559.
In I–XI libros Codicis commentaria. Lyon, 1561.
Lectura super prima et secunda parte Digesti veteris. Lyon, 1562.
Consiliorum sive responsorum volumina I–V. Venice, 1575 (anastatic reproduction, Turin, 1970).
Commentaria ad IV Institutionum libros. Lyon, 1585.
Commentaria in primam et secundam Digesti veteris partem. Lyon, 1585.
Commentaria in I–XI Codicis libros. Lyon, 1585.
In usus feudorum commentaria. Lyon, 1585.
Tractatus. Lyon, 1585.
In Decretalium volumen commentaria. Venice, 1595 (anastatic reproduction, Turin, 1971).
Praelectiones in IV Institutionum libros. Venice, 1615.
In primam Digesti veteris partem commentaria. Venice, 1616.
In secundam Digesti veteris partem commentaria. Venice, 1615.
In primam et secundam Infortiati partem commentaria. Venice, 1615.
In I–XI Codicis libros commentaria. Venice, 1615.
Tractatus. Venice, 1615.
Repetitio ad l. Cunctos populos, in Meijers, E. M. (ed.) *Tractatus duo de vi et potestate statutorum*. Haarlem, 1939.
Bartholomaeus de Saliceto *In primam et secundam partem Codicis*. Venice, 1574.

Bibliography

Bartolus de Sassoferrato *In primam et secundam Digesti novi partem.* Milan, 1491.
Super Constitutione 'Ad reprimendum' in *Corpus Iuris Civilis.* Venice, 1497.
Super Constitutione 'Qui sint rebelles' in *Corpus Iuris Civilis.* Venice, 1497.
In primam et secundam Digesti veteris partem. Turin, 1577.
In primam et secundam Infortiati partem. Turin, 1577.
In primam et secundam Digesti novi partem. Turin, 1577.
In primam et secundam Codicis partem commentaria. Turin, 1577.
In tres Codicis libros commentaria. Turin, 1577.
Super Authenticis commentaria. Turin, 1577.
Consilia. Turin, 1577.
Tractatus represaliarum. Turin, 1577.
In tres Codicis libros commentaria. Basel, 1588.
In primam et secundam Digesti novi partem commentaria. Basel, 1589.
Tractatus de Guelphis et Gebellinis, ed. Quaglioni in *Politica e diritto.*
Tractatus de regimine civitatis, ed. Quaglioni in *Politica e diritto.*
Tractatus de tyranno, ed. Quaglioni in *Politica e diritto.*
Biblia sacra iuxta vulgatam Clementinam. Rome-Tournai-Paris, 1947.
Bodin, J. *Les six livres de la république.* Paris, 1576.
Cicero *De finibus bonorum et malorum,* ed. Schiche, T., Teubner series. Repr. Stuttgart, 1967.
De republica, ed. Ziegler, K., Teubner series. Leipzig, 1960.
Corpus Iuris Canonici, I: *Decretum Magistri Gratiani;* II: *Decretalium Collectiones,* ed. Friedberg, E. Repr. Graz, 1959.
Corpus Iuris Civilis. Venice, 1497–8.
Corpus Iuris Civilis, I: *Institutiones,* ed. Krueger, P. and *Digesta,* ed. Mommsen, T. and Krueger, P. 15th ed. Berlin, 1928; II: *Codex,* ed. Krueger, P. 11th ed. Berlin, 1954; III: *Novellae,* ed. Schoell, R. and Kroll, W. 6th ed. Berlin, 1954.
Cynus de Pistoia *In Codicem et aliquot titulos primi Pandectarum tomi commentaria.* Frankfurt, 1578.
Dante Alighieri *Monarchia,* ed. Moore, E. Oxford, 1916.
Diplovataccius *De claris iuris consultis,* ed. Schulz, F., Kantorowicz, H. and Robotti, G. in *Studia Gratiana,* x (1968), 297–307.
Franciscus Zabarella *Super I–V Decretalium commentaria.* Venice, 1602.
Gregory VII *Registrum,* ed. Caspar, E., in *M.G.H.: Epistolae selectae,* II, fasc. II. 2nd ed. Berlin, 1955.
Guilelmus de Cuneo *Super Codice.* Lyon, 1513 (anastatic reproduction, Bologna, 1968).
Lectura super Digesto veteri, Proem, in Brandi, B. *Notizie intorno a Guillelmus de Cunio.* Rome, 1892.
Guilielmus Durantis *Speculum iuris* [with *additiones* of Baldus de Ubaldis and Johannes Andreae]. Frankfurt, 1592.
Hostiensis *Summa aurea super titulis Decretalium.* Venice, 1570.
Lectura in V Decretalium libros. Paris, 1512.
Innocent III *Die Register Innocenz' III.,* I: *Pontifikatsjahr, 1198/99 – Texte,* eds Hageneder, O. and Haidacher, A., Publikationen der Abteilung für Historische Studien des Österreichischen Kulturinstituts in Rom: II. Abteilung – Quellen, I. Reihe. Graz-Cologne, 1964.

Bibliography

Innocent IV *Super libros quinque Decretalium.* Lyon, 1525.

Super libros quinque Decretalium. Frankfurt, 1570.

Jacobus de Arena *Commentarii in universum ius civile.* Lyon, 1541.

Jacobus de Belvisio *Commentarii in Authenticum et consuetudines feudorum.* Lyon, 1511 (anastatic reproduction, Bologna, 1971).

Jacobus Butrigarius *Lectura super Codice.* Paris, 1516.

In primam et secundam veteris Digesti partem. Rome, 1606 (anastatic reproduction, Bologna, 1978).

Jacobus de Ravannis *Lectura super prima et secunda parte Codicis.* Paris, 1519 (wrongly attributed to Petrus de Bellapertica by the sixteenth-century editor).

Jason de Maino *In primam Digesti veteris partem commentaria.* Lyon, 1540.

Johannes Andreae *Novella super Decretalibus.* Venice, 1505.

Commentarii in sextum Decretalium. Lyon, 1550.

Johannes de Imola *Commentaria super Clementinis.* Lyon, 1525.

Johannes Monachus *Glosa aurea super Sexto Decretalium.* Paris, 1535.

John of Paris *De regia potestate et papali,* ed. Bleienstein, F., in *Johannes Quidort von Paris über königliche und päpstliche Gewalt,* Frankfurter Studien zur Wissenschaft von der Politik, 4. Stuttgart, 1969.

Lucas de Penna *Commentaria in tres posteriores libros Codicis.* Lyon, 1597.

Marinus de Caramanico *Super libro Constitutionum,* Proem, in Calasso, F. *I Glossatori e la teoria della sovranità.* 3rd ed. Milan, 1957.

Macrobius *Commentarii in somnium Scipionis,* ed. Willis, J., Teubner series. Leipzig, 1963.

Marsilius of Padua *Defensor pacis,* ed. Scholz, R. in *M.G.H.: Fontes iuris germanici antiqui.* Hannover, 1932–3.

Monumenta Germaniae historica: Constitutiones et acta publica imperatorum et regum, I and II. Repr. Hannover, 1963; *Leges,* IV, *Const.,* I. Repr. Hannover, 1981.

Ockham, William of *Tractatus contra Benedictum,* in Sikes, J. G., Bennett, R. F. and Offler, H. S. (eds) *Guilelmi de Ockham opera politica,* III. Manchester, 1956.

Odofredus de Denariis *Interpretatio in XI primos Pandectarum libros.* Lyon, 1550.

In secundam Digesti veteris partem praelectiones. Lyon, 1552.

In primam Codicis partem praelectiones. Lyon, 1552.

Oldradus de Ponte *Consilia.* Lyon, 1550.

Panormitanus (Nicholas de Tudeschis) *Commentaria in V Decretalium libros.* Venice, 1605.

Paulus de Castro *In primam et secundam Digesti veteris partem commentaria.* Venice, 1593.

In primam et secundam Codicis partem commentaria. Venice, 1593.

Consilia. Frankfurt, 1582.

Petrus de Bellapertica *Lectura Institutionum.* Lyon, 1586 (anastatic reproduction, Bologna, 1972).

Repetitiones in aliquot divi Iustiniani imperatoris Codicis leges. Frankfurt, 1571 (anastatic reproduction Bologna, 1968).

Quaestiones et Distinctiones. Lyon, 1517 (anastatic reproduction, Bologna, 1970).

Tractatus de feudis (contained in *Quaestiones et Distinctiones*). Lyon, 1517.

Bibliography

Philippus Decius *In Decretales commentaria*. Turin, 1575.

Practica iudiciaria. Lyon, 1534 (wrongly attributed to Baldus).

Pseudo – Aristotle *Secretum secretorum*, Latin text in Möller, R. (ed.) *Hiltgart von Hürnheim: Mittelhochdeutsche Prosaübersetzung des 'Secretum secretorum'*, Deutsche Texte des Mittelalters herausgegeben der deutschen Akademie der Wissenschaften zu Berlin, 56. Berlin, 1963.

Raynerius de Forlì *Repetitio ad l. Omnes populi*, in Albericus de Rosciate *Commentariorum pars prima super Digesto veteri*. Lyon, 1545.

Statuti di Perugia dell'anno MCCCXLII, ed. degli Azzi, G., Corpus statutorum italicorum, 4. 2 vols. Milan, 1913–16.

Theiner, A. (ed.) *Caesaris S.R.E. Card. Baronii, Od. Raynaldi, et Jac. Laderchii… annales ecclesiastici*, XXVI. Bar-le-Duc, 1872.

Thomas Aquinas *Commentum in sententias*. Parma, 1856.

In decem libros Ethicorum Aristotelis ad Nicomachum expositio, ed. Spiazzi, R. M. 3rd ed. Turin-Rome, 1964.

In octo libros politicorum Aristotelis expositio, ed. Spiazzi, R. M. Turin-Rome, 1966.

Quaestiones quodlibetales, ed. Mandonnet, R. P. Paris, 1926.

De regimine principum, in *Aquinas Selected Political Writings*, ed. with an introduction by D'Entrèves, A. P. Oxford, 1970.

Summa theologiae. Leonine ed. Rome, 1889—.

Summa theologiae, ed. Marietti. Turin-Rome, 1948–50.

Summa theologiae, Ia IIae, 90–7, with a trans. by Gilby, T., Blackfriars ed. London, 1966.

Summa theologiae, Ia IIae, 71–80, with a trans. by Fearon, J., Blackfriars ed. London, 1969.

Tractatus universi iuris. 17 vols. Lyon, 1549.

Tractatus illustrium iurisconsultorum. 29 vols. Venice, 1584.

2. SECONDARY SOURCES

a) *Unprinted*

Evans, D. P. 'The idea of the *populus* in later medieval Roman law' (doctoral dissertation, University of London, 1979).

Wahl, J. A. 'Baldus de Ubaldis' concept of state: a study in fourteenth-century legal theory' (doctoral dissertation, University of St Louis, 1968).

b) *Printed*

Ascheri, M. *Saggi sul Diplovatazio*, Quaderni di 'Studi senesi', 25. Milan, 1971.

Aubert, J.-M. *Le droit romain dans l'œuvre de Saint Thomas*. Paris, 1955.

Austin, J. *Lectures on Jurisprudence or the Philosophy of Positive Law*, 5th ed. revised and edited by Campbell, R. 2 vols. London, 1911.

Barraclough, G. *The Origins of Modern Germany*. Oxford, 1962.

Bartolo da Sassoferrato – studi e documenti per il VI centenario. 2 vols. Milan, 1962.

Baskiewicz, J. 'Quelques remarques sur la conception de dominium mundi dans l'œuvre de Bartolus', in *Bartolo da Sassoferrato*, II, 9–25.

Bibliography

Bizzari, D. 'Ricerche sul diritto di cittadinanza nella costituzione comunale', *Studi senesi*, XXXII (1916), 19–136.

Black, A. J. *Monarchy and Community: Political Ideas in the Later Conciliar Controversy, 1430–1450*, Cambridge Studies in Medieval Life and Thought, 3rd series, 2. Cambridge, 1970.

Blanshei, S. R. *Perugia, 1260–1340: Conflict and Change in a Medieval Italian Urban Society*, Transactions of the American Philosophical Society, new series, LXVI, 2 (1976).

Bonolis, L. G. *Questioni di diritto internazionale in alcuni consigli inediti di Baldo degli Ubaldi. Testo e commento.* Pisa, 1908.

Bowsky, W. M. '*Cives silvestres*: Sylvan citizenship and the Sienese commune (1287–1355)', *Bolletino senese di storia patria, Miscellanea di studi in memoria di Giovanni Cecchini*, III, 64–74. Siena, 1965.

Breschi, B. 'Alcune osservazioni sul contributo recato da Bartolo alla teoria degli statuti', in *Bartolo da Sassoferrato*, II, 51–9.

Brie, S. *Die Lehre vom Gewohnheitsrecht: eine historische-dogmatische Untersuchung, I: Geschichtliche Grundlegung.* Breslau, 1899.

Buckland, W. W. *A Text-Book of Roman Law from Augustus to Justinian*, 3rd ed. revised by Stein, P. Cambridge, 1963.

Bueno de Mesquita, D. M. *Giangaleazzo Visconti, Duke of Milan (1351–1402).* Cambridge, 1941.

Buisson, L. *Potestas und Caritas. Die päpstliche Gewalt im Spätmittelalter*, Forschungen zur kirchlichen Rechtsgeschichte und zum Kirchenrecht, II. Cologne-Graz, 1958.

Calasso, F. *Gli ordinamenti giuridici del rinascimento medievale.* 2nd ed. Milan, 1949.
I Glossatori e la teoria della sovranità: studio di diritto comune pubblico. 3rd ed. Milan, 1957.
Medio evo del diritto, I: Le fonti. Milan, 1954.
'Bartolo da Sassoferrato', in *Dizionario biografico degli italiani*, VI. Rome, 1964.

Campitelli, A. and Liotta, F. 'Notizia del Ms. Vat. Lat. 8069', *Annali di storia del diritto*, VI (1962), 387–406.

Canning J. P. 'The corporation in the political thought of the Italian jurists of the thirteenth and fourteenth centuries', *History of Political Thought*, I, 1 (1980), 9–32.
'A fourteenth-century contribution to the theory of citizenship: political man and the problem of created citizenship in the thought of Baldus de Ubaldis', in Tierney, B. and Linehan, P. A. (eds), *Authority and Power: Studies on Medieval Law and Government Presented to Walter Ullmann on his Seventieth Birthday*, pp. 197–212. Cambridge, 1980.
'Ideas of the state in thirteenth and fourteenth-century Commentators on the Roman law', *Transactions of the Royal Historical Society*, 5th series, XXXIII (1983), 1–27.

Carlyle, R. W. and A. J. *A History of Medieval Political Theory in the West.* 6 vols. Edinburgh and London, 1903–36.

Chevrier, G. 'Baldi de Ubaldi', in *Dictionnaire de droit canonique*, II (Paris, 1937), cols 39–52.

Coing, H. (ed.) *Handbuch der Quellen und Literatur der neueren europäischen*

Bibliography

Privatrechtsgeschichte, I: *Mittelalter (1100–1500) – Die Gelehrten Rechte und die Gesetzgebung*; II: *Neuere Zeit, 1500–1800*. Munich, 1973 and 1977.

Cortese, E. *La norma giuridica: spunti teorici nel diritto comune classico*. 2 vols. Milan, 1964.

Costa, P. *Iurisdictio: semantica del potere politico nella pubblicistica medievale, 1100–1433*, Università di Firenze – pubblicazioni della Facoltà di Giurisprudenza, I. Milan, 1969.

Curcio, C. 'La politica di Baldo', *Rivista internazionale di filosofia del diritto*, XVII (1937), 113–39.

Cuturi, T. 'Baldo degli Ubaldi in Firenze', in *L'opera di Baldo*, pp. 365–95.

David, M. *La souveraineté et les limites juridiques du pouvoir monarchique du IXe au XVe siècle*. Paris, 1954.

'Le contenu de l'hégémonie impériale dans la doctrine de Bartole', in *Bartolo da Sassoferrato*, II, 201–16.

Davis, C. T. *Dante and the Idea of Rome*. Oxford, 1957.

Dean, T. 'Lords vassals and clients in Renaissance Ferrara', *English Historical Review*, C (1985), 106–19.

Dolezalek, G. *Verzeichnis der Handschriften zum römischen Recht bis 1600. Materialsammlung, System und Programm für elektronische Datenverarbeitung*. 4 vols. Frankfurt-am-Main, 1972.

Duff, P. W. *Personality in Roman Private Law*. Cambridge, 1938.

Engelmann, W. *Die Wiedergeburt der Rechtskultur in Italien durch die Wissenschaftliche Lehre*. Leipzig, 1938.

Ercole, F. *Dal comune al principato: saggi sulla storia del diritto pubblico del rinascimento italiano*. Florence, 1929.

Da Bartolo all'Althusio – saggi sulla storia del pensiero pubblicistico del rinascimento italiano. Florence, 1932.

'Studi sulla dottrina politica e sul diritto pubblico di Bartolo', *Rivista italiana per le scienze giuridiche*, LVIII (1916), 177–276.

Ermini, G. *Storia della Università di Perugia*. Bologna, 1947.

'Diritto Romano comune e diritti particolari nelle terre della Chiesa', *Ius romanum medii aevi*, V, 2c. Milan, 1975.

Eschmann, T. 'Studies on the notion of society in St Thomas Aquinas, I: St Thomas and the Decretal of Innocent IV *Romana ecclesia: Ceterum*', *Mediaeval Studies*, VIII (1946), 1–42.

Feenstra, R. 'L'histoire des fondations à propos de quelques études récentes', *Tijdschrift voor Rechtsgeschiedenis*, XXIV (1956), 381–448.

Figgis, J. N. 'Bartolus and the development of European political ideas', in *The Divine Right of Kings*, pp. 343–72. 2nd ed. Cambridge, 1914.

Fiumi, F. 'Alcune ricerche sui manoscritti delle opere di Baldo degli Ubaldi nelle principali biblioteche d'Italia', in *L'opera di Baldo*, pp. 397–406.

Fop, M. P. 'Il comune di Perugia e la chiesa durante il periodo avignonese con particolare riferimento all'Albornoz', *Bolletino della Deputazione di Storia Patria per l'Umbria*, LXV, fasc. 2 (1968), 5–100.

Franklin, J. H. *Jean Bodin and the Rise of Absolutist Theory*. Cambridge, 1973.

Gewirth, A. *Marsilius of Padua – the Defender of Peace*. 2 vols. New York, 1951 and 1956.

Gierke, O. *Das deutsche Genossenschaftsrecht*, III. Berlin, 1881.

Bibliography

Political Theories of the Middle Age, trans. with an introduction by Maitland, F. W. Cambridge, 1900.

Giesey, R. A. 'Medieval jurisprudence in Bodin's concept of sovereignty', in Denzer, H. (ed.) *Jean Bodin. Verhandlungen der internationalen Bodin Tagung in München*, pp. 167–86. Munich, 1973.

Gilby, T. *Principality and Polity: Aquinas and the Rise of State Theory in the West.* London, 1958.

Gillet, P. *La personnalité juridique en droit ecclésiastique, spécialement chez les Décrétistes et les Décrétalistes et dans le code de droit canonique.* Malines, 1927.

Gilmore, M. P. *Argument from Roman Law in Political Thought, 1200–1600,* Harvard Historical Monographs, 15. Cambridge, Mass., 1941.

Gordon, W. M. 'Cinus and Pierre de Belleperche', in Watson, A. (ed.) *Daube noster: Essays in Legal History for David Daube*, pp. 105–17. Edinburgh, 1974.

Hamesse, J. *Les auctoritates Aristotelis: un florilège médiéval – Etude historique et édition critique.* Louvain-Paris, 1974.

Hay, D. *The Italian Renaissance in its Historical Background.* 2nd ed. Cambridge, 1977.

Heywood, W. *A History of Perugia.* London, 1910.

Hoffmann, H. 'Die Unveräusserlichkeit der Kronrechte im Mittelalter', *Deutsches Archiv für Erforschung des Mittelalters*, xx (1964), 389–474.

Holthofer, E. 'Die Literatur zum gemeinen und partikularen Recht in Italien, Frankreich, Spanien und Portugal', in Coing, *Handbuch*, II, 103–499.

Horn, N. *Aequitas in den Lehren des Baldus*, Forschungen zur neueren Privatrechtsgeschichte, 11. Cologne-Graz, 1968.

'Philosophie in der Jurisprudenz der Kommentatoren: Baldus philosophus', *Ius commune*, Veröffentlichungen des Max-Planck-Instituts für Europäische Rechtsgeschichte, Frankfurt-am-Main, 1 (1967), 104–49.

'Die legistische Literatur der Kommentatoren und der Ausbreitung des gelehrten Rechts', in Coing, *Handbuch*, I, 261–364.

Izbicki, T. M. 'Notes on late medieval jurists: I. Juan de Mella: cardinal and canonist. II. Baldus on the Sext', *Bulletin of Medieval Canon Law*, new series, IV (1974), 49–54.

Jolowicz, H. F. *Historical Introduction to the Study of Roman Law.* Cambridge, 1932.

Jones, P. J. 'Communes and despots: the city-state in late-medieval Italy', *Transactions of the Royal Historical Society*, 5th series, xv (1965), 71–96.

Kantorowicz, E. H. *The King's Two Bodies: a Study in Medieval Political Theology.* Princeton, 1957.

'Inalienability: a note on canonical practice and the English coronation oath in the thirteenth century', *Speculum*, xxix (1954), 488–502.

Kantorowicz, H. 'Introduzione: la vita di Tommaso Diplovataccio', *Studia Gratiana*, x (1968), 1*–140*.

Kelley, D. R. *Foundations of Modern Historical Scholarship: Language, Law and History in the French Renaissance.* New York, 1970.

Kempf, F. *Papsttum und Kaisertum bei Innocenz III. Die geistigen und rechtlichen Grundlagen seiner Thronstreitpolitik*, Miscellanea historiae pontificiae edita a Facultate Historiae Ecclesiasticae in Pontificia Universitate Gregoriana, 19, collectionis n. 58. Rome, 1954.

285

Bibliography

Kirshner, J. 'Paolo di Castro on *cives ex privilegio*: a controversy over the legal qualifications for public office in early fifteenth-century Florence', in Molho, A. and Tedeschi, J. A. *Renaissance Studies in Honor of Hans Baron*. De Kalb, Illinois, 1971.

'Messer Francesco di Bici degli Albergotti d'Arezzo, Citizen of Florence (1350–1376)', *Bulletin of Medieval Canon Law*, new series, II (1972), 84–90.

'"Civitas sibi faciat civem": Bartolus of Sassoferrato's doctrine of the making of a citizen', *Speculum*, XLVIII (1973), 694–713.

'"Ars imitatur naturam": a *consilium* of Baldus on naturalization in Florence', *Viator*, V (1974), 289–331.

'Between nature and culture: an opinion of Baldus of Perugia on Venetian citizenship as second nature', *The Journal of Medieval and Renaissance Studies*, IX, 2 (1979), 179–208.

Kirshner, J. and Pluss, J. 'Two fourteenth-century opinions on dowries, paraphernalia and non-dotal goods', *Bulletin of Medieval Canon Law*, new series, IX (1979), 65–77.

Kisch, G. *Consilia: eine Bibliographie der juristischen Konsiliensammlungen*. Basel, 1970.

Köstler, R. 'Consuetudo legitime praescripta. Ein Beitrag zur Lehre vom Gewohnheitsrecht und vom Privileg', *Zeitschrift der Savigny Stiftung für Rechtsgeschichte*, XXXIX, Kan. Abt., VIII (1918), 154–94.

Laehr, G. *Die Konstantinische Schenkung in der abendländischen Literatur des Mittelalters bis zur Mitte des 14. Jahrhunderts*. Repr. Vaduz, 1965.

'Die Konstantinische Schenkung in der abendländischen Literatur des ausgehenden Mittelalters', *Quellen und Forschungen aus italienischen Archiven und Bibliotheken*, XXIII (1931–2), 120–81.

Lange, H. 'Die Consilien des Baldus de Ubaldis (†1400)', *Akademie der Wissenschaften und der Literatur, Mainz* (Abhandlungen der Geistes- und Sozialwissenschaftlichen Klasse), XII (1973), 3–47.

Lewis, E. *Medieval Political Ideas*. 2 vols. London, 1954.

'Organic tendencies in medieval political thought', *American Political Science Review*, XXXII (1938), 849–76.

Lewis, J. D. *The Genossenschaft-Theory of Otto von Gierke: a Study in Political Thought*. University of Wisconsin Studies in the Social Sciences and History, 25. Madison, Wisconsin, 1935.

Lucrezi, F. *Leges super principem: la 'monarchia costituzionale' di Vespasiano*, Pubblicazioni della Facoltà Giuridica dell'Università di Napoli, 195. Naples, 1982.

Maccarrone, M. *Vicarius Christi. Storia del titolo papale*, Lateranum n.s., 18. Rome, 1952.

Maffei, D. *Gli inizi dell'umanesimo giuridico*. Milan, 1956.

La *'Lectura super Digesto veteri' di Cino da Pistoia. Studio sui MSS Savigny 22 e Urb. Lat. 172*. Milan, 1963.

La *donazione di Costantino nei giuristi medievali*. Milan, 1964.

'Giuristi medievali e falsificazioni editoriali del primo cinquecento: Iacopo di Belvisio in Provenza?', *Ius commune*, Sonderhefte, Texte und Monographien, X. Frankfurt, 1979.

Magni, C. *Il tramonto del feudo lombardo*. Milan, 1937.

Bibliography

Martines, L. *Power and Imagination: City-States in Renaissance Italy*. New York, 1979.

Meijers, E. M. *Etudes d'histoire du droit*, ed. Feenstra, R. and Fischer, H. F. W. D. 4 vols. Leiden, 1966.

Michaud-Quantin, P. *Universitas – expressions du mouvement communautaire dans le moyen âge latin*. Paris, 1970.

Mochi Onory, S. *Fonti canonistiche dell'idea moderna dello stato – imperium spirituale, iurisdictio divina, sovranità*, Publ. dell'Università Cattolica del Sacro Cuore, n.s., 38. Milan, 1951.

Offler, H. S. 'Aspects of government in the late medieval empire', in Hale, J. R., Highfield, J. R. L. and Smalley, B., *Europe in the Late Middle Ages*, pp. 217–47. London, 1965.

L'opera di Baldo, per cura dell'Università di Perugia nel V centenario dalla morte del grande giureconsulto, ed. Scalvanti, O. Perugia, 1901.

Paradisi, B. 'Le glosse di Bartolo da Sassoferrato' in *La critica del testo*, Atti del secondo congresso internazionale della società italiana di storia del diritto, II, 575–618. Florence, 1971.

'Il pensiero politico dei giuristi medievali', in Firpo, L. (ed.) *Storia delle idee politiche economiche e sociali*, II, 1–160. Turin, 1973.

Partner, P. *The Lands of St Peter: the Papal State in the Middle Ages and the Early Renaissance*. London, 1972.

Perugia, *Archivio di Stato di Perugia: Archivio Storico del Comune di Perugia – Inventario*, Ministero dell'Interno Pubblicazioni degli Archivi di Stato, 31. Rome, 1956.

Pescatore, G. *Miscellen*, Beiträge zur mittelalterlichen Rechtsgeschichte, 2. Berlin, 1889.

Prosdocimi, L. *Il diritto ecclesiastico dello stato di Milano dall'inizio della signoria viscontea al periodo tridentino (sec. XIII–XVI)*. Repr. Milan, 1973.

Quaglioni, D. 'Per una edizione critica e un commento moderno del *Tractatus de regimine civitatis* di Bartolo da Sassoferrato', *Il pensiero politico: rivista di storia delle idee politiche e sociali*, IX, 1 (1976), 70–93.

'Il "Tractatus de tyrannia" di Bartolo', *Il pensiero politico*, X, 2 (1977), 268–84.

'"Regimen ad populum" e "regimen regis" in Egidio Romano e Bartolo da Sassoferrato', *Bullettino dell'Istituto Storico Italiano per il Medio Evo*, LXXXVII (1978), 201–28.

'Alcune osservazioni sul testo di due trattati bartoliani: "De regimine civitatis" e "De Guelphis et Gebellinis"', *Il pensiero politico*, XII, 1 (1979), 3–18.

'Un "Tractatus de tyranno": il commento di Baldo degli Ubaldi (1327?–1400) alla lex Decernimus, C. De sacrosanctis ecclesiis (C.1,2, 16)', *Il pensiero politico*, XIII, 1 (1980), 64–77.

Politica e diritto nel trecento italiano: il 'De tyranno' di Bartolo da Sassoferrato (1314–1357), con l'edizione critica dei trattati 'De Guelphis et Gebellinis', 'De regimine civitatis' e 'De tyranno', 'il pensiero politico', biblioteca, 11. Florence, 1983.

Quillet, J. *La philosophie politique de Marsile de Padoue*. Paris, 1970.

Renouard, Y. *The Avignon Papacy, 1305–1403*. London, 1970.

Riccobono, S. (ed.) *Fontes iuris romani anteiustiniani*, 1. Florence, 1941.

Richardson, H. G. 'The English coronation oath', *Speculum*, XXIV (1949), 44–75.

Bibliography

Riesenberg, P. N. *Inalienability of Sovereignty in Medieval Political Thought.* New York, 1956.

'The consilia literature: a prospectus', *Manuscripta*, VI, 1 (1962), 3–22.

'Civism and Roman law in fourteenth-century Italian society', in Herlihy, D., Lopez, R. S. and Slessarev, V. (eds) *Economy, Society and Government in Medieval Italy*, pp. 237–54. Ohio, 1969.

'Citizenship and equality in late medieval Italy', *Studia Gratiana*, XV (1972), 425–39.

'Citizenship at law in late medieval Italy', *Viator*, V (1974), 333–46.

Rivière, J. *Le problème de l'église et de l'état au temps de Philippe le Bel.* Louvain and Paris, 1926.

Roberti, M. 'Il corpus mysticum di S. Paolo nella storia della persona giuridica', in *Studi in onore di Enrico Besta*, IV, 37–82. Milan, 1939.

Rodriguez, M. J. 'Innocent IV and the element of fiction in juristic personalities', *The Jurist* (A Quarterly Review Published by the School of Canon Law, The Catholic University of America, Washington, D.C.), XXII (1962), 287–318.

Rubinstein, N. 'Florence and the despots: some aspects of Florentine diplomacy in the fourteenth century', *Transactions of the Royal Historical Society*, 5th series, II (1952), 21–45.

'Marsilius of Padua and Italian political thought of his time', in Hale, J. R., Highfield, J. R. L. and Smalley, B. (eds) *Europe in the Late Middle Ages*, pp. 44–75. London, 1965.

'Le dottrine politiche nel rinascimento' in *Il rinascimento: interpretazioni e problemi*, pp. 183–237. Rome-Bari, 1979.

Rummer, J. 'A fourteenth-century legal opinion', *The Quarterly Journal of the Library of Congress*, XXV, 3 (1968), 179–93.

Savigny, F. C. von *Geschichte des römischen Rechts im Mittelalter.* 7 vols. 2nd ed. Heidelberg, 1834–51.

Scalvanti, O. 'Un opinione del Bartolo sulla libertà perugina', *Bollettino della Società Umbra di Storia Patria*, II (1896), 59–98.

'Notizie e documenti sulla vita di Baldo, Angelo e Pietro degli Ubaldi', in *L'opera di Baldo*, pp. 181–359.

Scholz, R. *Die Publizistik zur Zeit Philipps des Schönen und Bonifaz' VIII.* Stuttgart, 1903.

Schulte, F. L. von *Die Summa des Stephanus Tornacensis über das Decretum Gratiani.* Giessen, 1891.

Segoloni, D. 'Bartolo da Sassoferrato e la civitas perusina', in *Bartolo da Sassoferrato*, II, 513–671.

Seibt, F. *Karl IV. Ein Kaiser in Europa 1346–1378.* Munich, 1978.

Skinner, Q. R. D. *The Foundations of Modern Political Thought*, I: *The Renaissance*; II: *The Age of Reformation.* 2 vols. Cambridge, 1978.

Solmi, A. 'Di un'opera attribuita a Baldo', *Archivio giuridico*, 'Filippo Serafini', LXVII (1901), 401–34.

Steinwenter, A. 'Νόμος ἔμψυχος: zur Geschichte einer politischen Theorie', *Anzeiger der Akademie der Wissenschaften in Wien*, phil.-hist. Kl., CXXXIII (1946), 250–68.

Swanson, R. N. *Universities, Academics and the Great Schism*, Cambridge Studies in Medieval Life and Thought, 3rd series, 12. Cambridge, 1979.

Bibliography

Tamassia, N. 'Baldo studiato nelle sue opere', in *L'opera di Baldo*, pp. 3–35.

Tierney, B. *Foundations of the Conciliar Theory: the Contribution of the Medieval Canonists from Gratian to the Great Schism.* Cambridge, 1955.

'Some recent works on the political theories of the medieval canonists', *Traditio*, x (1954), 594–625.

'"The prince is not bound by the laws". Accursius and the origins of the modern state', *Comparative Studies in Society and History*, v, 4 (July, 1963), 378–400.

Tiraboschi, G. *Storia della letteratura italiana*, v. Venice, 1823.

Ullmann, W. *The Medieval Idea of Law as Represented by Lucas de Penna.* London, 1946.

Origins of the Great Schism: a Study in Fourteenth-Century Ecclesiastical History. London, 1948.

A History of Political Thought: the Middle Ages. Harmondsworth, 1965.

Principles of Government and Politics in the Middle Ages. 2nd ed. London, 1966.

The Individual and Society in the Middle Ages. London, 1967.

The Carolingian Renaissance and the Idea of Kingship. London, 1969.

The Growth of Papal Government in the Middle Ages. 3rd ed. London, 1970.

A Short History of the Papacy in the Middle Ages. London, 1972.

Law and Politics in the Middle Ages: an Introduction to the Sources of Medieval Political Ideas. London, 1975.

Medieval Foundations of Renaissance Humanism. London, 1977.

'Bartolus on customary law', *Juridical Review*, LII (1940), 265–83.

'Baldus' conception of law', *Law Quarterly Review*, LVIII (1942), 386–99.

'The delictal responsibility of medieval corporations', *Law Quarterly Review*, LXIV (1948), 78–96.

'The development of the medieval idea of sovereignty', *English Historical Review*, LXIV (1949), 1–33.

'Cardinal Roland and Besançon', *Sacerdozio e regno da Gregorio VII a Bonifacio VIII* (= *Miscellanea historiae pontificiae*, XVIII, 1954), 107–26.

'De Bartoli sententia: Concilium repraesentat mentem populi', in *Bartolo da Sassoferrato*, II, 707–33.

'The Bible and principles of government in the Middle ages', *Settimane di studio del Centro italiano di studi sull'alto medioevo*, x (Spoleto, 1963), 183–227.

'Juristic obstacles to the emergence of the concept of the state in the Middle Ages', *Annali di storia del diritto – rassegna internazionale*, XII–XIII (1968–9), 43–64.

'Schranken der Königsgewalt im Mittelalter', *Historisches Jahrbuch*, XCI (1971), 1–21.

'A note on inalienability in Gregory VII', *Studi Gregoriani*, IX (1972), 117–40.

'Boniface VIII and his contemporary scholarship', *Journal of Theological Studies*, n.s., XXVII (1976), 58–87.

'Arthur's homage to King John', *English Historical Review*, XCIV (1979), 356–64.

'This realm of England is an empire', *The Journal of Ecclesiastical History*, XXX, 2 (1979), 175–203.

Vaccari, P. 'Vtrum jurisdictio cohaereat territorio: la dottrina di Bartolo', in *Bartolo da Sassoferrato*, II, 737–53.

Vergottini, G. de *Studi sulla legislazione imperiale di Federico II in Italia: Le leggi*

Bibliography

del 1220, Pubblicazioni straordinarie dell'Accademia delle Scienze di Bologna, 11. Milan, 1952.

Vermiglioli, G. B. *Biografia degli scrittori perugini e notizie delle opere loro*, 1. Perugia, 1829.

Wahl, J. A. 'Immortality and inalienability: Baldus de Ubaldis', *Mediaeval Studies*, XXXII (1970), 308–28.

'Baldus de Ubaldis: A study in reluctant conciliarism', *Manuscripta*, XVIII (1974), 21–9.

'Baldus de Ubaldis and the foundations of the nation-state', *Manuscripta*, XXI, 2 (1977), 80–96.

Waley, D. *The Italian City-Republics*. London, 1969.

Walther, H. G. *Imperiales Königtum, Konziliarismus und Volkssouveränität*. Munich, 1976.

Watt, J. A. *The Theory of Papal Monarchy in the Thirteenth Century: the Contribution of the Canonists*. London, 1965.

Weigand, R. *Die Naturrechtslehre der Legisten und Dekretisten von Irnerius bis Accursius und von Gratian bis Johannes Teutonicus*, Münchener Theologische Studien, III. Kanonistische Abteilung, 26. Munich, 1967.

Weimar, P. 'Die legistische Literatur der Glossatorenzeit', in Coing, *Handbuch*, I, 129–260.

Weisheipl, J. A. 'The interpretation of Aristotle's *Physics* and the science of motion', in *The Cambridge History of Later Medieval Philosophy*, ed. Kretzmann, N., Kenny, A. and Pinborg, J., pp. 521–36. Cambridge, 1982.

Wilks, M. J. *The Problem of Sovereignty in the Later Middle Ages – the Papal Monarchy with Augustinus Triumphus and the Publicists*, Cambridge Studies in Medieval Life and Thought, 2nd series, 9. Cambridge, 1963.

'The idea of the church as "Unus homo perfectus" and its bearing on the medieval theory of sovereignty', *Miscellanea historiae ecclesiasticae*, pp. 32–49. Stockholm, 1960.

'Corporation and representation in the Defensor Pacis', *Studia Gratiana*, XV (1972), 253–92.

Will, E. *Die Gutachten des Oldradus de Ponte zum Prozesse Heinrichs VII. gegen Robert von Neapel*. Berlin, 1917.

Wolter, U. *Ius canonicum in iure civili: Studien zur Rechtsquellenlehre in der neueren Privatrechtsgeschichte*, Forschungen zur neueren Privatrechtsgeschichte, 23. Cologne-Vienna, 1975.

Woolf, C. N. S. *Bartolus of Sassoferrato – His Position in the History of Medieval Political Thought*. Cambridge, 1913.

INDEX

Lightning Source UK Ltd.
Milton Keynes UK
UKHW012138110722
405719UK00001B/4